Books in the Security Series

Computer Security Fundamentals
ISBN: 0-13-171129-6

Information Security: Principles and Practices
ISBN: 0-13-154729-1

Firewalls and VPNs: Principles and Practices
ISBN: 0-13-154731-3

Security Policies and Procedures: Principles and Practices
ISBN: 0-13-186691-5

Network Defense and Countermeasures: Principles and Practices
ISBN: 0-13-171126-1

Intrusion Detection: Principles and Practices
ISBN: 0-13-154730-5

Disaster Recovery: Principles and Practices
ISBN: 0-13-171127-X

Computer Forensics: Principles and Practices
ISBN: 0-13-154727-5

Information Security
Principles and Practices

MARK S. MERKOW, CISSP, CISM
JIM BREITHAUPT

PEARSON

Prentice Hall

Upper Saddle River, New Jersey 07458

Library of Congress Cataloging-in-Publication Data

Merkow, Mark S.
  Principles of information security : principles and practices / Mark Merkow, James Breithaupt.
    p. cm.
  Includes bibliographical references and index.
  ISBN 0-13-154729-1
  1. Computer security. I. Breithaupt, Jim, 1955- II. Title.
  QA76.9.A25M485 2005
  005.8--dc22

                                        2005016854

Vice President and Publisher: Natalie E. Anderson
Executive Acquisitions Editor, Print: Stephanie Wall
Executive Acquisitions Editor, Media: Richard Keaveny
Executive Editor, Emerging Technologies: Chris Katsaropoulos
Editorial Project Manager: Emilie Herman
Editorial Assistants: Brian Hoehl, Alana Meyers, Sandra Bernales
Senior Media Project Managers: Cathi Profitko, Steve Gagliostro
Marketing Manager: Sarah Davis
Marketing Assistant: Lisa Taylor
Managing Editor: Lynda Castillo
Production Project Manager: Vanessa Nuttry
Manufacturing Buyer: Natacha Moore
Design Manager: Maria Lange
Art Director/Interior Design/Cover Design: Blair Brown
Cover Illustration/Photo: Gettyimages/Photodisc Blue
Composition/Full-Service Project Management: Custom Editorial Productions Inc.
Cover Printer: Courier/Stoughton

Credits and acknowledgments borrowed from other sources and reproduced, with permission, in this textbook appear on appropriate page within text.

Microsoft® and Windows® are registered trademarks of the Microsoft Corporation in the U.S.A. and other countries. Screen shots and icons reprinted with permission from the Microsoft Corporation. This book is not sponsored or endorsed by or affiliated with the Microsoft Corporation.

Pearson Education LTD.
Pearson Education Singapore, Pte. Ltd
Pearson Education, Canada, Ltd
Pearson Education–Japan

Pearson Education Australia PTY, Limited
Pearson Education North Asia Ltd
Pearson Educación de Mexico, S.A. de C.V.
Pearson Education Malaysia, Pte. Ltd

10 9 8 7 6 5 4 3 2
ISBN 0-13-154729-1

To a safer computing frontier.

Contents in Brief

Table of Contents

Security Series Walk-Through

The Prentice Hall Security Series prepares students for careers in IT security by providing practical advice and hands-on training from industry experts. All of the books in this series are filled with real-world examples to help readers apply what they learn to the workplace. This walk-through highlights the key elements in this book created to help students along the way.

Chapter Objectives. These short-term, attainable goals outline what will be covered in the chapter text.

Chapter Objectives

After reading this chapter and completing the exercises, you will be able to do the following:

- Evaluate an organization's security policy.
- Create a basic security policy.
- Update a target system's patches.
- Shut down unnecessary ports.
- Scan a system for vulnerabilities.
- Activate port filtering in Windows 2000 or Windows XP.
- Use a port scanner.

Chapter Introduction. Each chapter begins with an explanation of why these topics are important and how the chapter fits into the overall organization of the book.

Introduction

As you learn more about computer security you will learn new techniques for securing a particular system. However it is critical to be able to assess a system's security. This chapter discusses the essential steps in assessing a system for vulnerabilities. It is also important to assess a system's security level prior to implementing any security measures. Information about the current state of affairs will help you appropriately address any vulnerabilities.

IN PRACTICE: Using NetCop

Let us begin with NetCop, since it is one of the easiest to use port scanners available. IT can be obtained from many sites. You can download NetCop at http://www.cotse.com/pscan.htm.

When you download NetCop you get a simple self-extracting executable that will install the program on your machine and will even put a shortcut in your program menu. When you launch NetCop, it has a very simple and intuitive screen.

You can type in a single IP address, or a range of IP addresses. That makes this tool particularly useful for network administrators that wish to check for open ports on their entire network. Four our purposes we will begin by scanning a single IP address, our own machine. You can either type your machines actual IP address, or simply the loop back address (127.0.0.1). When you type in a single IP address and click on scan now, you can see it checking each and every port. This is very methodical but also a bit slow.

You can, of course, stop the scan at any time you desire. These results are from a machine the author used specifically for this book. You would, of course, get different results on different machines.

You can see that NetCop gives you useful information about open ports. Before you choose to close any port, you should make sure that the port is not one that you actually need for system operations. The following websites list all well-known ports.

In Practice. Takes concepts from the book and shows how they are applied in the workplace.

FYI. Additional information on topics that go beyond the scope of the book.

FYI: The Microsoft Patch

Go to http://www.microsoft.com and on the left hand side of the website you will find a link under the sub heading Resources, entitled Windows Update. If you select that option and follow the very clear instructions you will be able to correct any and all Windows patch issues on a target machine.

7

...twork is to probe the network. This means using ...or vulnerabilities. These tools are often the same ...tempting to breach your security, so it is critical ...n this section we will use three separate analysis ...other tools freely available on the Internet, and ...ver these three are the most commonly used. We ...er, NetBrute, and NetCop. Also this section will ...ions in this book. We will conduct the exercise ...d of the chapter. The reason for this is simply that ...tical aspects of applying these tools Additional ...f the chapter.

Caution

Security Audit

When conducting a security audit, it's critical that you document the specific steps taken during the audit, any flaws found, and what corrective actions where taken.

Caution. Critical, not to be forgotten information that is directly relevant to the surrounding text.

Test Your Skills

Each chapter ends with exercises designed to reinforce the chapter objectives.
Four types of evaluation follow each chapter.

Multiple Choice Questions. Test the reader's understanding of the text.

Exercises. Brief, guided projects designed around individual concepts found in the chapter.

Projects. Longer, guided projects that combine lessons from the chapter.

Case Study. A real-world scenario to resolve using lessons learned in the chapter.

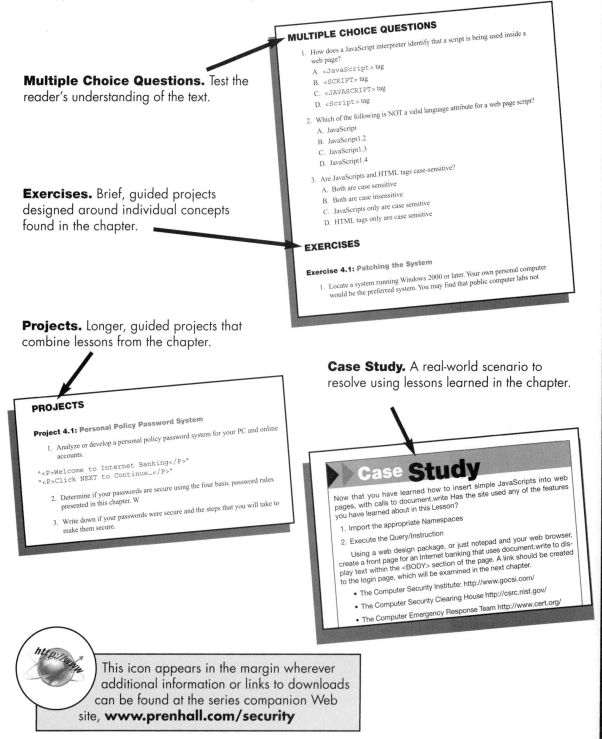

MULTIPLE CHOICE QUESTIONS

1. How does a JavaScript interpreter identify that a script is being used inside a web page?
   A. `<JavaScript>` tag
   B. `<SCRIPT>` tag
   C. `<JAVASCRIPT>` tag
   D. `<Script>` tag

2. Which of the following is NOT a valid language attribute for a web page script?
   A. JavaScript
   B. JavaScript1.2
   C. JavaScript1.3
   D. JavaScript1.4

3. Are JavaScripts and HTML tags case-sensitive?
   A. Both are case sensitive
   B. Both are case insensitive
   C. JavaScripts only are case sensitive
   D. HTML tags only are case sensitive

EXERCISES

Exercise 4.1: Patching the System

1. Locate a system running Windows 2000 or later. Your own personal computer would be the preferred system. You may find that public computer labs not

PROJECTS

Project 4.1: Personal Policy Password System

1. Analyze or develop a personal policy password system for your PC and online accounts.

```
"<P>Welcome to Internet Banking</P>"
"<P>Click NEXT to Continue…</P>"
```

2. Determine if your passwords are secure using the four basic password rules presented in this chapter. W

3. Write down if your passwords were secure and the steps that you will take to make them secure.

Case Study

Now that you have learned how to insert simple JavaScripts into web pages, with calls to document.write Has the site used any of the features you have learned about in this Lesson?

1. Import the appropriate Namespaces

2. Execute the Query/Instruction

Using a web design package, or just notepad and your web browser, create a front page for an Internet banking that uses document.write to display text within the <BODY> section of the page. A link should be created to the login page, which will be examined in the next chapter.

• The Computer Security Institute: http://www.gocsi.com/
• The Computer Security Clearing House http://csrc.nist.gov/
• The Computer Emergency Response Team http://www.cert.org/

This icon appears in the margin wherever additional information or links to downloads can be found at the series companion Web site, **www.prenhall.com/security**

Preface

When teaching a complex and ever-changing discipline like information security, students are best served by beginning with a high-level understanding of the subject before tackling the details. A solid grasp of the objectives, terminology, principles, and framework will help them understand how to place issues in a context to find working solutions. That is the goal of this text: to introduce students to the most important topics of information security and hopefully pique their interest to learn more.

The Body of Knowledge (as it is called in the IT security industry) is vast, deep, and at times baffling. Solutions are not always straightforward, because the problems they address are rarely intuitive. There is no cookbook or universal recipe for IT security success. Ideally, protecting computer systems from attacks and unauthorized access means anticipating problems and devising strategies to address how people, processes, and technologies interact. The goal, while not always realistic, is to prevent these problems from happening and not simply to react to them as so many organizations do today.

This is rarely easy.

This book navigates through the ocean of information technology (IT) security topics and issues while keeping the technical jargon to a minimum. Chapters are ordered to follow the major "domains" of the Common Body of Knowledge to help you organize your course and prepare students for a more detailed examination of the topics if that is their desire. If some students are already familiar with some of the concepts of information security, the book should be sufficiently detailed to hold their interest and discuss topics they may not have previously considered.

IT security specialists are rarely experts in all areas of the discipline. They must focus on carefully selected areas of the field if they want to succeed. This book guides students through the critical topics and helps them to decide which areas are of greatest interest to them.

According to the Bureau of Labor Statistics, the need for IT security specialists will continue to grow into the foreseeable future (**www.bls.gov/oco/ocos042.htm**). With the growth of computers in offices, homes, and public areas, the need for effective security has grown while the availability of trained and experienced personnel is inadequate. Businesses, governments, and civic organizations alike need security experts to help assure that the computing resources they have grown to depend upon are secure and reliable. Should students decide to enter the field of information security, they will find this book helpful in charting their course and joining the ranks of specialists in this discipline. If student interest is more general and part of a broader information science curriculum, they should find the topics covered not only informative but useful in their own lives.

Audience

The book is designed for introductory courses in information security. A background for instructing a course on IT security includes a basic understanding of telecommunications networks and how the Internet operates. The textbook is a useful foundation for advanced studies in CBK Domains and related topics. Content, review material, exercises, and end-of-section questions are designed to test whether section objectives were met.

Overview of the Book

This textbook is designed for anyone who desires a tighter grasp of security principles and practices or is considering entering the field as a practitioner or researcher. Topics were selected and organized using the widely accepted Common Body of Knowledge (CBK) defined by the International Information Systems Security Certifications Consortium, Inc. (**www.isc2.org**). While the CBK is used for organization of the content, the book should not be considered a study guide for the CISSP exam or other ISC[2] exams based on the information security Common Body of Knowledge.

Chapters 1 and 2 offer an overview of the fundamental principles and concepts of Information Security (InfoSec) that are needed for setting the context and the objectives for the remainder of the book. Chapter 3 introduces the Information Security Common Body of Knowledge and provides an overview of each of the 10 domains.

Chapters 4-13 follow the content–at the principles and concepts level–of the 10 domains, specifically:

- Security Management (Chapter 4) examines the policies, standards, and other documents that form the basis of an IT Security Management Programme. It includes the principles and industry best practices to codify a successful management system.

- Security Architecture and Models (Chapter 5) provides the framework and fundamental principles of common security architectures and information assurance models that are applied in various security mechanisms described throughout the text.

- Business Continuity Planning/Disaster Recovery Planning (Chapter 6) looks at the principles, methods, and tools needed to assure continued business operations in the event of a loss of access or a disaster that affects a business' information systems.

- Law, Investigations, and Ethics (Chapter 7) covers fundamental principles and practices related to the collection of evidence for forensics purposes when computer security incidents occur. Chapter 7 also looks at the ethical standards that IT Security personnel must uphold. Physical Security (Chapter 8) examines the mechanisms, building, and safety requirements for installations housing computer equipment needed to operate a business.

- Operations Security (Chapter 9) offers principles and practices that apply to data center personnel security to prevent abuses of privilege and to assure the reliability of IT systems and their related security requirements.

- Access Control Systems and Methodology (Chapter 10) examines in the depth the aspects of controlling access to IT systems to implement the principles of "Least Privilege" and Need-to-Know controls.

- Cryptography (Chapter 11) examines basic cryptography mechanisms and techniques that are used to disguise information from everyone except who are permitted to see it. It includes shared key and public key cryptography and some of the modern algorithms that are used to protect sensitive business information. No advanced mathematics background is assumed of the students, and topics are covered with the intent of illustrating application of techniques and not development of new or enhanced cryptosystems.

- Telecommunications, Network, and Internet Security (Chapter 12) covers the gamut of security mechanisms that are found throughout computer networks to implement a networking "defense in depth" strategy.

- Application Development Security (Chapter 13) looks at the security needs for in-house developed and customized programs to need business needs. It provides a set of recommended controls and techniques that are used to assure that obvious security flaws are not introduced as the System Development Life Cycle (SDLC) progresses.

Each chapter covers the topics at the principles and concepts level and helps students build a foundation and framework to understanding the role of IT Security in the modern, networked world. Appendices included at the end of the book offer a listing of the key areas of knowledge in the Common Body of Knowledge (Appendix A), a taxonomy for security policies and standards (Appendix B), example security policies and standards to use as a model for developing customized documents (Appendix C), an inside look at one popular security management software system (Appendix D), and a review of the HIPPA Security Rules Standards (Appendix E).

Conventions Used in This Book

To help you get the most from the text, we've used a few conventions throughout the book.

IN PRACTICE: About In Practice

These show readers how to take concepts from the book and apply them in the workplace.

FYI: About FYIs

These boxes offer additional information on topics that go beyond the scope of the book.

About Cautions

Cautions appear in the margins of the text. They flag critical, not-to-be forgotten information that is directly relevant to the surrounding text.

Snippets and blocks of code are boxed and numbered, and can be downloaded from the companion Web site (**www.prenhall.com/security**).

New key terms appear in **_bold italics_**.

 This icon appears in the margin wherever more information can be found at the series companion Web site, **www.prenhall.com/security**.

Instructor and Student Resources

Instructor's Resource Center on CD-ROM

The Instructor's Resource Center on CD-ROM (IRC on CD) is distributed to instructors only and is an interactive library of assets and links. It includes:

- Instructor's Manual. Provides instructional tips, an introduction to each chapter, teaching objectives, teaching suggestions, and answers to end-of-chapter questions and problems.

- PowerPoint Slide Presentations. Provides a chapter-by-chapter review of the book content for use in the classroom.

- Test Bank. This TestGen-compatible test bank file can be used with Prentice Hall's TestGen software (available as a free download at: **www.prenhall.com/testgen**). TestGen is a test generator that lets you view and easily edit test bank questions, transfer them to tests, and print in a variety of formats suitable to your teaching situation. The program also offers many options for organizing and displaying test banks and tests. A built-in random number and text generator makes it ideal for creating multiple versions of tests that involve calculations and provides more possible test items than test bank questions. Powerful search and sort functions let you easily locate questions and arrange them in the order you prefer.

Companion Web Site

The Companion Web site (**www.prenhall.com/security**) is a Pearson learning tool that provides students and instructors with online support. Here you will find:

- Interactive Study Guide, a Web-based interactive quiz designed to provide students with a convenient online mechanism for self-testing their comprehension of the book material.

- Additional Web projects and resources to put into practice the concepts taught in each chapter.

About the Authors

Mark S. Merkow, CISSP, CISM works with his company's CIO office to establish the IT security strategy for financial services management and infrastructure to support a broad portfolio of credit card, banking, and brokerage products and services. Mark is a delegate to the ANSI X9F (Financial Services Security) committee and has worked closely with the National Institute of Standards and Technology (NIST) on the Common Criteria Security testing and evaluation methodology.

Mark also teaches online courses in IT Security and E-commerce for DeVry University Online and University of Phoenix Online. He holds a Masters of Science in Decision and Information Systems from Arizona State University and a Masters of Education in Learning Technologies from ASU. Mark also holds two industry security certifications, the Certified Information Systems Security Professional (CISSP) and the Certified Information Security Manager (CISM) certificate from ISACA. Mark has over 28 years of experience in Information Technology with experience in roles as programmer, systems designer, consultant, instructor, and IT Security professional.

Mark is also an author of eight books (six on IT Security) and a contributor to several other books including the *Internet Encyclopedia* (Wiley, 2004) and the *Computer Security Encyclopedia* (Wiley, 2005).

Jim Breithaupt is a Project Manager with a major manufacturing company in Phoenix, Arizona. He has over twenty years of IT experience, primarily in the financial services industry, and has co-authored several books with Mark Merkow including *The E-Privacy Imperative* (Amer Management Associates, 2001) and *Computer Security Assurance* (Thomson Delmar Learning, 2004).

Acknowledgments

From Mark Merkow:

Once again, I'm deeply grateful to my friend and co-author, Jim Briethaupt, who has a remarkable skill in turning the incomprehensible into the obvious. Without Jim, there would be no book.

Thanks to my wife, Amy Merkow, as always, for her positive attitude, full support, and unwavering encouragement for the written word.

To our scattered children, Josh Merkow, Jasmine Merkow, Brandon Bohlman, and Caitlyn Bohlman for their continuous support and patience throughout the writing process.

These people deserve gratitude beyond measure for their help, support, expertise, encouragement, and reassurance that's always needed for a successful book project: Michael Barrett, Shaunna Bell, Fred Bishop, Dr. H. M. and Mimi Bohlman, Joe Cavanaugh, Reza Chapman, Marilyn Corno, Michael Daniels, Soleil Dolce, Cindy Donaldson, Michael Donovan, Allen Forbes, Sean Franklin, Steve Gibbons, Michael Kibbe, John Kirkwood, Sean Lague, Wally Lake, Joe Lesko, John G McDonald, Douglas McGovern, Scott More, Jim Palmer, Jeff Palmeri, Harry Pearson, Jim Petrone, Angela Poletis, Kerry Sedwick, Jim and Candy Strassels, John Van Tussenbroek, Patricia Woodward, and Daniel Yong.

Tremendous thanks goes to Steve Elliot, Megan Smith-Creed, Tammy Staats, Emilie Herman, and the entire staff at Prentice Hall for their commitment to excellence, efficiency, and can-do attitudes that make working with them a total pleasure!

Special thanks goes to my agent, Carole McClendon at Waterside Production, for an amazing ability to keep good news coming along regularly!

From Jim Breithaupt:

To my parents, George and Martha of Mt. Vernon, who made this all possible and necessary. I also want to thank the fine editors at Prentice Hall who shepherded us through the editing process, to the reviewers who provided valuable insight about how the book might fit their curriculum, and to my friend and co-author Mark who keeps us on the playing field.

Quality Assurance

We would like to extend our thanks to the Quality Assurance team for their attention to detail and their efforts to make sure that we got it right.

Technical Editors

Jay Benson
Computer Science
Anne Arundel Community College

Michael L. Denn
Network Security Technology
Texas State Technical College

Reviewers

Jeff Dorsz
Business Science
Saddleback Community College

Jeanne Nelson Furfari
Information Systems Technology
New Hampshire Community Technical College,
Pease Emerging Technologies Campus

Murray Kirch
Computer Science and Information Systems
Richard Stockton College

Linda Woll
Computer Science
Montgomery County Community College

Chapter | 1

Why Study Information Security?

Chapter Objectives

After reading this chapter and completing the exercises, you will be able to do the following:

- Recognize the growing importance of information security specialists to the information technology (IT) infrastructure and how this can translate into a rewarding career.

- Develop a strategy for pursuit of a career in information security.

- Comprehend information security in the context of the mission of a business.

Introduction

With the rapid advances in networked computer technology during the past decade and the unprecedented growth of the Internet, the public has become increasingly aware of the threats to personal privacy through computer crime. Identity theft, pirated bank accounts, forgery: The list of electronic crimes is as unlimited as the imaginations of those who use technology in harmful and dangerous ways. As much as consumers and businesses like the convenience of the Internet and open computer networks, this ease of access also makes people vulnerable to technically savvy but unscrupulous thieves. To protect computers, networks, and the information they store, organizations are increasingly turning to information security specialists.

An information security specialist is more than a technician who prevents hackers from attacking a Web site. In fact, you might be surprised to learn that the discipline is actually as much a solid grounding in business management as it is an understanding of cryptography and firewalls—two of the tools security specialists use to protect information systems. In this book, we'll examine both practical and theoretical skills, but we begin by trying to answer the first question most students starting out in the field ask: Why study information security?

Growing IT Security Importance and New Career Opportunities

According to Chief Information Officers (**www.cio.com**), a Web site devoted to issues affecting CIOs and other information officers, information security is the process of protecting the confidentiality, integrity, and availability of data from accidental or intentional misuse. This discipline is a combination of technical and nontechnical approaches designed to reduce the risk to information systems that have increasingly open system architectures. This means that as organizations open more and more parts of their systems to customers, business partners, and employees, they also open themselves up to greater risk of attack from computer hackers. A bank that offers its customers an online, interactive Web site to manage checking accounts and credit cards opens itself to the threats of forged e-mails that appear to be from the bank but are in fact a clever attack to harvest the user IDs and passwords needed to access the site. Once these are acquired, bank customers are surprised to learn that their accounts have been cleaned out and they can't quite figure out why.

Other attacks in recent years have included virus and worm outbreaks that prevent internal users from accessing the systems they need to perform their jobs, and it falls upon the security professionals to find the source of the problem, eradicate it, and repair the damage it left behind. In 2003, the MS Blast worm exploited a flaw in a software feature found in most Microsoft desktop and server systems. In just 24 hours, MS Blast exploded onto some 120,000 computers around the world. A big part of the problem was that inattentive home users and overworked IT staffs hadn't been able to respond in time to prevent damage.

Large corporations use the Internet to transmit data back and forth with business suppliers, referred to as business-to-business, or B2B, processing. A manufacturing company might transmit shipping information to a third-party Web site where business partners can view the status of their orders. An internal company Internet, or intranet, might give its employees the ability to access coverage information from a health provider. Increased services to both vendors and employees create worlds of possibilities in satisfying customer needs, but they also create risks where none existed before: risks to the confidentiality, integrity, and availability of confidential or sensitive data.

The goal of this text is not to make you an expert in the technical details of information systems security. Rather, you will gain a solid foundation in the fundamental principles of information security and learn where to go in case you want to know more about a specific topic, perhaps in pursuit of a career in information security.

As custodians of this vast amount of information stored in corporate and public databases, information managers have created new positions within their organizations to address information security-related issues. Realizing that information security is no longer a "nice to have" in their IT budgets, these managers have added to their already overwhelming duties the obligation to protect the *confidentiality*, *integrity*, and *availability* of personal information—terms that you will know by heart by the end of this text. Although concern for the well-being of society can be a powerful motivator for information security managers, increasing governmental regulation such as privacy legislation and the fear of unwanted publicity over a hacked site often are what drive these managers to action. No one, from the personal computer user on a laptop to the CIO of a major corporation, can afford to ignore the importance of information security.

But why should a concern over information security translate into a possible career in information security?

Increasing Demand by Government and Private Industry

The U.S. Department of Labor predicts that the occupational outlook for computer and information systems managers will grow much faster than the average for all occupations through the year 2012. In practical terms, employment in this field is expected to increase 36 percent or more during the next decade.

In addition, the specialized training of information security professionals coupled with the growing importance of security in general could result in even higher demand for expertly trained individuals. The U.S. Bureau of Labor Statistics predicts the following:

> The security of computer networks will continue to increase in importance as more business is conducted over the Internet. The security of the Nation's entire electronic infrastructure has come under renewed focus in light of recent threats. Organizations need to understand how their systems are vulnerable and how to protect their infrastructure and Internet sites from hackers, viruses, and other acts of cyber-terrorism. The emergence of "cyber-security" as a key issue facing most organizations should lead to strong growth for computer managers. Firms will increasingly hire cyber-security experts to fill key leadership roles in their information technology departments, because the integrity of their computing environment is of the utmost concern. As a result, there will be a high demand for managers proficient in computer security issues.

Source: **www.collegegrad.com/careers/manag30.shtml.**

FYI: Corporate IT Security Jobs Pay

Base pay for corporate IT security jobs grew 3.1 percent annually over the last 36 months, while average IT pay declined nearly 6 percent overall according to a *Computerworld* magazine quarterly compensation survey. Bonuses for security professionals climbed an average of 9.5 percent, but bonus pay for IT jobs overall dropped a steep 34 percent. Premium pay for security certifications is up a whopping 23 percent since the first quarter of 2001, even though overall technical certification bonus pay declined 5 percent in that period. *Computerworld* expects security pay to continue to outperform the market. Beginning in late 2003, employers are much more aggressively recruiting security professionals with the right combination of skills, knowledge, experience, and character.

Source: Info Security Job Boom Inevitable (**www.computerworld.com/careertopics/careers/story/0,10801,73893,00.html**).

Becoming an Information Security Specialist

A specialty in information security does not come easily. The serious student must prepare himself for a challenging slate of classes in security architecture, laws and ethics, access control, disaster recovery planning, and other coursework that might not be an obvious prerequisite.

One major educational institution, Carnegie Mellon (**www.cmu.edu/**), established the Information Network Institute (INI) in 1989 as a leading research and education center in the field of information networking.

The INI offers three graduate degree programs in the areas of information networking, information technology, and information security. The degree in information security prepares students to:

- Identify the information security risks that an organization faces.

- Associate these risks with problems related to technology and human beings.

- Identify and evaluate the technology tools available to minimize risk, reduce system vulnerabilities, and maintain computer services.

- Oversee the development of a secure information security (IS) infrastructure.

- Keep abreast of IS policies, laws, and market forces and perform impact analysis for an organization.

- Maintain professional growth in IS disciplines.

The following is a sample of the curriculum for the Master of Science in Information Security from Carnegie-Mellon's Information Networking Institute:

Core Courses: 60 units	
Fundamentals of Telecommunication Networks	12 units
Intro to Information Security	12 units
Security Architecture & Analysis	12 units
Information Security Risk Management	12 units
Statistics for IT Managers/Decision Making under Uncertainty	12 units (6 units/each)
Possible Electives: 60 units	
Network Security	12 units
Security for Software Engineers	12 units
Privacy in the Digital Age	12 units
Database Management	12 units
Telecommunications Management	12 units
Curriculum Option	
MSIT-IS Project Course **OR** 24–36 units of electives from above	24–36 units
Total Program Units	**144 units**

Source: **www.ini.cmu.edu/academics/MSIT-ISJapan/index.htm.**

Although the path to becoming an information security specialist is not rigidly defined, most experts in the field believe that the following steps are becoming increasingly important to a professional interested in entering the InfoSec world:

- **Get the right certifications**, most notably the Certified Information Systems Security Professional (CISSP) certification. However, other certifications such as the Global Information Assurance Certification (GIAC) are becoming increasingly sought-after by large IT organizations. GIAC offers nine specialized security certifications ranging from the GIAC Security Essentials Certification (GSEC), which provides a foundation in basic security principles, to the more advanced GIAC Certified Forensic Analyst (GCFA), who specializes in advanced incident handling scenarios (you can learn more about such certificates at **www.giac.org**).

- **Consider earning a graduate degree in information security**, preferably one that combines technical with business training, connecting the Denial of Service (DoS) attack with the Denial of Revenue (DNR) fallout.

- **Increase your disaster recovery and risk management skills**, as not all security threats are detected before they happen. The individual who understands how to keep an operation running after an attack is that much more valuable to an organization.

- **Build a home laboratory** using the freeware and shareware readily available to individual users. The proliferation of once-private domain software allows the student to learn on his own as well as in the classroom.

- **Give something back to the information security community** by working with professional organizations and certification groups to develop best practices and enhance the Common Body of Knowledge.

- **Get on a project working with strategic partners**, something that will give you valuable experience working with vendors, business customers, and Internet service providers (ISPs) and broad exposure to the far-reaching issues of information security.

- **Consider an internship in IS if you're still in school**—good advice in any discipline.

- **Take a second look at government jobs.** Although some students may consider working for a government agency a less lucrative proposition than working in private industry, the fact is that the graying of the workforce is leading to a dearth of experienced and qualified personnel.

Schools Are Responding to Demands

Homeland security is a hot topic not only in corporate America. Higher education is responding to the need with new and robust certificate programs, degrees, and special interest courses.

Hundreds of community colleges, four-year universities, and postgraduate programs are offering degrees and certificates in emergency preparedness, counterterrorism, and security. Students study topics ranging from political science and psychology to engineering and biotechnology to prepare for possible disasters, cyber and physical.

"Homeland security will be the biggest government employer in the next decade or so. America continues to face threats, and terrorism will never go away," says Steven David, Chair of the Graduate Certificate Program in Homeland Security at Johns Hopkins University in Baltimore, Maryland.

Many companies have added homeland security sectors to their organizations, and individuals educated in the field are in demand, says Mel Bernstein, Director of University Programs for the U.S. Department of Homeland Security. "Some graduates will work in the financial sector, for the government, in insurance, for consulting companies. . . . If you look across the country, almost every company or agency has something they call a 'homeland security initiative,' and they will need people."

One of the programs that the Department of Homeland Security sponsors is an 18-month, highly selective professional training effort at the Naval Postgraduate School in Monterey, California. The school educates high-ranking emergency management and public safety officials about policy analysis, advanced strategy, and information technology. "We're taking the best and the brightest and giving them additional education so that they can go back to their cities and assume the highest positions," says Paul Stockton, associate provost at the school.

Some of the certificate programs and concentrations related to InfoSec majors include the following:

- At Ohio State University, students can get a degree in political science, sociology, or computer science with a concentration in homeland security, in which they focus on such areas as network security and bioterrorism.

- At George Washington University in Washington, D.C., certificates are offered in crisis and disaster management, telecommunications, and national security; the certificates are offered through the school's Homeland Security Policy Institute.

- Northeastern University in Boston offers programs in the law-enforcement aspect of homeland security through its College of Criminal Justice. Northeastern also received a grant from the National Institute of Justice to educate students about al-Qaeda banking and the *gray market*—the practice of transferring money from abroad to other countries, possibly to finance illicit activities.

- Monroe Community College in Rochester, New York, for example, has a $26 million Homeland Security Management Institute complete with a crime scene simulator, forensics lab, hazardous-materials training area, and aircraft simulator. It also offers training that educates community members on what to do if disaster strikes.

Multidisciplinary Approach

Information Security magazine offers this advice for people interested in pursuing a career in information security:

The best place to start is by establishing a major in either computer science or MIS, complemented with as many InfoSec courses as possible.

A good curriculum will include courses in logic, programming, operating systems, data structures, quality assurance, and cryptography and data communications. Whatever isn't offered in the classroom should be compensated for through outside, independent study—in other words, read a lot. In addition to these core computer subjects, students should augment their studies with courses in probability and statistics, psychology, English, foreign language, philosophy, ethics and history. Beyond the undergraduate level, a growing number of InfoSec students are continuing their education in law school, giving themselves a legal foundation to deal with the privacy and liability issues associated with security.

Source: **http://infosecuritymag.techtarget.com/articles/may01/ features_career_advice.shtml.**

What is the benefit of melding hard-core computer courses with liberal arts studies? The answer is perspective. Computer code is binary, but the real world isn't. Exposure to nontechnical areas gives InfoSec professionals a greater ability to address and solve the complex problems encountered in IT/IS environments. For instance, a computer science student could write a term paper on the history of cryptography and illustrate it with examples of the different encryption techniques used by intelligence agents throughout the ages. A programming class project could focus on the importance of good business practices and human-resource management. In other words, information security specialists need to have a holistic view of the world around them and avoid a strictly technical orientation.

Bottom line: A wide range of educational experiences is a good foundation for an InfoSec career.

Contextualizing Information Security

As the world's computers become more interconnected, and as more people and companies rely on the global village to communicate and transact, the more exposed these systems become to successful break-in attempts. As noted by Bruce Schneier, Principal of Counterpane Internet Security Inc. and foremost expert and authority on computer security, "The only secure computer is one that is turned off, locked in a safe, and buried 20 feet down in a secret location—and I'm not completely confident of that one either" (Schneier 1995).

Disconnected and buried computers don't serve anyone well, and eventually someone will connect it to the Internet. Understanding the risks in making these connections is comparable to launching an effective defense against a well-armed and well-prepared enemy. To defend yourself adequately, you need to prepare for anything the offense throws at you. This preparation begins with a comprehensive understanding of the security umbrella, as illustrated in Figure 1.1.

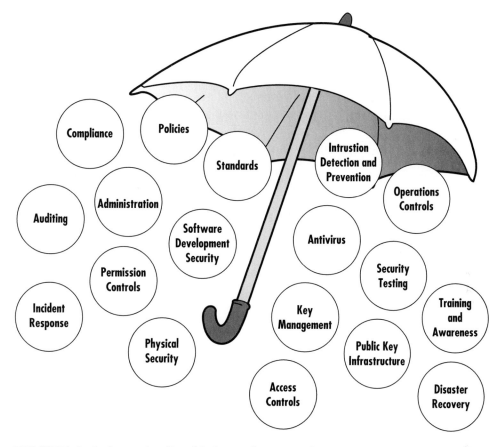

FIGURE 1.1 An umbrella of information security.

As you see in Figure 1.1, InfoSec is a discipline that's difficult to put your arms around. Each topic within the umbrella can easily fill an entire book, and many would require an encyclopedia for a more complete understanding. Information security draws upon the best practices and experiences from multiple domains but always begins with the nontechnical, human-centric aspects of a security posture. An organization's security posture defines its tolerance for risk and outlines how it plans to protect information and resources within its charge. This posture is documented in standards, guidelines, and procedures that must exist long before a single program is written or a computer is installed.

Information Security Careers Meet the Needs of Business

Companies are not spending millions of dollars in information security just for the sake of security. IT security is needed to protect the business both from itself and from outsiders who would cause it harm. To support business operations—regardless of the industry—a number of common positions and career opportunities are needed to prevent and respond to business needs.

- Security administrators work alongside system administrators and database administrators to assure that an appropriate separation of duties exists to prevent abuse of privilege when new computer systems are implemented and users begin to access these systems. The security administrators help to establish new user accounts, assure that auditing mechanisms are present and operating as needed, assure that communications between systems are securely implemented, and assist in troubleshooting problems and responding to incidents that could compromise confidentiality, integrity, or availability of the systems.

- Access coordinators are those who are delegated the authority on behalf of a system owner to establish and maintain the user base that is permitted to access and use the system in the normal course of their job duties.

- Security architects and network engineers design and implement network infrastructures that are built with security in mind. Skills needed here include understanding firewall designs, designing and developing intrusion detection systems and processes, and determining how to configure servers and desktop computers to comply with security policies.

- Security consultants work with project-development teams to perform risk analysis of new systems by balancing the needs of business with the threats that stem from opening up access to data or managing new information that could compromise the business if it fell into the wrong hands. Security consultants are usually internal personnel who are assigned to project-development teams and remain with the project from inception to implementation.

- Security testers are the *white-hat hacker*s paid to test the security of newly acquired and newly developed or redeveloped systems. Testers who can mimic the activities of outside hackers are hired to find software problems and bugs before the system is made available, and their work reduces the likelihood that the system will be compromised once it's in day-to-day operating mode.

- Policymakers and standards developers are the people who look to outside regulators and executive management to set the tone and establish the specific rules of the road when interacting or managing information systems. Policymakers formally encode the policies or management intentions in how information will be secured.

■ Compliance officers check to see that employees remain in compliance with security policies and standards as they use information systems in their daily work. Compliance officers usually work with outside regulators when audits are conducted and are often charged with employee security training and awareness programs to help maintain compliance.

■ Incident response team members are alerted when an intrusion or security incident occurs and decide how to stop the attack or limit the damage as they collect and analyze forensics data for interacting with law enforcement personnel and executive management.

■ Governance and vendor managers are needed to assure that outsourced functions are operating within security policies and standards. As the IT industry continues to rely on off-shore developers, managed security services, and outsourced computer operations, the growth of governance personnel is assured.

For a view of a typical structure and context of where IT Security fits within a typical large services corporation, see Figure 1.2.

Studying InfoSec is challenging and often overwhelming to beginners. It's easy to get lost or confused when studying security because there are many areas to understand. Rather than approaching the discipline with a focus on one or two major areas, students are better served by understanding

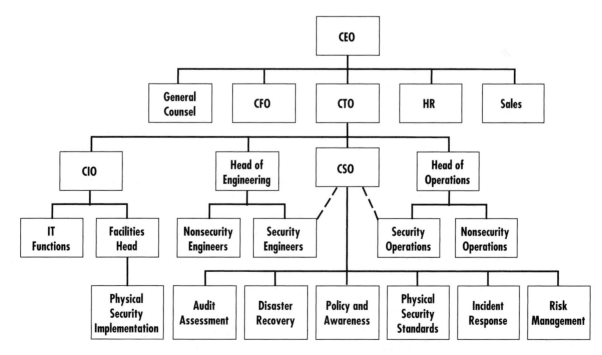

FIGURE 1.2 A typical information security organization structure.

InfoSec in context, as you'll begin to see in Chapter 2. This is best accomplished by understanding the principles, foundations, and durable, rarely changing "truths." With a principles-based view of InfoSec, you'll be able to analyze a security need in the right frame of reference or context so you can balance the needs of permitting access versus the risk of allowing such access.

Summary

Technology experts are recognizing the increasing importance of a rigorous information security discipline. This need is based on the expanding use of technology, primarily the Internet, and the risks posed to networked systems, many of which are not secure and remain vulnerable to attacks from within and without an organization.

This realization has led to a growing demand for professionals trained in information security. This is reflected in the growing job prospects for those seeking a career in information security, which look better than average through the year 2012. The explosive growth of e-commerce and the pervasive personal and business uses of the Internet have created a growing demand for information security specialists.

Homeland security and cyber terrorism have raised the stakes in the global village and have underscored the need for constant vigilance and preventative, detective, and corrective controls in order to counter threats sufficiently to conduct business in a safe, secure, and embracing environment that focuses on meeting business and personal needs.

The fundamentals of information security are mostly commonsense principles, approaches, and concepts that work together like a symphony orchestra to provide the harmonious mix of risk and reward that modern business demands.

Test Your Skills

MULTIPLE CHOICE QUESTIONS

1. Information security is primarily a discipline to manage the behavior of:

   A. technology

   B. people

   C. processes

   D. organizations

2. Careers in information security are booming because of which factors?

   A. threats of cyber terrorism

   B. government regulations

   C. growth of the Internet

   D. all of the above

3. The three objectives of information security are:

   A. confidentiality, integrity, and availability.

   B. resilience, privacy, and safety.

   C. confidentiality, secrecy, and privacy.

   D. safety, access control, and secrecy.

4. A good definition of *information security* should include:

   A. security policies and procedures.

   B. intentional attacks only.

   C. unintentional attacks only.

   D. none of the above.

5. The growing demand for InfoSec specialists is occurring predominantly in what types of organizations?

   A. government

   B. corporations

   C. not-for-profit foundations

   D. all of the above

6. Which college curriculum is more appropriate for a career in information security?

   A. business administration

   B. computer information sciences

   C. both A and B

   D. none of the above

7. What is meant by the *umbrella of information security*?

   A. When it rains, it pours.

   B. IS incorporates many different pursuits and disciplines.

   C. Just as it is bad luck to open an umbrella indoors, it is equally bad luck not to have an information security policy.

   D. IS policies, like umbrellas, should never be loaned to others as they are easily lost or misused.

8. The formal study of information security has accelerated primarily for what reason?

   A. the attack of September 11

   B. the formation of the U.S. Department of Homeland Security

   C. object-oriented programming

   D. increasingly interconnected global networks

9. Which of the following would make an individual seeking a career in information security more marketable?

   A. CISSP certification

   B. GIAC certification

   C. evaluating virus-protection software on a home computer

   D. all of the above

10. A career in information security:

    A. has a better job growth outlook than other areas within IT.

    B. is limited by the programming languages the candidate knows.

    C. will eventually disappear with improvements in IS tools.

    D. is a highly complex but narrow discipline.

11. Sound information security policy:

    A. is worth any price.

    B. is a balance between the cost of protecting information and the value of the information being protected.

    C. belongs exclusively to the IT department.

    D. results in unique practices and policies specific to the owning IT department.

12. Which of the following topics would not be part of a program in information security?

    A. laws and ethical practices

    B. file access control

    C. security architecture

    D. All of the above would be classes you could expect in an IS program.

13. Which of the following roles helps development teams with meeting security requirements?

    A. policymakers

    B. compliance officers

    C. security consultants

    D. security architects

14. Who is responsible for assuring that systems are auditable and protected from excessive privileges?

    A. compliance officers

    B. access coordinators

    C. security administrators

    D. policymakers

15. Which of the following roles are responsible for assuring that third-party suppliers and outsourced functions remain in security compliance?

    A. compliance officers

    B. vendor managers

    C. security architects

    D. access coordinators

EXERCISES

Exercise 1.1: Look at Salary Growth Among Information Security Careers

1. Visit *Information Security Magazine* online at **http://infosecurity mag.techtarget.com**.

2. Compare the growth in salaries since the year 2000 in careers related to InfoSec.

3. Record and graph the data in an Excel worksheet.

4. What are the year-over-year increases in wages from 2000 to 2005?

5. Can you predict how wages will continue to rise through 2012?

Exercise 1.2: Search for College Programs in IS

1. Use an Internet search engine of your choice to find certificate and degree programs in information security.

2. Use an Internet search engine of your choice to find certificate and degree programs in information assurance.

3. Use an Internet search engine of your choice to find certificate and degree programs in network security.

4. Use an Internet search engine of your choice to find certificate and degree programs in physical security.

5. What is common among these programs? What makes each one unique?

Exercise 1.3: National Security Agency Education in Information Assurance Programs

1. Visit the National Security Agency Centers of Academic Excellence home page at **www.nsa.gov/ia/academia/caeiae.cfm**.

2. Review the criteria for measurement of educational institutions that participate in the program.

3. Review the list of participating institutions and select a college or university in your region or state.

4. Compare the curriculum from that institution with the curriculum outlined in this chapter.

Exercise 1.4: Review NSA/DHS Partnership on Security Education

1. Visit the National Security Agency and Department of Homeland Security Partnership Announcement at **www.nsa.gov/releases/relea 00077.cfm**.

2. Determine what the partnership aims to achieve.

3. How does the program support the U.S. National Strategy to Secure Cyberspace (**www.whitehouse.gov/pcipb/**)?

Exercise 1.5: For-Profit Education

1. Visit the MIS Training Institute (**www.misti.com**).

2. Look for certification programs in information security.

3. Review the courses offered in these programs.

4. How do these course offerings compare with state university programs in information security?

PROJECTS

Project 1.1: Identifying the Multidisciplinary Approach

Based on what you have learned so far about information security, discuss what you think is meant by "information security in a business context." Think about other seemingly unrelated coursework you are taking and examine ways in which it may help build a foundation for a background in information security.

Project 1.2: Getting Some Practical Advice

Select a local business or organization with a sizeable IT department (e.g., more than 100 IT employees) and identify the person in charge of information security. Interview the individual and ask for practical advice about the kind of training and experience the IT security manager is looking for in candidates.

Project 1.3: Charting Your Course

What area of information security seems most interesting to you at this point? What motivates you to investigate this area further for career opportunities?

Case Study

Growth in career opportunities for information security professionals is all but assured over the next few decades. Between the efforts of the U.S. Department of Homeland Security to combat the threats of cyber terrorism, the rise in organized crime through electronic intrusions, the ever-rising threat of identity theft, and the general attack on personal privacy and credit card data, it's a never-ending battle between good and evil. As companies increasingly open access to their systems for customer self-service and as e-commerce continues to grow unabated, the needs for qualified personnel outstrip the ability to fill these positions.

Imagine that you are in a position to attract IT security personnel for a brick-and-mortar retailer that is establishing a new e-commerce site for nationwide sales of the retailer's products. Where would you begin to search? How much would you be willing to pay? How will you know you've built the right organization to respond appropriately to business needs?

Chapter 2

Information Security
Principles of Success

Chapter Objectives

**After reading this chapter and completing the exercises,
you will be able to do the following:**

- Build an awareness of 12 generally accepted basic principles of information security to help you determine how these basic principles are applied to real-life situations.

- Distinguish between the three main security goals.

- Learn how to design and apply the principle of "Defense in Depth."

- Comprehend human vulnerabilities in security systems to better design solutions to counter them.

- Explain the difference between functional and assurance requirements.

- Comprehend the fallacy of *security through obscurity* to avoid using it as a measure of security.

- Comprehend the importance of risk analysis and risk management tools and techniques for balancing the needs of business.

- Determine which side of the open disclosure debate you would take.

Introduction

Many of the topics information technology students study in school can be carried directly from the classroom to the workplace. For example, new programming and systems analysis and design skills can often be applied on new systems-development projects as companies espouse object-oriented analysis and programming to internal systems.

Security is a little different. Although their technical skills are certainly important, the best security specialists combine their practical knowledge of computers and networks with general theories about security, technology, and human nature. These concepts, some borrowed from other fields such as military defense, often take years of (sometimes painful) professional experience to learn. With a conceptual and principles view of information security, you'll be able to analyze a security need in the right frame of reference or context so you can balance the needs of permitting access versus the risk allowing such access. No two systems or situations are identical, and there are no cookbooks to consult on how to solve security problems, so it's imperative to rely on principle-based analysis and decision making.

This chapter introduces these key information security principles, concepts, and durable "truths."

Principle 1: There Is No Such Thing as Absolute Security

In 2003, the art collection of the Whitworth Gallery in Manchester, England, included three famous paintings by Van Gogh, Picasso, and Gauguin. Valued at more than $7 million, the paintings were protected by closed-circuit television, a series of alarm systems, and 24-hour rolling patrols. Yet, in late April 2003, thieves broke into the museum, evaded the layered security system, and made off with the three masterpieces. Several days later, investigators discovered the paintings in a nearby public restroom along with a note from the thieves saying, "The intention was not to steal, only to highlight the woeful security."

The burglars' lesson translates to the information security arena and illustrates the first principle of information security (IS): Given enough time, tools, skills, and inclination, a hacker can break through any security measure. This principle applies to the physical world as well and is best illustrated by using the analogy of safes or vaults, which businesses commonly use to protect their assets. Safes are rated according to their resistance to attacks using a scale that describes how long it could take a burglar to open them. They are divided into a number of categories based on the level of protection they can deliver and the testing they undergo. Four common classes of safe ratings are B-Rate, C-Rate, ULTL-15, and ULTL-30:

- **B-Rate:** B-Rate is a catchall rating for any box with a lock on it and describes the thickness of the steel used to make the lockbox. No actual testing is performed to gain this rating.

- **C-Rate:** This is defined as a variably thick steel box with a 1-inch-thick door and a lock. No tests are given to provide this rating either.

- **ULTL-15:** Safes with an Underwriters Laboratory (UL) TL-15 rating have passed standardized tests as defined in UL Standard

2

687 using tools and an expert group of safe-testing engineers. The UL TL-15 label requires that the safe be constructed of 1-inch solid steel or equivalent. The label means that the safe has been tested for a net working time of 15 minutes using ". . . common hand tools, drills, punches hammers, and pressure applying devices." Net working time means that when the tool comes off the safe, the clock is stopped. Engineers exercise more than 50 different types of attacks that have proved effective for safecracking.

- **ULTL-30:** UL TL-30 testing is essentially the same as the TL-15 testing except for the net working time. Testers get 30 minutes and a few more tools to help them gain access. Testing engineers usually have a safe's manufacturing blueprints and can disassemble the safe before the test begins to see how it works.

As you will see in Chapter 5, security testing of hardware and software systems employs many of the same concepts of safe testing, using computers and custom-developed testing software instead of tools and torches, but the outcomes of testing are just the same—like software, no safe is burglar proof; it will simply buy time. This leads to the second principle.

Principle 2: The Three Security Goals Are Confidentiality, Integrity, and Availability

All information security measures try to address at least one of three goals:

- Protect the *confidentiality* of data.
- Preserve the *integrity* of data.
- Promote the *availability* of data for authorized use.

These goals form the confidentiality, integrity, availability (CIA) triad (see Figure 2.1 for a diagram of the CIA triad). The CIA triad is the basis of all security programs. Information security professionals who create policies and procedures (often referred to as *models*) must consider each goal when creating a plan to protect a computer system.

Caution

Confidentiality Models

Confidentiality models are primarily intended to assure that no unauthorized access to information is permitted and that accidental disclosure of sensitive information is not possible. Common confidentiality controls are user IDs and passwords.

FYI: Confidentiality by Another Name

Confidentiality is sometimes referred to as the "principle of least privilege," meaning that users should only be given enough privilege to perform their duties, and no more. Some other synonyms for confidentiality you may encounter include privacy, secrecy, and discretion.

FIGURE 2.1 The CIA triad.

Integrity Models

Integrity models keep data pure and trustworthy by protecting system data from intentional or accidental changes. Integrity models have three goals:

- Prevent unauthorized users from making modifications to data or programs.

- Prevent authorized users from making improper or unauthorized modifications.

- Maintain internal and external consistency of data and programs.

An example of integrity checks would be balancing a batch of transactions to make sure that all the information is present and accurately accounted for.

Availability Models

Availability models keep data and resources available for authorized use, especially during emergencies or disasters. Information security professionals usually address three common challenges to availability:

- Denial of Service (DoS) due to intentional attacks or because of undiscovered flaws in implementation (e.g., a program written by a programmer who is unaware of a flaw that could crash the program if a certain unexpected input is encountered).

- Loss of information system capabilities because of natural disasters (e.g., fires, floods, storms, or earthquakes) or human actions (e.g., bombs or strikes).

- Equipment failures during normal use

Some of the activities that preserve confidentiality, integrity, and/or availability are the granting of access only to authorized personnel, applying

---

Caution

CIA Triad

The principle of information security protection of confidentiality, integrity, and availability cannot be overemphasized and is central to all studies and practices in IS. You'll often see the term *CIA triad* to illustrate the overall goals for IS throughout the research, guidance, and practices you encounter.

encryption to information that will be sent out over the Internet, periodic testing of operating system security to uncover new vulnerabilities, and developing a disaster recovery plan to assure that the business can continue to exist in the event of a disaster or loss of access by personnel.

Principle 3: Defense in Depth as Strategy

A bank would never leave its assets inside an unguarded safe alone. Typically, access to the safe requires passing through layers of protection that may include human guards and locked doors with special access controls. Furthermore, the room where the safe resides may be monitored by closed-circuit television, motion sensors, and alarm systems that can quickly detect unusual activity. The sound of an alarm may trigger the doors to automatically lock, the police to be notified, or the room to fill with tear gas.

Layered security, like the example described above, is called *defense in depth*. Defense in depth is security implemented in overlapping layers that provide the three elements needed to secure assets: prevention, detection, and response. Defense in depth also means that the weaknesses of one security layer are offset by the strengths of two or more layers.

In the information security world, defense in depth means you should layer security devices in a series that protects, detects, and responds to attacks on systems. For example, a typical Internet-attached network designed with security in mind includes routers, firewalls, and intrusion detection systems (IDS) to protect the network from would-be intruders; it employs traffic analyzers and real-time human monitors who watch for anomalies as the network is being used to detect any breach in the layers of protection; and it relies on automated mechanisms to turn off access or remove the system from the network in response to detection of an intruder.

Finally, the security of each of these mechanisms must be thoroughly tested before deployment to ensure that the integrated system is suitable for normal operations. After all, a chain is only as good as its weakest link.

Principle 4: When Left on Their Own, People Tend to Make the Worst Security Decisions

The primary reason that identity theft, viruses, worms, and stolen passwords are so common is that people are easily duped into giving up the secrets that technologies use to secure systems. Organizers of Infosecurity Europe 2003, Britain's biggest information technology security exhibition, sent researchers to London's Waterloo Station to ask commuters to hand over their office computer passwords in exchange for a free pen. Three-quarters of respondents revealed the information immediately and an additional 15 percent did so after some gentle probing. Study after study like this one shows how little it takes to convince someone to give up their credentials in exchange for trivial or worthless goods.

Virus writers know all too well how easy it is to fool people into spreading their viruses for them. A good example is the Anna Kournikova VBS.SST computer virus, informally known as "Anna." This viral worm swept through the computing world in 2001. It used Visual Basic to infect Windows systems when a user unwittingly opened an e-mail note with an attachment that appeared to be a graphic image of Russian tennis star Anna Kournikova. When the file was opened, a clandestine code extension enabled the worm to copy itself to the Windows directory and then send the file as an attachment to all the addresses listed in the victim's Microsoft Outlook e-mail address book.

The virus arrived as an e-mail with the following subject, message, and attachment:

```
Subject: Here you have, ;o)
Message body: Hi: Check This!
Attachment: AnnaKournikova.jpg.vbs
```

That's all it took. Despite the primitive nature of this attack, many people were easily convinced to double-click on the attachment hoping for a quick peek at Anna. Because of Anna and other viruses like it, computer users are now much more wary of opening e-mail attachments from unknown sources. However, today's virus writers are far more sophisticated and use dozens of other ways to convince people to open an attachment or visit a rogue Web site.

IN PRACTICE: Phishing for Dollars

Phishing is another good example of how easily intelligent people can be duped into breaching security. Phishing is a dangerous Internet scam, named after the hacking community's use of "ph" instead of "f," which comes from the days of phone *phreaking* in the 1970s. Phone phreakers, with the most famous among them named Captain Crunch (John Draper), discovered that the free whistle that used to come packaged with Captain Crunch cereal produced the identical tone to coins dropped in a pay-phone slot, thus permitting the phreaker to make unlimited and untraceable long-distance telephone calls. A phishing scam typically operates as follows:

- The victim receives an "official looking" e-mail message purporting to come from a trusted source, such as an online banking site, Paypal, eBay, or other service where money is exchanged, moved, or managed.

■ The e-mail tells the user that his or her account needs updating immediately or will be suspended within *X* number of days.

■ The e-mail contains a URL (link) and instructs the user to click on the link to access their account and update their information. The link text appears as though it will take the user to the site they expect. The link itself is actually a link to the attacker's site, which is made to look exactly like the site the user expects to see.

■ Once at the spoofed site, the user enters his or her credentials (ID and password) and clicks on submit.

■ The site returns an innocuous message, such as "We're sorry—we're unable to process your transaction at this time" or a similar message and the user is none the wiser.

■ At this point, the victim's credentials are stored on the attacker's site or sent via e-mail to the perpetrator where they can be used to log-in to the *real* banking or exchange site and empty it before the user knows what happened.

Phishing and the resultant ID theft and monetary losses are on the increase and will only begin to slow down once the cycle is broken through awareness and education. Protect yourself by taking the following steps:

■ Look for telltale signs of a fraud—rather than addressing you by name, a phishing e-mail will address you as "User" or by your e-mail address—a legitimate message from a legitimate company will use your name as they know it.

■ Do not click on links embedded in unsolicited finance-related e-mail messages. It's simple to make a link look legitimate, but when you click on it, you may be redirected to the site of a phisher. If you believe that your account is in jeopardy, type in the known URL of the site in a new browser window and look for messages from the provider after you're logged in.

■ Check with your provider for messages related to phishing scams that they are aware of. Your bank or other financial services provider wants to make sure that you don't fall victim and often go out of their way to educate users on preventing problems.

Principle 5: Computer Security Depends on Two Types of Requirements: Functional and Assurance

Functional requirements describe what a system *should* do, and *assurance requirements* describe how functional requirements should be implemented and tested. Both sets of requirements are needed to answer the following questions:

- Does the system do the right things (i.e., behave as promised)?

- Does the system do the right things in the right way?

These are the same questions that others in noncomputer industries face with verification and validation. Verification is the process of confirming that one or more predetermined requirements, or specifications, are met. Validation then is a determination of the correctness or quality of the mechanisms used in meeting the needs. In other words, you can develop software that addresses a need, but it may contain flaws that could compromise data when placed in the hands of a malicious user.

Using car safety testing as an example, verification testing for seat belt functions may include stress tests on the fabric, testing the locking mechanisms, and making certain the belt will fit the intended application, thus completing the functional tests. Validation, or assurance testing, might then include crashing the car with crash-test dummies inside to "prove" that the seat belt is indeed safe when used under normal conditions and can survive under harsh conditions.

With software, you need both verification and validation answers to gain confidence in products prior to launching them into a wild, hostile environment like the Internet. Most of today's *commercial off-the-shelf (COTS)* software and systems stop at the first step, verification, without bothering to test for obvious security vulnerabilities in the final product. Developers of software generally lack the wherewithal and motivation needed to try and break their own software. More often, developers will test that the software meets the specifications in each function that is present but usually do not try to find ways of circumventing the software in an attempt to make it fail. You'll learn more about security testing of software in Chapter 5, Security Architectures and Models.

Principle 6: Security Through Obscurity Is Not an Answer

Many in the information security industry believe that if hackers don't know *how* software is secured, security is better. Although this may seem logical, it's actually untrue. Security through obscurity means that hiding the details of the security mechanisms is sufficient to secure the system alone. An example of security through obscurity might involve closely guarding the written specifications for security functions and preventing all but the most trusted people from seeing it. Obscuring security leads to a *false* sense of security, which is often more dangerous than not addressing security at all.

If the security of a system is maintained by keeping the implementation of the system a secret, once the first person discovers how the security mechanism works, the entire system collapses—and someone is always determined to discover these secrets. The better bet is to make sure that no one mechanism is responsible for the security of the entire system. This again is defense in depth in everything related to protecting data and resources.

In Chapter 11, Cryptography, you'll see how this principle applies and why it makes no sense to keep an algorithm for cryptography secret when the security of the system should rely on the cryptographic keys used to protect data or authenticate a user. You can also see this in action with the open-source movement where anyone can gain access to program (source) code and analyze it for security problems and then share with the community improvements that eliminate vulnerabilities and/or improve the overall security through simplification (see Principle 9).

Principle 7: Security = Risk Management

It's critical to understand that spending more on securing an asset than the intrinsic value of the asset is a waste of resources. For example, buying a $500 safe to protect $200 worth of jewelry makes no practical sense. The same is true when protecting electronic assets. All security work is a careful balance between the level of risk and the expected reward of expending a given amount of resources. Security is not concerned with eliminating all threats within a system or facility but with eliminating known threats and minimizing losses if an attacker succeeds in exploiting a vulnerability. Risk analysis and risk management are central themes to securing information systems. Once risks are well understood, there are three possible outcomes:

- The risks are mitigated (countered).

- Insurance against the losses that would occur should a system be compromised is acquired.

- The risks are accepted and the consequences are managed.

Risk assessment and risk analysis are concerned with placing an economic value on assets to best determine appropriate countermeasures that protect them from losses.

Likelihood	Consequences				
	1. Insignificant	2. Minor	3. Moderate	4. Major	6. Catastrophic
A (almost certain)	High	High	Extreme	Extreme	Extreme
B (likely)	Moderate	High	High	Extreme	Extreme
C (moderate)	Low	Moderate	High	Extreme	Extreme
D (unlikely)	Low	Low	Moderate	High	Extreme
E (rare)	Low	Low	Moderate	High	High

FIGURE 2.2 Consequences/likelihood matrix for risk analysis.

The simplest form of determining the degree of a risk is by looking at two factors:

■ What is the consequence of a loss?

■ What is the likelihood that this loss will occur?

Figure 2.2 illustrates a matrix you can use to determine the degree of a risk based on these factors.

Once a risk rating has been determined, one of the following actions may be required:

■ Extreme risk: immediate action required.

■ High risk: senior management attention needed.

■ Moderate risk: management responsibility must be specified.

■ Low risk: manage by routine procedures.

In the real world, risk management is more complicated than simply making a human judgment call based on intuition or previous experience with a similar situation. Recall that every system has unique security issues and considerations, so it's imperative to understand the specific nature of data the system will maintain, what hardware and software will be used to deploy the system, and the security skills of the development teams. Determining the likelihood of a risk coming to life requires understanding a few more terms and concepts:

■ Vulnerability

■ Exploit

■ Attacker

Vulnerability refers to a known problem within a system or program. A common example in InfoSec is called the *buffer overflow* or *buffer overrun* vulnerability. Programmers tend to be trusting and do not worry about who will attack their programs but rather about who will use their programs legitimately. One feature of most programs is the ability for a user to "input" information or requests. The program instructions (source code) then will contain an "area" in memory (buffer) for these inputs and act upon them when told to do so. Sometimes the programmer won't check to see if the input is proper or innocuous. A malicious user, however, might take advantage of this weakness and overload the input area with more information than it can handle, crashing or disabling the program. This is called *buffer overflow* and might permit the malicious user to gain control over the system. This is a very common vulnerability in nearly all versions of all software and must be addressed when developing systems. This will be covered in greater detail in Chapter 13, "Application Software Development Security."

An *exploit* is a program or a "cookbook" on how to take advantage of a specific vulnerability. It might be a program that a hacker can download over the Internet and then use to search for systems that contain the vulnerability it's designed to exploit. It might also be a series of steps that are documented on how to exploit the vulnerability once an attacker finds a system that contains it.

An attacker, then, is the link between a vulnerability and an exploit. The attacker has two characteristics: skill and will. He is either skilled in the art of attacking systems or has access to tools that do the work for him. He has the will to perform attacks on systems he does not own and usually cares little about the consequences of his actions.

In applying these concepts to risk analysis, the IS practitioner must anticipate who might want to attack the system, how capable the attacker may be, how available the exploits to a vulnerability are, and which systems have the vulnerability present.

Risk analysis and risk management are specialized areas of study and practice, and the IS professionals who concentrate in these areas must be skilled and current in their techniques. You'll find more on Risk Management in Chapter 4, Security Management.

Principle 8: The Three Types of Security Controls Are Preventative, Detective, and Responsive

Controls (such as documented processes) and countermeasures (such as firewalls) must be implemented as one or more of these above types, else the controls are not there for the purposes of security. Shown in another triad, the principle of defense in depth dictates that a security mechanism serves a purpose by preventing a compromise, detecting that a compromise or compromise attempt is underway, or responding to a compromise while it's happening or after it has been discovered.

Referring to the example of the bank vault in Principle 3, access to a bank's safe or vault requires passing through layers of protection that may include human guards and locked doors with special access controls (prevention). In the room where the safe resides, closed-circuit televisions, motion sensors, and alarm systems quickly detect any unusual activity (detection). The sound of an alarm may trigger the doors to automatically lock, the police to be notified, or the room to fill with tear gas (response).

These controls are the basic toolkit for the security practitioner who mixes and matches them to carry out the objectives of confidentiality, integrity, and/or availability by using people, processes, or technology (see Principle 11) to bring them to life.

Principle 9: Complexity Is the Enemy of Security

The more complex a system gets, the harder it is to secure. With too many "moving parts" or interfaces between programs and other systems, the system or interfaces become difficult to secure while still permitting them to operate as intended. You'll learn in Chapter 5 how complexity can easily get in the way of comprehensive testing of security mechanisms.

Principle 10: Fear, Uncertainty, and Doubt Do *Not* Work in Selling Security

There was a time where it was effective to "scare" management into spending resources on security to avoid the unthinkable. The tactic of fear, uncertainty, and doubt (FUD) no longer works: Information security management is now too mature. Now, IS managers must justify all investments in security using techniques of the trade. Although this makes the job of information security practitioners more difficult, it also makes them more valuable because of management's need to understand what is being protected and why. When spending resources can be justified with good, solid business rationale, security requests are rarely denied.

Principle 11: People, Process, and Technology Are *All* Needed to Adequately Secure a System or Facility

As described in Principle 3, "Defense in Depth as Strategy," the information security practitioner needs a series of countermeasures and controls to implement an effective security system. One such control might be *dual control*, a practice borrowed from the military. The U.S. Department of Defense uses a dual control protocol to secure the nation's nuclear arsenal. This means that at least two on-site people must agree in order to launch a nuclear weapon. If one person were in control, she could make an error in judgment or act maliciously for whatever reason. But with dual control, one person acts as a countermeasure to the other: Chances are less likely that both people will make an error in judgment or act maliciously. Likewise, no one person in an organization should have the ability to control or close down a security activity. This is commonly referred to as *separation of duties*.

Process controls are implemented to assure that different people can perform the same operations exactly in the same way each time. Processes are documented as procedures on how to carry out an activity related to security. The process to configure a server operating system for secure operations is documented as one or more procedures that security administrators use and can be verified as done correctly.

Just as the information security professional might establish process controls to make sure that a single person cannot gain complete control over a system, she should never place all of her faith in technology. Technology can fail, and without people to notice and fix technical problems, computer systems would stall permanently. This type of waste would be illustrated by installing an expensive firewall system (a network perimeter security device that blocks traffic), and then turning around and opening all the ports that are intended to block certain traffic from entering the network.

People, process, and technology controls are essential elements of several areas of practice in information technology (IT) security including operations security, applications development security, physical security, and cryptography. These three pillars of security are often depicted as a three-legged stool (see Figure 2.3).

Process

People   **Technology**

FIGURE 2.3 The people, process, and technology triad.

IN PRACTICE: How People, Process, and Technology Work in Harmony

To illustrate how people, process, and technology work together to secure systems, let's take a look a how the security department grants access to users for performing their duties. The process, called *user access request*, is initiated when a new user is brought into the company or switches her department or role within the company. The user access request form is initially completed by the user and approved by her manager.

Once the user access request is approved, it's routed to information security access coordinators to process using the documented procedures for granting access. Once access is granted and the process for sharing the user's ID and password are followed, the system's technical access control system takes over to protect the system from unauthorized access by requiring a user ID and password and preventing password guessing by an unauthorized person by limiting the number of attempts to three before locking the account from further access attempts.

Principle 12: Open Disclosure of Vulnerabilities Is Good for Security!

A raging and often heated debate within the security community and software developing centers concerns whether to let users know about a problem before a fix or patch can be developed and distributed. Principle 6 tells us that security through obscurity is not an answer: Keeping a given vulnerability secret from users and from the software developer can only lead to a false sense of security. Users have a right to know about defects in the products they purchase, just as they have a right to know about automobile recalls because of defects. The need to know trumps the need to keep secrets in order to give users the right to protect themselves.

IN PRACTICE: To Disclose or Not to Disclose; That Is the Question!

Having specific knowledge of a security vulnerability gives administrators the knowledge to properly defend their systems from related exploits. The ethical question is how should that valuable

2

information be disseminated to the good guys while keeping it away from the bad guys? The simple truth is that you can't! Hackers tend to communicate among themselves *far* better than professional security practitioners ever could. Hackers know about most vulnerabilities long before the general public gets wind of them. By the time the general public is made aware, the hacker community has already developed a workable exploit and disseminated it far and wide to take advantage of the flaw before it can be patched or closed down.

Because of this, open disclosure benefits the general public far more than is acknowledged by the critics who claim that it gives the bad guys the same information.

Bottom Line: If you uncover an obvious problem, raise your hand and let someone who can do something about it know. You'll sleep better at night!

Summary

To be most effective, computer security specialists must not only know the technical side of their jobs but also must understand the principles behind information security. No two situations that security professionals review are identical, and there are no recipes or cookbooks on universal security measures. Because each situation calls for a distinct judgment to address the specific risks inherent in information systems, principles-based decision-making is an imperative. There's an old saw that states, "If you only have a hammer, every problem looks like a nail." This approach simply does not serve today's businesses, which are always striving to balance risk and reward of access to electronic records. The goal is to help you create a toolkit and develop the skills to use these tools like a master craftsman. Learn these principles, take them to heart, and you'll start out much farther along than your peers who won't take the time to bother learning them!

As you explore the rest of the Common Body of Knowledge (CBK) domains, try to relate the practices you find to one or more of these. For example, Chapter 8 covers physical security, which addresses how to limit access to physical spaces and hardware to authorized personnel. This helps prevent breaches in confidentiality, integrity, and availability and implements the principle of defense in depth. As you will find, these principles are mixed and matched to describe why certain security functions and operations exist in the real world of IT.

Test Your Skills

MULTIPLE CHOICE QUESTIONS

1. The three goals of information security are:

   A. confidentiality, integrity, and availability.

   B. prevention, detection, and response.

   C. people controls, process controls, and technology controls.

   D. network security, PC security, and mainframe security.

2. Making sure that data has not been changed unintentionally due to an accident or malice is:

   A. availability.

   B. confidentiality.

   C. integrity.

   D. auditability.

3. Related to information security, confidentiality is the opposite of which of the following?

   A. closure

   B. disclosure

   C. disaster

   D. disposal

4. The CIA triad is often represented by a:

   A. triangle.

   B. diagonal.

   C. ellipse.

   D. circle.

5. Defense in depth is needed to assure that which three mandatory activities are present in a security system?

   A. prevention, response, and prosecution

   B. response, collection of evidence, and prosecution

   C. prevention, detection, and response

   D. prevention, response, and management

6. The weakest link in any security system is the:
   A. technology element.
   B. process element.
   C. human element.
   D. B and C.

7. The two types of IT security requirements are:
   A. functional and logical.
   B. logical and physical.
   C. functional and assurance.
   D. functional and physical.

8. Security functional requirements describe:
   A. what a security system should do by design.
   B. what controls a security system must implement.
   C. quality assurance description and testing approach.
   D. how to implement the system.

9. Security assurance requirements describe:
   A. how to test the system.
   B. how to program the system.
   C. to what degree the testing of the system is conducted.
   D. implementation considerations.

10. The probability that a threat to an information system will material-
    ize is called _____.
    A. threat
    B. vulnerability
    C. hole
    D. risk

11. The absence or weakness in a system that may possibly be exploited
    is called a(n):
    A. vulnerability.
    B. threat.
    C. risk.
    D. exposure.

12. Controls are implemented to:
    A. eliminate risk and eliminate the potential for loss.
    B. mitigate risk and reduce the potential for loss.
    C. eliminate risk and reduce the potential for loss.
    D. mitigate risk and eliminate the potential for loss.

13. A cookbook on how to take advantage of a vulnerability is called a(n):
    A. risk.
    B. exploit.
    C. threat.
    D. program.

14. The three types of security controls are:
    A. people, functions, and technology.
    B. people, process, and technology.
    C. technology, roles, and separation of duties.
    D. separation of duties, processes, and people.

15. Process controls for IT security include:
    A. assignment of roles for least privilege.
    B. separation of duties.
    C. documented procedures.
    D. All of the above.

EXERCISES

Exercise 2.1: The Importance of Information Confidentiality

Why is confidentiality important to corporate information? What kinds of abuses can you think of in the absence of controls to confidentiality? What criminal activities could be reduced or eliminated if confidentiality controls were effectively implemented?

Exercise 2.2: Real-World Defense in Depth

Find some analogies to the principle of defense in depth in the physical world and make some diagrams of the mechanism that you locate.

Exercise 2.3: Avoiding Security Through Obscurity

Why is security through obscurity a bad idea to the overall security of a system?

Exercise 2.4: Finding Poor Security Within Society

Locate and summarize stories that you find on the Internet about users who make poor security decisions related to viruses, giving up passwords, and so forth.

Exercise 2.5: Risk Management in Action

Every day you make risk management decisions in your daily life. Should you get in the car and drive to the store? Should you jaywalk or cross at the light? Should you get on that airplane or not? Think about the risk management decisions you make when using your PC:

1. What kinds of judgments do you make before downloading a piece of software? Or writing an e-mail to your boss?

2. What are the mental steps you go through before taking some action?

PROJECTS

Project 2.1: E-mail–Borne Viruses

1. Visit one or more of the antivirus software developer sites (Symantec, MacAfee, Computer Associates, Trend Micro, and so forth) and see if you can identify which viruses and worms require a user to click on an e-mail attachment to replicate.

2. Trace the sophistication of the virus writers over time and try to determine how they circumvent any improvements in user awareness of and education toward preventing viruses from spreading.

Project 2.2: Hackers Come in Many Colors

Open disclosure of software vulnerabilities is often associated with *gray-hat hackers*, described as security researchers who aren't particular about who learns of their findings. Research the three types of hackers (white hat, gray hat, and black hat) and try to determine their typical positions on full disclosure of software problems prior to patches or new versions of the software being made available in the marketplace. Use Google.com or your favorite Internet search engine with a query of "Open Disclosure of Software Vulnerabilities" to help you formulate your answers.

Project 2.3: Comparing Physical and
Virtual Risk Management Techniques

1. How is risk management for physical systems similar to computer systems? How are they different? What skill sets would be required for each type?

Case Study

The Maginot Line was built between 1929 and 1940 to protect France from her longtime enemy, Germany, and to defend the traditional invasion routes across France's eastern frontier. It was built to provide time for the French army to mobilize and to make up for a potentially disastrous shortfall of manpower that was predicted for the late 1930s. Most of all, it was built to provide a place behind which the French army could hide, a so-called Great Wall of France where the nation could feel secure in a doctrine that would become known as the *Maginot mentality.*

The World War II German invasion plan of 1940 was designed to deal with the line. A decoy force sat opposite the line while a second army group cut through the Low Countries of Belgium and The Netherlands, as well as through the Ardennes Forest, which lay north of the main French defenses, thus bypassing the Maginot Line and going around it. The Germans were able to avoid assaulting the Maginot Line directly. Attacking from May 10, the German forces were well into France within 5 days, and they continued to advance until May 24, when they stopped near Dunkirk. By early June, the German forces had cut the line off from the rest of France, and the French government was preparing for surrender.

This famous story highlights several of the principles found in the chapter, the most notable one being defense in depth.

What other defenses could the French have deployed to protect their entire border? What other principles did the French violate that led to such catastrophic results?

Chapter 3

Certification Programs and the Common Body of Knowledge

Chapter Objectives

After reading this chapter and completing the exercises, you will be able to do the following:

- Analyze the Certified Information Systems Security Professional (CISSP) certificate program as the gold standard in information technology (IT) security certification.
- Define and describe the role of the International Information Systems Security Certifications Consortium.
- Distinguish the contents of the 10 domains of the Common Body of Knowledge.
- Distinguish the CISSP from other security certification programs in the industry.

Introduction

This chapter outlines the more prominent information security certifications available to individuals interested in becoming security professionals or those already in the field who are interested in advancing their careers. To help you in those efforts, we begin with the most prominent and most demanded certification that's available to professionals and practitioners: the Certified Information Systems Security Professional (CISSP) and the System Security Certified Practitioner (SSCP) certificates, administered by The International Information Systems Security Certifications Consortium (*IISSCC*, or *ISC²*).

The CISSP and SSCP are based on formal testing of content knowledge and practical experience found in the security professional's ***Common Body of Knowledge (CBK)***. The CBK is a compilation and distillation of all security information collected internationally that is relevant to information security professionals. This book uses the CBK and its 10 domains as the organizing framework to introduce the field of information security (commonly referred to as *InfoSec*) and to help students decide what area(s) of InfoSec they may wish to pursue.

Once you get an idea of the structure of the CBK, you'll then find other industry certification programs that are complementary to the CISSP and SSCP.

Certification and Information Security

Information security professionals invest corporate resources in information assets, such as technology, architecture, and processes. Industry standards, ethics, and certification of information systems (IS) professionals and practitioners is critical to ensuring that a high standard of security is achieved. Certification benefits both the employer and the employee.

Benefits of ISC^2 certification to employers include the following:

■   Establishes best practices.

■   Provides a broad, solution-based orientation, particularly of the CBK (covered later in this chapter), which practitioners find useful when faced with solving IT security issues and problems. Many times, great value is derived from knowing what questions to ask and where to locate practical, hands-on solutions to common problems, and the CBK makes that effort simple.

■   Allows access to a network of global industry and subject matter/ domain experts.

■   Acts as a resource for broad-based security information.

■   Adds to credibility of the employee because of the rigor and regimen of the certification examinations.

■   Provides a business and technology orientation to risk management.

The benefits of ISC^2 certification to professionals include the following:

■   Confirms a working knowledge of information security.

■   Confirms the passing of a rigorous examination.

■   Differentiates career, with peer networking and added IS credibility.

■   Broadens career expectations because of credentials.

Oversight and governance of the professional certification process is needed to help maintain its relevance and currency and to aid professionals in networking with other professionals for collaboration in problem solving and in job seeking. To meet that need, the ISC^2 organization was created.

International Information Systems Security Certifications Consortium

The ISC^2 is a global, not-for-profit organization dedicated to:

- Maintaining a Common Body of Knowledge for information security.

- Certifying industry professionals and practitioners according to the international IS standard.

- Administering training and certification examinations.

- Ensuring credentials are maintained, primarily through continuing education.

Governments, corporations, centers of higher learning, and other organizations worldwide demand a common platform to use in administering and mastering the dynamic nature of information security. ISC^2 helps fulfill these needs. Thousands of IS professionals in more than 60 countries worldwide have attained certification in one of the two primary designations administered by ISC^2:

- Certified Information Systems Security Professional (CISSP)

- System Security Certified Practitioner (SSCP)

Both credentials indicate that those certified have demonstrated experience in the field of information security, passed a rigorous examination (6 hours, 250 questions), subscribed to a Code of Ethics, and will maintain certification with continuing education requirements. The CISSP is intended for those who are in managerial positions or for senior personnel who have oversight for multiple areas of information security, whereas the SSCP is intended for people who specialize in areas of security operations. It's possible to attain both certificates beginning with the SSCP and then, with further exposure to other areas of InfoSec and advanced experience, gain the CISSP.

In 2004, the International Standards Organization (ISO) gave its stamp of approval to the CISSP security certification for IT professionals.

The American National Standards Institute (ANSI), the U.S. representative to the Geneva-based ISO, announced that the standards bodies are granting certificate accreditation to the CISSP credential. Roy Swift, an ANSI program director, said the CISSP is the first IT certification to be accredited under ISO/IEC 17024, the standard that is a global benchmark for workers in various professions.

FYI: ISO/IEC 17024

The ISO/IEC 17024:2003 *"Conformity assessment—General re-quirements for bodies operating certification of persons"* standard outlines the requirements for bodies operating a certification of persons program and was developed with the objective of achiev-ing and promoting a globally accepted benchmark for organiza-tions offering certifications programs. Certifying people is one means of providing assurance that the certified person meets the requirements of the certification scheme. Confidence in the re-spective certification schemes is achieved by means of a globally accepted process of assessment, subsequent surveillance, and pe-riodic reassessments of the competence of certified persons.

You can find out more about ISO/IEC 17024 at **www.iso. org/iso/en/CatalogueDetailPage.CatalogueDetail?CS NUMBER=29346&scopelist=**.

ISO's accreditation of CISSP reduces some of the uncertainty that currently exists because of competing certification programs (see **www.computerworld.com/securitytopics/security/story/0,10801,94169, 00.html**).

The Information Security Common Body of Knowledge

The CBK is a compilation and distillation of all security information col-lected internationally that is relevant to information security professionals. The ISC^2 was formed, in part, to aggregate, standardize, and maintain this information because no industry standards previously existed.

ISC^2 works to ensure that accomplished and experienced IS profes-sionals with CISSP certification have a working knowledge of all 10 do-mains of the CBK as described on the ISC^2 Web site (**www.isc2.org**). Note that you will not find material in this book that covers all of the in-formation found in the CBK. To do so would require a much more com-prehensive text. Rather, you will gain a good understanding of the underlying principles for each of the 10 domains and the topics needed to make an informed decision on whether information security is right for you as a career choice, and if so, which areas of concentration you may find most appealing.

There are many books on specialized areas of InfoSec that you may wish to acquire for a more complete examination of the domains. The goal here is not to prepare you for industry certification exams but rather to provide you sufficient detail to make an informed choice for a possible career in information security.

These ten domains of the CBK are described below.

Security Management Practices

The Security Management Practices domain (covered in Chapter 4) emphasizes the importance of a comprehensive security plan that includes security policies and procedures for protecting data and how it is administered. Topics include:

- Types of security controls

- Components of a security program

- Security policies, standards, procedures, and guidelines

- Risk management and analysis

- Information classification

- Employee management issues

- Threats and corresponding administrative controls

Security Architecture and Models

The Security Architecture domain (covered in Chapter 5), one of the more technical areas of study within the CBK, discusses network layering, configuration, access control lists, and types of attacks. Specific topics cover:

- Critical components of every computer

- Processes and threads

- The OSI model

- Operating system protection mechanisms

- Ring architecture and trusted components

- Virtual machines, layering, and virtual memory

- Access control models

- *Orange Book*, ITSEC, and Common Criteria

- Certification and accreditation

- Covert channels and types of attacks

- Buffer overflows and data validation attacks

Business Continuity Planning

Business Continuity Planning (BCP), along with the Business Impact Assessment (BIA) and the Disaster Recovery Plan (DRP), is the core of this domain. Topics included in this domain are

- Roles and responsibilities
- Business impact analysis
- Development process of BCP
- Backup options and technologies
- Types of off-site facilities
- Implementation and testing of BCP

This domain is covered in Chapter 6.

Law, Investigations, and Ethics

This domain covers the different targets of computer crimes, bodies of law, and the different types of laws as they apply to computer security. Other topics included in this domain are

- Computer criminal profiles
- Types of crimes
- Liability topics
- Privacy laws and concerns
- Complications of computer crime investigation
- Types of evidence and how to collect it
- Forensics
- Legal systems
- The role of ethics in information security professionalism

This domain is covered in Chapter 7.

Physical Security

Topics covered in this domain include securing the physical site using policies and procedures coupled with the appropriate alarm and intrusion detection systems, monitoring systems, and so forth. Topics include:

- Facility location and construction issues
- Physical vulnerabilities and threats

- Doors, windows, and secure room concerns

- Hardware metrics and backup options

- Electrical power issues and solutions

- Fire detection and suppression

- Fencing, lighting, and perimeter protection

- Physical intrusion detection systems

This domain is covered in Chapter 8.

Operations Security

This domain covers the kind of operational procedures and tools such as firewalls, antivirus scanners, and network sniffers that may be familiar to IT specialists and users alike. Specific topics include:

- Operations department responsibilities

- Personnel and roles

- Resource protection

- Types of intrusion detection systems

- Vulnerability and penetration testing

This domain is covered in Chapter 9.

Access Control Systems and Methodology

Who may access the system and what can they do once they are signed on? That is the focus of this CBK domain. Specific topics include:

- Identification, authentication, and authorization techniques and technologies

- Biometrics, smart cards, and multifactor authentication

- Password management

- Single sign-on technologies and their risks

- Discretionary versus mandatory access control models

- Rule-based and role-based access control

- Social engineering issues

- Specific attacks and countermeasures

This domain is covered in Chapter 10.

Cryptography

This domain contains the stuff of espionage and spy novels. It involves encrypting data so that authorized individuals may view the sensitive data and unauthorized individuals may not. Cryptography is a highly complex topic. The InfoSec specialist needs to understand the function but not necessarily the mechanics of cryptography. Topics in the Cryptography domain include:

- Historical uses of cryptography
- Block and stream ciphers
- Explanation and uses of symmetric key algorithms
- Explanation and uses of asymmetric key algorithms
- Public key infrastructure components
- Data integrity algorithms and technologies
- IPSec, SSL, and PGP

This domain is covered in Chapter 11.

Telecommunications, Network, and Internet Security

This domain covers another technical segment of the CBK. Topics include not just network topologies but also their weaknesses and defenses. Many of the operational tools such as firewalls are covered in this domain along with the following subject areas:

- Open system interconnect (OSI) seven-layer model
- TCP/IP suite
- LAN, MAN, and WAN topologies and technologies
- Network devices, like routers and firewalls
- Firewall types and architectures
- Dial-up and VPN protocols
- Domain Name Service (DNS)
- Wireless LANs and security issues
- Types of network attacks

This domain is covered in Chapter 12.

Application Development Security

Application development in a networked environment (covered in Chapter 13) focuses on sound and secure application development techniques. Topics covered in this domain include:

- Software development models

- Software development life cycle

- Object-oriented programming

- ActiveX and Java

- Database security

- Relational database components

- Types of malware

Chapter 4 through Chapter 13 are devoted to the domains listed above in a level of detail that will help you to decide if a career in InfoSec is for you.

Other Certificate Programs in the IT Security Industry

Although the CISSP and SSCP are the gold standards for IT security, many other certification programs also exist. Some of these programs are complementary to the CISSP, and others demonstrate a proficiency in specific areas within information security. A few of these programs are discussed in the following section.

Certified Information Systems Auditor

Once the exclusive domain of IT auditors, the Certified Information Systems Auditor (CISA) has become a sought-after certification for senior-level personnel and management. The subject areas of the CISA have moderate overlap with the CISSP, but it focuses more on business procedures than technology. The CISA certification is administered by the Information Systems Audit and Control Association and Foundation (ISACA) (**www.isaca.org**), founded in 1969. The CISA certification itself has been around since 1978. As of late 2002, about 28,000 individuals worldwide held the CISA certification.

Certified Information Security Manager

In 2003, ISACA deployed the Certified Information Security Manager (CISM) certification. This certification recognizes the knowledge and experience of an IT security manager. The CISM is ISACA's next-generation credential and is specifically geared toward experienced information security managers and those who have information security management responsibilities. The CISM is designed to provide executive management with assurance that those earning the designation have the required knowledge and ability to provide effective security management and consulting. It is business-oriented and focuses on information risk management while addressing management, design, and technical security issues at a conceptual level. Although its central focus is security management, all those in the IS profession with security experience may find value in CISM.

Global Information Assurance Certifications (GIAC)

The SANS Institute (**www.sans.org**) is also on the certification bandwagon with its suite of certifications under the GIAC (Global Information Assurance Certification) program. Although GIAC certifications are intended primarily for practitioners or hands-on personnel such as system administrators and network engineers, there are a few that would be appropriate for early-career managers. The GIAC Information Security Officer (GISO) is an entry-level certification that includes knowledge of threats, risks, and best practices. The GIAC Security Essentials Certification (GSEC) is an intermediate-level certification that requires basic information security knowledge for both practitioners and managers. Information on GIAC certifications can be found at **www.giac.org**.

CompTIA Security+ Certification

The CompTIA Security+ certification exam tests the security knowledge mastery of an individual with two years on-the-job networking security experience. The exam covers industry-wide topics, including communication security, infrastructure security, cryptography, access control, authentication, external attack, and operational and organization security. CompTIA Security+ is taught at colleges, universities, and commercial training centers around the globe. There are approximately 10,000 CompTIA Security+ certified professionals worldwide. The objectives of CompTIA Security+ were derived through input from industry, government, and academia, a job task analysis, a survey of more than 1,100 subject matter experts, and a beta exam with responses from subject matter experts around the world.

Vendor-Specific Certification Programs

Vendor-neutral certification programs like those described above differ in focus and objectives from vendor-specific certification programs. In the IT security industry, dozens of vendor-specific certificates are available for practitioners. A few of these programs are listed below. For a comprehensive list of what's available in the industry, visit **www.certmag.com**.

Check Point Certified Security Principles Associate An entry-level certification, the Check Point Certified Security Principles Associate (CCSPA) focuses on security fundamentals, concepts and best practices, and incorporation of network and systems security with business needs. This credential covers the information security triad (described in Chapter 1), threat and vulnerability assessments, security policies, business-continuity plans, safeguards and countermeasures, security and network architecture, encryption algorithms, and access control technologies (see **www.checkpoint.com**).

Cisco Qualified Specialist Program Cisco Qualified Specialists can pursue midlevel certification across a broad array of subjects and technologies. This program includes several credentials with strong—if not exclusive—security components, including:

- Cisco Firewall Specialist

- Cisco IDS Specialist

- Cisco VPN Specialist

- Cisco Wireless LAN Design Specialist

- Cisco Wireless LAN Support Specialist

For more information, visit **www.cisco.com**.

INFOSEC (Information Systems Security) Professional In early 2003, the National Security Agency and the Committee on National Security Systems granted Cisco the authority to recognize INFOSEC professionals who are responsible for the security of key networks. Candidates must pass four exams based on Cisco products (IOS, PIX Firewall, Cisco VPN, and Cisco IDS). For more information, visit **www.cisco.com**.

Microsoft Certified Systems Engineer Security Specializations (MCSE: Security) These two credentials take the standard MCSE for Windows 2000 and Windows Server 2003 and transform elective exams into security specialization exams (and add one exam to the total count required, so that this credential requires passing eight exams instead of seven for Windows Server 2003, and seven exams instead of six for Windows Server 2000). The idea is to allow MCSEs to demonstrate their interest in and focus on Microsoft-related security topics, tools, and technologies (all Microsoft Certified Systems Administrator [MCSA] requirements also carry over to the MCSE for security specializations). For more information, visit **www.microsoft.com**.

RSA Certified Systems Engineer The RSA Certified Systems Engineer (RSA/CSE) is designed for security professionals who install and configure enterprise security solutions built around RSA SecureID, ClearTrust, and KEON PKI Core products (three separate credentials, one for each product family). Candidates must be able to design client solutions based on analysis of business needs, match implementations to client environments and infrastructures, and carry a solution from design through prototyping, pilot, and full-scale deployment phases. For more information, visit **www.rsa.com**.

Sun Certified Security Administrator for the Solaris Operating System This credential aims to identify experienced Solaris administrators with security interest and experience. It's a midrange credential that focuses on system lockdown, best security practices, a good understanding of file and system resources protection, and encryption and authentication methods. A single exam, 310-301, is required to obtain this credential. For more information, visit **www.sun.com**.

Symantec Technology Architect A single-product-focused and entry-level credential, Symantec Technology Architects must pass any one of the security solutions exams. Security solutions topics include virus protection and content filtering, intrusion detection, vulnerability management, and firewall and VPN technologies. For more information, visit **www.symantec.com**.

Tivoli Certified Consultant Tivoli is part of the IBM family of companies. Tivoli's Certified Consultant credential covers security topics: the IBM Tivoli Access Manager for Business Integration V3.8.1. Certified consultants must have a strong working knowledge of InfoSec concepts, tools, and technologies and understand how to design, deploy, manage, maintain, and troubleshoot Access Manager environments. For more information, visit **www.ibm.com**.

Windows Server 2003 Security Certified Professional This credential recognizes individuals with thorough knowledge of managing and configuring a Windows Server 2003 environment, deploying local and network security, configuring Active Directory to manage organization-wide security, administering patch management and vulnerability scans, and creating and enforcing security policies and procedures. For more information, visit **www.learningtree.com**.

FYI: Is 2005 the Year of the Security Pro?

In late 2004, ISC[2] declared 2005 as the "Year of the Information Security Professional" with the goal of recruiting new candidates to the profession and educating organizations and the public on the growing importance of certification as a measure of competence, commitment, and professionalism.

Summary

The International Information Systems Security Certification Consortium maintains the ever-evolving Common Body of Knowledge through ongoing reviews of references and best practices to ensure its relevance and effectiveness.

The information security CBK consists of 10 domains that cover all the areas of InfoSec that practitioners and managers are encouraged to know in order to excel in their careers and provide their employers with industry best practices that have proved successful.

The benefits of certification and immersion into the CBK are clear to both employers and professionals who commit to life-long learning and to the betterment of themselves and their careers. The role of the security professional is expanding, fueled by growing demands from the IT industry and national governments that are experiencing a growing threat to computing systems and operations.

Test Your Skills

MULTIPLE CHOICE QUESTIONS

1. ISC^2 was formed for which of the following purposes?

   A. maintaining a Common Body of Knowledge for information security

   B. certifying industry professionals and practitioners in an international IS standard

   C. ensuring credentials are maintained, primarily through continuing education

   D. all of the above

2. The information security Common Body of Knowledge is

   A. a compilation and distillation of all security information collected internationally of relevance to information security professionals

   B. a volume of books published by ISC^2

   C. a reference list of books and other publications put together by practitioners in information security

   D. an encyclopedia of information security principles, best practices, and regulations

3. The CBK contains:
   A. 5 domains
   B. 10 domains
   C. 7 domains
   D. 3 domains

4. The Security Management Practices domain includes:
   A. identification of security products
   B. documented policies, standards, procedures, and guidelines
   C. managiement of risk to corporate assets
   D. B and C only

5. The Security Architecture and Models domain includes:
   A. concepts and principles for secure operations
   B. concepts and principles for secure programs
   C. concepts and principles for secure designs of computing resources
   D. concepts and principles for secure application development

6. The Access Control Systems and Methodology domain includes:
   A. a collection of mechanisms to create secure architectures for asset protection
   B. instructions on how to install perimeter door security
   C. a methodology for applications development
   D. a methodology for secure data center operations

7. The Application Development Security domain includes:
   A. an outline for the software development environment to address security concerns
   B. a recipe book for developers to follow in building secure application software
   C. a language guide on programming security functions
   D. quality assurance testing of custom-developed software

8. The Operations Security domain includes:
   A. mechanisms for secure access to a data center
   B. identification of controls over hardware, media, and personnel
   C. help-desk support for security incidents
   D. evidence collection and preservation for computer crimes

9. The Physical Security domain includes:

   A. a code of conduct for employees

   B. perimeter security controls and protection mechanisms

   C. data center controls and specifications for physically secure operations

   D. B and C

10. The Cryptography domain includes:

    A. principles, means, and methods to disguise information to assure confidentiality, integrity, and authenticity

    B. tools and techniques to intercept competitive secrets

    C. procedures on how to protect Internet communications

    D. procedures on how to discover cryptographic keys

11. The Telecommunications, Network, and Internet Security domain includes:

    A. technology, principles, and best practices to secure telephone networks

    B. technology, principles, and best practices to secure corporate networks

    C. technology, principles, and best practices to secure Internet-attached networks

    D. all of the above

12. The Business Continuity domain includes:

    A. plans for recovering business operations in the event of loss of access by personnel

    B. management practices to determine business risks

    C. documented plans for interacting with law enforcement

    D. maintenance of current versions of all software in use by the organization

13. The Law, Investigations, and Ethics domain includes:

    A. teams of lawyers to determine the legality of security decisions

    B. private law-enforcement personnel

    C. methods to investigate computer crime incidents

    D. a council to determine the ethical behavior of security personnel

3

14. People more interested in certifying themselves as security experts in a business context should consider preparing for which certification?

    A. GIAC

    B. CISA

    C. CompTIA Security+

    D. SSCP

15. People more interested in certifying themselves as security technical practitioners should consider preparing for which certification(s)?

    A. CISM and GIAC

    B. GIAC and CompTIA Security+

    C. CISSP and CISM

    D. SSCP and CISA

16. The growth in the security profession is driven by:

    A. new technology

    B. growth of the Internet

    C. demands by industry and government for scarce resources

    D. overseas hackers

EXERCISES

Exercise 3.1: Benefits Gained Through Industry Certification

1. Think about how certification benefits employees and employers in job-seeking efforts. (Refer to advantages listed in this chapter if necessary.)

2. Name three advantages certified professionals have over noncertified professionals when applying for a job.

3. Explain how an employer could use information about certifications to evaluate potential employees.

Exercise 3.2: Preparing for Certification Tests

1. Search your favorite online bookstore for books in print that help prepare professionals to sit for the CISSP and CISM certificates.

2. Aside from the organization of the books, what can you find in common among them?

3. Do you believe that drills from exam test banks is a good method for the beginner to prepare for certifications? Why or why not?

Exercise 3.3: Hot Topics in Information Security

1. Off the top of your head, list some of the current topics and issues in information security that you think concern IT and business managers.

2 Visit the Search Security Web site (**www.searchsecurity.com**) to see how your list maps to hot topics found on the Web site.

3. As a practitioner, how would you respond to these concerns when company management looks to you for information and recommendations?

Exercise 3.4: Growth in Internal Security Departments

1. Describe the composition and size of the security department at your place of employment or at your school. You may need to talk to the IT professionals within your organization to develop this description as well as to address the following steps.

2. Explain whether the department has grown in size during the past few years. If it has grown, by how much and for what reasons? (Has the organization grown? Or is there more work for the security professionals to do?)

3. Explain whether the managers feel that it has been difficult to recruit qualified employees. What sort of experience or certifications do the managers look for in potential employees?

Exercise 3.5: BS7799 and CBK Domains

1. Research the British Standard 7799 Part One (**www.bsi-global.com/ Education/Information_Security/explained.xalter**).

2. Determine how its organization is similar to the CBK. List the similarities.

3. List the area(s) that are different and how they are different.

PROJECTS

Project 3.1: Comparing Certificate Programs

1. Consider security industry certification like the SSCP and CISSP versus security vendor certifications like those from Cisco Systems (**www.cisco.com**) and Symantec Corporation (**www.symantec.com**). Why do you think someone might pursue vendor certification rather than industry certification?

2. Are there any situations in which it would be beneficial to have both? If so, describe the situations in which having both would be beneficial.

3. What certifications would make good combinations for certain domain areas?

4. Which certificates do you think would be more valuable to hiring managers?

5. Which certificates do you think employers are demanding for security personnel?

Project 3.2: Supplemental ISC^2 Certifications

In addition to the CISSP and SSCP, ISC^2 offers specialty concentration certifications for management (ISSMP), security architecture (ISSAP), and one specific for the United States National Security Agency (NSA): the ISSEP.

1. Research these concentrations at the ISC^2 Web site (**www.isc2.org**).

2. Try to determine why professionals might want to attain one or more of them beyond the CISSP credential.

3. Do you see additional personal value beyond the CISSP for these certificates? If so, list the values you see.

4. Explain why employers might seek personnel who hold these certificates.

5. Why would the NSA require a concentration specific only to their organization?

Project 3.3: Information Privacy and Information Security

Information privacy and information security are two sides of the same coin. You can't have privacy without security.

1. Using an Internet search engine, distinguish between those issues related to privacy versus those related to security.

2. What overlapping issues do you find?

3. Why are U.S. lawmakers seemingly more concerned with privacy controls and protections than requiring U.S. companies to maintain effective IT security programs?

4. What are some of the controls being mandated through legislation?

5. Do you believe these controls are (will be) effective?

3

▶▶ Case Study

Sue and Barbara both have an equivalent of eight years of IT security consulting experience in the banking industry. Barbara has earned her CISSP and has held it for five years. Sue decided not to pursue the certificate because she could not find the time, and she has focused her efforts solely on internal company issues. A headhunter in IT security has recently contacted both of them for an opportunity that has recently come along, and both have decided to interview for the position.

Which candidate do you think will be more appealing to the hiring manager? What is it about professional certification that makes the difference among employers?

Some of the resources you may find helpful to research in finding the answers include:

- *Infoworld* Magazine Online (**http://iwsun4.infoworld.com/**).

- *Internet Week* Magazine Online (**www.internetweek.com**).

- *Windows IT Pro* Magazine Online (**www.win2000mag.com/**).

- *Tech Republic* Magazine Online (**http://techrepublic.com/**).

Chapter 4

Security Management

Chapter Objectives

After reading this chapter and completing the exercises, you will be able to do the following:

- Choose the appropriate type of policies to document a security programme.
- Distinguish between the roles of standards, regulations, baselines, procedures, and guidelines.
- Organize a typical standards and policies library.
- Classify assets according to standard principles.
- Incorporate the separation of duties principle when creating a security policy.
- Outline the minimum preemployment hiring practices for organizations.
- Analyze and manage risk.
- Outline the elements of employee security education, awareness, and training.
- List the eight types of people responsible for security in an information technology (IT) setting.

Introduction

This chapter describes the first domain of the Certified Information Systems Security Professional (CISSP) Common Body of Knowledge (CBK): Security Management Practices. This domain appears first because it establishes the framework and foundation for all the other domains to build upon.

Security management is a broad set of executive support and management activities that define an IT security programme. (*Note:* This spelling is used to distinguish a management programme from a computer program.)

A *programme*, unlike a project, is an ongoing management activity that is constantly funded and intended for the preservation and advancement of the organization.

Like any programme, an IT security programme begins with statements of management's intent. These goals are translated into security ***policies*** (statements of management intent) and then used to drive the details of how the programme will run, who will be responsible for day-to-day work, how training and awareness will be conducted, and how compliance to policies will be handled.

Other areas addressed within the Security Management Practices domain are activities related to information classification, risk management concepts and techniques, and security roles and responsibilities to assure ongoing organizational security consciousness.

Security Policies Set the Stage for Success

Policies are the most crucial element in a corporate information security infrastructure and must be considered long before security technology is acquired and deployed. Security industry expert Marcus Ranum explains, ". . . If you haven't got a security policy, you haven't got a firewall. Instead, you've got a thing that's sort of doing something, but you don't know what it's trying to do because no one has told you what it should do" (Ranum 2003). Implementing security technology with no predetermined rules about what it *should* do results in accidental protection at best—even a broken clock is right twice a day!

Effective policies can rectify many of the weaknesses from failures to understand the business direction and security mission and can help to prevent or eliminate many of the faults and errors caused by a lack of security guidance.

An organization faces many technology and strategic choices when deciding how to protect its computer assets. Some choices are made based on trade-offs, but others involve conflicting trade-offs, questions about an organization's strategic direction, and other factors that don't easily lend themselves to quantitative analysis. Technology providers are at times overly anxious to push product out the door that unwitting managers may choose to buy without determining what problem(s) it might solve. Once established, policies become the basis for protecting both information and technology resources and for guiding employee behavior but are not sufficient on their own. Familiarity with these types of policies is required to aid people within a company in addressing computer security issues that are important to the organization as a whole. Effective policies ultimately result in the development and implementation of better computer security and better protection of systems and information.

Policies may be published on paper or electronically via a corporate intranet. Tools used to automate the mechanics of policy creation, management, maintenance, and dissemination are commercially available. (For more information about these tools, visit Archer Technologies at **www.archer-tech.com** and NetIQ for the Vigilent Policy Center at **www.netiq.com**).

Figure 4.1 illustrates a typical structure of a corporate policy and standards library.

An effective policy contains the following information:

- Title

- Purpose

- Authorizing individual-

- Author/sponsor

- Reference to other policies

- Scope

- Measurement expectations

- Exception process

- Accountability

- Compliance management and measurements description

- Effective/expiration dates

- Definitions

This structure is a best practice within the industry for comprehensive coverage of the topics found in security policies. As people gain experience and exposure to policies, a common structure helps them to quickly locate the information they seek.

Four Types of Policies

According to the National Institute of Standards and Technology (NIST) Computer Systems Laboratory (CSL)—a division of the U.S. Department of Commerce—there are four types of computer security policies. Policies and the follow-up documents in the library start out at a very high level of understanding and become more specific (granular) at the lower levels.

- *Programme-level policy* is used for creating a management-sponsored computer security program. A programme-level policy, at the highest level, might prescribe the need for information security and may delegate the creation and management of the program to a role within the IT department. Think of this as the mission statement for the IT security program.

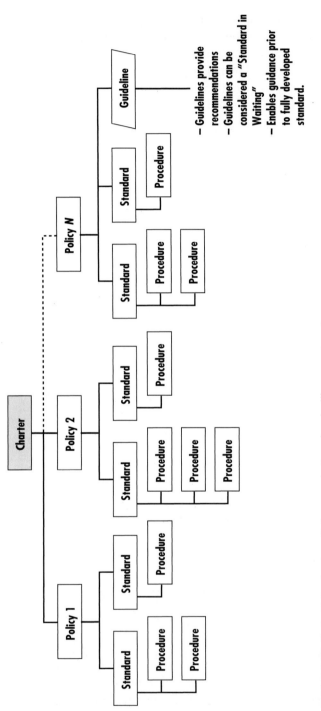

- Guidelines provide recommendations
- Guidelines can be considered a "Standard in Waiting"
- Enables guidance prior to fully developed standard.

FIGURE 4.1 A typical policies and standards library structure.

- *Programme-framework policy* establishes the overall approach to computer security (i.e., a computer security framework). A framework policy adds detail to the program by describing the elements and organization of the program and department that will carry out the security mission.

- *Issue-specific policy* addresses specific issues of concern to the organization.

- *System-specific policy* focuses on policy issues that management has decided for a specific system.

A complete IT security policy and standards library taxonomy may be found in Appendix B. Specific types of policy and standards examples may also be found in Appendix C at the back of this book.

Each policy type is described in greater detail in the following sections.

Programme-Level Policies

Management needs programme-level policy to help establish a security programme, assign programme management responsibilities, state an organization-wide computer security purpose and objectives, and establish a basis for policy compliance.

The head of the organization or other senior officials, such as the organization's top management officers, typically will issue programme-level policy. Programme-level policy, sometimes called an information security charter, establishes the computer security program and its basic framework. This high-level policy defines the purpose of the programme and its scope within the organization, assigns responsibilities for direct programme implementation (to the computer security organization) as well as responsibilities to related offices, and addresses compliance issues.

The components of programme-level policy are

- **Purpose** clearly states the purpose of the programme. This includes defining the goals of the computer security programme as well as its management structure. Security-related needs, such as integrity, availability, and confidentiality, can form the basis of organizational goals established in policy. For instance, in an organization responsible for maintaining large mission-critical databases, reduction in errors, data loss, or data corruption might be specifically stressed. In an organization responsible for maintaining confidential personal data (as in most e-commerce systems), the goals might emphasize stronger protection against unauthorized disclosure. A programme management structure should be organized to best address the goals of the programme and respond to the particular operating and risk environment of the organization. Important issues for the structure of the central computer security programme include management and coordination of security-related resources, interaction with diverse communities, and the ability to relay issues of concern to upper management. The policy could also establish operational security offices for major systems, particularly those at high risk or most critical to organizational operations.

- **Scope** specifies which resources (including facilities, hardware, and software), information, and personnel the programme covers. Often, the programme will cover all systems and agency personnel, but this is not always the case. In some instances, a policy may name specific assets, such as major sites and large systems. Sometimes, tough management decisions arise when defining the scope of a program, such as determining the extent to which the programme applies to contractors and outside organizations using or connected to the organization's systems. Scope should also consider home-based employers (telecommuters) and mobile employees who access company resources from remote locations.

- **Responsibilities** addresses the responsibilities of officials and offices throughout the organization, including the role of line managers, applications owners, users, and the information processing or IT organization. The policy statement distinguishes between the responsibilities of computer services providers and the managers of applications using the computer services. It can also establish the basis for employee accountability. Overall, the programme-level assignment of responsibilities covers those activities and personnel who will be vital to the implementation and continuity of the computer security policy.

- **Compliance** authorizes and delineates the use of specified penalties and disciplinary actions for individuals who fail to comply with the organization's computer security policies. Because the security policy is a high-level document, penalties for various infractions are normally not detailed therein. However, the policy may authorize the creation of compliance structures that include violations and specific penalties. Infractions and associated penalties are usually defined in issue-specific and system-specific policies.

When establishing compliance structures, an organization must consider that employee violations of policy can be unintentional. For example, nonconformance can be due to a lack of knowledge or training. Each policy and standard should contain a section on compliance management and metrics to help management educate employees on their responsibilities and provide a measurement tool to help determine the document's effectiveness. The Web-based policy and standards management systems (mentioned above), offer facilities to "push" a new or revised standard or policy to the audience that needs to be aware of changes, and then provide awareness training (if needed), quizzes to gauge user understanding of the changes, and a mechanism to record a user's decision to comply with the new standard or request intervention from the security department.

Programme-Framework Policies

Programme-framework policies provide an organization-wide direction for broad areas of programme implementation. These policies may be issued to assure that everyone complies with acceptable use rules (e-mail, Internet, and so on) or that they address disaster planning and risk analysis issues correctly. Managers or departments with sufficient authority to direct all organization components on computer security issues create programme-framework policies. This may be the organization's management official or the head of the computer security programme (e.g., chief information officer or more commonly chief information security office).

Programme-framework policies define the organization's security programme elements that form the foundation for the computer security programme. The programme-framework policy reflects information technology management's decisions about priorities for protection, resource allocation, and assignment of responsibilities.

The areas addressed by programme-framework policy vary within each organization, as does the way in which the policy is expressed. Some organizations issue policy directives, whereas others issue handbooks that combine policy, regulations, standards, and guidance.

Many organizations issue policy on "key" areas of computer security, such as life-cycle management, contingency planning, and network security. If the policy and associated standards and guidance are too rigid, cost-effective implementations and innovation could be negatively affected. For an example of programme-framework policy, consider a typical organization policy on contingency planning. An organization may require that all contingency plans categorize the criticality of computer programs and IT processes according to a standard scale. This will assist the organization in preparing a master plan (in the event the physical plant is destroyed) by supporting prioritization across departmental boundaries. Programme-framework policies may be composed of components similar to those contained in programme-level policy but may be in different formats (organizational handbooks, and so forth) Examples of possible programme-framework policies include

- Business continuity planning (BCP) framework (see Chapter 6).

- Physical security requirements framework for data centers (see Chapter 7).

- Application development security framework (see Chapter 13).

Issue-Specific Policies

Issue-specific and system-specific policies identify and define specific areas of concern and state an organization's position or posture on the issue. Depending on the issue and its controversy—as well as potential impact— issue-specific policy may come from the head of the organization, the top management official, the chief information officer (CIO), or the computer security programme manager (e.g., CISO).

System-specific policy is normally issued by the manager or owner of the system (which could be a network or application) but may originate from a high-level executive or official. This is especially true if all affected departments don't agree with the policy and may be tempted to create conflicting policies addressing their own needs to the detriment of the overall organization.

IN PRACTICE: An Issue-Specific Policy Scenario

Trying to stay on top of ever-evolving technology and the security risks posed by these technologies is one of the most challenging aspects of being an IT security professional. For example, hand-held PDAs and laptop computers have become ubiquitous in private medical offices, clinics, hospitals, and even blood banks because of the convenience and ease of wireless local area networks (WLANs). They allow physicians and nurses to access patient records remotely, add observations and diagnoses, and check on medications—among other things. This increased access poses new and difficult security questions:

- How can office managers be sure that no unauthorized computers can eavesdrop on the wireless communications?
- How can patients be sure that the doctor's convenience is not at the price of patient record privacy?

Covered health care entities need to consider whether they should postpone deploying an initial WLAN until planned improvements in wireless network security standards are adopted and have been implemented in commercial products. Those who are charged with maintaining the security of health care information systems carry a heavy burden. As technology changes constantly, covered entity managers and their lawyers are required to regularly evaluate the impact of those changes on the security of their networks. (*Source:* **www.dwt.com/practc/hc_ecom/ bulletins/05-03_BNAarticle.htm.**)

System-specific policies

- State security objectives of a specific system.

- Define how the system should be operated to achieve the security objectives.

- Specify how the protections and features of the technology will be used to support or enforce the security objectives.

Issue-specific policies focus on areas of current relevance and concern to an organization. Although programme-level policy is usually broad enough that it requires little modification over time, issue-specific policies require more frequent revision due to changes in technology and related factors. As new technologies are developed, some issues diminish in importance, and new ones continually appear. It may be appropriate, for example, to issue a policy on the proper use of a cutting-edge technology (like Wi-Fi networks)—the security vulnerabilities of which are still largely unknown.

A useful structure for issue-specific policy is to break the policy into its basic components:

- **Issue statement** defines a security issue, along with any relevant terms, distinctions, and conditions. For example, an organization might want to develop an issue-specific policy on the use of "Internet access," which may define what Internet activities it will permit and those it won't permit. Additionally, other distinctions and conditions may need inclusion, for instance, Internet access that's gained using a personal dial-up or broadband ISP connection from an employee's desktop PC that makes the internal network vulnerable to interlopers when the connection is alive.

- **Statement of the organization's position** clearly states an organization's position on the issue. Continuing with the example of Internet access, the policy should state what types of sites are prohibited in all or some cases (e.g., porn sites or brokerage sites), whether or not there are further guidelines for approval and use, or whether case-by-case exceptions will be granted, by whom, and on what basis.

- **Applicability** clearly states where, how, when, to whom, and to what a particular policy applies. For example, the hypothetical policy on Internet access may apply only to the organization's own on-site resources and employees and not to contractor organizations with offices at other locations. Additionally, the policy's applicability to employees traveling among different sites or working at home who will require Internet access from multiple sites might require further clarification.

- **Roles and responsibilities** assigns roles and responsibilities to the issue. Continuing with the Internet example above, if the policy permits private ISP access given the appropriate approvals, then the approving authority should be identified. The office or department(s) responsible for compliance should also be named.

- **Compliance** gives descriptions of the infractions and states the corresponding penalties. Penalties must be consistent with organizational personnel policies and practices and need to be coordinated with appropriate officials, offices, and, perhaps, employee bargaining units.

- **Points of contact and supplementary information** lists the names of the appropriate individuals to contact for further information and lists any applicable standards or guidelines. For some issues, the point of contact might be a line manager; for other issues it might be a facility manager, technical support person, or system administrator. For yet other issues, the point-of-contact might be a security programme representative. Using the Internet access example, employees need to know whether the point of contact for questions and procedural information would be the immediate superior, a system administrator, or a computer security official. Examples of an issue-specific policy include:
  - E-mail acceptable use
  - Internet acceptable use
  - Laptop security policy

System-Specific Policies

Programme-level policies and issue-specific policies both address policies from a broad level, usually involving the entire organization. System-specific policies, on the other hand, are much more focused, as they address only one system. Many security policy decisions apply only at the system level. Examples include

- Who is allowed to read or modify data in the system?

- Under what conditions can data be read or modified?

- Are users allowed to dial into the computer system from home or while on travel?

Development and Management of Security Policies

To develop a comprehensive set of system security policies, a management process is required that derives security rules from security goals such as a three-level model for system security policy:

- Security objectives

- Operational security

- Policy implementation

Security Objectives

The first step is to define the security objectives. This step must extend beyond analyzing the need for integrity, availability, and confidentiality. Security objectives must be more specific and concrete. They should be clearly stated in order to achieve the objective. The security objectives should consist of a series of statements to describe meaningful actions about specific resources. These objectives should be based on system functionality or mission requirements but should also state the security actions to support the requirements.

Operational Security

The next section is concerned with the operational policies that list the rules for operating a system. Using data integrity as an example, the operational policy would define authorized and unauthorized modification: who, (by job category, by organization placement, or by name) can do what (modify, delete, and so forth) to which data (specific fields or records) and under what conditions. Managers need to make decisions in developing this policy, as it is unlikely that all security objectives will be fully met. Cost, operational, technical, and other constraints will intervene.

Also worth consideration is the degree of formality needed in documenting the policy. Once again, the more formal the documentation, the easier it will be to enforce and follow policy. Formal policy is published as a distinct policy document; less formal policy may be written in memos. Informal policy may not be written at all. As would be expected, unwritten policy is extremely difficult to follow or enforce. On the other hand, very granular and formal policy at the system level can also be an administrative burden. In general, good practice suggests a granular formal statement of the access privileges for a system due to its complexity and importance. Documenting access control policy makes it substantially easier to follow and to enforce.

Another area that normally requires a granular and formal statement is the assignment of security responsibilities. Some less formal policy decisions may be recorded in other types of computer security documents such as risk analyses, accreditation statements, or procedural manuals. However, any controversial or uncommon policies may need formal policy statements. Uncommon policies include any areas where the system policy is different from organization policy or from normal practice within the organization—being either more or less stringent. Uncommon policies should also contain a statement explaining the reason for deviating from the organization's standard policy.

An example of the need for an uncommon policy or standard is where a specialty-computer system may be unable to meet the organization's overall policy on password lengths. Suppose this oddball system allows only five-character passwords using only letters of the alphabet, but the organizational policy on passwords dictates that passwords be eight or more characters in length and must contain at least one number. In this case, a standard that requires additional controls over this system to mitigate the risk of the inability to comply with the organizational policy may be developed.

Policy Implementation

Finally, the organization must determine the role technology plays in enforcing or supporting the policy. Security is normally enforced through a combination of technical and traditional management methods. This is especially true in the areas of Internet security where security devices protect the perimeter of the company's information management systems. Although technical means are likely to include the use of access control technology, there are other automated means of enforcing or supporting security policy.

For example, technology can be used to block telephone systems users from calling certain numbers. Intrusion detection software can alert system administrators to suspicious activity or take action to stop the activity. Personal computers can be configured to prevent booting from a floppy disk. Automated security enforcement has both advantages and disadvantages. A computer system, properly designed, programmed, and installed, consistently enforces policy, although users can't be forced to follow all procedures. In addition, deviations from the policy may sometimes be necessary and appropriate. This situation occurs frequently if the security policy is too rigid.

Policy Support Documents

Although policies are defined as statements of management's intent, the embodiment of policies and details on how to comply with them show up in other documents that are derived from policy statements. These documents provide levels of detail supporting the policy and explaining the system development, management, and operational requirements. Procedures then provide a recipe for the execution of steps that are intended to comply with a policy directive. These supporting documents include

- **Regulations:** laws passed by regulators and lawmakers.

- **Standards and baselines:** topic-specific (standards) and system-specific (baselines) documents that describe overall requirements for security.

- **Guidelines:** documentation that aids in compliance with standard considerations, hints, tips, and best practices in implementation.

- **Procedures:** step-by-step instructions on how to perform a specific security activity (configure a firewall, install an operating system, and others).

Regulations

Often, the standards related to information security (InfoSec) are dictated by the nature of an organization's business. The Federal Trade Commission (FTC) and Department of Commerce govern U.S. retail operators, among others. Federal banking standards regulate U.S. banks (FFIEC), U.S. medical device manufacturers or suppliers fall under Federal Drug Administration (FDA) regulations, and so forth. By selecting the most robust or strictest sets of published standards governing a particular business, an organization is most likely to meet the requirements outlined by any applicable less-stringent standards.

In 2004, the Sarbanes–Oxley Corporate Responsibility and Accountability Act—passed by the U.S. Senate in the wake of the collapse of Enron, Arthur Anderson, Worldcom, and several other large firms—gained the attention of all U.S. corporate CEOs. The act requires internal controls in order to foster regulator confidence in the integrity of financial statements to the Securities and Exchange Commission (SEC) and shareholders. It also requires that CEOs attest to the integrity of financial statements to the SEC.

Because of this mandate, controls related to information processing and management have been placed under a magnifying glass. As the effective date of the regulation draws closer, the need for a comprehensive library of current operating documents is underscored.

Many of the regulations on the books are drawn from existing and evolving sources of information security industry standards and best practices. Policies and standards are always changing as best practices are learned, documented, and shared with others in the same industry.

IN PRACTICE: HIPAA Privacy

The Health Insurance Portability and Accountability Act of 1996 (HIPAA) includes a section titled "Medical Privacy Rule," which specifies new privacy protections for patients and lays out the privacy obligations for employers and health care providers. Because of the privacy rule, health care providers and health plan providers can no longer release protected health information to patients' employers unless certain conditions are met. Human resources

▶▶ CONTINUED ON NEXT PAGE

▸▸ **CONTINUED**

departments in all companies that offer employee health-care coverage must now look at HIPAA as it relates to workers compensation, drug testing, physical exams, Family Medical Leave Act (FMLA), maternity leaves, sick days, and health care plan communications.

Suddenly, developers of HR systems are no longer immune from privacy and security controls, and retrofitting existing (legacy) systems is not only costly but also detracts from new development work and adds new risks of security controls that may not be well implemented. Demands on security specialists are increased, too, as companies are forced to bring these old systems into compliance.

IT security policies and standards have been around for many years, and many are already available as *de facto* (accepted practices in the industry) and *dejure* (official standards passed by international and industry standards committees). One such standard that is regularly used in IT security is ISO/IEC 17799—Code of Practice for Information Security Management. ISO/IEC 17799 is based on British Standard (BS) 7777 Part I. It defines a series of domains or subject areas—similar to the CISSP CBK—that management is expected to address and is more suggestive in nature (e.g., management *should* address the area of preemployment background checks). On the other hand, British Standard 7799 Part II is the actual standard that prescribes activities that management must address in order to be compliant to the standard. It refers to dictates, such as management SHALL put into place preemployment background checks, and may be used as an assessment tool to verify compliance.

Although ISO/IEC 17799 and BS 7799 are widely used throughout the industry, other documents prepared by international and industry bodies are available for the asking. The National Institute of Standards and Technology, formerly the National Bureau of Standards, has a complete library of documents that serve as the basis for IT security within U.S. federal agencies and the Federal Information Processing Standards (FIPS).

The Control Objectives for Information and Related Technology (COBIT) is another widely accepted set of documents that is commonly found as the basis for an information security programme throughout the world. COBIT is an initiative from the Information Systems Audit and Control Association (ISACA) and is preferred among IT auditors.

The U.S. National Security Telecommunications and Information Systems Security Committee (NSTISSC) Standard 4011, otherwise known as National Training Standard for Information Systems Security Professionals, establishes the minimum training standard for the training of information systems security professionals in the disciplines of telecommunications and automated information systems security. The body of knowledge listed in the standard may be obtained from a variety of sources (e.g., the National Cryptologic School, contractors, adaptations of existing department/agency training programs) or a combination of experience and formal training. The instruction is applicable to all departments and agencies of the U.S. government, their employees, and contractors who are responsible for the security oversight or management of national security systems during each phase of the life cycle. For more on NSTISSC Number 4011, see **www.cnss.gov/As sets/pdf/nstissi_4011.pdf**.

Standards and Baselines

There's an old saw within the IT industry about standards being great because there are so many to choose from. But the point is that there's little need to reinvent your own standards when you can simply reuse what people have found to be best practices.

FYI: Security Experts Are Never Alone

You cannot invent best practices—you simply adopt them from others and thank those who have documented them for making mistakes that you can avoid. This is a primary reason for being fully involved in the IT security industry when you're a practitioner. It's folly to operate in a corporate vacuum, especially when others who share your concerns and problems have already traversed the trails that led them to improved processes and technologies. Security is not an area where competition is admired. Companies are better served by not competing on security when interdependence is present. For example, a bank offering better security on credit card payments is not helping the industry as a whole if it uses security as a market differentiator. If any bank suffers a breach in security, the entire banking industry is adversely affected.

Below the layer of policies, you'll find a more populated layer of standards and baselines (refer to Figure 4.1). Often, you'll see the terms *standards* and *baselines* interchanged. A **standard** refers to specific security requirements, or what is needed for a system or process to be considered secure. An example is a password standard that covers the requirements for password creation, distribution, use, changing, and revocation in support of the policy that mandates appropriate access controls and accountability measures. A **baseline** is a specific set of requirements for a technology implementation, such as Windows 2003 Server security settings or Oracle DBMS protection mechanisms.

Baselines and standards are the enforceable element in the security pro-gramme. Compliance with standards and baselines is what the auditors check, and exceptions are filed against a baseline or a standard. If a standard cannot be met because of time or budget constraints to implementing a control, an ex-ceptions or variance process is usually present to accommodate the messy re-ality of software development and implementation. Exceptions should be temporary and include a plan for meeting compliance to the standard. In any event, the risks of failing to comply with a standard must be understood, and compensating controls to contain these risks should be implemented.

Guidelines

Guidelines, guidance documents, or advisories provide the people who need to implement a standard or baseline more detailed information and guidance (hints, tips, processes, advice, and so forth) to aid in compliance. These documents are optional in a library but are often helpful.

Procedures

Procedures are the detailed, step-by-step activities that are followed to im-plement a process or configure a system for compliance to a guideline. They may also be step-by-step security processes that assure repeatability and accountability of personnel performing the procedure.

Suggested Standards Taxonomy

Standards are formal written documents that describe several security concepts that are fundamental to all successful programmes. The highest level includes

- Asset and data classification

- Separation of duties

- Pre-employment hiring practices

- Risk analysis and management

- Education, awareness, and training

For a complete taxonomy of standards that would be expected in a comprehensive library, see Appendix B.

Asset Classification

Asset and data classification is needed by businesses and agencies to help determine how much security is needed for appropriate protection. A rule of thumb states that one should never spend more on security than the value of the asset being protected. Sometimes determining value is straightfor-ward, but other times—for example, when trying to place a value on a brand icon—it is not so clear. That's where classification helps.

Some of the obvious benefits to a classification system are

- Data confidentiality, integrity, and availability are improved because appropriate controls are used throughout the enterprise.

- Protection mechanisms are maximized.

- A process exists to review the values of company business data.

- Decision quality is increased because the quality of the data upon which the decision is being made has been improved.

In the military, a strict classification system exists to protect national secrets and information. This classification system is covered in-depth in Chapter 5, but a common taxonomy for commercial businesses may provide for the following classes:

- **Public information:** information intended for public dissemination. This may include marketing content on a Web site, direct mail inserts, directories of contact information, published annual reports, and so forth.

- **Business sensitive or business confidential:** information needed by employees and other insiders to perform their duties. This may include company directories (address books, e-mail addresses, and so forth), invoice information, department budget information, internal policies, and so forth.

- **Customer confidential:** information that identifies individual customers of the business or institution and may include their purchase activity, account-specific information, credit card numbers, social security numbers (when needed), grades or course information in the case of a university, or any other information considered personally identifiable information (PII) that dictates *need to know* or least privilege controls to assure confidentiality and integrity.

- **Trade secret:** information in this classification is severely restricted and protected through more strict need to know controls than customer confidential information. Some examples of trade secret information may include the recipe for Coca-Cola, employee disciplinary actions, prereleased financial statement information, or proprietary secrets that offer a competitive advantage to the business.

Separation of Duties

Separating duties within a business or organization helps limit any individual's ability to cause harm or perpetrate theft. For an illegal act to succeed, two or more employees would be forced to conspire. This concept is similar to accounting controls, where it's imprudent, for example, for a person approving an invoice to also be responsible for preparing a vendor payment.

FYI: U.S. Regulations Covering PII

Many of the newly enacted regulations by the U.S. Congress are aimed at protecting PII. Two notable regulations are the Gramm–Leach–Bliley Act (GLBA) for banking, insurance, and finance, and the Health Insurance Portability and Accountability Act (HIPAA) for health care providers, pharmacies, and health care insurance providers. HIPAA caused a flurry of activity throughout 2002 to 2004. In order to comply with the act, health care providers required all patients to sign a release form that authorized them to share personal health-related information for purposes of treatment. You may remember signing these forms each time you used a health care service (dentists, doctors, pharmacy visits, and so forth).

You may also remember a mass mailing in 2003 by your credit card issuers of privacy statements that detailed your rights as a user of a credit product. This activity was in response to the enforcement date of GLBA, which took effect in late 2003.

No single person should be responsible for completing a task involving sensitive, valuable, or critical information from beginning to end. Likewise, a person must not be responsible for approving his own work. Following are some suggestions for separating critical activities:

- Separate development, testing, and production environments and different personnel to manage and operate these environments.

- Separate security management and audit mechanisms and personnel.

- Separate accounts payable and accounts receivable processing and personnel.

- Separate controls over encryption key generation or changing of keys (split knowledge: see Chapter 11 for more details).

- Separate encryption keys into two (or more) components, each of which does not reveal the contents to the two (or more) key signing officers (dual control: see Chapter 11 for more details).

Preemployment Hiring Practices

Policies, standards, and procedures issued by human resources should address internal information security processes and functions. These documents should address preemployment screening and background checks, how to handle employee termination, creating and revoking employee accounts, forwarding e-mail and voice mail after departure, lock keys and safe combination changes, system password changes, and collecting company property upon departure (badges, credit cards, and so forth).

Employee Screening Companies hiring people into areas of responsibility (especially security personnel!) should have policies and practices in place to perform background checks or to get a new employee cleared by the government with security clearances when acting as a contractor for the government. Preemployment background checks should refer to public records because they often provide critical information needed to make the best hiring decision. Conducting these and other simple checks verifies the information provided on the application is current and true and gives the employer an immediate measurement of an applicant's integrity.

Other items that can easily be checked include

- Credit report

- SSN searches

- Worker's compensation reports

- Criminal records

- Motor vehicle report

- Education verification and credential confirmation

- Reference checks

- Previous employer verification

Military Security Clearance One of the most meticulous background checks is the U.S. Department of Defense (DOD) security clearance. The steps are contained in the 30-page Defense Industrial Personnel Security Clearance Review. A defense security clearance is generally only requested for individuals in the following categories whose employment involves access to sensitive government assets:

- Members of the military.

- Civilian employees working for the Department of Defense or other government agencies.

- Employees of government contractors.

A DOD review, known as the *personnel security investigation*, can take a year or longer and includes these activities:

- Search of investigative files and other records held by federal agencies, including the FBI and, if appropriate, international checks.

- Financial check.

- Field interviews of references (in writing, by telephone, or in person), to include coworkers, employers, personal friends, educators, neighbors, and other individuals.

- A personal interview with the applicant conducted by an investigator.

Risk Analysis and Management

Security in any system should be in proportion to the risk under which it operates. The process to determine which security controls are appropriate and cost effective is quite often a complex and sometimes a subjective matter. One of the prime functions of security risk analysis is to put this process onto a more objective basis.

There are two basic types of risk analysis: quantitative and qualitative.

Quantitative Risk Analysis Quantitative, or a quasisubjective, risk analysis attempts to establish and maintain an independent set of risk metrics and statistics. Some of the calculations used for quantitative risk analysis include

- **Annualized loss expectancy (ALE):** single loss expectancy multiplied by annualized rate of occurrence.

- **Probability:** chance or likelihood, in a finite sample, that an event will occur or that a specific loss value may be attained should the event occur.

- **Threat:** an event, the occurrence of which could have an undesired impact.

- **Control:** risk-reducing measure that acts to detect, prevent, or minimize loss associated with the occurrence of a specified threat or category of threats.

- **Vulnerability:** the absence or weakness of a risk-reducing safeguard.

To compute risk value, multiply the probability of an event occurring by the likely loss it would incur. The result is a single value called the annual loss expectancy. Risk managers use the ALE to rank events by magnitude of risk and to make investment decisions based on this ranking. The problems with quantitative risk analysis are usually associated with the unreliability and inaccuracy of the data. Probability can rarely be precise and can, in some cases, promote complacency. In addition, controls and countermeasures often tackle a number of potential events, and the events themselves are frequently interrelated.

Qualitative Risk Analysis Qualitative risk analysis is the most widely used approach to risk analysis. Probability data is not required, and only estimated potential loss is used. Most qualitative risk analysis methodologies make use of a number of interrelated elements:

- Threats

- Vulnerabilities

- Controls

Threats are things that can go wrong or that can "attack" the system. Examples might include fire or fraud. Threats are present for every system no matter what you try to do to eliminate them completely.

Vulnerabilities make a system more prone to attack or make an attack more likely to have some success or impact. For example, fire vulnerability would be the presence of flammable materials (e.g., paper).

Controls are the countermeasures for vulnerabilities and come in five types:

- Deterrent controls reduce the likelihood of a deliberate attack.

- Preventative controls protect vulnerabilities and make an attack unsuccessful or reduce its impact.

- Corrective controls reduce the effect of an attack.

- Detective controls discover attacks and trigger preventative or corrective controls.

- Recovery controls restore lost computer resources or capabilities to recover from security violations.

A risk is real when there is a presence of threat (e.g., a willing and capable attacker), a vulnerability that the attacker can exploit, and a high likelihood that the attacker will carry out the threat.

Figure 4.2 illustrates the qualitative risk analysis process.

Risk analysis is required because it's impossible to protect assets if you do not know what you are protecting against. A risk analysis answers three fundamental questions:

- What am I trying to protect?

- What is threatening my system?

- How much time, effort, and money am I willing to spend?

After risks are classified either as metrics or relative to one another, you can then develop policies and procedures needed to reduce them.

Education, Training, and Awareness

Because people are the weakest link in any security-related process, it's crucial that a security programme address user education, awareness, and

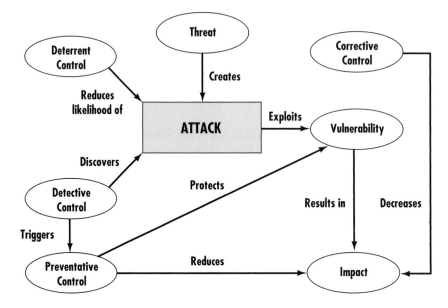

FIGURE 4.2 A model of the risk analysis process.

training on policies and procedures that affect them. Education must be driven top-down and must be comprehensive, all the way from high-end servers down to the desktop systems, peripherals, and hard copies of business documents.

Training may be offered in any number of forms and formats, including paper-based, intranet-based, classroom-based, self-study, and so forth. It should also include mechanisms to make sure that management keeps track of which employees have completed security training and which have agreed to live up to the programme expectations. Furthermore, training must be ongoing (at least annually) and also take place whenever policies change. All employees (including contractors and third-party service providers) need to be made aware of changes.

Training materials and content will vary by the roles or job duties of personnel. A computer user, for example, may only need basic security training (do not write down or share passwords, and so forth), whereas a developer would require application development security training, and IT support personnel or administrators would require more technical security training on the specific assets for which they're responsible.

Who Is Responsible for Security?

Everyone who uses information technology is responsible for maintaining the security and confidentiality of information resources and must comply with security policies and procedures. Certain individuals, however, have specific information security responsibilities that are established by the security programme:

- **Chief information security officer (CISO)**: establishes and maintains security and risk management programmes for information resources.

- **Information resources manager:** maintains policies and procedures that provide for security and risk management of information resources.

- **Information resources security officer:** directs policies and procedures designed to protect information resources (e.g., identifies vulnerabilities, develops security awareness programme, and so forth).

- **Owners of information resources:** responsible for carrying out the programme that uses the resources. This does not imply personal ownership. These individuals may be regarded as programme managers or delegates for the owner.

- **Custodians of information resources:** provide technical facilities, data processing, and other support services to owners and users of information resources.

- **Technical managers (network and system administrators):** provide technical support for security of information resources.

- **Internal auditors:** conduct periodic risk-based reviews of information resources security policies and procedures.

- **Users:** people who have access to information resources in accordance with the owner-defined controls and access rules.

For a comprehensive example of a policy and standards library that is open to the public, visit the University of Houston Security Manual Web site at: **www.uh.edu/infotech/php/template.php?nonsvc_id=268**.

Summary

The Security Management Practices domain is most concerned with the establishment and ongoing operation of the organization's security programme. This programme begins with documentation in the form of policies, standards, baselines, procedures, and guidance for compliance.

An effective security programme includes top-down sponsorship to establish and enforce these policies and standards and to develop and maintain procedures within a comprehensive library of documents that clearly spell out the responsibilities and consequence of noncompliance for all users of IT resources.

The library of documents is arranged as a hierarchy with the highest level consisting of a few policies, followed by an increasing number of standard and baseline documents and further supplemented with guidance documents to aid in implementation, and finally lots of procedure documents that explicitly describe how to implement a security control or process.

The library should be developed and managed by dedicated personnel who are experts in the subject matter related to the organization's industry or mission. Because information security does not stand still for long, policies and standards libraries must be living and breathing in order to be effective for use in preventing, detecting, and responding to security risks.

Test Your Skills

MULTIPLE CHOICE QUESTIONS

1. Which of the following choices is *not* part of a security policy?

    A. definition of overall steps of information security and the importance of security

    B. statement of management intent, supporting the goals and principles of information security

    C. definition of general and specific responsibilities for information security management

    D. description of specific technologies used in the field of information security regulations

2. Which of the following would be the first step in establishing an information security programme?

    A. adoption of a corporate information security policy statement

    B. development and implementation of an information security standards manual

    C. development of a security awareness–training program for employees

    D. purchase of security access control software

3. An effective information security policy should not have which of the following characteristics?

    A. include separation of duties

    B. be designed with a short- to mid-term focus

    C. be understandable and supported by all stakeholders

    D. specify areas of responsibility and authority

4. What is the difference between advisory and regulatory security policies?

   A. There is no difference between them.

   B. Regulatory policies are high-level policy, whereas advisory policies are very detailed.

   C. Advisory policies provide recommendations.

   D. Advisory policies are mandated, whereas regulatory policies are not.

5. What can best be defined as high-level statements, beliefs, goals, and objectives?

   A. standards

   B. policies

   C. guidelines

   D. procedures

6. A deviation or exception from a security standard requires which of the following?

   A. risk acceptance

   B. risk assignment

   C. risk reduction

   D. risk containment

7. Why would an information security policy require that communications test equipment be controlled?

   A. The equipment is susceptible to damage.

   B. The equipment can be used to browse information passing on a network.

   C. The equipment must always be available for replacement if necessary.

   D. The equipment can be used to reconfigure network devices.

8. Step-by-step instructions used to satisfy control requirements are called a

   A. policy.

   B. standard.

   C. guideline.

   D. procedure.

9. Which of the following embodies all the detailed actions that personnel are required to follow?

    A. standards

    B. guidelines

    C. procedures

    D. baselines

10. Which of the following would be defined as an absence or weakness of a safeguard that could be exploited?

    A. a threat

    B. a vulnerability

    C. a risk

    D. an exposure

11. Within IT security, which of the following combinations best defines risk?

    A. threat coupled with a breach

    B. threat coupled with a vulnerability

    C. vulnerability coupled with an attack

    D. threat coupled with a breach of security

12. IT security measures should

    A. be complex.

    B. be tailored to meet organizational security goals.

    C. make sure that every asset of the organization is well protected.

    D. not be developed in a layered fashion.

13. Which of the following should *not* be addressed by employee termination practices?

    A. removal of the employee from active payroll files

    B. return of access badges

    C. employee bonding to protect against losses due to theft

    D. deletion of assigned logon ID and passwords to prohibit system access

14. What would best define risk management?

    A. the process of eliminating the risk

    B. the process of assessing the risks

    C. the process of reducing risk to an acceptable level

    D. the process of transferring risk

15. Controls are implemented to

    A. eliminate risk and reduce the potential for loss.

    B. mitigate risk and eliminate the potential for loss.

    C. mitigate risk and reduce the potential for loss.

    D. eliminate risk and eliminate the potential for loss.

16. Which of the following is an advantage of a qualitative over a quantitative risk analysis?

    A. It prioritizes the risks and identifies areas for immediate improvement in addressing the vulnerabilities.

    B. It provides specific quantifiable measurements of the magnitude of the impacts.

    C. It makes a cost–benefit analysis of recommended controls easier.

    D. It can easily be automated.

17. What can be defined as an event that could cause harm to the information systems?

    A. a risk

    B. a threat

    C. a vulnerability

    D. a weakness

18. One purpose of a security awareness program is to modify

    A employees' attitudes and behaviors.

    B. management's approach.

    C. attitudes of employees with sensitive data.

    D. corporate attitudes about safeguarding data.

19. Which of the following should be given technical security training?

    A. operators

    B. security practitioners and information systems auditors

    C. IT support personnel and system administrators

    D. senior managers, functional managers, and business unit managers

EXERCISES

Exercise 4.1: Security Organizational Structures

1. Using your school or employer, document the organization structure of the department responsible for IT security management.

2. Which security concepts (separation of duties, risk management, and so forth) do you find that influenced the current structure?

3. Which security concepts (if any) appear to be missing from the structure?

Exercise 4.2: Policy Manual Analysis

1. Locate the security policy manual for your organization or school.

2. How does its content compare to the content described in this chapter?

3. How does its structure compare to the structure described in this chapter?

Exercise 4.3: Security Awareness and Training

1 Describe the education, awareness, and training activities that you have encountered as an employee or student.

2. Describe the opportunities for education and awareness that are offered to you as an employee or student.

Exercise 4.4: Finding Analogies to Separation of Duties

1. Explain the principle of separation of duties.

2. How does this principle compare to checks and balances found within the U.S. government?

3. How does this principle compare to checks and balances found within your state government?

Exercise 4.5: Risk Analysis Application

1. Apply the information related to qualitative risk analysis to your personal or family's vehicle as an asset.

2. Which risks can you determine, and how would you manage each one?

3. What might you do differently once you complete the exercise?

PROJECTS

Project 4.1: Comparing Standards Libraries Across Organizations

1. Visit the University of Houston Information Security Manual Web site at **www.uh.edu/infotech/php/template.php?nonsvc_id=268**.

2. Compare what you find there to the taxonomy of documents presented in this chapter.

3. Do you find many differences? How might you attribute differences between security manuals for corporations over those for educational organizations?

4. What are some of the similarities?

Project 4.2: Best Practices Standards

1. Visit the InfoSec Reading Room at SANS.org (**www.sans.org/rr**).

2. Search for documented best practices in information security.

3. What types of best practices are commonly documented?

4. How could you incorporate these best practices into the development of a security manual?

5. How would you distribute these to personnel requiring the information?

Project 4.3: Employee Prescreening and Termination Processes

1. Develop a list of recommended steps to include in a preemployment hiring process.

2. Develop a list of recommended steps to include in an employee termination process.

3. Which areas within the organization need to be included?

4. Suggest some ways for the security department to communicate with these other departments to assure that nothing falls through the cracks.

5. How would you help to assure that outside departments follow these recommendations?

Case Study

A small medical office of four physicians and support staff decides they want to set up a wireless LAN to permit them to take their laptops with them from room to room for real-time data entry on patient records. The doctors know they need to comply with HIPAA controls over patient records and are concerned that a Wi-Fi LAN could compromise security.

What advice would you offer to the medical office manager about implementing a Wi-Fi access point on the network? What elements would a policy contain? Develop a high-level standard to address the considerations for implementing Wi-Fi under HIPAA security rule constraints.

There are several ways that wireless access points are being deployed to make them more secure.

You may find these sites helpful when developing your policy:

Wi-Fi Planet: **www.wi-fiplanet.com/columns/article.php/1550241**

HIPAA Advisory: **www.hipaadvisory.com/tech/wireless.htm**

Chapter | 5

Security Architecture and Models

Chapter Objectives

After reading this chapter and completing the exercises, you will be able to do the following:

- Summarize the concept of a trusted computing base (TCB).
- Illustrate the concept of rings of trust.
- Distinguish among the protection mechanisms used in a TCB.
- Defend the purposes of security assurance testing.
- Apply the Trusted Computer Security Evaluation Criteria (TCSEC) for software evaluations.
- Apply the Trusted Network Interpretation of the TCSEC.
- Categorize the role of the Federal Criteria for Information Technology Security.
- Apply the Common Criteria for Information Security Evaluation.
- Summarize the principles behind confidentiality and integrity models and their role in security architectures.

Introduction

The Security Architecture and Models domain of the Common Body of Knowledge contains the concepts, principles, structures, and standards used to design, monitor, and secure operating systems, equipment, networks, and applications. It also contains the controls used to enforce various levels of availability, integrity, and confidentiality. These ideas and controls stem from research in computer science and the development of systems requiring strict attention to computer security.

Several new terms and concepts are introduced in this domain, including the concepts of trusted computing base (TCB), formal security evaluations and testing, and, finally, models of access control behavior.

Defining the Trusted Computing Base

While the tools and methodologies to implement access controls are found in Chapter 10, the principles behind these mechanisms will be found in this chapter.

The ***trusted computing base*** (TCB) is the totality of protection mechanisms within a computer system including hardware, firmware, and software. A TCB consists of one or more components that together enforce a unified security policy over a product or system. It describes the isolation of objects on which the protection is based, following the concept of the ***reference monitor***. The reference monitor is a software model or ***abstract machine*** that mediates all access from any subject (user or other device) to any object (resource, data, and so forth) and cannot be bypassed. An abstract machine mediates accesses to objects by subjects. In principle, a reference monitor should be

- complete in that it mediates every access.

- isolated from modification by other system entities (objects and processes).

- verifiable in that it only does what it's programmed to do and cannot be circumvented by malicious acts or programmer error.

A security kernel is an implementation of a reference monitor for a specific hardware base such as Sun Solaris, Red Hat Linux, or Mac OS X. The TCB, reference monitor, and security kernel are essential for military- and government-grade information technology (IT) security to prevent unauthorized access or threats to the integrity of programs, operating systems, or data.

A trusted system, according to the TCB, is a system that can be expected to meet users' requirements for reliability, security, and effectiveness due to having undergone formal testing and validation. Trusted computing is an essential element for governments and agencies managing national secrets. Because no single person is responsible for data ownership when it comes to national secrets (as they are in a commercial setting), the operating systems that are relied on use a concept called ***mandatory access control*** (MAC) for deciding who may gain access to what. MAC requires that access control policy decisions are beyond the control of the individual owner of an object, thus requiring the system to make the decisions. The reference monitor makes these decisions and permits or denies access based on labels and clearance levels.

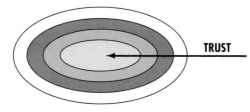

FIGURE 5.1 The unidirectional layered model of trust.

An *object* is something within a trusted system that people wish to access or use (such as a program). Objects are labeled with a sensitivity level (see Chapter 4). *Subjects* (people or other processes) that wish to access these objects must be cleared to the same level of classification or higher. Several security models covered later in this chapter have been developed to address confidentiality and integrity.

Rings of Trust

The TCB concept is illustrated using what is called a ***ring of trust***. Trust in a system moves from the outside to the inside in a unidirectional mode. The ring model of security was originally derived from the concept of execution domains developed by the Multics project. Figure 5.1 illustrates the concept of rings of trust.

FYI: What Is Multics?

Multics (Multiplexed Information and Computing Service) was a timesharing operating system project begun in 1965. The system was started as a joint project by MIT Project MAC, Bell Telephone Laboratories, and General Electric. Multics never caught much in the way of commercial attention, but it had a powerful impact in the computer field, due to its many novel and valuable ideas. In particular, the Unix system (produced by Bell Labs personnel who had worked on Multics), the GNU project, and much later the Linux kernel, are in part descended from Multics.

Among its new ideas, Multics was the first operating system to provide a hierarchical file system, a feature that now can be found in virtually every operating system. It had numerous features intended to result in high availability, so that it would produce a computing utility, similar to the telephone and electricity services.

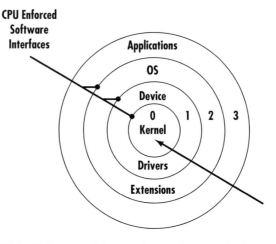

FIGURE 5.2 Rings of trust in stand-alone systems.

Figure 5.2 shows the rings of trust concept in the context of a single computer system. In this model, outer rings contain a lower level of security, and systems requiring higher levels of security are located inside the inner rings. Extra security mechanisms must be navigated to move from an outer ring into an inner ring. The operating system (OS) enforces how communications flow between layers using the reference monitor (within the kernel) to mediate all access and protect resources.

It's also possible to use the concepts of rings of trust to design security domains or operating environments for networks of systems. This concept is illustrated in Figure 5.3.

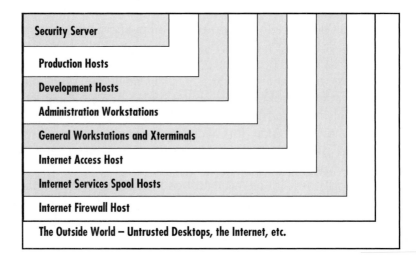

FIGURE 5.3 Rings of trust in networked environments.

This model divides the hosts into rings, based on the security rating of the services they provide to the network, and then uses these rings as the basis for trust between hosts.

To help determine the hierarchy of the rings, some questions must be answered:

- Is the host in a physically secured computer room?

- Does the host have normal (as opposed to privileged) user accounts?

- Is this host at a remote site and hence less trustworthy than the ones in the central computer room?

- Does this host operate software that relies on data obtained from the Internet?

- Does this host provide mission-critical services? How many people in the company would be affected by downtime on this host?

The following general rules apply to constructing rings of trust in networked systems:

- Each host trusts those hosts in a more inner ring than itself.

- No host trusts any host in a more outer ring than itself.

- Each host may trust those hosts in the same ring as itself.

- Where a ring has been segmented into separate subnetworks, a host in one segment does not trust hosts in other segments.

As you can see, rings of trust apply equally well for stand-alone systems, small business or home networks, and large-scale corporate and government networks where security requirements are absolute.

To implement the rings of trust model, a number of software constructs and design objectives are used for security and protection of resources.

Protection Mechanisms in a Trusted Computing Base

There are a number of standard design concepts and software processes that are often found in a TCB and are described below.

Process isolation is a design objective in which each process has its own distinct address space for its application code and data. In this way, it is possible to prevent each process from accessing another process's data. This prevents data or information leakage and prevents modification of the data while it is memory.

Principle of least privilege dictates that a process (program) has no more privilege than what it really needs in order to perform its functions.

Any modules that require "supervisor" or "root" access (that is, complete system privileges) are embedded in the operating system kernel. The kernel handles all requests for system resources and mediates the access from external modules to privileged modules when required.

Hardware segmentation specifically relates to the segmentation of memory into protected segments. The kernel allocates the required amount of memory for the process to load its application code, its process data, and its application data. The system prevents user processes from being able to access another process's allocated memory. It also prevents user processes from being able to access system memory.

Layering is a process operation that is divided into layers by function. Each layer deals with a specific activity. The lower (outer) layers perform basic tasks, whereas the higher (inner) layers perform more complex or protected tasks.

Abstraction is a process that defines a specific set of permissible values for an object and the operations that are permissible on that object. This involves ignoring or separating implementation details in order to concentrate on what is important to maintain security.

Data hiding—also known as information hiding—is a mechanism to assure that information available at one processing level is not available in another, regardless of whether it is higher or lower. It is also a concept in the object-oriented programming (OOP) technique (see Chapter 13 for more details on OOP) when information is encapsulated within an object and can be directly manipulated only by the services provided within the object.

Information storage refers to the parts of a computer system that retain a physical state (information) for some interval of time, possibly even after electrical power to the computer is removed. There are a number of different types used for data or information storage. These include the following types:

- *Primary storage* is the computer's main memory that is directly addressable by the central processing unit (CPU). Primary storage is a volatile storage medium, meaning that the contents of the physical memory are lost when the power is removed.

- *Secondary storage* is a nonvolatile storage format, where application and system code plus data can be stored when the system is not in use. Examples of secondary storage are disk drives or other persistent data storage mechanisms (e.g., Flash [USB] drives, memory sticks, and tapes).

- *Real memory* is where a program has been given a definite storage location in memory and direct access to a peripheral device. This is common with database management systems that control how storage is used outside of the control of the operating system.

- *Virtual memory* extends the volume of primary storage by using secondary storage to hold the memory contents. In this way, the operating system can run programs larger than the available physical memory. Virtual memory (memory contents stored on disk) is swapped in and out of primary memory when needed for processing.

- *Random memory* is the computer's primary working and storage area. It is addressable directly by the CPU and stores application or system code in addition to data.

- *Sequential storage* is computer memory that is accessed sequentially. An example of this is magnetic tape.

- *Volatile memory* means that there is a complete loss of any stored information when the power is removed.

Closed systems are of a proprietary nature. They use specific operating systems and hardware to perform the task and generally lack standard interfaces to allow connection to other systems. The user is generally limited in the applications and programming languages available.

An *open system*, on the other hand, is based on accepted standards and employs standard interfaces to allow connections between different systems. It promotes interoperability and allows the user to have full access to the total system capability.

Multitasking is a technique used by a system that is capable of running two or more tasks in a concurrent performance or interleaved execution.

A *multiprogramming system* allows for the interleaved execution of two or more programs on a processor.

Multiprocessing provides for simultaneous execution of two or more programs by a processor (CPU). This can alternatively be done through parallel processing of a single program by two or more processors in a multi-processor system that all have common access to main storage.

A *finite-state machine* is any device that stores the status or state of something at a given time that can operate based on inputs to change the stored status and/or cause an action or output to take place. The importance of finite-state machines is that the machine has distinct states that it remembers. In Multics, for example, there was a state associated with each ring of trust. Each computer's data register also stores a state. The read-only memory from which a boot (computer start-up) program is loaded stores a state. In fact, the boot program is an initial state. The operating system is itself a state, and each application that it runs begins with some initial state that may change as it handles input. Thus, at any moment in time, a computer system can be seen as a very complex set of states and each program in it as a state machine. In practice, however, state machines are used to develop and describe specific device or program interactions for purposes of discovery or evaluation.

System Security Assurance Concepts

When considering IT security systems (firewall software, intrusion detection devices, access control mechanisms, and so forth), the requirements or needs, decided by those who sponsor the development, appear in two forms: functional requirements and assurance requirements.

Functional requirements describe what a system should do by design, and *assurance requirements* describe how the functional requirements should be implemented and tested. Both sets of requirements are needed to answer the following questions:

- Does the system do the right things?

- Does the system do the right things in the right way?

These are the same questions that others in noncomputer industries face with verification and validation. You need both answers to gain confidence in products prior to launching them into a wild, hostile environment, like the Internet, or to use them to protect national secrets and data (like income tax returns). Both types of requirements must be tested (and retested) and are included in the scope of security assurance testing.

Software testing focused only on functionality testing for user acceptance will uncover errors (bugs) in how the software operates. If the system responds to input in the ways the users expect it to respond, it's stamped as ready to ship. If the system responds differently, the bugs are worked out in successive remediation and retesting until it behaves as desired.

Goals of Security Testing

Security testing flips this technique on its head and takes it a step further. It not only verifies that the functions designed to meet a security requirement operate as expected but also validates that the implementation of the function is not flawed or haphazard.

This kind of security testing can only be performed effectively by experts—never by casual users or developers. Programmers can't uncover flaws in their own programs that affect security—they can only find the flaws in its operation.

Security assurance and testing is laced with lots of odd concepts and principles that truly do fly in the face of conventional thinking and are foreign to most people involved in IT development. Gaining confidence that a system does not do what it's not supposed to do is akin to proving a negative, and most everyone knows that you can't prove a negative! What you can do, however, is subject a system to brutal security testing, and with each resistance to an attack, gain additional confidence that it was developed with security in mind.

Formal Security Testing Models

Beginning with the widespread adoption of affordable computers by both the military and government bodies, the *Trusted Computer System Evaluation Criteria* (TCSEC) was born in the United States in the early 1980s. Over the succeeding decade, other countries around the world began the work of developing their own evaluation criteria, building upon the concepts of the TCSEC but adding more flexibility to adapt to evolving computing technology.

In Europe, the *Information Technology Security Evaluation Criteria* (ITSEC) version 1.2 was published in 1991 by the European Commission after joint development by France, Germany, the Netherlands, and the United Kingdom. In Canada, the *Canadian Trusted Computer Product Evaluation Criteria* (CTCPEC) version 3.0 was published in early 1993 as a combination of the ITSEC and TCSEC approaches.

Back in the United States, the draft *Federal Criteria for Information Technology Security* (FC) version 1.0 was published in early 1993 as an attempt to develop criteria to replace the TCSEC and harmonize North American and European concepts for security evaluation criteria. A draft version of the Federal Criteria was released for public comment in December 1992 but was supplanted by the *Common Criteria* standardization efforts.

Beginning with TCSEC, in the next few sections we'll examine the evolution of security testing models that led to today's Common Criteria standard.

5

Trusted Computer Security Evaluation Criteria

The U.S. Department of Defense (DOD) Trusted Computer System Evaluation Criteria (TCSEC) was a collection of criteria used to grade or rate the security claimed for a computer system product. The now-obsolete TCSEC was often called the *Orange Book* because of its orange cover. The last version is dated 1985 (DOD 5200.28-STD, Library No. S225,711). TCSEC is one part of a series of DOD documents called the "Rainbow Series" because of the multiple colored covers on each document.

TCSEC is most interested in confidentiality and sets forth criteria used to rate the effectiveness of trusted systems in terms of how well they can protect the secrecy of objects contained within them.

The TCB described by the *Orange Book* is a complete description of all the protection mechanisms used within computer systems. The combination of all protection mechanisms are used to enforce security policy. The TCB consists of the hardware, software, and firmware that make up the system. Security policy is a formal description of the rules for subjects and objects that a trusted system needs to determine if a given subject is authorized to access a specific object. Trusted systems are evaluated products (hardware, software, or combinations of the two) that are expected to meet the requirements for reliability, security, and operational effectiveness. They're both verified and validated as being implemented correctly through formal evaluation methods that use established criteria for testing.

The earlier efforts to formalize security assurance included groupings of requirements that described the desired levels of security for a product or a system. TCSEC and other assurance criteria documents outlined both security functional requirements (what functions must be present) along with security assurance requirements (i.e., how thoroughly the functions should be tested) to arrive at an overall rating.

TCSEC provided classes (or divisions) of trust that are roughly equivalent to object classifications of Unclassified, Secret, Top Secret, and beyond Top Secret, using the letters D, C, B, and A, respectively.

Division D: Minimal Protection

Division D is reserved by the TCSEC for those systems that have either been formally evaluated but fail to meet the requirements for a higher evaluation class or it is used on unrated or untested systems. TCSEC does not contain specific requirements for Division D evaluations, but some of the TCSEC interpretations documents (other Rainbow Series documents) do permit specifying Division D levels of evaluation.

Division C: Discretionary Protection

Classes in Division C provide for discretionary protection, based on the need-to-know, or least privilege, principle and for audit control mechanisms that enforce the personal accountability of subjects for the actions they take while using the system. Discretionary protection is what is seen in the commercial world protecting objects from unauthorized subjects through the assignment of privilege to the subject by the object's owner. In other words, a data owner (human being) gets to decide who is authorized to access his or her objects (data, programs, and so forth).

Class C1: Discretionary Security Protection The TCB of a Class C1 system satisfies the discretionary access control requirements by separating users and data. It incorporates mechanisms that are capable of enforcing access limitations on an individual basis. C1 requirements are suitable for allowing users the ability to protect project or private information and to keep other users from accidentally reading or destroying their data. Class C1 systems are typically used among a group of users who share the same level of clearance (e.g., workgroups).

Class C2: Controlled Access Protection Systems in this class enforce a more finely grained discretionary access control than C1 systems, making users individually accountable for their actions through login procedures, auditing of security-relevant events, and resource isolation. This means that no program can gain access to the memory areas used by other programs.

Security assurance divisions above Division C are usually reserved for governmental systems and are rarely found in the commercial world unless the company acts as a subcontractor to government agencies requiring such protections. Similarly, assurance levels in the Common Criteria above Evaluation Assurance Level (EAL) 4 are typically reserved for national government systems.

Division B: Mandatory Protection

A major requirement in this division is that a TCB preserves the integrity of sensitivity labels and uses them to enforce a set of mandatory access control rules. Systems in this division must carry the sensitivity labels (secret or top secret, for example) with major data structures in the system. The system developer provides the security policy model on which the TCB is based and furnishes a specification of the TCB. Evidence is needed to demonstrate that the reference monitor concept has been implemented. The reference monitor refers to the concept of an abstract machine (a machine within a machine) that mediates the access of subjects to objects. The reference monitor must be protected from unauthorized changes, must always be used to mediate all access (cannot be circumvented), and must be verified as implemented correctly.

Mandatory protections are what the military is most interested in to protect national secrets. With mandatory access controls, the system or TCB decides who can access what according to the security policy that's implemented by the reference monitor.

Class B1: Labeled Security Protection Class B1 systems require all the features required for Class C2. In addition, an informal statement of the security policy model, data labeling, and mandatory access control over named subjects and objects must be present. The capability must exist for accurately labeling exported information from the system, and any flaws identified during testing must be removed.

Class B2: Structured Protection In Class B2 systems, the TCB is based on a clearly defined and documented formal security policy model that requires the discretionary and mandatory access control enforcement found in Class B1 systems be extended to all subjects and objects in the system. In addition, covert channels are addressed. Covert channels are possible wherever there's an opportunity for a system to provide unintended communications. One example of a covert channel is a back door in a system that circumvents the security mechanisms and enables the movement of data from a higher classification level to an area where lower classifications of data are accessible.

The TCB must be carefully structured into protection-critical and non-protection-critical elements. The TCB interface is well defined and well understood, and the TCB design and implementation should enable the system to be subjected to more thorough testing and more complete review. During this testing and review, authentication mechanisms are strengthened, trusted facility management is offered via an interface for system administrator and operator functions, and strict configuration management controls are imposed. The system is then deemed relatively resistant to penetration.

Class B3: Security Domains For Class B3, the TCB must satisfy the reference monitor requirements to

- mediate all accesses of subjects to objects.

- be tamperproof.

- be small enough to be subjected to analysis and tests.

To this end, the TCB is structured to exclude program code that's not essential to security policy enforcement. This requires significant system engineering during TCB design and implementation with the goal of minimizing its complexity. A security administrator role is supported, audit mechanisms are expanded to signal (trace) security-relevant events, and system recovery procedures are required. This system is deemed highly resistant to penetration.

Division A: Verified Protection

Division A is characterized by the use of formal security verification methods to assure that the mandatory and discretionary security controls employed within the system effectively protect classified or other sensitive information stored or processed by the system. Extensive documentation is required to demonstrate that the TCB meets the security requirements in all aspects of design, development, and implementation.

Class A1: Verified Design Systems in Class A1 are functionally equivalent to those in Class B3, with no additional architectural features or policy requirements added. The distinguishing feature of systems in this class is the analysis derived from formal design specification and verification techniques and the resulting high degree of assurance that the TCB is correctly implemented. This assurance is developmental in nature, starting with a formal model of the security policy and a formal top-level specification of the design. There are five important criteria for Class A1 design verification independent of the particular specification language or verification system used:

- A formal model of the security policy must be clearly identified and documented, including a mathematical proof that the model is consistent with its axioms and is sufficient to support the security policy.

■ A formal top-level specification must be produced that includes abstract definitions of the functions the TCB performs and of the hardware and/or firmware mechanisms that are used to support separated execution domains.

■ The formal top-level specification of the TCB must be shown to be consistent with the model using formal techniques where possible (i.e., where verification tools exist) or informal ones where formal techniques are unavailable.

■ The TCB implementation (i.e., in hardware, firmware, and software) must be informally shown to be consistent with the formal top-level specification. The elements of the formal top-level specification must be shown, using informal techniques, to correspond to the elements of the TCB. The formal top-level specification must express the unified protection mechanism required to satisfy the security policy. It is the elements of this protection mechanism that are mapped to the elements of the TCB.

■ Formal analysis techniques must be used to identify and analyze covert channels. Informal techniques may be used to identify covert timing channels (unwanted communications based on temporal activities). Any continued existence of identified covert channels in the system must be justified by the developer.

To preserve the extensive design and development analysis of the TCB required of systems in Class A1, additional stringent configuration management is required along with procedures for securely distributing the system to sites. System security administrator functions are also required.

The Trusted Network Interpretation of the TCSEC

The Trusted Network Interpretation (TNI) of the TCSEC is also referred to as the *Red Book* of the Rainbow Series. The TNI restates the requirements of the TCSEC in a network context as contrasted with TCSEC on stand-alone and non-networked environments.

Information Technology Security Evaluation Criteria

The Information Technology Security Evaluation Criteria (ITSEC) is a European-developed criterion that fills a role roughly equivalent to the TCSEC for use throughout the European Community. Although the ITSEC and TCSEC have many similar requirements, there are some important distinctions. The ITSEC places increased emphasis on integrity and availability and attempts to provide a uniform approach to the evaluation of both products and systems.

ITSEC introduces the concept of the *target of evaluation* (TOE), which refers to the product or system under evaluation. It adds to the TCB security-relevant functions in addition to security-enforcing functions (like TCSEC). ITSEC provides for functionality classes, assurance classes, and profiles for systems. It also introduces the security target (ST), a written document that contains

- a system security policy.

- required security enforcing functions.

- required security mechanisms.

- claimed ratings of minimum strength.

- target evaluation levels, expressed as both functional and evaluation (F-xx and E-yy).

Comparing ITSEC and TCSEC

ITSEC functionality and assurance classes map closely to the TCSEC divisions and classes and are shown below in Table 5.1. You can use these to roughly compare implementations and testing requirements between products manufactured in the U.S. and Europe.

ITSEC classes are hierarchical; each class adds to the class above it and contains specific functions and mechanisms that correspond to TCSEC. ITSEC also supports other specialized classes that stand alone (nonhierarchical):

- F-IN for high-integrity

- F-AV for high-availability

- F-DI for high data integrity

- F-DC for high data confidentiality

- F-DX for networks that require high demands for confidentiality and integrity during data exchanges

These five classes only describe additional functional requirements above the preset requirements found in Table 5.1.

ITSEC Assurance Classes

The assurance classes, listed as the second value in Table 5.1 for ITSEC, describe the testing requirements and are listed in Table 5.2.

TABLE 5.1 TCSEC and ITSEC classes compared.

TCSEC Classes	ITSEC Functional and Assurance Classes
C1	F-C1, E1
C2	F-C2, E2
B1	F-B1, E3
B2	F-B2, E4
B3	F-B3, E5
A1	F-B3, E6

TABLE 5.2 ITSEC assurance classes.

ITSEC Assurance Class	Description
E0	Inadequate assurance: fails to meet E1 requirements
E1	Security target document that provides an informal description of the TOE's architectural design and functional testing that the TOE satisfies target requirements
E2	E1 requirements plus an informal description of detailed designs, testing evidence, configuration control requirements, and approved distribution procedures
E3	E2 requirements plus source code and drawings that are evaluated and testing evidence of security mechanisms that are evaluated
E4	E3 requirements plus a formal model of security policy, semiformal specification of security enforcing functions, architectural design documents, and detailed design documents
E5	E4 requirements plus evidence of close correspondence between detailed design and source code (traceability of design into implementation)
E6	E5 requirements plus a formal specification of security enforcing functions and architectural design, along with consistency with the formal security policy model

5

Canadian Trusted Computer Product Evaluation Criteria

In August 1988, the Canadian System Security Centre (CSSC) at the Communications Security Establishment of the Government of Canada was formed to develop a set of criteria and to set up a Canadian evaluation capability among other tasks. In April 1992, a draft of version 3.0 of the Canadian Trusted Computer Product Evaluation Criteria (CTCPEC) was published.

The Canadian Trusted Computer Product Evaluation Criteria is the Canadian equivalent of the TCSEC. It is somewhat more flexible than the TCSEC (along the lines of the ITSEC) while maintaining fairly close compatibility with individual TCSEC requirements. The CTCPEC and its approach to structure security functionality separate from assurance functionality influenced international standardization through the Common Criteria. In January 1993, the final and last version (version 3) of CTCPEC was published.

Federal Criteria for Information Technology Security

To further meet organizational needs for handling both classified and unclassified information, the Federal Criteria for Information Technology Security (Federal Criteria, or FC) was developed as a joint project by the National Institute of Standards and Technology (NIST) and the National Security Agency (NSA). The Federal Criteria was an attempt to develop a set of newer criteria to replace the aging TCSEC. It introduces the concept of a protection profile (PP) that empowers users or buyers of technology to specify their security requirements for hardware and software.

A draft version of the FC was released for public comment in December 1992. The effort was supplanted by the international Common Criteria development efforts, and the Federal Criteria never moved beyond the draft stage (although many of its ideas are retained in the Common Criteria). No final version of the FC was ever published.

The Common Criteria

Joint efforts between the United States (TCSEC), Canada (CTCPEC), and Europe (ITSEC) began in 1993 to harmonize security evaluation criteria to enable true comparability between the results of independent security evaluations. These joint activities were designed to align international separate criteria into a single set of IT security criteria that could be broadly used. The activity was named the Common Criteria (CC) Project, and its purpose was to resolve the conceptual and technical differences found in the various source criteria and to deliver the results to the International Organization for Standardization (ISO) as a proposed international standard under development.

FYI: Formal Security Testing in the Real World

While these concepts and processes may seem a bit of overkill, assurance of commercial products is nothing that serious buyers of security products should ever ignore. To better understand how security evaluations work in practice and what their value is to government and commercial buyers of security products, visit the Common Criteria Portal at **www.commoncriteriaportal.org**.

Representatives of the sponsoring organizations formed the CC Editorial Board (CCEB) to develop the CC, and a liaison relationship was established between the CCEB and ISO Working Group 3 (WG3). The CCEB contributed several early versions of the CC to WG3 via the liaison. As a result of the interaction between WG3 and the CCEB, successive versions of the CC were adopted as working drafts of the various parts of the CC beginning in 1994. Work continued for the next 5 years on harmonizing requirements. In June 1999, the Common Criteria for IT Security Evaluation became ISO International Standard 15408. It focuses on security objectives, the related threats (malicious or otherwise), and the functional requirements relevant to security.

The market force driving the need for harmonized criteria is best understood by an example. Say a vendor of firewalls in Germany wanted to sell its ITSEC evaluated product to an American government agency. If the U.S. agency required the product for a classified government system, the German firewall vendor would have no choice but to sponsor a separate evaluation of its product in the United States using TCSEC criteria—adding tremendous cost and time to the process of successfully selling its products outside the German border.

The Common Criteria addresses this problem through a mutual recognition of the final certificates granted to successfully evaluated products and eliminates the need for multiple evaluations and their associated costs and time requirements.

The Common Criteria, also known as ISO 15408, combines the best features of the TCSEC with the ITSEC and the CTCPEC and synergizes them into a single international standard.

Many countries and organizations participated in the development of the Common Criteria:

- **Canada:** Communications Security Establishment

- **France:** Service Central de la Securite des Systèmes d'Information

- **Germany:** Bundesamt fur Sicherheit in der Informationstechnik

- **The Netherlands:** Netherlands National Communications Security Agency

- **United Kingdom:** Communications-Electronics Security Group

- **United States:** National Institute of Standards and Technology and the National Security Agency

The CC provides a common language and structure to express IT security requirements and enables the creation of catalogs of standards broken down into components and packages. The CC breaks apart the functional and assurance requirements into distinct elements that users can select for customized security device implementation.

Packages permit the expression of requirements that meet an identifiable subset of security objectives. Packages are reusable and can be used to construct larger packages as well. Using the CC framework, users and developers of IT security products create ***protection profiles*** (PPs) as an implementation-independent collection of objectives and requirements for any given category of products or systems that must meet similar needs (e.g., firewalls). Protection profiles are needed to support defining functional standards and serve as an aid in specifying needs for procurement purposes.

Whereas protection profiles serve as a generic description of product and environmental requirements, targets of evaluation (TOE) are the specific products or systems that will fall into an evaluation against an existing PP. The sets of evidence about a TOE and the TOE itself form the inputs to a security target (ST) that's used by certified independent evaluators as the basis for evaluation.

Once again, there are two types of security requirements: functional and assurance. Functional requirements describe what a product needs to do, and assurance requirements describe how well it meets the functional requirements. Consumers need both of these pieces of data to effectively judge the merits of one product over another.

In defining security requirements for a trusted product or system, users and developers need to consider the threats to the environment. The Common Criteria provides a catalog of components (Part 2 of the CC) that developers of PPs use to form the requirements definition. Assurance requirements (defined in Part 3 of the CC) contain two classes from which evaluation assurance requirements may be selected, along with a class for assurance maintenance.

Protection Profile Organization

A protection profile is organized as follows:

- Introduction section, which provides descriptive information that's needed to identify, catalog, register, and cross-reference a PP. The overview provides a summary of the PP as a narrative.

- Target of evaluation (TOE) description, which describes the TOE to aid in understanding its security requirements and addresses the product type and the general features of the TOE, providing a context for the evaluation.

- Security environment, which consists of three subsections:
  - Assumptions
  - Threats
  - Organizational security policies

These sections describe the security aspects of the environment in which the TOE will be used and the manner in which it will be used. Assumptions describe the security aspects of the environment in which the TOE will be used, including information about the intended usage, aspects about the intended applications, potential asset value, and possible limitations of use. The threats section covers all the threats where specific protection within the TOE or its environment is needed. Only those threats that are relevant to secure TOE operation are included. Organizational security policies identify and explain any security policies or rules that govern the TOE or its operating environment.

- Security objectives address all of the security environment aspects identified in earlier sections of the PP. These objectives define the intent of the TOE to counter identified threats and include the organizational security policies and assumptions. This section defines in detail the security requirements that must be satisfied by the TOE or its environment. TOE security requirements describe what supporting evidence is needed to satisfy security objectives. Functional requirements are selected from the CC functional components (Part 2).

- Assurance requirements are stated as one of the evaluation assurance levels (EALs) from the CC Part 3 assurance components.

- Rationale presents the evidence used by a PP evaluation. This evidence supports the claims that the PP is a complete and cohesive set of requirements and that a compliant TOE provides an effective set of IT security countermeasures within the security environment.

Security Functional Requirements

The classes of security functional requirements (component catalog) include

- **Audit:** Security auditing functions involve recognizing, recording, storing, and analyzing information related to security-relevant activities. The resulting audit records can be examined to determine which security-relevant activities took place and which user is responsible for them.

- **Cryptographic support:** These functions are used when the TOE implements cryptographic functions in hardware, firmware, or software.

- **Communications:** These functional requirements are related to assuring the identity of a transmitted information originator and assuring the identity of the recipient. These functions ensure that an originator cannot deny having sent the message, nor can the recipient deny having received it.

- **User data protection:** This class of functions is related to protecting user data within a TOE during import, export, and storage.

- **Identification and authentication:** These functions ensure that users are associated with the proper security attributes (e.g., identity, groups, roles).

- **Security management:** These functions are intended to specify the management of several aspects of the TOE security functions security attributes and security data.

- **Privacy:** These requirements provide a user protection against discovery and misuse of identity by other users.

- **Protection of the TOE security functions (TSF):** These requirements relate to the integrity and management of the mechanisms that provide the TSF and to the integrity of TSF data.

- **Resource utilization:** Support the availability of required resources such as CPU and/or storage capacity. Fault tolerance provides protection against unavailability of capabilities caused by failure of the TOE. Priority of service ensures that the resources will be allocated to the more important or time-critical tasks and cannot be monopolized by lower priority tasks.

- **TOE access:** Control the establishment of a user's session.

Evaluation assurance classes include

- Configuration management to help ensure that the integrity of the TOE is preserved through required discipline and control in the processes of refinement and modification of the TOE and other related information. Configuration management prevents unauthorized modifications, additions, or deletions to the TOE and provides assurance that the TOE and documentation used for evaluation are the ones prepared for distribution.

- Delivery and operation classes define the requirements for the measures, procedures, and standards concerned with secure delivery, installation, and operational use of the TOE, assuring that the security protection offered by the TOE is not compromised during transfer, installation, start-up, and operation.

■ Development classes define the requirements for the stepwise (proceeding in steps) refinement of the TOE security functions (TSF) from the summary specification in the security target down to the actual implementation. Each of the resulting TSF representations provides information to help the evaluator determine whether the functional requirements of the TOE have been met.

■ Guidance documents define the requirements for understandability, coverage, and completeness of the operational documentation provided by the developer. This documentation, which provides two categories of information—for users and for administrators—is an important factor in the secure operation of the TOE.

■ Life-cycle support defines the requirements for the adoption of a well-defined life-cycle model for all the steps of the TOE development, including flaw remediation procedures and policies, correct use of tools and techniques, and the security measures used to protect the development environment.

■ Tests cover the testing requirements needed to demonstrate that the TSF satisfies the TOE security functional requirements. This class addresses coverage, depth of developer testing, and functional tests for independent lab testing.

■ Vulnerability assessment defines the requirements directed at identifying exploitable vulnerabilities. Specifically, it addresses those vulnerabilities introduced in the construction, operation, misuse, or incorrect configuration of the TOE.

■ Protection profile evaluation is used to demonstrate that the PP is complete, consistent, technically sound, and that an evaluated PP is suitable as the basis for developing an ST.

■ Security target evaluation: The goal of an ST evaluation is to demonstrate that the ST is complete, consistent, technically sound, and is suitable as the basis for the corresponding TOE evaluation.

■ Maintenance of assurance provides the requirements intended for application after a TOE has been certified against the Common Criteria. Maintenance of assurance requirements help to assure that the TOE will continue to meet its security target as changes are made to the TOE or its environment. Such changes include the discovery of new threats or vulnerabilities, changes in user requirements, and the correction of bugs found in the certified TOE.

TABLE 5.3 Security criteria compared.

Common Criteria Assurance Level	Orange Book Criteria Level	ITSEC Criteria Level
—	D: Minimal protection	E0
EAL1	—	—
EAL2	C1: Discretionary security protection	E1
EAL3	C2: Controlled access protection	E2
EAL4	B1: Labeled security protection	E3
EAL5	B2: Structured protection	E4
EAL6	B3: Security domains	E5
EAL7	A1: Verified design	E6

Evaluation Assurance Levels

Assurance levels define a scale for measuring the criteria for evaluating PPs and STs. Evaluation Assurance Levels (EALs) provide an increasing scale that balances the levels of assurance claimed with the cost and feasibility of acquiring such assurance. Table 5.3 indicates the CC EAL levels, along with backward compatibility to the Orange Book and ITSEC criteria levels.

Evaluation Assurance Level 1 EAL1 applies where some confidence in correct operation is required but the threats to security are not viewed as serious. It is of value where independent assurance is required to support the contention that due care has been exercised in protecting personal or similar types of information. It's intended that an EAL1 evaluation could be successfully conducted without assistance from the developer of the TOE at a low cost. An evaluation at this level provides evidence that the TOE functions in a manner consistent with its documentation and that it provides useful protection against identified threats. Think of EAL1 as kicking the tires on a vehicle that you're considering for purchase.

Evaluation Assurance Level 2 EAL2 requires the cooperation of a developer in terms of the delivery of design information and test results but does not demand more effort on the part of the developer than is consistent with good commercial practice and should not require a substantially increased investment of money or time. EAL2 is applicable where developers or users require a low to moderate level of independently assured security in the absence of ready availability of the complete development record. Such a situation may arise when securing legacy systems or where access to the developer may be limited.

Evaluation Assurance Level 3 EAL3 permits a conscientious developer to gain maximum assurance from positive security engineering at the design stage without substantial alteration of existing sound development practices. EAL3 applies in those circumstances where developers or users require a moderate level of independently assured security and requires a thorough investigation of the TOE and its development without substantial reengineering.

Evaluation Assurance Level 4 EAL4 permits a developer to gain maximum assurance from positive security engineering based on good commercial development practices that, though rigorous, do not require substantial specialist knowledge, skills, and other resources. EAL4 is applicable in those circumstances where developers or users require a moderate to high level of independently assured security in conventional off-the-shelf TOEs and are prepared to incur additional security-specific engineering costs.

Evaluation Assurance Level 5 EAL5 permits a developer to gain maximum assurance from security engineering based on rigorous commercial development practices supported by moderate application of specialist security engineering techniques. Such a TOE will likely be designed and developed with the intent of achieving EAL5 assurance. EAL5 is applicable in those circumstances where developers or users require a high level of independently assured security in a planned development and require a rigorous development approach without incurring unreasonable costs for special security engineering techniques.

Evaluation Assurance Level 6 EAL6 permits developers to gain high assurance from the application of security engineering techniques to a rigorous development environment in order to produce a premium TOE for protecting high-value assets against significant risks. EAL6 is applicable to the development of security TOEs for application in high-risk situations, where the value of the protected assets justifies additional costs.

Evaluation Assurance Level 7 EAL7 applies to the development of security TOEs for application in extremely high-risk situations where the value of such assets justifies the costs for higher assurance levels.

Once an ST is independently evaluated and is found to meet the desired assurance level, the CC provides for a certification process that's recognized across all CC-using countries. The implication is that products developed and tested abroad can compete on equal footing with similar products developed within the United States.

The Common Evaluation Methodology

The Common Evaluation Methodology Editorial Board (CEMEB), with members from all of the organizations that produced the Common Criteria for Information Technology Security Evaluation, is responsible for producing an agreed upon methodology for conducting evaluations to apply the CC to security targets.

The Common Evaluation Methodology (CEM) is a companion document to the CC. It is focused on the actions that evaluators must take to determine that CC requirements for a TOE are present. CEM is a tool that's used by evaluation schemes to ensure consistent application of the requirements across multiple evaluations and multiple schemes. As such, it is an important component of the Mutual Recognition Arrangement (MRA) that enables any country to accept a certified evaluation from any other member country. So far, agreement has been reached for evaluation levels EAL1 to EAL4, which are deemed adequate for most commercial security products. The CCMEB is continuing the work on common evaluations for levels EAL5, EAL6, and EAL7.

The CEM contains three parts:

- **Part 1:** Introduction and General Model: Describes agreed upon principles of evaluation and introduces agreed upon evaluation terminology dealing with the process of evaluation.

- **Part 2:** CC Evaluation Methodology: This is based on CC Part 3 evaluator actions. It uses well-defined assertions to refine CC Part 3 evaluator actions and tangible evaluator activities to determine requirement compliance. In addition, it will offer guidance to further clarify the intent evaluator actions. Part 2 provides for

  Methodology to evaluate PPs

  Methodology to evaluate STs

  Methodology to evaluate to EAL1

  Methodology to evaluate to EAL2

  Methodology to evaluate to EAL3

  Methodology to evaluate to EAL4

  Methodology to evaluate to EAL5

  Methodology to evaluate to EAL6

  Methodology to evaluate to EAL7

  Methodology to evaluate components not included in an EAL

- **Part 3:** Extensions to the Methodology: These extensions are needed to take full advantage of the evaluation results. It will include topics such as guidance on the composition and content of evaluation document deliverables.

The Common Criteria is currently in use worldwide and is rapidly gaining acceptance and use in common commercial off-the-shelf (COTS) systems. Several large software and hardware developers have embraced the CC, and their products (including Oracle databases, Apple Computer's MAC OS X, Windows Server 2003, and others) are poised for widespread government procurement activities.

Confidentiality and Integrity Models

Security models are mathematical representations of abstract machines that describe how a reference monitor is designed to operate and to help evaluators determine if the implementation meets the design requirements. The following are some of the more commonly used models:

- Bell-LaPadula model

- Biba integrity model

- Clark and Wilson

- Noninterference

- State machine model

- Access matrix model

- Information flow model

The Bell-LaPadula model and the Biba integrity model are explained in-depth below, as they were major influencing models for TCSEC and ITSEC. Other models that follow are minor improvements to Bell-LaPadula and Biba or provide more analysis tools.

Bell-LaPadula Model

An early and popular security model, called Bell-LaPadula, was developed by Leonard J. LaPadula and David E. Bell in the 1970s and forms the basis of the TCSEC. It is a formal model of security policy that describes a set of access control rules. By conforming to a set of rules, the model inductively proves that the system is secure. A subject's (usually a user's) access to an object (usually a file) is allowed or disallowed by comparing the object's security classification with the subject's security clearance.

Bell-LaPadula is a *confidentiality model* intended to preserve the principle of least privilege. It is a formal description of allowable paths of information flow in a secure system and is used to define security requirements for systems handling data at different sensitivity levels. The model defines a secure state and access between subjects and objects in accordance with specific security policy.

Biba Integrity Model

The Biba model covers integrity levels, which are analogs to the sensitivity levels from the Bell-LaPadula model. Integrity levels cover inappropriate modification of data and prevent unauthorized users from making modifications to resources and data.

The Biba model uses a ***read up, write down*** approach. Subjects cannot read objects of lesser integrity and subjects cannot write to objects of higher integrity. Think of CIA analysts and the information that they need to perform their duties. Under Biba, an analyst with top secret clearance can only see information that's labeled at top secret with respect to integrity (confirmed by multiple sources, and so forth) and can only contribute information at their clearance level. Those with higher clearances will not be "poisoned" with data from a lower level of integrity and cannot poison those with clearances higher than theirs.

Advanced Models

Some of the other models improve upon earlier models or provide more in-depth analysis tools.

- **Clark and Wilson model:** Proposes "Well Formed Transactions." It requires mathematical proof that steps are performed in order exactly as they are listed, authenticates the individuals who perform the steps, and defines separation of duties.

- **Noninterference model:** Covers ways to prevent subjects operating in one domain from affecting each other in violation of security policy.

- **State machine model:** An abstract mathematical model consisting of state variables and transition functions.

- **Access matrix model:** A state machine model for a discretionary access control environment.

- **Information flow model:** Simplifies analysis of covert channels. A covert channel is a communication channel that allows two cooperating processes of different security levels (one higher than the other) to transfer information in a way that violates a system's security policy.

As you see, security models are required to help developers and evaluators with widely accepted criteria and functions that are proven reliable and acceptable for even a nation's most closely guarded secrets.

FYI: How Does a Covert Channel Work?

Following is an example of a human covert channel: A group of managers decide they don't want to waste too much time with an interview of a prospective employee and have come up with a communications protocol to let other interviewers know of their impression of the interviewee to either continue the interview or cut it short. The managers decide to cough if they decide to end the interview and sneeze if they are interested in pursuing the candidate. Without the candidate having any idea what they're up to, the managers can quickly agree to make the best use of their time.

Now here's an example of a computer-based covert channel: A program written by one programmer wants to communicate with another program written by a different programmer in collusion to violate the system's security policy. One possible motivation for doing so would be to span across a "Chinese Wall" that separates a banking company from a brokerage company to share information about a high-value customer with the intent of defrauding them outside the scope of the business. These programs may be written to agree beforehand on a protocol based on the programmers' desires. When program PostCreditToBill wants to send covert data to program SellStock, program PostCreditToBill may be programmed to cause lots of sudden CPU activity that program SellStock can detect and begin reading memory channels or communication channels to gain information about checking account data that would not be found in the brokerage system.

5

Summary

The Security Architecture and Models domain of the Common Body of Knowledge embodies the study of formal models for design and evaluation of systems needed for the highest levels of information security, including those that protect national secrets and other government property.

The trusted computing base, or TCB, is the portion of a computer system that contains all elements of the system responsible for supporting the security policy and supporting the isolation of objects on which the protection is based. Included are several mechanisms, properties, and concepts that are required for a formal evaluation prior to being used to protect resources and information.

Several evolving models of evaluation and assurance cover various aspects of confidentiality, integrity, and availability. TCSEC, otherwise known as the *Orange Book*, is primarily concerned with confidentiality and is based on the Bell-LaPadula model. ITSEC adds concerns about integrity and availability. The Canadian Criteria (CTCPEC) advances the work of TCSEC and ITSEC.

Finally, the Common Criteria harmonizes the work of the various international efforts into a unified evaluation methodology that replaces the former methods.

Test Your Skills

MULTIPLE CHOICE QUESTIONS

1. What can best be defined as the sum of protection mechanisms inside the computer, including hardware, firmware, and software?

    A. trusted system

    B. security kernel

    C. trusted computing base

    D. security perimeter

2. Which of the following statements pertaining to protection rings is false?

    A. They provide strict boundaries and definitions on what the processes that work within each ring can access.

    B. Programs operating in inner rings are usually referred to as existing in a privileged mode.

    C. They support the CIA triad requirements of multitasking operating systems.

    D. They provide users with a direct access to peripherals.

3. Which of the following places the *Orange Book* classifications in order from most secure to least secure?

    A. Division A, Division B, Division C, Division D

    B. Division D, Division C, Division B, Division A

    C. Division D, Division B, Division A, Division C

    D. Division C, Division D, Division B, Division A

4. The *Orange Book* describes four hierarchical levels to categorize security systems. Which of the following levels require mandatory protection?

    A. Divisons A and B

    B. Divisions B and C

    C. Divisions A, B, and C

    D. Divisions B and D

5. Which of the following *Orange Book* ratings represents the highest security level?

    A. B1

    B. B2

    C. F6

    D. C2

6. Which *Orange Book* security rating introduces security labels?

    A. C2

    B. B1

    C. B2

    D. B3

7. The *Orange Book* is founded upon which security policy model?

    A. the Biba model

    B. the Bell-LaPadula model

    C. Clark-Wilson model

    D. TEMPEST

8. The Information Technology Security Evaluation Criteria (ITSEC) was written to address which of the following that the *Orange Book* did not address?

    A. integrity and confidentiality

    B. confidentiality and availability

    C. integrity and availability

    D. none of the above

9. What does CC stand for?

    A. enCrypted Communication

    B. Common Criteria for Information Security Evaluation

    C. Certificate Creation

    D. Circular Certificate rollover

10. What is it called when a computer uses more than one CPU in parallel to execute instructions?
    A. multiprocessing
    B. multitasking
    C. multithreading
    D. parallel running

11. Which of the following choices describe a condition when RAM and secondary storage are used together?
    A. primary storage
    B. secondary storage
    C. virtual storage
    D. real storage

12. What is the Biba security model concerned with?
    A. confidentiality
    B. reliability
    C. availability
    D. integrity

13. Which of the following is not a method to protect subjects, objects, and the data within the objects?
    A. layering
    B. data mining
    C. abstraction
    D. data hiding

14. What is the main concern of the Bell-LaPadula security model?
    A. accountability
    B. integrity
    C. confidentiality
    D. availability

15. What would best define a covert channel?
    A. an undocumented back door that has been left by a programmer in an operating system
    B. an open system port that should be closed
    C. a communication channel that allows transfer of information in a manner that violates the system's security policy
    D. a Trojan horse

EXERCISES

Exercise 5.1: Trusted Computing Base

1. Describe the concept and main features of the trusted computing base (TCB).

2. What elements are found in the TCB?

3. What types of software should implement the concept of the TCB?

Exercise 5.2: Security Evaluations

1. Describe the concept of security evaluation (security assurance).

2. What are some of the general criteria used for evaluation?

Exercise 5.3: TCSEC (*Orange Book*)

1. Describe TCSEC in terms of its overall purposes.

2. What are the different TCSEC divisions and classes?

3. Why are different classes needed for different types of security classifications?

Exercise 5.4: ITSEC

1. Describe ITSEC in terms of purposes and differences in classes.

2. How does ITSEC differ from TCSEC?

Exercise 5.5: Common Criteria (CC)

1. Describe the Common Criteria in terms of its purpose.

2. How does the CC differ from TCSEC and ITSEC?

PROJECTS

Project 5.1: Security Testing for Obvious Vulnerabilities

1. Research the Internet for several common software vulnerabilities (examples: buffer-overflow conditions, cross-site scripting).

2. Describe several ways that security testing can uncover the conditions.

3. Describe the limitations of security testing.

4. To what degree should testing be performed if the software is intended for commercial uses?

5. To what degree should testing be performed if the software is intended for commercial, governmental, and military uses?

Project 5.2: MS Windows and Common Criteria Testing

1. Visit the Microsoft Web Site at **www.microsoft.com**.

2. Search for what MS is doing with the Common Criteria for Windows Operating Systems.

3. How does their involvement in CC testing fit into their Trustworthy Computing Initiatives?

4. What advantages does a CC-certified version of Windows bring about?

5. What criticisms of the CC-certified versions of Windows can you find?

Project 5.3: Trusted Computing in the Marketplace

1. Research a few of the user authentication products in the marketplace:
   - Netegrity Siteminder: **www.netegrity.com**
   - Computer Associates eTrust: **www.ca.com**
   - BMC Software's Control SA: **www.bmc.com**

2. What elements of trusted computing can you find in these products?

3. What kinds of commercial security testing have these products undergone?

4. Which product(s) are certified?

Case Study

A manufacturer of intrusion detection systems that is based in Canada wishes to offer its product for sale to the U.S. government. The marketing group has asked your advice on the requirements for selling information assurance products to the United States. As a lead security analyst for the firm, prepare a list of the steps that the manufacturer should go through to prepare the product for a Common Criteria evaluation. What documents do you need to prepare in advance of an evaluation? How long would an evaluation be expected to take?

Use the following Web sites to assist your research:

- Common Criteria Portal: **www.commoncriteriaportal.org**

- Science Applications International Corporation (a U.S.-based CC Lab): **www.saic.com**

- CGI Information Systems and Management Consultants: **http://infosec.cgi.com**

5

Chapter | 6

Business Continuity Planning and Disaster Recovery Planning

Chapter Objectives

After reading this chapter and completing the exercises, you will be able to do the following:

- Distinguish between the business continuity plan (BCP) and the disaster recovery plan (DRP).
- Follow the steps in the BCP.
- Inform business executives why planning is important.
- Define the scope of the business continuity plan.
- Identify types of disruptive events.
- Outline the contents of a business impact analysis (BIA).
- Discuss recovery strategies and the importance of crisis management.
- Explain backup and recovery techniques including shared-site and alternate site agreements.

Introduction

Upon reading this chapter, you may feel like you are preparing for a project management role rather than an information security role, but you'll soon see that the interests of those who manage the business and those who safeguard it are intertwined. This chapter, more so than any of the other domains of the Common Body of Knowledge, deals with business management concerns: how to prepare for an emergency or calamity and how to respond and continue operations under suboptimal business conditions.

In this chapter, you will learn about the goals of sound business continuity planning and disaster recovery planning, how these two types of planning differ, the types of threats that could invoke emergency planning and procedures, and several of the more prominent techniques organizations are using to plan for and hopefully prevent a disruption in business activities.

Overview of the Business Continuity Plan and Disaster Recovery Plan

In the early 1990s, the focus of most businesses concerned about the health and safety of their organization and its continued operation centered on disaster recovery planning. This type of planning primarily included information technology (IT) systems and applications, application data, and the networks supporting the IT infrastructure. In the case of highly regulated industries such as government, health care, and financial services, organizations had to meet recovery-time objectives and recovery-point objectives to minimize the loss of operations and the transaction data upon which they depend.

As the millennium change (or, Y2K) approached, such organizations began to broaden their approach to disaster recovery planning, implementing more encompassing business continuity planning to address fail points not in just IT operations but throughout the organization. Such a shift in view from a strictly IT-centric to a company-wide plan accelerated after the September 11 terrorist attack, when the loss of life dramatically emphasized the need to protect an organization's most important resource, its employees.

The business continuity plan (BCP) describes the critical processes, procedures, and personnel that must be protected in the event of an emergency and uses the business impact analysis (BIA) to evaluate risks to the organization and to prioritize the systems in use for purposes of recovery. Mission-critical systems—those systems that are essential for the ongoing operation of the business—are at the top of the list, followed by less critical systems and those down the line that are "nice to have" systems but nonessential for the business to remain in business.

The disaster recovery plan (DRP) describes the exact steps and procedures personnel in key departments, specifically the IT department, must follow in order to recover critical business systems in the event of a disaster that causes the loss of access to systems required for business operations. For example, one credit card company's mission-critical system is the authorization system for charge requests at the point of sale: Without this capability, no revenue could be generated and the company would be out of business in a matter of days or weeks.

Business continuity planning and disaster recovery planning share the common goal of keeping a business running in the event of an emergency or interruptions. They are alike in that both the BCP and DRP strive to prevent costly disruptions in critical business processes after disaster strikes.

Anticipating, planning for, and preventing problems is generally less costly than simply reacting to them after they occur. At a minimum, outages to IT systems can cost millions of dollars in lost revenue, lost productivity, and lost resources because of legal issues. At the extreme, a sustained outage can threaten the viability of an organization. According to the Gartner Group, "two out of every five enterprises that experience a disaster go out of business within five years." Failing to plan is indeed planning to fail when it comes to business and IT operations.

The following steps must be included when business and security experts create a business continuity plan. They are designed to ensure continued operations and to protect people and property within the business in the event of an emergency. They must:

1. Identify the scope and boundaries of the business continuity plan while communicating the importance of such a plan throughout the organization. What are the critical aspects of the business that must be considered as part of the plan? This step typically involves an audit analysis of the organization's assets including people, facilities, applications, and IT systems, and a risk analysis that identifies the types of threats to the organization, both man-made and natural.

2. The result of the thorough analysis in step 1 is the creation of the business impact assessment. The BIA measures the operating and financial loss to the organization resulting from a disruption to critical business functions (the BIA will be explained more thoroughly later in this chapter).

3. Once the BIA is complete, those responsible for creating the plan must sell the concept of the BCP to key senior management and obtain organizational and financial commitment. Without the support of top management, the BCP will remain an abstraction, mere words on a page, and nothing more. The presenters must be prepared to answer such questions as, is the BCP cost-effective and practical? If the cost of implementing the plan outweighs the benefit derived from it, the BCP will need to be reviewed and modified where appropriate. And if the plan is too cumbersome and impractical to implement, chances of its succeeding are slim.

4. Once the BCP has gained the approval of upper management who have signed off on the plan and released the necessary resources to implement it, each department will need to understand its role in the plan and support and help maintain it. This happens through a thorough examination of "best practices" within the organization and the tasks, processes, roles, and resources needed to meet the stated objectives of the continuity plan.

5. Finally, the BCP project team must implement the plan. This includes the necessary training, testing, and ongoing review and support of the BCP, both in financial and practical terms. Business processes are rarely static, and the project team must ensure that the BCP adapts to changes within the organization.

Why the BCP Is So Important

Although never an absolute guarantee, the BCP reduces the risk to the business in the event of a disruption in the continuity of business (more below on exactly what these disruptions can be). Many of the same reasons we plan for emergencies in our personal lives apply to the BCP: to save time and money, reduce stress, maintain a steady flow of income, protect lives, and to minimize disruptions.

Businesses, however, have responsibilities beyond personnel and property. They are chartered with protecting shareholder investments while meeting federal and state legal requirements. They also have to worry about public image. Any significant disruption in business will quickly drive away partners, investors, and consumers. You may have heard the phrase "due diligence" in the work place or in other course work. Although the phrase has no precise definition, the intent is that a business will act responsibly and protect its assets according to generally accepted business practices and management. In fulfilling this responsibility, being "proactive" is preferable to being "reactive."

According to AbleOne Systems, a provider of high-tech consulting services, some telling statistics related to business continuity planning and disaster recovery planning include

- Eighty percent of businesses without a recovery plan went bankrupt within 1 year of a major data loss.

- Fifty-nine percent of companies cannot conduct business during unscheduled IT downtime.

- Forty percent of companies that cannot conduct business during a major IT outage go out of business within 5 years.

- Fifty percent of companies in the World Trade Center went out of business after September 11, 2001.

(Source: **www.ableone.com/Web%20PDF%20files/Business%20Continuity%20Plan-no%20pic.pdf.**)

Types of Disruptive Events

You will learn about some of the specific types of threats to a business in Chapter 8 in a discussion of the Physical Security Domain. Part of the definition of business continuity planning involves identifying realistic threats to the business. Keep in mind that the BCP defines plans and processes to be invoked after an event occurs. Many of the preventative controls belong to the Operations Security Domain in Chapter 9.

Natural events capable of disrupting a business could include

- earthquakes, fires, floods, mudslides, snow, ice, lightning, hurricanes, tornadoes, and so forth

- explosions, chemical fires, hazardous waste spills, smoke and water damage

- power outages caused by utility failures, high heat and humidity, solar flares, and so forth

Examples of natural events causing dramatic challenges to continuity planning include the 1989 San Francisco earthquake, Hurricane Hugo, the 1997 floods in the Midwestern United States, the 1998 Florida tornadoes, and the series of summer 2004 hurricanes in Florida and on the Gulf Coast of the United States.

Events where man and not nature is directly responsible for disruptive events could include

- strikes, work stoppages, walkouts

- sabotage, burglary, and other forms of hostile activity

- massive failure of technology including utility and communication failure caused by human intervention or error

Memories of the Tylenol scare in 1982, the bombings in 1992 in the London Financial District, the 1993 bombing of the World Trade Center, the Oklahoma City bombing in 1995, the Tokyo sarin gas attack in 1995, and the September 11, 2001, attacks on the World Trade Center in New York and the Pentagon in Washington, D.C., loom large in the minds of millions. Although these are some of the most dramatic examples of recent man-made actions resulting in significant loss of lives and money, a relatively minor event such as theft or sabotage performed by a disgruntled employee can seriously jeopardize a business and go unnoticed for a long period of time.

Defining the Scope of the Business Continuity Plan

The formal implementation of the BCP requires a close examination of business practices and services that constitute the boundaries and define the scope of the plan. Obviously, for a large business or organization, this process can be time consuming and labor intensive. For that reason, one of the most overlooked but important steps is obtaining executive management buy-in and sign-off for the plan. The project team must make a business case for continuity planning, especially in those instances where the BCP is not mandatory. They will have to compare the cost of implementing the BCP with the benefits derived from meeting its objectives.

Other steps involved in defining the scope of the BCP include

■ Identifying critical business processes and requirements for continuing to operate in the event of an emergency.

■ Assessing risks to the business if critical services are discontinued. This process is sometimes referred to as *business impact analysis*.

■ Prioritizing those processes and assigning a value to each process. Which processes are absolutely critical and must be kept "online" without interruption? For example, keeping a continuous supply of power in a hospital emergency room is obviously more important than in the employee cafeteria.

■ Determining the cost of continuous operation and the value ascribed to each service.

■ Establishing the priority of restoring critical services. Which must be restored within the hour? the day? within a week? Which services cannot withstand any interruption?

■ Once executive management has approved the concept of the BCP and the scope and definition of the project is identified, the BCP team must establish the rules of engagement. This involves identifying roles and responsibilities of the project team members and establishing the means of communication and the mechanisms for tracking progress.

Creating the Business Impact Analysis

The BIA identifies the risks that specific threats pose to the business, quantifies the risks, establishes priorities, and performs a cost versus benefit analysis for countering risks. In pursuit of these goals, the three most important steps include

1. Prioritize the business processes, most likely at the department level, possibly using a scoring system to assign a weight or value to each process. For example, in a manufacturing environment, processes such as materials receipt, inventory, production, shipping, and accounting among others would deserve consideration. This makes the task of prioritizing easier and hopefully less subjective, assuming that all business units accept the scoring method. This approach gives prioritization more objective scientific validity.

2. Once critical processes have been identified and prioritized, determine how long each process can be down before business continuity is seriously compromised. Keep in mind that processes usually are interrelated and may need to be grouped together in order to assess downtime tolerance.

3. Identify the resources required to support the most critical processes. What equipment, which people, and how much money beyond normal operating costs do you need to maintain critical ("life support" in industry jargon) systems?

The committee responsible for drafting the BIA must present it to the executive team for evaluation and recommendation when it is complete. Senior management will review the contents of the document including the identification and prioritization of critical processes, cost-benefit analyses and the method of supporting the plan once implemented. Then, most importantly, the plan is communicated to all employees and support personnel including outside vendors and contractors. All personnel, not just those individuals supporting the critical processes, must have a basic awareness of what the business continuity plan contains. This is one case where "on the job" training does not work.

Disaster Recovery Planning

In order to keep the business running, what actions must be taken until normal operations can be restored? In most organizations today, IT plays a critical role in supporting key business processes, thus the importance of the disaster recovery plan. The DRP most typically involves running operations at a remote off-site location until the business deems it safe to restart at its primary location.

The goals of the DRP include

- Keeping the computers running. Computer services are an integral part of most businesses, especially those such as Internet service providers where it is the business.

- Meeting formal and informal service-level agreements with customers and suppliers.

- Being proactive rather than reactive. A carefully rehearsed DRP must be second nature to critical personnel. The DRP should include a comprehensive checklist of activities to perform through practice runs to help make sure those people who are responsible for recovery are not caught by surprise.

Identifying Recovery Strategies

The BCP will identify the critical business processes that must be protected through the BIA documents. The function of the DRP is to identify the exact strategy for recovering those processes, specifically IT systems and services that are struck by a disaster. Because information technology is critical to almost every business these days and is the focus of this text, you will need to understand several disaster recovery strategies that are available to an organization.

Shared-Site Agreements

Shared-site agreements are arrangements between companies with similar if not identical data processing centers. This compatibility in hardware, software, and services allows companies who enter into an agreement to back up each other when one of the partners has an emergency. Rather than build an entire infrastructure to back up its applications and data, Company A enters an agreement with Company B to share resources in the event of a disaster. Such an arrangement can save substantial time and money because the computers and software already exist and do not have to be procured. In theory, when Company A loses its data processing center resources, a figurative switch flips and it begins to run its applications on Company B's computers as if nothing ever happened.

Despite the advantages of reduced costs, there are problems with this scenario. First, the data centers must be highly compatible in terms of the hardware and software they run. In fact, if Company A is not a subsidiary of Company B or if they aren't regional offices of the same corporation, a shared-site agreement is difficult to implement. If the companies are not part of the same corporate charter, other difficulties arise such as assured data security, privacy protection, and data synchronization. Shared-site agreements are feasible when companies are closely related and share common processing platforms, but the challenges are greater when this is not the case.

Alternate Sites

A company seeking DRP assistance can also use a third-party vendor to provide emergency backup services. Instead of entering a reciprocal agreement with another business, the company uses the services of a vendor whose business is to provide DRP services. You might be wondering who provides backup services for the third-party vendor. The vendor is responsible for providing backup services in case they experience a critical failure in their systems.

These alternate-site services providers are the most commonly used form of DRP assistance and generally take on one of three forms: a hot site, a warm site, or a cold site.

Hot Site A hot-site facility assumes the entire burden of providing backup computing services for the customer. This includes hosting the application software and data in a so-called mirror site. The vendor should be prepared to assume all responsibility for processing transactions for the customer, with little to no interruption of service. The vendor is responsible for maintaining the facility including all environmental controls such as heating, air conditioning, and power; hardware, including servers and printers; data backups; and all other services you would associate with a data processing center.

Although a hot-site facility offers several advantages, most importantly providing uninterrupted service in a relatively quick time, it can also be the most expensive solution as a DRP. Also, the hot site poses some security risk as the data is now stored, backed up, and theoretically accessible to a third party. Still, for those companies that can afford a hot-site facility, it is the most attractive solution.

Cold Site Unlike the hot site, the cold site provides the facilities including power, air conditioning, heat, and other environmental systems necessary to run a data processing center without any of the computer hardware or software. The customer must literally deliver the hardware and software necessary to bring their site up. The cold site is a cheaper solution than hot-site services, but you get what you pay for. When you consider the logistical problems of moving hardware that is highly sensitive to both temperature fluctuations and movement and quickly installing software on it, you will appreciate the challenges that a cold-site facility poses. In the event of a true disaster, where a company cannot afford to suffer a protracted outage, the cold-site alternative, although economically feasible, may give the customer the illusion of security that may not be grounded in reality. Unfortunately, this lesson may be learned the hard way.

Warm Site As you might suspect, the warm-site facility is a compromise between the services offered by hot- and cold-site vendors. A warm-site facility provides the building and environmental services previously mentioned, with the addition of the hardware and communication links already established. However, the customer's applications are not installed nor are workstations provided. In this case, the customer restores application software from backups using workstations it provides. Warm sites are cheaper than hot sites but require more effort. On the other hand, they are more expensive than cold-site facilities but less labor intensive and more likely to be effective in a disaster.

An important part of the BCP is determining the constraints, both financial and operational, under which the company is working and choosing the most realistic solution that meets the minimal needs of the BCP.

Additional Arrangements

Several other arrangements exist, affording a company more options with their business continuity planning. They are:

- Multiple centers: in this case, processing is distributed across multiple sites that may be in-house or part of a shared-site agreement. As with distributed networks, a multiple center arrangement spreads the processing across sites and offers redundancy in processing as an added safeguard. Although less costly than a hot site, administering multiple centers could be a burdensome chore and cost-prohibitive.

- Service bureaus: Known for their quick response but high cost, service bureaus provide backup processing services at a remote location. Service bureaus also perform primary application processing such as payroll systems and have extra capacity available for DRP services.

- Mobile units: In this scenario, a third-party vendor provides a data processing center on wheels, complete with air conditioning and power systems.

How to Test a Disaster Recovery Plan

Testing the DRP thoroughly is an absolutely necessary and non-negotiable step in planning for a disaster. A plan may look great on paper, but until it is tested in a situation that resembles a true disaster, its value cannot be determined. Testing the plan not only shows that the plan is viable, but it also prepares personnel for a disaster by teaching them their responsibilities and removing all uncertainty and thus mitigating risk.

The Certified Information Systems Security Professional, or CISSP, recognizes five methods of testing the DRP. They are

- **Walk-throughs:** Members of the key business units meet to trace their steps through the plan, looking for omissions and inaccuracies.

- **Simulations:** During a practice session, critical personnel meet to perform a "dry run" of the emergency, mimicking the response to a true emergency as closely as possible.

- **Checklists:** A more passive type of testing, members of the key departments "check off" the tasks for which they are responsible and report on the accuracy of the checklist. This is typically a first step toward a more comprehensive test.

- **Parallel testing:** The backup processing occurs in parallel with production services that never stop. This is a familiar process for those who have installed complex computer systems that run in parallel with the existing production system until the new system proves to be stable. An example of this might be when a company installs a new payroll system: Until the new system is deemed ready for full cut-over, the two systems are operated in parallel.

- **Full interruption:** Also known as the true/false test, production systems are stopped as if a disaster had occurred to see how the backup services perform. They either work (true) or they fail (false) in which case the lesson learned can be as painful as a true disaster.

Without the Walls and Within

A well-tested DRP should anticipate the unanticipated. It should predict how employees will behave in the event of an emergency within its walls and consider how they will interact with external agents such as firemen, ambulance drivers, and policemen. The goal of the DRP is to reassure and not alarm personnel about the outcome of a disaster and to remind them, above all, that the company will make every effort to protect them. The company must also protect its image to outsiders by proving that the DRP procedures are well thought-out and tested. Should the company survive a disaster in spite of its DRP rather than because of it, the message sent to customers, suppliers, and investors is not a comforting one.

Summary

Buisness continuity planning (BCP) and disaster recovery planning (DRP) are formal processes in any business that is concerned about maintaining its operation in the face of a disaster or interruption that prevents people from gaining access to their place of employment.

The DRP has its roots in the early 1990s when securing IT operations was the focus of most organizations. This concern spread to other areas of the organization with dramatic punctuation after the September 11 attack.

To implement its DRP, a company typically uses outside services such as a shared-site arrangement or third-party vendor to replicate critical data processing services. Several of the alternatives are hot-site, cold-site, and warm-site arrangements.

Regardless of which arrangement a company chooses, the plan must be thoroughly tested using one or more of the five testing techniques such as simulation or parallel testing. Although a true disaster cannot absolutely be recreated, a close approximation should reassure employees that their safety is the company's highest priority and also serve to clarify their responsibilities in the event of a true disaster.

Test Your Skills

MULTIPLE CHOICE QUESTIONS

1. Which of the following is NOT true about the BCP and DRP?
   A. Both plans deal with security infractions after they occur.
   B. Both plans describe preventative, not reactive, security procedures.
   C. The BCP and DRP share the goal of maintaining "business-as-usual" activities.
   D. They belong to the same domain of the Common Body of Knowledge.

6

2. According to the Gartner Group:

   A. Organizations with sound business continuity plans will never experience an interruption of business.

   B. Approximately 40 percent of businesses experiencing a disaster of some sort go out of business.

   C. The BCP and DRP are interchangeable in most organizations.

   D. Organizations with fewer than 100 employees generally do not need a DRP.

3. Place the following steps of the BCP in the correct sequence: (a) create the BIA; (b) obtain signoff of the tested BCP; (c) identify the scope of the BCP; (d) write the BCP:

   A. a, c, d, b

   B. c, b, a, d

   C. c, a, d, b

   D. d, b, c, a

4. Why is the BCP important?

   A. It minimizes disruption in business continuity.

   B. It eliminates risk in an organization.

   C. It has spawned a new cottage industry for business planning experts.

   D. The public will be unaware of problems within the organization.

5. What is the purpose of the BIA?

   A. To create a document that's used to help management understand what impact a disruptive event would have on the business.

   B. To define a strategy that minimizes the effect of disturbances and to allow for the resumption of business processes.

   C. To emphasize the organization's commitment to employees and vendors.

   D. To work with executive management to develop a DRP.

6. The scope definition of the BCP should include all of the following *except*:

   A. prioritizing critical business processes.

   B. calculating the value and cost of continuing important business processes.

   C. performing a dry run of emergency fire and medical evacuation procedures.

   D. assessing the cost to the business if critical services are disrupted.

7. Which of the following would be considered a man-made disaster?

    A. earthquake

    B. tornado

    C. flooding caused by a broken water main

    D. wildcat strike

8. What is the number one priority of disaster response?

    A. protecting hardware

    B. protecting software

    C. transaction processing

    D. personnel safety

9. What is *not* a benefit of cold sites?

    A. no resource contention with other organizations

    B. quick recovery

    C. geographical location that is not affected by the same disaster

    D. low cost

10. Which of the following computer recovery sites is only partially equipped?

    A. nonmobile hot site

    B. mobile hot site

    C. warm site

    D. cold site

11. An organization short on funding but long on its ability to assume risk would most likely use what kind of recovery site?

    A. alternate site

    B. cold site

    C. global site

    D. tepid site

12. Which of the following is an advantage of using hot sites as a backup alternative?

    A. The costs associated with hot sites are low.

    B. Hot sites can be made ready for operation within a short period of time.

    C. Hot sites can be used for an extended amount of time.

    D. Hot sites do not require that equipment and systems software be compatible with the primary installation being backed up.

13. Using multiple centers as a recovery site has what main disadvantage?

    A. Multiple centers are more difficult to administer than other types of recovery sites.

    B. Processing is shared by multiple sites.

    C. Multiple centers offer redundant processing.

    D. Services may be shared between in-house and outside services.

14. What is a mobile unit site?

    A. a convenient means for employees to give blood

    B. a fully equipped recovery site on wheels

    C. a SWAT team that provides first-response services

    D. a backup power supply, typically a diesel or gasoline generator

15. The primary goal of the DRP is to:

    A. alarm employees as a call to arms.

    B. protect the image of the organization above all.

    C. educate employees about emergency evacuation procedures.

    D. reassure employees that the organization puts their safety above all else.

16. The most extensive type of disaster recovery testing is

    A. checklists

    B. full interruption

    C. simulation

    D. parallel testing

EXERCISES

Exercise 6.1: Define the Attributes of an Effective DRP

1. Develop a DRP for an elementary school to respond to the building catching fire. Remember that the DRP must address the following concerns:

   - **It's practical.** Include useful information. Leave out unnecessary information.

   - **It's understandable.** Test instructions before implementing them.

   - **It's accessible.** Give copies to all concerned individuals, offices, and service points.

   - **It's kept current.** Revise pages as needed.

2. Share your DRP with other students in the class. What are the similarities? What are the differences?

Exercise 6.2: Investigate September 11 Emergency Procedures

1. Investigate BCP/DRP disaster recovery stories from the September 11, 2001, catastrophe in New York and Washington, D.C. (for example, visit the following Web site: **www.recoverychronicles.com/eNewsletter/August2004/378/Article.asp**).

2. What did companies that successfully recovered do right?

3. What did companies that failed do wrong?

4. What lessons have we learned from such a calamity?

Exercise 6.3: Determine Local DRP Considerations

1. Identify the types of natural disasters prevalent in the area in which you live.

2. Research the types of disaster recovery services ready to respond to such disasters (you might research your local government Web site devoted to emergency management and homeland security).

3. Do you feel your community is prepared for such events?

6

Exercise 6.4: Revisit a Family Emergency

Think about a particular time in your own life, for example a family emergency, when you feel you were not adequately prepared to respond to the event. For example, imagine you went on an overnight backpacking trip with a small child and didn't take adequate supplies to get you through the hike.

1. What could you have done beforehand to avert some of the consequences of a lack of preparedness?

2. What could you have done to foresee events requiring contingency responses?

PROJECTS

Project 6.1: Create an Imaginary Company

1. Create a fictitious company or organization and describe the nature of its business, its location, the number of employees, and so forth.

2. Identify the challenges you would face in keeping your company running in the event of a disaster or interruption.

3. Prioritize the assets and determine what mission-critical functions and systems would need to be recovered first, second, and so forth.

4. Decide on some strategies on how to recover these systems and processes.

Project 6.2: Your BCP and DRP

1. Search the Internet to locate a business continuity plan or disaster recovery plan checklist for a small business. Several online sites you may want to visit include

   - The Business Continuity Planning & Disaster Recovery Planning Directory: **www.disasterrecoveryworld.com/**
   - Disaster Recovery Made Easy: **www.disaster-recovery-plan.com/**
   - Disaster Recovery Journal: **www.drj.com**

2. Draft your own business continuity plan or disaster recovery plan including a checklist of critical recovery tasks.

3. Share your plans with your classmates.

4. What are the similarities between the plans? What are the differences?

5. How would you revise your plan(s) now that you've seen some others?

Project 6.3: Compare Off-Site Services

1. Using the Internet, identify two or more off-site companies providing third-party backup services and compare their services and costs.

2. What kind of common services do they offer?

3. How do their costs compare?

4. Does one company offer services that another doesn't?

5. How do you account for this difference?

Case Study

You have just been hired as the chief information officer (CIO) for a high-tech firm in Silicon Valley. You know that the Bay Area in California is susceptible to earthquakes as it sits on top of a major fault line. However, what you didn't know was that your first project in your new position is to relocate the company's data center to a more geographically stable area that is not as susceptible to seismic disturbances. Your quandary, as you see it, is how to do so without losing your highly talented staff.

Most of your employees live in your current location for the lifestyle it offers and would be unlikely to move with the company to what they would consider a less desirable location. Your company provides highly specialized data processing services, and finding replacements for your current staff in a less urban setting would be difficult.

Weighing the financial health of the organization and the safety of your employees, how would you proceed?

6

Chapter 7

Law, Investigations, and Ethics

Chapter Objectives

After reading this chapter and completing the exercises, you will be able to do the following:

- Identify the types and targets of computer crime.
- Summarize the major types of attacks performed by cyber criminals.
- Understand the context of the computer in the legal system.
- Appreciate the complexities of intellectual property law.
- Discuss the issues surrounding computer security and privacy rights.
- Articulate the challenges of computer forensics.
- Recognize ethical issues related to information security.

Introduction

This chapter focuses on the obligations and responsibilities of the information security (IS) specialist. It will cover appropriate ethical behavior for working with sensitive data and systems and the laws governing the profession. It is a constant challenge for IS specialists to keep up with the latest laws, codes of ethics, and other rules governing the use of information technology. They rely on legal experts from both the private and public sectors who scramble to understand and respond to issues created by emerging technologies—issues that may have never existed before. The speed of technological change in most cases simply outstrips the speed in which our governing bodies can create applicable laws.

This gap between technology and the laws governing its use makes the IS specialist's role even more critical. She is duty-bound to her employers, the public, and to governing bodies such as the Information Systems Security Certification Consortium (ISC²) to uphold the law and act ethically in all cases. In this chapter, you will be exposed to some of the legal and ethical implications of being an information security specialist through an overview of the nature and types of computer crime, the laws created to deal with it, and the IS specialist Code of Ethics that governs professional behavior.

Types of Computer Crime

The pervasiveness of sensitive customer, government, and corporate information on the Web has created a million-dollar cottage industry of computer crime. The losses are difficult to gauge accurately, partly because many businesses, and individuals, are reluctant to advertise vulnerabilities. Letting the world know that the company site has been hacked simply is not good advertising. Corporations shun bad news such as this because it undermines public confidence, rattles stockholders, and can result in a sell-off on Wall Street.

Still, the 2004 Computer Security Institute (CSI)/FBI Computer Crime and Security Survey estimated that, based on 489 responses from information security practitioners across a broad range of industries, more than $141 million was lost through computer crimes (*source*: **http://i.cmp net.com/gocsi/db_area/pdfs/fbi/FBI2004.pdf**). The graph in Figure 7.1 reveals the dollar amount lost as a result of each type of computer crime.

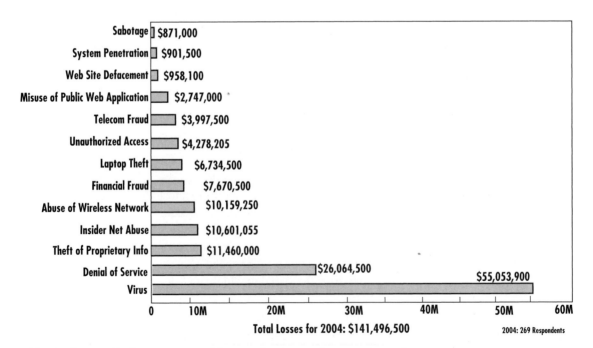

FIGURE 7.1 Dollar amount of losses by type of computer crime.

The CSI/FBI report also revealed that:

■ The greatest financial loss ($55 million) came from virus attacks.

■ The second most prevalent crime ($26 million) was the Denial of Service (DoS) attacks (more on this later in this chapter).

■ Only 20 percent of companies experiencing an attack reported it to the authorities—down 10 percent from 2003.

The last point is telling. No one knows exactly how much is lost through computer crime, but it would be safe to say that the dollar amount is significantly higher than the amount reported by surveys.

Who are the victims of these acts? Practically everyone, as it turns out. According to the Certified Information Systems Security Professional (CISSP) Common Body of Knowledge, computer crimes are so widespread that identifying specific targets is too cumbersome. Instead, the CISSP has identified these major categories of computer crimes:

■ **Military and intelligence attacks:** Criminals and intelligence agents illegally obtain classified and sensitive military information and police files.

■ **Business attacks:** Increasing competition between companies frequently leads to illegal access of proprietary information. Even higher education is not immune from these activities. Yale accused Princeton of hacking its admissions site to obtain candidate information in July 2002 (see **www.usatoday.com/tech/news/comput ersecurity/2002-07-25-ivy-hack_x.htm**).

■ **Financial attacks:** Banks and other financial institutions provide attractive targets for computer criminals for obvious reasons.

■ **Terrorist attacks:** The U.S. Department of Homeland Security monitors the level of "chatter" on the Internet, looking for evidence of planned terrorist attacks against computer systems and geographic locations.

■ **"Grudge" attacks:** Companies are increasingly wary of disgruntled employees who feel mistreated and exact their revenge using computer systems.

■ **"Thrill" attacks:** Unlike grudge attackers who want some kind of revenge, thrill attackers hack computer systems for the "fun of it," bragging rights, or simply for a challenge.

Now that we've categorized the types of crimes that take place, we can take a look at the means of how these crimes are pulled off and what the consequences may be.

How Cyber Criminals Commit Crimes

The methods available to the computer criminal are extensive and too numerous for a complete treatment in this text, but several of the most prevalent types of computer crimes are listed below.

- **Denial of Service (DoS) attacks:** This is an overloading of a computer's resources (in particular, the temporary storage area in computers called "buffers") from any number of sources until the system is so bogged down that it cannot honor requests. The distributed Denial of Service attack in February 2000 on Yahoo! took the site down for three hours. A day later, eBay, Amazon.com, Buy.com, and CNN.com were hit with the same type of attack. The following day, ETrade and ZDNet were struck.

- **Rogue code:** The user inadvertently launches software that can log a user's keystrokes and send them to a remote server or perform other undesirable activities such as deleting files or destroying the operating system, rendering the computer useless.

- **Software piracy:** Copying or downloading software and using it without permission.

- **Social engineering:** Using deception to solicit information such as a password or personal identification number (PIN) from an unwitting victim; for example, a thief calls up a help desk pretending to be a user whose password needs resetting.

- **Dumpster diving:** A no-tech criminal technique that is pointed to as the primary cause of ID theft, where a criminal digs through your trash and recycling bins looking for receipts, checks, and other personal and sensitive information. Tip: If you don't shred all your receipts or lock up your recycling bin where you dispose of protected information, someone may be rummaging through your personal or proprietary information at this very moment.

- **Spoofing of Internet Protocol (IP) addresses:** Sending a message with a false originating IP address to convince the recipient the sender is someone other than who he really is. Every computer on the Internet is assigned a unique IP address. In this case, the attacker masquerades as a legitimate Internet site by using that site's IP address.

- **Emanation eavesdropping:** Intercepting radio frequency (RF) signals emanated by wireless computers to extract sensitive or classified information. This problem is addressed by the U.S. Government's TEMPEST program (requiring shields on computers transmitting such data). Operated by the U.S. Department of Defense (DOD), the

TEMPEST program has created a cottage industry of companies who create protective equipment to prevent foreign spies from collecting stray computer signals issued from DOD labs or U.S. embassies.

- **Embezzlement:** In the movie *Office Space*, three disgruntled employees modify computer software to collect round-off amounts (i.e., fractions of a penny) from a company's accounting program. This is an old crime in a new garb. Now criminals steal money by manipulating software or databases.

- **Information warfare:** A concern of the newly created U.S. Department of Homeland Security, information warfare includes attacks upon a country's computer network to gain economic or military advantage. You can learn more about information warfare at the Institute for the Advanced Study of Information Warfare (**www.psycom.net/iwar.1.html**).

The more highly publicized instances of these attacks are generally dramatic because they are so far-reaching. Some of these with which you might be familiar are the DoS attack against 3Com Corp and Nike.com in 2000, Kevin Mitnick's well-documented hacker exploits against phone companies, the Nigerian e-mail fraud, the Melissa Microsoft Word virus, the Bubbleboy worm, and the theft of 300,000 credit card numbers by the Russian hacker Maxus in 1999.

Then there are the more pedestrian methods: chain letters, pyramid schemes, outright fraud, cyberstalking, and phishing, where a scammer poses as a legitimate enterprise or organization in order to extract personally identifying information from a naïve or gullible user.

A common theme among most of these methods is the presence of vulnerabilities because of flaws in popular computer operating systems and application software or flaws in system implementation (i.e., failing to activate security controls or not configuring a system properly). The Application Development Domain (Chapter 13) covers specific vulnerabilities, but it is important to recognize now that most computer crime is preventable with sufficient, and competent, attention to security detail when deploying software.

The Computer and the Law

There are many laws that address computer crime. Legal issues have become more complex in the past decade with the extension of the U.S. economy to nations with emerging economies and the proliferation of companies with international or offshore sites. Computer crime issues were once strictly a matter of national law, but the movement of data across time zones and international boundaries has complicated the issue of legal jurisdiction.

As a consequence, an entirely new set of international computer security and privacy laws has been forged, often with conflicting goals. When the European Union passed the 1998 EU Data Protection Directive, it caused a great deal of controversy in the United States. This directive contains protections and safeguards of individual privacy that are generally much stricter than they are in the United States. Rather than examine the conflicts between countries over competing computer security regulations, this text will focus primarily on the legal system within the United States, discussing international law only in the context of how it may differ from U.S. laws.

Legislative Branch of the Legal System

As you are undoubtedly aware, the three branches of government that create and administer the laws defining the legal system in the United States are the legislative, executive, and judicial branches. The legislative branches (Congress and Senate) are responsible for passing statutory laws. A statutory law is a law written through the act of a legislature declaring, commanding, or prohibiting something. They are arranged by subject matter in the order in which they are enacted, thus they are referred to as *session laws*. Federal and state law codes incorporate statutes into the body of laws, and the judiciary system interprets and enforces them. State statutes govern matters such as wills, probate administration, and corporate law; federal statutes cover matters such as patent, copyright, and trademark laws.

Later in this chapter, you will read about copyright law and see how a basic understanding of statutory law is important to the information security specialist.

Administrative Branch of the Legal System

Administrative law is also referred to as *natural justice*. We owe this legal concept to the Romans, who believed certain legal principles were "natural" or self-evident and did not need to be codified by statute. In this case, disputes are resolved before an administrative tribunal and not in a court. For example, the Workmen's Compensation Board reviews and resolves disputes between the employee and his employer, aiming to provide workers and their dependents financial relief in the case of injuries arising out of job-related accidents without requiring a formal court proceeding. Administrative law is expanding rapidly because it normally offers a more expeditious and inexpensive resolution to disputes.

Judicial Branch of the Legal System

Common law arose from unwritten law that developed from judicial cases based on precedent and custom. The United States inherited the common law system from England as the basis for most of its legal systems. Common law is either unwritten or written as statutes or codes. The three primary categories of laws within the common law system are

- **Civil law:** Civil laws are written to compensate individuals who were harmed through wrongful acts known as *torts*. A tort can be either intentional or unintentional in the case of negligence. Common law is generally associated with civil disputes whereby compensation is financial but does not involve imprisonment.

- **Criminal law:** Criminal law punishes those who violate government laws and harm an individual or group. Unlike civil law, criminal law includes imprisonment in addition to financial penalties.

- **Regulatory law:** Administrative laws that regulate the behavior of administrative agencies of government. Considered part of public law, regulatory law addresses issues that arise between the individual and a public entity. Regulatory laws may also exact financial penalties and imprisonment.

The common laws governing matters of information systems include laws regulating intellectual property and privacy, which are discussed next in this chapter.

Intellectual Property Law

If you have ever downloaded music from a Web site without paying for it, you have likely broken one of the laws that protect intellectual property; that is, committed *copyright infringement*. Such an act may seem, at first, innocuous. But multiply this event by millions of users, then by the cost of the CDs they would have purchased, and the sum of the lost revenue is staggering. The magnitude of the problem is immense, costing the recording industry millions of dollars in revenue yearly. According to the Irish Recorded Music Association, a nonprofit organization facilitating discussion between the Irish recording industry and the government, annual losses from downloaded music exceed 3.8 million euros—at the current exchange rate about US$5 million—within the European Union. The association estimates the worldwide music piracy problem to be $5 billion annually (**www.irma.ie/piracy.htm**). This is why the artists and their recording labels go to court.

It is also why you need to know something about the legal framework protecting intellectual property, as the computer and its Internet connection makes the theft of music, video, and software files possible. The Internet also makes plagiarism a breeze. With the sheer volume of content on the Internet, it's difficult at times to determine what's covered by copyright and what is not, but more than one term paper turned in by students is certain to have violated someone's copyrights!

Besides copyright protection, designed to protect the distribution and reproduction rights of the owner, intellectual property law includes several other categories: patent law, trademarks, and trade secrets. These are discussed in detail in the following sections.

Patent Law

Inventors rush to patent their ideas to prevent others from using them. *Patents* "grant an inventor the right to exclude others from producing or using the inventor's discovery or invention for a limited period of time" (**www.uspto.gov**). In the United States, a patent is good for 17 years. The Patent and Trademark Office (PTO) oversees patent law for the federal government. However, the PTO has historically resisted patenting software. In the 1970s, the PTO would not grant a patent if the invention required a computer to perform a computation. The PTO was geared to the world of processes, manufactured articles, and machinery and did not recognize original claims to scientific truth or mathematical expressions. (Mathematical formulas or algorithms still cannot be patented.) This reluctance on the part of the PTO did not prevent a number of companies from filing patent applications for software. In 1963, for example, Bell Telephone Laboratories filed an application on behalf of its employees entitled "Conversion of Numerical Information" for its method of processing data, specifically the programmatic conversion of numeric data to other data types. The patent examiner from the PTO rejected the claim because of a "lack of novelty or non-obviousness." He felt that "mental processes" or "mathematical steps" were not the stuff of statutory law (**http://digital-law-online.info/lpdi1.0/treatise61.html**).

With the rapid advance of computer technology and its rapid spread from government offices to business and public use, the PTO had to devise new guidelines to address the issue of software patents. After numerous U.S. Supreme Court challenges in the early 1980s, the PTO had, by the mid-1990s, developed new guidelines to determine when a software invention was protected by patent law. For example, the PTO now grants patents for software such as instructions on a disk that guide machines or computers.

More famously, Amazon.com won an injunction against Barnes & Noble, who used the "one click" software similar to the software Amazon.com introduced for storing buyer preferences and other identifying information. The courts overturned the injunction in 2001, but Amazon still holds six patents related to ordering books (*source*: **www4.ncsu.edu/~baumerdl/Burgunder.04/Ch.%205.ppt#11**).

Trademarks

The Trademark Act defines *trademark* as "any word, name, symbol, or device, or any combination thereof" that the individual intends to use commercially and wants to distinguish as coming from a unique source. Again, the PTO was originally reluctant to sail the uncharted waters of granting trademarks to intellectual property such as software. But over time they have. Software giant Microsoft currently holds more than 200 trademarks, from "Actimates" to "Zoo Tycoon."

Trade Secrets

If you just gulped down your favorite sports drink, answered a telemarketing survey, or performed a routine task on your computer that used an obscure algorithm, chances are you have unwittingly taken advantage of a company trade secret. Unlike trademarks or patents, ***trade secrets*** do not benefit from legal protection. As long as no one but you knows about your idea, it belongs to you. Usually, a trade secret is a patent in process, an embryonic but unofficial and legally unprotected idea.

The story of the protection of software as intellectual property is a book unto itself. Enter the keyword search "software intellectual property" on Amazon.com and you should receive more than 20,000 hits, beginning with the contentious issue of "open sourcing." The courts are still debating the question of when an idea manifested as software moves from protection under intellectual property law to the public domain.

Privacy and the Law

Perhaps you have received privacy statements from your bank or other financial lenders explaining exactly what they plan on doing with your personally identifying information (e.g., a PIN). Maybe you have signed a statement at your doctor's office agreeing that you have read and fully comprehend the fine print contained in the Health Insurance Portability and Accountability Act (HIPAA) of 1996. These privacy documents often give rise to confusion. Do you "opt in" or "opt out" when being asked to share personally identifying information? What about privacy issues you might not be aware of like cookies (text files that remember information about you) stored on your hard drive without your knowledge? There are many privacy issues confronting companies that keep personal information about customers and employees.

The Federal Trade Commission's May 2000 report, "Fair Information Practices in the Electronic Marketplace," is pertinent to this discussion. Although the FTC does not mandate privacy practices, the report lists four privacy practices that all companies engaged in electronic commerce should observe, namely:

- ■ **Notice/awareness:** In general, the Web site should tell the user how it collects and handles user information. The notice should be conspicuous, and the privacy policy should clearly state how the site collects and uses information.

■ **Choice/consent:** Web sites must give consumers control over how their personally identifying information is used. Abuse of this practice is the gathering of information for a stated purpose but using it in another way, one to which the consumer might object.

■ **Access/participation:** Perhaps the most controversial of the fair practices, users would be able to review, correct, and in some cases delete personally identifying information on a particular Web site. Most companies that currently collect personal information have no means of allowing people to review what the company collected, nor do they provide any way for a person to correct incorrect information. Implementing this control would be a burden to companies to retrofit onto an existing system. As you have likely seen with commercial credit reports, inaccurate information or information used out of context can make people's lives problematic.

■ **Security/integrity:** Web sites must do more than reassure users that their information is secure with a "feel-good" policy statement. The site must implement policies, procedures, and tools that will prevent unauthorized access and hostile attacks against the site.

International Privacy Issues

The issue of protecting privacy in the United States has grown more complicated with the expansion of e-commerce across international borders and into the domain of different and sometimes much more rigorous and exacting privacy protection laws. The European Union's Data Protection Directive of 1998 was the result of several years of tough negotiation among EU members. The directive addressed the disparity between European privacy protection laws and what the EU viewed as the more porous and inconsistent state and federal privacy laws in the United States.

The U.S. Department of Commerce, wishing to head off a privacy law impasse with the European Union, negotiated the Safe Harbor Privacy Principles, a framework that allowed U.S. entities wishing to do business in the European Union to meet the minimum privacy controls of the EU directive. The International Safe Harbor Principles include the following privacy guidelines:

■ **Notice:** Companies must notify individuals what personally identifying information they are collecting, why they are collecting it, and how to contact the collectors.

■ **Choice:** Individuals must be able to choose whether and how their personal information is used by, or disclosed to, third parties.

■ **Onward transfer:** Third parties receiving personal information must provide the same level of privacy protection as the company from whom the information is obtained.

- **Security:** Companies housing personal information and sensitive data must secure the data and prevent its loss, misuse, disclosure, alteration, and unauthorized access.

- **Data integrity:** Companies must be able to reassure individuals that their data is complete, accurate, current, and used for the stated purposes only.

- **Access:** Individuals must have the right and ability to access their information and correct, modify, or delete any portion of it.

- **Enforcement:** Each company must adopt policies and practices that enforce the aforementioned privacy principles.

Privacy Laws in the United States

Unless you are an employee of a U.S. corporation working in the European Union, you are probably more aware of privacy matters in your day-to-day life. For example, the Kennedy-Kassenbaum Health Insurance Portability and Accountability Act (HIPAA), passed in August 1996, codifies the right of individuals to control and protect their own health information. Although the European continent has adopted a more comprehensive and consistent set of privacy principles, the United States has been more willing to allow different industries, such as banking and health care, and different levels of government, to draft their own privacy guidelines. The effect has been a more piecemeal and disjointed approach to privacy protection. The following partial list of computer security and privacy laws shows a less than holistic approach to privacy protection in the United States:

- 1970 U.S. Fair Credit Reporting Act: a federal law that regulates the activities of credit bureaus.

- 1986 U.S. Electronic Communications Act: protects the confidentiality of private message systems through unauthorized eavesdropping.

- 1987 U.S. Computer Security Act.

- 1996 U.S. Kennedy-Kassenbaum Health Insurance and Portability Accountability Act (HIPAA): protects the confidentiality and portability of personal health care information.

- 2000 National Security Directive 42 (NSD-42): signed by President Bush, this directive established the Committee on National Security Systems (CNSS). The CNSS gives guidance on the security of national defense systems, among other roles.

- 2001 U.S. Patriot Act HR 3162, a.k.a. "Uniting and Strengthening America by Providing Appropriate Tools Required to Intercept and Obstruct Terrorism (USA PATRIOT ACT) Act of 2001."

- 2002 Federal Information Security Management Act: defines the basic statutory requirements for protecting federal computer systems.

The sheer numbers of laws related to computers has made it difficult for owners, operators, legislators, and law enforcement to stay on top of all regulations because of a number of factors:

- Enactment of new laws in a rapidly changing technology environment at times causes more problems than are solved.

- Globalization of the economy results in unclear international legal boundaries and jurisdiction questions.

- Standards are not always adopted by all countries, and conflicting security standards and practices result in varying levels of compliance and enforcement.

Without a more comprehensive and consolidated approach to privacy law, legislation in the United States most likely will continue to be a series of industry-specific rules and regulations.

Computer Forensics

Investigating crimes committed with computers is known as *computer forensics*. According to the National Data Conversion Institute, an organization specializing in facilitating the conversion and exchange of data between disparate computer systems as well as providing litigation data management services to law firms, corporations, and governments, an increasing number of civil and criminal lawsuits involve computerized data stored on some form of computer medium. Sherlock Holmes never could have envisioned that the physical evidence he once detected such as a lock of hair, a smudge on a topcoat, or mud caked on boots would evolve into the nearly invisible world of computer evidence.

The intangibility of computer evidence makes the job of prosecuting cyber crime even more difficult than traditional crime. Specialized expert knowledge is usually required, and jurisdictions become murky because of the difficulty of determining the locus of the crime. Furthermore, gathering evidence is complicated by the high-tech sleight-of-hand that computer criminals have mastered. Many know how to cover their tracks and distract investigators from their true locations.

The National Data Conversion Institute (NDCI) makes a case for using expert investigative services to solve computer crimes. Among the many arguments for such services are

- Successful litigation frequently depends on obtaining irrefutable computer evidence. Without solid computer evidence, you may not have a case.

- Your evidence may not be as good as the opposition's if you are using less sophisticated data-detection techniques.

- Your adversaries do not want you to obtain the data you need.

- The technology used to create the data you need may have already disappeared. Time is of the essence.

Additionally, all of the other requirements of successful litigation are still in play: the admissibility of evidence, the types of legal evidence, and the legal search and seizure of evidence. Those prosecuting a crime must still play by the rules when conducting an investigation. But instead of looking for a smoking gun, they may be trying to restore a hard drive that was "permanently" erased.

The Information Security Professional's Code of Ethics

Security specialists are held to a high standard because they have access to a vast amount of information that, if used improperly, could ruin lives and even nations. Ethical behavior is easier to define than display. Although most people intuitively know what proper conduct is, it is difficult for anyone to admit that they are wrong or have done something wrong. It is very tempting to find ways to reinterpret behavior when caught committing a crime. For example, is an IT security specialist with access to sensitive payroll information acting unethically when confirming that a coworker is making substantially less money than another employee with the same job grade and performance rating?

In an effort to make the ethical behavior of information security specialists more explicit, the International Information Systems Security Certification Consortium (ISC^2) developed the code of conduct for Certified Information Systems Security Professionals (CISSPs).

According to the ISC^2 Web site, "All information systems security professionals who are certified by ISC^2 recognize that such certification is a privilege that must be both earned and maintained. In support of this principle, all Certified Information Systems Security Professionals (CISSPs) commit to fully support this Code of Ethics. CISSPs who intentionally or knowingly violate any provision of the Code will be subject to action by a peer review panel, which may result in the revocation of certification" (**www.isc2.org**). The ISC^2 Code of Ethics is mandatory for certified professionals. There are four mandatory canons in the code listed below. General guidance is not intended to substitute for the sound ethical judgment of the professional.

- Protect society, the commonwealth, and the infrastructure.

- Act honorably, honestly, justly, responsibly, and legally.

- Provide diligent and competent service to principals.

- Advance and protect the profession.

> ## FYI: A Security Professional's Ethical Dilemma
>
> Suppose you're an IT employee at a pharmaceutical manufacturer, and a high-level manager's PC has been hit hard with a virus attack that requires a desk-side visit to determine the prognosis. You find that the system will no longer boot up but, with your hard-drive recovery and antivirus tools, you're able to recover her files. In the process, you discover an internal memo that the company is trying to suppress from the FDA that discusses the surprising number of deaths during the field trials of a new anticancer drug.
>
> What should you do? Should you ignore what you've found? Should you notify someone? Should you blow the whistle through the media? How can you apply the Code of Ethics to this dilemma? Which canon(s) apply?
>
> This type of dilemma is one you might face as an IT security professional at some point in your career. Your decision at that point will be easier if this is a scenario that you have already thought about.

Although the tools used to commit crimes may change over the years with the advances in technology, the principles of investigation and prosecution, as well as the standards of ethical behavior, remain the same.

Other Ethics Standards

The ISC^2 Code of Ethics is one of the more prominent attempts at specifying ethical conduct for computer specialists. Other codes include

- Computer Ethics Institute's Ten Commandments of Computer Ethics

- Internet Activities Board's Ethics and the Internet

- U.S. Department of Health, Education, and Welfare Code of Fair Information Practices

Each of these efforts to codify ethical behavior share a common goal: establishing a code of conduct for anyone using computer resources. We will now cover each in more detail.

Computer Ethics Institute

The Ten Commandments of Computer Ethics was originally presented by Dr. Ramon C. Barquin in a paper titled "In Pursuit of a 'Ten Command-ments' for Computer Ethics" (Computer Ethics Institute, May 7, 1992; **www.brook.edu/its/cei/cei_hp.htm**). They are

1. Thou Shalt Not Use a Computer to Harm Other People.
2. Thou Shalt Not Interfere with Other People's Computer Work.
3. Thou Shalt Not Snoop Around in Other People's Computer Files.
4. Thou Shalt Not Use a Computer to Steal.
5. Thou Shalt Not Use a Computer to Bear False Witness.
6. Thou Shalt Not Copy or Use Proprietary Software for Which You Have Not Paid.
7. Thou Shalt Not Use Other People's Computer Resources Without Authorization or Proper Compensation.
8. Thou Shalt Not Appropriate Other People's Intellectual Output.
9. Thou Shalt Think About the Social Consequences of the Program You Are Writing or the System You Are Designing.
10. Thou Shalt Always Use a Computer in Ways That Ensure Consideration and Respect for Your Fellow Humans.

Although many of these commandments are just good common sense, it's useful to remind people that there are consequences for unacceptable behavior. You may consider including these Ten Commandments in a security training and awareness program (see Chapter 4).

Internet Activities Board: Ethics and the Internet

Computer uses are pervasive; no industry or profession can survive this day and age without the aid of computer technology. Because of the potential for abuse of information or damage to resources from malicious uses of computer technology, the Internet Activities Board published a standard—Ethics and the Internet—intended for wide distribution and acceptance from the Internet-using communities. The introduction to RFC 1087 - Ethics and the Internet reads:

> At great human and economic cost, resources drawn from the U.S. Government, industry and the academic community have been assembled into a collection of interconnected networks called the Internet...

> ...As is true of other common infrastructures (e.g., roads, water reservoirs and delivery systems, and the power generation and distribution network), there is widespread dependence on the Internet by its users for the support of day-to-day research activities.

The reliable operation of the Internet and the responsible use of its resources is of common interest and concern for its users, operators and sponsors...

...Many of the Internet resources are provided by the U.S. Government. Abuse of the system thus becomes a Federal matter above and beyond simple professional ethics.

The complete RFC 1087 is available at **www.faqs.org/rfcs/rfc1087 .html**. It outlines a statement of policy and lists a number of unacceptable behaviors that would violate ethical behavior.

Code of Fair Information Practices

The Code of Fair Information Practices was adopted in 1973 by the U.S. Department of Health, Education and Welfare—now called the U.S. Department of Health and Human Services. It states that:

1. There must be no personal data record-keeping systems whose very existence is secret.
2. There must be a way for an individual to find out what information is in his or her file and how the information is being used.
3. There must be a way for an individual to correct information in his or her records.
4. Any organization creating, maintaining, using, or disseminating records of personally identifiable information must assure the reliability of the data for its intended use and must take precautions to prevent misuse.
5. There must be a way for an individual to prevent personal information obtained for one purpose from being used for another purpose without his or her consent.

   (*Source*: **www.epic.org/privacy/consumer/code_fair_info.html.**)

The Code of Fair Information Practices, related more to the privacy of individuals on computerized record-keeping systems, complements the ethics standards for people to consider when using information systems. Because no one stands alone when connected to public networks, it's vital to lay the ground rules for what's acceptable and what's not acceptable.

Source: **U.S. Department of Health, Education, and Welfare (1973)**.

Summary

Laws, investigative principles, and professional ethics, often thought of as abstract topics, are as important to information security professionals as knowing how to design firewall architecture. Understanding how different laws affect security practices across the globe gives the practitioner the correct perspective with which to operate internationally with the same confidence as working close to home. Understanding the relationships of computer crime investigations and the laws that govern property is critical to becoming a productive member of a team that can effectively protect, detect, and respond to security incidents.

     Ethics are the ties that bind one's behavior to the world of computer security—balancing the authority one is given while working in the field with the checks and balances that prevent the abuse of power.

Test Your Skills

MULTIPLE CHOICE QUESTIONS

1. Business losses that are a result of computer crime are difficult to estimate for which of the following reasons?

    A. Companies are not always aware that their computer systems have been compromised.

    B. Companies are sometimes reluctant to report computer crime because it is bad advertising.

    C. Losses are often difficult to quantify.

    D. All of the above.

2. According to a 2004 Computer Security Institute CSI/FBI Computer Crime and Security Survey, what percentage of organizations experiencing computer attacks reported them to law enforcement agencies?

    A. 75 percent

    B. 20 percent

    C. 10 percent

    D. 90 percent

3. The CISSP categorizes computer attacks by type. Which of the following is not one of the categories identified by the CISSP?

    A. terrorist attack

    B. thrill attack

    C. subterfuge attack

    D. business attack

4. What type of individual is most likely to perform a "grudge attack?"

   A. an employee who feels he has been mistreated by his employer

   B. a political exile

   C. a libertarian

   D. all of the above

5. Computer crime is generally made possible by which of the following?

   A. the perpetrator's obtaining advanced training and special knowledge

   B. victim carelessness

   C. collusion with others in information processing

   D. system design flaws

6. The computer criminal who calls a help desk trying to obtain another user's password is most likely a:

   A. dumpster diver

   B. black-hat hacker

   C. social engineer

   D. spammer

7. Which of the following computer crimes involves overtaxing a computer's resources until it is no longer functional?

   A. spoofing IP addresses

   B. Denial of Service (DoS)

   C. rogue code

   D. information warfare

8. We inherited which of our legal systems from England?

   A. administrative law

   B. patent law

   C. Ccommon law

   D. byways

9. Computer laws have become increasingly difficult to enforce for which of the following reasons?

   A. the inability of legislation in the United States to keep pace with technological advances

   B. the globalization of the economy resulting in unclear international legal boundaries

   C. conflicting security standards within the United States and between the United States and other nations

   D. all of the above

10. "Natural justice" is

    A. primitive and thus "natural."

    B. enforced by judge and jury.

    C. considered self-evident and thus requires no statutes.

    D. unsuited for arbitration.

11. The Patent and Trademark Office (PTO) resisted patenting software for years for what primary reason?

    A. Software was too intangible.

    B. Software was the product of scientific truth or mathematical expressions.

    C. The average shelf life of software was estimated to be less than the life span of a patent (17 years).

    D. It was too interconnected with the computer's operating system.

12. Which of the following statements is true about a "trade secret"?

    A. It offers legal protection just as a trademark does.

    B. It is a patent "in the works."

    C. It is widely known but rarely discussed.

    D. All of the above.

13. Which of the following *is not* one of the FTC's four Fair Information Practices?

    A. Individuals should be given the choice of "opting out" when sharing their personal information.

    B. Personal information should be accurate and stored securely.

    C. Web sites must have 100 percent availability in case the user wishes to change his personal information.

    D. Web sites must tell the user how his personal information will be used and notify him of any changes to that policy.

7

14. What can be said about the European Union Data Protection Directive of 1998?

    A. The United States was exempted from privacy standards in the EU.

    B. The directive's goal was to standardize privacy protection among the EU members.

    C. It resulted in the "Safe Harbor Privacy Principles" that allowed the United States to meet minimum privacy controls in the European Union.

    D. Both B and C are correct.

15. Which of the following definitions best describes "computer forensics"?

    A. using computers to investigate crime

    B. investigating crimes committed using computers

    C. probing the operating system for signs of malfeasance

    D. predicting behaviors of cyber criminals

16. The ISC^2 Code of Ethics is intended to

    A. help certificate holders in resolving dilemmas related to their practice.

    B. provide guidance on encouraging good behavior.

    C. provide guidance on discouraging poor behavior.

    D. All of the above.

17. What bearing does ethics have on the information security specialist?

    A. Ethical conduct is expected of all IS specialists.

    B. It helps define a high moral code of professional behavior.

    C. It speaks to the credibility of the individual.

    D. All of the above.

18. Which of the following is not one of the provisions of the ISC^2 Code of Ethics?

    A. Act honorably, responsibly, and legally.

    B. Provide thorough and competent service to your customers and peers.

    C. Judge not lest you be judged.

    D. Strive to protect society and its components.

EXERCISES

Exercise 7.1: Research Current Computer Crimes

1. Perform a Google search on computer crime and compile a list of recent attacks and data compromises.

2. Where possible, identify the nature and source of the attacks.

Exercise 7.2: Research the Details of a Computer Crime

1. Select one of the types of computer attacks (e.g., DoS) and research the details of the attack.

2. What has the industry done in response to these attacks?

3. What became of the perpetrators of the crime(s)?

Exercise 7.3: Investigate the Current State of the EU Directive

1. Investigate further the current status of the European Union's Data Protection Directive on information privacy.

2. How many countries currently belong to the Safe Harbor group?

3. If you can determine, how well is Safe Harbor working out for information providers based in the United States?

Exercise 7.4: Investigate the Different Types of Computer-Based Legal Evidence

1. Research the different kinds of legal evidence used in computer crime investigations.

2. What are the differences between admissible and inadmissible evidence?

3. Who should be responsible for maintaining the chain-of-custody for computer crimes evidence?

Exercise 7.5: Brainstorm Unethical Uses of the Computer

1. Try to think of 10 examples of what you would consider to be unethical uses of the computer.

2. How might you mitigate these threats?

3. How would a set of codified ethics that users of the computer must subscribe to for using the system help in mitigating these threats?

PROJECTS

Project 7.1: Interview an IS Specialist

1. Identify and interview an IS specialist whose job it is to gather evidence for computer crimes.

2. Ask him/her to discuss as fully as possible the nature of the crimes. (*Note*: Investigators *love* talking about their jobs!)

3. What tools and techniques did he or she use to determine the culprit(s)?

4. How successful were any prosecutions of lawsuits brought against the perpetrators?

Project 7.2: Investigate the Complexities of Intellectual Property Law

1. Research the topic of intellectual property as related to copyright law.

2. What are some of the difficulties in proving a copyright infringement case, such as that brought by the RIAA against those who download free MP3 files?

3. What are some of the other recent and famous cases related to copyright, trademark, or trade secret infringements?

4. Who should govern the Internet to prevent intellectual property law infringements?

5. Can anyone or any one country govern how the Internet is used (and abused)?

Project 7.3: Examine a Recent Governmental Privacy Act

1. Select a recent governmental regulation such as HIPAA or the Gramm-Leach-Bliley Act (GLBA) to research the privacy aspects of the act.

2. What are some of the conflicting interests to business and the individual related to privacy matters?

3. What privacy concerns do you have as an Internet user and shopper?

4. How will your behavior change as a result of reading this chapter?

Case Study

In fall 2003, The University of Calgary began offering a new course called "Computer Viruses and Malware," intended for fourth-year students. In the course, students learn to write and test their own viruses. The move touched off a wave of criticism within the antivirus community.

As a school administrator, you wound up getting the phone calls from both the supporters and the protesters who accuse you of being irresponsible and demand that you cancel the class immediately.

Will you cancel the class? Can you defend the course and the reasoning behind offering it to students? Is there an ethical dilemma here? Write a press release that you would want to share with the local papers and TV stations that reflects your decision to continue or cancel the course.

7

Chapter **8**

Physical Security Control

Chapter Objectives

After reading this chapter and completing the exercises, you will be able to do the following:

- Distinguish between logical and physical security, and explain the reasons for placing equal emphasis on both.
- Recognize the importance of the Physical Security domain.
- Outline the major categories of physical security threats.
- Classify the techniques to mitigate risks to an organization's physical security.
- Classify the five main categories of physical security controls, including their strengths and limitations.
- Propose how smart cards can be used for physical access control.
- Categorize the different types of biometric access controls and determine their respective strengths and weaknesses.

Introduction

An often overlooked connection between *physical systems* (computer hardware) and *logical systems* (the software that runs on it) is that in order to protect logical systems, the hardware running them must be physically secure. If you can't physically protect your hardware, you can't protect the programs and data running on your hardware!

Physical security deals with who has access to buildings, computer rooms, and the devices within them. Controlling physical security involves protecting sites from natural and man-made physical threats through proper location and by developing and implementing plans that secure devices from unauthorized physical contact.

Information security experts, however, usually focus more on the problems related to logical security because of the greater likelihood that remotely located computer hackers will analyze, dissect, or break into computer networks. A hacker's physical proximity to a network has less to do with its vulnerability than porous interfaces or operating systems with more holes in them than Swiss cheese.

The idea of physical security may seem almost arcane and anachronistic in an age of remote high-tech stealth and subterfuge, but no aspect of computer security can be taken for granted. We are reminded by surveys, including the National Retail Security Survey (NRSS), that employee (insider) theft is on the rise and shows no sign of abating in light of downsizing, rightsizing, and layoffs. According to the 2001 NRSS, retailers attributed more than 45 percent of their company's losses to employee theft, including the trafficking of proprietary information. As you shall see, physical security applies not only to external attacks but also to "inside jobs" perpetrated by disgruntled employees who frequently feel that the company "owes them something" or by employees who are simply thieves.

The NRSS describes the more traditional view of loss of tangible goods (e.g., clothing, DVDs, manufacturing parts, etc.) through theft; however, loss of intellectual property and company information complicates the more traditional definition of property and has forced organizations to take internal theft as seriously as external theft.

Some of the information in this chapter may seem intuitive or obvious. Unfortunately, too many organizations, big and small, neglect some of the most basic aspects of physical security. That is why physical security is one of the 10 domains of the Certified Information Systems Security Professional (CISSP) Common Body of Knowledge (CBK).

Understanding the Physical Security Domain

The Physical Security domain includes the more traditional safeguards against threats, both intentional and unintentional, to the physical environment and the surrounding infrastructure. If you have ever worked for a large company or entered a municipal building, you most likely have experienced some of these security checks first-hand: badge readers, television monitors, bag and "airport" X-ray devices, and the ever-present armed security guards. The level of physical security is typically proportional to the value of the property that is being protected. Organizations such as the government or corporations conducting high-level research generally use more sophisticated physical security checks, including biometrics (explained later), as the property inside might be highly classified. Organizations that keep less sensitive information, however, still must worry about compromising customer and employee information, which could result in damaging or fatal lawsuits. Regardless of the size or the nature of the organization, the goal of the Physical Security domain is to set safeguards in place to protect an organization's assets and assure the continuity of business in the event of man-made or natural disasters.

Challenges related to physical security lay in the need to make it simple for people who belong in a building to get in and get around but make it difficult for those who do not belong to enter and navigate. Thus, physical security, like many other areas of security, is a careful balancing act that requires trusted people, effective processes that reduce the likelihood of harm from inadvertent and deliberate acts, and appropriate technology to maintain vigilance.

If you have an interest in the security field, you'll need to understand the following areas of physical security:

- How to choose a secure site (location) and guarantee the correct design.

- How to secure a site against unauthorized access.

- How to protect equipment, for example personal computers and the information contained on them, against theft.

- How to protect the people and property within an installation.

These four areas of physical security are the focus of this chapter.

Physical Security Threats

You need to understand the threats physical security control systems address before learning about design and implementation. As you will learn later in this chapter, site selection depends heavily on a list of potential physical security threats for a given location. The goal of identifying these threats beforehand is to help assure uninterrupted business and/or computer service, lessen the risk of physical damage to a site from natural or man-made causes, and reduce the risk of internal and external theft. Most importantly, the safety of personnel takes precedence over the safety of structures, computers, data, and other systems.

The major categories of physical security threats, as defined in the CBK, are

- **Weather:** tornadoes, hurricanes, floods, fire, snow, ice, heat, cold, humidity, and so forth.

- **Fire/chemical:** explosions, toxic waste/gases, smoke, fire.

- **Earth movement:** earthquakes, mudslides.

- **Structural failure:** building collapse because of snow/ice or moving objects (cars, trucks, airplanes, and so forth).

- **Energy:** loss of power, radiation, magnetic wave interference, and so forth.

- **Biological:** virus, bacteria, infestations of animals or insects.

- **Human:** strikes, sabotage, terrorism, and war.

A number of factors such as geographic locale determine the likelihood of specific physical security threats. A data center located in the San Francisco Bay area should be more concerned about earthquakes than a comparable data center in Kansas. And because tornados are more prevalent in Kansas than on the West Coast, data centers in the Great Plains should be more concerned about wind shears and snow and ice storms.

Providing Physical Security

The remainder of this chapter discusses in some detail the five areas of physical security that address the aforementioned types of physical security threats. These areas are

- educating personnel

- administrative controls, such as site selection

- physical controls, such as keys and locks, fencing, lighting, and guards

- technical controls, such as smart cards, audit trails, intrusion detection systems, and biometrics

- environmental/life-safety controls

Educating Personnel

An educated staff, made aware of the potential for theft and misuse of facilities and equipment, is the best weapon a company can have against illegitimate and accidental acts by others. Just as the staff should be prepared for the potential of unforeseen acts of nature, employees should be reminded periodically of the importance of helping to secure their surroundings, including

- Being mindful of physical and environmental considerations required to protect the computer systems.

- Adhering to emergency and disaster plans.

- Monitoring the unauthorized use of equipment and services and reporting suspicious or unusual activity to security personnel.

- Recognizing the security objectives of the organization.

- Accepting individual responsibilities associated with their own security and that of their coworkers as well as the equipment they use and how they use it.

An organization can educate its staff on the importance of their physical security through the use of self-paced or formal instruction, security education bulletins, posters, training films and tapes, or awareness days that drive home the importance of constant vigilance.

Administrative Access Controls

The second category of physical access controls, administrative access controls, addresses the procedural and codified application of physical controls. For example, you will learn about several different physical control devices that make a site more secure. And one of the administrative access controls that will be reviewed in this section, site selection, involves the planning for and the design of the site before it is constructed.

Restricting Work Areas A *physical security plan*, developed by executive management, department managers, and physical security site personnel as one of the many policy and standards documents that all effective security programmes require (see Chapter 4), should first identify the access rights to the site (e.g., campus) in general and then the various access rights required by each location (building) within the site. Within a manufacturing plant, an individual may need different access privileges depending on the department or area they are attempting to enter even though they have gained general admittance to the plant. A single mechanism usually controls various levels of security access. This could be a badge reader encoded to allow the individual into specific areas of the facility based on function or business need. The important point to remember is that, just as security experts assign data to specific security classes, there can also be varying degrees of physical access based on security requirements within the facility.

Escort Requirements and Visitor Control Controlling visitor access to a building is not a new concern. Most companies have long had some kind of procedure for requiring visitors to "sign in" and specify a purpose for their visit and wait for an escort that authorizes their presence before granting access to the visitor. However, with heightened post–September 11 security and the formation of the U.S. Department of Homeland Security, visitor control has taken on increased importance because of concern over foreign nationals in the workplace. The U.S. Department of Commerce (DOC) defines a foreign national as "a person who was born outside the jurisdiction of the United States, who is subject to some foreign government, and who has not been naturalized under U.S. law." In many government facilities or facilities with strong government ties, foreign nationals are not allowed unescorted access to any site within the facility. To gain access to any DOC site, for example, a foreign national must provide more than 17 identifying pieces of information including passport number, country of issuance, and sponsor information.

For less secure and nongovernment sites, visitors typically must have a clear purpose for their visit and a confirmed contact within the site such as an employee or another individual with the appropriate clearance. Visitors are usually required to sign in at the security desk and are given a temporary badge or other identifying moniker that clearly defines them as a visitor.

In addition, visitors may be required to pass through a metal detector and should be prepared to have handbags, satchels, and laptop briefcases checked and to surrender, at least temporarily, recording devices such as cameras, tape recorders, and other questionable items (e.g., pocketknives).

Site Selection Site designers and planners must make at least the following considerations when deciding on the location for a facility. As an example, the location of a data operations center for a major corporation will be used.

- **Visibility:** How conspicuous will the facility be at a particular site? Most data centers look nondescript for a reason. They don't want to advertise what they are and attract undue attention. You will never find signs along the highway stating, "Highly Secure but Anonymous-Looking Data Operations Facility, Exit Here!" Low-key is the byword.

- **Locale considerations:** The wise prospective homeowner should always inspect the neighborhood before purchasing a new house. The same rules apply in many ways to site-selection committees. What are the local ordinances and variances? What is the crime rate of the surrounding neighborhood? Are potentially hazardous sites nearby, such as landfills, hazardous waste dumps, or nuclear reactors?

- **Natural disasters:** Several major corporations (e.g., Charles Schwab) have moved their computer operations centers from the West Coast, particularly the San Francisco Bay area, to more geologically stable locations because of the risk of earthquakes. Other obvious natural threats to consider are tornadoes, hurricanes, floods, wildfires, chemical fires, vermin, pest damage, and snow and ice. Mother Nature's hand is far-reaching, but site planners can minimize risk by examining local weather patterns, the history of weather-related disasters, and determining their risk tolerance.

- **Transportation:** Are transportation routes such as airports, highways, and railroads nearby, and if so, are they navigable? A good transportation system is important not only for the delivery of goods and services but also for emergency evacuation procedures as part of a disaster recovery plan (DRP).

Physical Security Controls

A spectrum of physical controls are needed to support the principle of defense in depth. These include controls for the perimeter of the data center, employee and visitor badging, guard dogs when deemed appropriate, and building lighting.

Perimeter Security Controls Controls on the perimeter of the data center are designed to prevent unauthorized access to the facility. These types of controls may have different "states" or behaviors based on the time of day or the day of the month. A gate may allow controlled access during the day but be locked or closed at night, for example.

Fences in some respects model the various levels of security in the virtual world. A fence 3 to 4 feet high will discourage the casual passerby. A fence 6 to 7 feet high will deter general intruders. A fence 8 feet high topped with razor-edge wire signals an even greater need to keep intruders out (and sometimes, unfortunately, to keep people in). A perimeter intrusion and detection assessment system (PIDAS) is fencing that uses passive vibration sensors to detect intruders or any attempts to compromise the system.

Turnstiles are less effective than either gates or fences. They dissuade rather than prevent intruders from entering a site without authorization. Anyone who has ever taken the New York City subway system undoubtedly has witnessed individuals leaping over the turnstile without depositing a token or, in today's age, swiping a Metrocard. Turnstiles usually do not authenticate a user but simply control access based on the use of a token.

Mantraps, as the name implies, are enclosed areas with a secure door on either end that literally "trap" an individual between doors. They address the problem of "piggybacking" whereby an individual without proper authorization will enter a secure area behind a person who enters legitimately. In order to pass through the second door of the Mantrap, the individual must pass a second level of validation—perhaps the authorization of a security guard, the entering of a password, or some other mechanism (see Figure 8.1 for an example of a mantrap).

Badging Issued by a site security office, the photo identification badge is a perimeter security control mechanism that not only authenticates an individual but also continues to identify the individual while inside the facility. Most sites issuing photo identification require that the individual displays the badge where it is most visible, usually on the upper torso. The badge alone is no guarantee that unauthorized individuals are denied access—badges can be stolen and photos replaced—but combined with other perimeter controls, the badge offers a familiar and comfortable sense of security in most organizations.

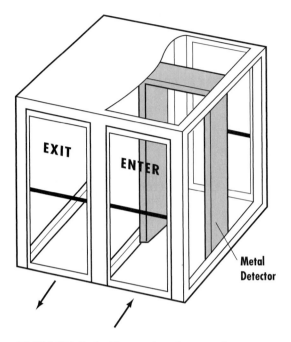

FIGURE 8.1 Example of a mantrap.

Keys and Combination Locks Keys and combination locks are how most people know physical security, mainly because they are the least complicated and expensive devices. Beyond the mechanical door lock opened with a key, locks are now programmable and opened with a combination of keys (e.g., the five-key pushbutton lock once popular in IT operations), a security badge with a magnetic strip, or some other mechanism. Locks are typically unguarded and are meant to delay an intruder, not absolutely deny him access. For that reason, you rarely find these devices any more in areas where a high level of access authorization is required.

Security Dogs What some home security experts don't tell you is that dogs are not just a man's best friend, but they can also make great security guards! Dogs can be unflinchingly loyal and rely on all of their senses to detect intruders. They can also be trained to perform specialized services such as sniffing out drugs or explosives at airports or alerting the blind to fire before it engulfs them. The image of the German shepherd tethered to the door behind an auto junkyard may be the first thing that comes to mind when thinking about security dogs, but dogs are a highly effective and threatening perimeter security control when handled properly and humanely.

Lighting Lighting is another form of perimeter protection that discourages intruders or other unauthorized individuals from entering restricted areas. You are likely familiar with how shopping malls use streetlights to discourage parking lot break-ins, and many homeowners have motion-detector lights installed on garages and back porches. Critical buildings and installations should use some form of lighting as a deterrent, whether it be floodlights, streetlights, or searchlights. According to the National Institute of Standards and Technology, critical areas (e.g., fire escapes, emergency exits, and so forth) require safety lighting to be mounted 8 feet high and burn with a candlepower of 2 candelas (the equivalent of a strong spotlight).

Technical Controls

The next group of physical security controls involves the use of computer hardware and software to protect facilities as opposed to some of the other more traditional physical security techniques described earlier in the chapter. The more prominent technical controls include:

- smart/dumb cards

- audit trails/access logs

- intrusion detection

- biometric access controls

Smart Cards A *smart card* resembles a regular payment (credit) card with the major difference that it carries a semiconductor chip with logic and nonvolatile memory (see Figure 8.2). Unlike a security access card (badge with magnetic strip), the smart card has many purposes, including storing value for consumer purchases, medical identification, travel ticketing and identification, and building access control. The card may also store software that detects unauthorized tampering and intrusions to the chip itself and, if

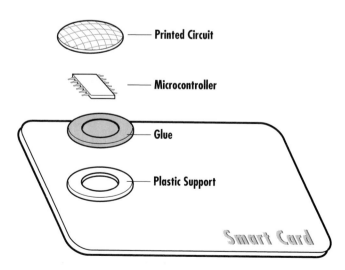

Printed Circuit

Microcontroller

Glue

Plastic Support

Smart Card

FIGURE 8.2 A smart card.

detected, can lock or destroy the contents of the chip to prevent disclosure or unauthorized uses.

FYI: A Taxonomy of Smart Cards

Smart cards are essentially working computers with an infinite possibility of uses. On the physical level, smart cards are classified as contact, contact-less, or as combinations of the two. Contact smart cards require a reader (and/or writer) in which the card is inserted when it's needed. Contact-less cards contain an antenna that may be read by remote receivers. Combination cards may be used both ways, depending on the applications intended. Logically, you'll find smart cards classified three different ways. Memory cards (the simplest form) are used to store values for future uses.

The most common example of a memory card is a prepaid phone card redeemable through the bright-yellow reader slot found on modern pay phones. Protected memory cards require the entry of a secret code or PIN before a stream of data can be sent to or received from the chip. Microprocessor cards contain a semiconductor chip to hold microcode that defines command structures, data file structures, and security structures. They're present when more "intelligence" or storage of information is needed and are often found used in multiapplication products and services, such as combined access and stored-value cards.

Smart cards—used much more extensively in Asia and Europe than in the United States—can also store banks of passwords. A user, for example, can store network, application, and Internet URLs and login passwords on a smart card. When smart cards are integrated with a biometrics (see Chapter 5) login (such as a fingerprint; discussed in more detail later in this chapter), security can further be enhanced.

Smart cards can also facilitate file encryption by storing the user's private key for use with a public key infrastructure (or PKI, a mechanism allowing the use of multiple "keys," one private, one public, to lock and unlock files; see Chapter 11). They work well for mobile users because such users are inclined to carry their smart card with them as they would one of their credit cards. This means that the user's encryption keys are not stored on a workstation, thus providing a more secure environment than when the cryptographic functions are performed on the workstation itself, which is subject to Trojan Horse attacks, or attacks where a seemingly innocuous object contains something harmful to the interests of the recipient.

Still, smart cards alone are not completely secure. If an attacker were to steal a user's PIN number or password along with the card, he could gain complete access to the network. However, using a fingerprint along with the card to authenticate the user greatly reduces the chance for intrusion.

The use of smart cards in conjunction with biometrics authentication, for example fingerprint readers or retinal scan techniques, can be extremely effective, especially in situations where controlling physical access is of the utmost importance. This kind of layered security goes beyond the use of passwords or passwords and smart cards alone. A company that has already committed to using smart cards for many of its applications could benefit from adding an additional level of security using a biometrics logon.

So why aren't these techniques more widely used? Several factors, namely cost, reliability, and practicality, have hampered the deployment of smart cards and biometrics. However, as more companies build smart card readers into their workstations and as the use of biometrics increases in manageability and flexibility and decreases in price, their use will become increasingly important and prevalent.

Audit Trails/Access Logs In financial settings such as banks, audit trails allow examiners to trace or follow the history of a transaction through the institution. Bank auditors or examiners, for example, are able to determine when information was added, changed, or deleted within a system with the purpose of understanding how an irregularity occurred and hopefully how to correct it. The immediate goal is to detect the problem in order to prevent similar problems in the future. The audit trail should contain the following information:

- The user ID or name of the individual who performed the transaction.

- Where the transaction was performed (hopefully using a fixed terminal ID).

- The time and date of the transaction.

- A description of the transaction, that is, what function did the user perform, and on what.

Creating an audit log is not enough, however, to protect a site. The retention period of the audit logs, recovery time (i.e., how long does it take to recall an archived log file), and, perhaps most importantly, the integrity of the data must also be considered and the logging system designed appropriately.

Intrusion Detection *Intrusion detection* is another type of technical control. In this case, intrusion detectors and alarms alert security personnel when an unauthorized person attempts to access a system or building. Unlike security guards, guard dogs, and security fencing discussed in the section on facility access control, this type of physical security control distinguishes itself by using technology. The burglar alarm is the most commonly known intrusion detection device, but, as you can imagine, the technology has become much more sophisticated since the first devices were used. The two categories of devices are

- **Perimeter intrusion detectors:** These devices are based on dry contact switches or photoelectric sensors. The former consists of metallic foil tape placed on windows or doorframes using contact switches. An alarm is set off when the switches are disturbed. Dry contact switches are used in residential homes and shop fronts where cost is important. Photoelectric sensors receive light beams, typically infrared, from a light-emitting device. When an intruder breaks the beams of light, he trips an alarm. This type of intrusion detection device is more expensive and usually found in larger facilities.

- **Motion detectors:** These devices detect unusual movements within a well-defined interior space. Included in this category of intrusion detection devices are wave pattern detectors that detect changes to light-wave patterns and audio detectors that passively receive unusual sound waves and set off an alarm.

Alarm Systems The implementation of a series of the aforementioned intrusion detectors is referred to as an alarm system. A local alarm system sets off an alarm on the premises, alerting guards on the premises to respond. Private security firms manage central-station systems, such as home alarms from ADT and other well-known home security companies. They monitor a system 24 hours a day and respond to alerts from a central location.

Company established, owned, and operated alarm systems (also called dedicated alarm systems) resemble a commercial central station system in that it serves many customers but differs because the focus is on the company exclusively. Dedicated systems may be more sophisticated than a local alarm system and share many of the same features as the centralized version. Additional alarms may be triggered at police or fire stations, with the permission and knowledge of the company being protected.

Biometrics The use of biometrics (Greek for "life measurements") in conjunction with more standard forms of authentication such as fixed passwords and PINs is beginning to attract attention as the cost of the technology decreases and its sophistication increases. In fact, the traditional scheme of password-based computer security could lose stature as the use of smart card–based cryptographic credentials and biometrics authentication become commercially viable. Some companies such as the American Biometrics Corporation claim that using an individual's unique physical characteristics along with other identification and authentication (I&A) techniques can almost unequivocally authenticate a user. Biometrics authentication uses characteristics of the human face, eyes, voice, fingerprints, hands, signature, and even body temperature, each technique having its own strengths and weaknesses.

Once the domain of TV spy shows and science fiction stories, the use of human characteristics to allow access to secure systems is quickly becoming a reality. (If you have ever seen Tom Cruise in any of his *Mission Impossible* movies, you will recognize many of these devices; oftentimes, science fiction is several decades ahead of reality.)

Any security system, especially biometrics systems, must balance convenience with security. A system that is too intrusive or cumbersome will discourage or prevent an authorized user from accessing a system. A security system should also be scaleable. In other words, not all systems and users need the same level of security, and security procedures and techniques should be flexible enough to reflect this. Still, any computer system requires a minimal level of security, and that is where authenticating the user at system logon becomes an issue.

A user's first access to a PC is during system logon, thus much attention focuses on the use of passwords, PINs, and more recently biometrics. With older versions of PC desktop operating systems, such as Windows 98 and Windows ME, no system logon was required, so whoever had physical access had complete control over the operating system and all the programs and data on the PC. Windows NT, however, was one of the first popular PC operating systems that required a network-level logon, which can be secured by authenticating a user's credentials on an authentication server before he can access the operating system and its file system.

How Best Can Authentication Be Achieved? Today, the use of fingerprints appears to be the cheapest and most reliable form of biometrics authentication, although other techniques such as retina scanning and thermal patterns are currently being developed. The tip of the finger has characteristics called "friction ridges," enclosures, and bifurcation points that uniquely differentiate one print from the print of any other individual. Because the fingerprint can vary in appearance throughout the day due to changes in temperature, skin moisture, dryness, oiliness, or cuts and abrasions, any direct comparison of digital images of the fingerprint cannot guarantee true authentication. Doing so would also require storing a complete image of the fingerprint in a database, something that attracts the attention of civil liberties groups and government agencies.

Instead, fingerprints are compared based on their characteristics described above and are thus characterized. How does this process work? The following steps generally describe the use of authenticating an individual using a fingerprint:

1. Multiple images of the individual's fingerprint are taken, using the center of the image as the reference point for the orientation and placement of other features.

2. The minutia features (ridges and other points) of importance surrounding the center of the image are computed as coordinate (XY) points and are catalogued in a database.

3. Each sample is scored based on the number and quality of coordinate values. The image with the highest (best sample) score becomes the "template" for the individual. This template is stored on a database and becomes the user's baseline or foundational template. Because it only contains a subset of the fingerprint detail, the template cannot be used to reconstruct the fingerprint or be used to impersonate a sample fingerprint.

4. When a user wants to authenticate, an algorithm is used to process the template stored in the database against the minutiae of his sample fingerprint. The level of security required determines the number of coordinate values that must match.

Environmental/Life-Safety Controls

Think of the infrastructure required to maintain the optimal operating environment for man and machine and you have environmental and life-safety controls. The three most critical areas are

- power (electrical, diesel)
- fire detection and suppression
- heating, ventilation, and air conditioning (HVAC)

Each of these areas will be discussed briefly below. For a more complete discussion, see the CISSP Common Body of Knowledge description (**www.isc2.org/**).

Power Whereas human beings can light candles when the power goes out, computers depend on an uninterrupted and regulated supply of power to assure constant voltage and current—computer equipment is highly sensitive to fluctuations in either voltage or current. We hardly need mention the importance of electricity in our working and private lives, but whereas the consumer patiently waits for the lights to come back on, businesses count the minutes in terms of lost revenue and productivity. As part of their DRP (see Chapter 6), most sites have backup power sources such as diesel generators, a kind of private energy source that kicks in when the primary power source is interrupted or inadequate. Threats to power systems include "noise," more specifically electrical radiation in the system, brownouts when a prolonged drop in voltage occurs, and humidity. When the humidity is too high, normally above 60 percent, condensation on computer parts can occur, resulting in lost efficiency.

Fire Detection and Suppression It is outside the scope of this book to discuss at length the details surrounding this extremely important technical control. Those planning on studying more about physical security will need to understand these particulars. Below we briefly touch on the main areas of this control, but you should consult one of the Web sites or CISSP exam prep books recommended at the end of this text for further information.

- **Fire types:** Fires are classified according to the types of combustibles and recommended methods of suppression. The four types of fires include common combustibles (e.g., wood, paper, and so forth), liquids (e.g., petroleum products, coolants, and so forth), electrical, and combustible metal (e.g., magnesium).

- **Fire detectors:** Fire detectors can be one of several types. Heat-sensing systems respond either to a predetermined threshold or a rapid rise in temperature. Flame detectors sense infrared energy or the pulsation of the flame. Smoke detectors use photoelectric sensors to respond to variations in the light hitting the photoelectric cells.

- **Fire-extinguishing systems:** When a fire occurs, the heating, ventilation, and air conditioning system (HVAC) must be stopped immediately to prevent the flow of oxygen. To extinguish the fire, either a water-sprinkler system or a gas-discharge system is used.

Water-sprinkler systems have four classifications: wet pipe, dry pipe, deluge, and preaction. Wet-pipe systems hold water in the pipes that is released when heat opens a valve. Dry-pipe systems do not have standing water in the pipes. Dry-pipe systems are used to eliminate the potential damage of a flood from a burst pipe in a wet-pipe system. When water is needed, a central valve outside the data center is opened (automatically when a fire is sensed), and water flows into the plumbing only when it's required to extinguish a fire. The deluge system is a dry-pipe system where the volume of water is substantially higher. The preaction system combines elements of both wet- and dry-pipe systems and is the recommended fire-extinguishing system for computer rooms.

Heating, Ventilation, and Air Conditioning The classifieds always seem to have ads for HVAC repairmen. That's because reliable and uninterrupted heating, ventilation, and air-conditioning systems are critical environmental controls. Computers are particularly sensitive to the smallest fluctuations in temperature and humidity. We frequently take the HVAC environmental controls for granted, but the IT manager or the person or persons responsible for these systems should know exactly what to do and whom to contact in the event of failure. Routine maintenance of critical infrastructure systems should prevent any significant failure of HVAC systems.

Summary

Physical security is often underemphasized by security experts when discussing strategies for protecting critical resources such as computers and the data stored on them. The ability of intruders and unauthorized personnel to access computer systems remotely does not take anything away from the need to secure physical sites. The Physical Security domain includes traditional safeguards against intentional and unintentional threats. Physical security threats can be man-made (e.g., labor strikes) or natural (e.g., earthquakes). Educating personnel about the importance of emergency response and accepting responsibility for their actions is critical. One type of physical security control is administrative access controls that use procedural and codified applications of physical security controls.

Another type of physical security control involves the use of mechanisms such as fences and gates to control access to a facility. Yet another type of physical security control, technical controls, uses computer hardware and software such as smart cards to protect facilities. One rapidly growing area of technical security controls is biometrics—the use of human traits such as fingerprints to identify and authenticate an individual.

Test Your Skills

MULTIPLE CHOICE QUESTIONS

1. Physical security pertains to
   A. guaranteeing the safety of equipment before people.
   B. annual health checkups for all employees.
   C. protecting an organization's assets and assuring the continuity of business in the event of a disaster.
   D. installing smoke alarms in every doorway of every building.

2. The level of physical security
   A. has no limits.
   B. is proportional to the value of the property being protected.
   C. depends on management involvement.
   D. is indexed to employee insecurities.

3. Which of the following does not pertain to physical security?

   A. site selection

   B. securing a site against unauthorized access

   C. protecting people and property

   D. installing firewalls on all computers

4. Natural disasters include

   A. earthquakes.

   B. chemical fires.

   C. rat infestations.

   D. All of the above.

5. Why is it important to educate personnel on the physical security of their facility?

   A. Doing so makes them more employable should they seek a career in facility management.

   B. They are protecting shareholder investments.

   C. They become more aware of the safety of coworkers and equipment.

   D. They become more "in tune" with their environment.

6. Which of the following is *not* a major concern when reviewing site selection?

   A. local crime rate

   B. proximity of restaurants, banks, and other conveniences for employees

   C. transportation systems

   D. weather

7. Why might San Francisco not be an optimal site for a data center?

   A. The cost of doing business is higher than in other parts of the country.

   B. San Francisco is near a major fault zone.

   C. Employees are easily distracted by local attractions.

   D. A and B.

8

8. Which of the following is not considered a physical security protection device?

   A. mantrap

   B. razor-edge wire

   C. German shepherd

   D. police helicopter

9. Security dogs

   A. are always German shepherds.

   B. once trained provide effective perimeter control.

   C. bark but don't bite.

   D. pose a biohazard.

10. Which of the following is true about smart cards?

    A. They are used more extensively in Europe and Asia than in the United States.

    B. They can store passwords such as personal identification numbers (PINs).

    C. Although promising great strides in authenticating users, smart cards are not infallible.

    D. All of the above.

11. What is an audit trail?

    A. a fitness path for quality inspectors

    B. a sound recording of conversations taped through perimeter devices

    C. a history of transactions indicating data that has been changed or modified

    D. all of the above

12. Which of the following is *not* true about the use of fingerprints for identification and authentication (I&A)?

    A. They are an infallible physical security control.

    B. They contain friction ridges and minutia points.

    C. They change based on fluctuations in temperature, skin moisture, and dryness.

    D. The practice has alarmed civil libertarians.

13. Environmental controls include

    A. heating and air conditioning.

    B. barometers.

    C. diesel backup generators.

    D. Both A and C.

14. Power supplies

    A. need to be clean and uninterrupted.

    B. come in unlimited quantities.

    C. are not a major physical security concern because municipalities are responsible for supplying power.

    D. are becoming increasingly inexpensive.

15. What is an HVAC system?

    A. a growing career choice for unemployed IT workers

    B. a medical response team

    C. backup computer power supply

    D. a type of environmental control system

EXERCISES

Exercise 8.1: Examine Your Personal Security Systems

1. Develop a checklist for your home or place of employment to help you decide if the level of physical security is adequate to protect your personal assets or your business's assets and data.

2. Complete the checklist by taking a walk around your site.

3. Recommend what you think needs to be done to improve the physical site's security.

Exercise 8.2: Explain the Codependency of Physical and Logical Security Controls

1. Describe how physical security controls are needed to augment logical security controls in a typical data center.

2. What physical security controls would you recommend for server rooms or network switching equipment closets if a full-blown data center is not practical?

Exercise 8.3: Observe the Security Controls Around You

1. Pick a typical day, and from dawn to dusk make note of the ways in which you interacted with security controls (e.g., you used a badge reader to enter an office building) and record your reaction. Remember that security controls include the unseen as well as the visible.

2. After you complete your list of security controls, describe how you feel about your observations.

3. Do you feel like your personal privacy is being invaded or are the security controls necessary in the highly technological age in which we live?

Exercise 8.4: Evaluate a Locale for a Data Center Operation

1. Select a specific geographic location, perhaps your hometown or the place where a friend or relative lives, and describe the suitability of the location for a major data center operation.

2. What criteria does the location meet for a viable operations center?

3. What are the drawbacks/limitations?

4. How do you go about weighing the advantages against the disadvantages?

Exercise 8.5: Evaluate the Practicality of Biometrics

1. Research in greater detail an aspect of biometrics (e.g., palm print recognition) and discuss the practicality of the security control.

2. Are specific biometric devices more realistic than others?

3. If so, what factors determine the reliability of a biometric control?

PROJECTS

Project 8.1: Tour Your School's Enrollment Systems

1. Arrange for a tour of your local school's information-keeping systems for student and faculty records.

2. Determine if their systems of controls seem appropriate for the nature and sensitivity of their record keeping.

3. Write down your impressions of their physical security controls to share with the class.

4. How do your findings differ from the findings by other students in the class?

Project 8.2: Compare Built-in and Add-on Physical Security

Masonryarts (**http://physicalsecurity.masonryarts.com/default.aspx**) is just one example of a company specializing in the design and implementation of blast-resistant building materials for government buildings (the U.S. embassy in Moscow is their "signature" project).

1. Examine how a company such as Masonryarts or a similar company "builds in" physical security.

2. How does their approach differ from "add-on" physical security devices and protections?

3. For what types of installations is their approach required?

4. Who is their largest customer?

8

Project 8.3: Research the Effectiveness of Home Alarm Systems

Americans spend millions of dollars each year on antitheft systems for their homes and offices from companies like ADT (**www.adt.com**) and Brinks Security (**www.brinkshomesecurity.com**).

1. How effective are these systems?

2. Are Americans shelling out hard-earned dollars for no reason or do such systems truly work?

3. What impacts do home alarm systems have on homeowner insurance premiums?

4. How much security is enough security? How can you determine how much of a system you should buy?

Case Study

A software development firm currently located in Wichita, Kansas, is becoming increasingly concerned about the safety and reliability of their data center, which has been struck by tornadoes over the past three summer seasons. They are considering relocating their data center and operations to another state with fewer risks of natural disasters. Management has asked you to prepare a proposal for three alternative sites within the continental United States.

How do you begin to determine what's best for the company? What do the company's competitors do for their data center operations? Which three locations would you choose?

Chapter 9

Operations Security

Chapter Objectives

After reading this chapter and completing the exercises, you will be able to do the following:

- Outline the types of controls needed for secure operations of a data center.
- Explain the principle of least privilege.
- Differentiate between the principle of least privilege and the principle of separation of duties.
- Define the control mechanisms commonly found in data center operations.
- Create a model of controls that incorporate people, process, and technology-based control mechanisms.

Introduction

Operations security is used to identify the controls over software, hardware, media, and the operators and administrators who possess elevated access privileges to any of these resources. Operations security is primarily concerned with data center operations processes, personnel, and technology and is needed to protect assets from threats during normal use. Audits and monitoring are the mechanisms that permit the identification of security events, define the key elements of these events, and serve as the source of pertinent event information given to the appropriate individual, group, or process.

Specific types of controls are needed to implement the security necessary to protect assets. The controls covered in this chapter include

- Preventative controls reduce the frequency and impact of errors and prevent unauthorized intruders.
- Detective controls discover errors once they've occurred.

- Corrective or recovery controls help mitigate the impact of a loss.

- Deterrent controls encourage compliance with external controls.

- Application-level controls minimize and detect software operational irregularities.

- Transaction-level controls provide control over various stages of a transaction.

Operations Security Principles

The *principle of least privilege*, or *need-to-know*, defines a minimum set of access rights or privileges needed to perform a specific job description. For example, a system administrator would have the necessary privileges to install a server operating systems and software but would not have the permission to add new users to the server. *Separation of duties* is a type of control that shows up in most security processes to make certain that no single person has excessive privileges that could be used to conduct hard-to-detect business fraud or steal secrets from a government system. The idea is to force collusion among two or more insiders in order for them to perpetrate fraud or theft.

Separation of duties is one of the six key elements of a strong system of internal and security controls and is similar in scope and practice to those found in financial systems (e.g., accounting departments). These six elements are

- Employing competent, trustworthy people with clear lines of authority and responsibility.

- Having adequate separation of job and process duties.

- Having proper procedures for authorizing transactions or changes to information.

- Maintaining adequate documents and records.

- Maintaining appropriate physical controls over assets and records.

- Executing independent checks on performance.

One of the primary benefits of separation of duties is that it enables one person's work to serve as a complementary check on another person's work. This implies that no one person has complete control over any transaction or process from beginning to end.

There are two fundamental reasons why separation of duties is important within all security-related processes. The first is that people are an integral part of every operations process. They authorize, generate, and approve all work that's needed. Having different people engaged in critical positions within the process is a common, sensible practice that ensures consistent and successful execution of the process. The second reason is an acknowledgment that people have shortcomings. When individuals perform complementary checks on each other, there is an enhanced opportunity for someone to catch an error before a process is fully executed and before a decision is made based on potentially erroneous data or activity. In spite of these checks and balances, some people may still be inclined to engage in fraud, theft, or malicious activities. They usually do so because they possess:

- **Motivation:** usually caused by some financial crisis that may be the result of health problems, drugs, overspending, gambling, extortion, or relationships.

- **Justification:** a sense that they have not been treated fairly, the employer owes them, or any explanation that they use to give good reason for their actions.

- **Opportunity:** knowledge or belief that a fraud can be committed and remain undetected ("I'll never get caught") because internal controls are either not in place, inadequate, or because they believe that no one is minding the store.

FYI: Separation of Duties

Separation of duties is essential to maintain the integrity of production operations and should always be present. A typical computer operation in most companies divides separation of duties into various environments. There's one environment for the software developers, another for quality assurance testing, and a third for production, or the environment that end users access, to perform their duties. As software is deemed ready, it's promoted from environment to environment by systems and security administration personnel other than the programmer. This separation of duties prevents a programmer from launching into production software that can perpetrate fraud or cause damage to production data or resources.

Operations Security Process Controls

Process controls are necessary for secure data center operations. The process controls help to assure that the principles outlined above are implemented in human-based process activities and software-based utilities and other data center management systems (e.g., tape libraries and program directories).

Trusted recovery controls ensure that security is not breached when a computer system crashes. Fail-secure system controls preserve the state of the system prior to the crash and prevent further damage or unauthorized access to the system. One example of this is a bank vault located in a high-security room. The trusted recovery control is the room itself that can detect any attempt at an unauthorized entry and lock the perpetrator in an area where he cannot escape (see mantrap in Chapter 8).

Configuration and change management controls are used for tracking and approving changes to a system. This process identifies, controls, and audits any changes by administrative personnel to reduce the threats or negative impacts of security violations. One threat to configuration and change management is called a block upgrade, which is when a requestor asks for a large number of simultaneous changes during an upgrade and change management is impossible, so it's bypassed. To prevent the threats from a block upgrade, changes should be packaged so they're readily managed and easily understood to preserve system security and integrity. You can find more on configuration and change management in the "Operations Security Controls in Action" section later in this chapter.

Personnel security involves pre-employment screening and mandatory vacation time. This prevents people from hiding illegal activities while performing their duties. (For instance, when other people take over the work while the person is on vacation, they may detect hidden activity.) Other personnel security measures include job rotation and a series of escalating warnings that lead up to termination of employment or prosecution in the criminal justice system in cases of unauthorized or illegal activity.

Record retention processes refers to how long transactions and other types of computerized or process records should be retained. These controls deal with computer files, disk directories, and libraries of software and utilities.

Resource protection is needed to protect company resources and assets. Some resources that require protection are modem pools, network routers, storage media, and documentation.

Privileged entity controls are given to operators and system administrators as special access to computing resources. Included are controls to assure individual accountability of all actions taken while logged-in as administrator.

IN PRACTICE: Controlling Privileged User IDs

To best control administrative rights and access to a system, it's essential to issue individual accounts (IDs) and passwords that can be tied to a single person. Those accounts can then be granted account privileges of an administrator. Rather than sharing the password associated with a default account ID "Administrator" or "Root" (UNIX-based systems), a better practice is to tag the default account so that it cannot be used (or delete it entirely if possible) and make sure that each administrator has a unique and personally identifiable account to perform his or her duties.

Media viability controls are needed for the proper marking and handling of assets. These include clearly marking media with contents, dates, classification (if needed), and other information that would help operators with locating and using the correct media more often.

Operations process controls are a necessary element in the overall security of a computer installation. Because operators tend to possess privilege beyond other users, it's vital to impose controls to limit the damage they can cause and protect them from themselves.

FYI: Sarbanes-Oxley and Data Center Security

The Sarbanes-Oxley (SOX) Act of 2002, passed by the U.S. Congress after the accounting scandals at firms such as Enron and WorldCom, has captured the attention of internal auditors and CEOs nationwide. SOX requires executives to review and modernize companies' financial reporting systems to comply with its regulations. One specific section of SOX—Section 404—calls for company executives and third-party auditors to certify the *effectiveness* of technologies and processes (internal controls) that are put in place to assure the integrity of financial reports.

Complying with Section 404 means looking into conditions where sensitive corporate data might be accessible, processed, or stored. The Statement on Auditing Standards (SAS) 70 is found useful in meeting these requirements. A SAS 70 is an auditing standard developed by the American Institute of Certified Public Accountants for service organizations. SAS 70 prescribes methods for an auditor to examine control activities. Two types of SAS 70 audits exist. A Type 1 audit focuses on general controls at a snapshot in time and doesn't include testing by auditors. A Type 2 audit, which can be more appropriate for SOX compliance, looks at conditions over a prolonged period of time and prescribes that auditors perform testing to verify the effectiveness of controls.

9

Operations Security Controls in Action

The Achilles' heel of many organizations is a failure to pay close and ongoing attention to operations security. The following section provides more details on specific areas of operations used as protection against this Achilles' heel. It will emphasize the principles needed for secure operations of data center assets. Without a robust set of controls, it is easy to undermine expensive security measures. This may be because of poor documentation, old user accounts, conflicting software versions or products, or poor control over maintenance of default accounts that come preloaded on new computer systems.

To ensure operations security, the individuals in charge of information security must keep a number of things in mind at all times, including these considerations:

- software support

- configuration and change management

- backups

- media controls

- documentation

- maintenance

- interdependencies

Each of these is discussed in more depth in the sections that follow.

Software Support

Software is the heart of an organization's computer operations, regardless of the size and complexity of the system. As such, it's essential that software functions correctly and is protected from corruption. Several elements of control are needed for software support.

One type of control within this category is limiting what software is used on a given system. If users or systems personnel can load and execute any software on any system, these systems become more vulnerable to viruses, worms, malware, unexpected software interactions, or software that may subvert or bypass security controls.

A second method of controlling software is to inspect or test software before it is loaded (e.g., to determine compatibility with custom applications or identify other unforeseen interactions). This applies to new software packages, upgrades, off-the-shelf products, and custom software. In addition to controlling the loading and execution of new software, organizations should be cautious with off-the-shelf or downloaded system utilities. Some of the system utilities are designed to compromise the integrity of operating systems or breach logical access controls.

Many organizations also include on their agendas a program to help assure that software is properly licensed. For example, an organization may audit systems for illegal copies of copyrighted software. This problem is primarily associated with PCs and local area networks (LANs) but can apply to any type of system.

Another element of software support is to assure that software is not modified without proper authorization. This involves protecting all software and backup copies. This is often accomplished using a combination of logical and physical access controls (see Chapter 8).

Configuration and Change Management

Configuration and change management, which is closely related to software support, tracks, and if needed, approves changes to the system. It normally addresses hardware, software, networking, documentation, and other changes and can be formal or informal. The primary security goal of configuration management is ensuring that users don't cause unintentional changes to the system that could diminish security. Some of the methods discussed under software support can be used to reach this goal; for example, inspecting and testing software changes and periodic review of software security controls and parameter settings in the software.

For networked systems, configuration management should include a consideration of external connections. Is the computer system connected to a network? What other systems are involved? To what systems are these other systems and organizations connected? Note that the security goal is to know what changes occur—you cannot manage what you do not know about!

A second security goal of configuration and change management is ensuring that changes to the system are reflected in up-to-date documentation, such as the contingency or continuity plan, as discussed in Chapter 6 (business continuity planning/disaster recovery planning). If the change is major, it may be necessary to reanalyze some or all of the system's security.

Backups

Support and operations personnel—and sometimes users—back up software and data. This function is critical to contingency planning. The frequency of backups will depend on how often data changes and the importance of those changes. Also, as a safety measure, it is useful to test the backup copies to ensure that they are actually usable. Finally, backups should be stored securely and preferably in a different site should there be an inability to access the building where the computing equipment is located.

Users of smaller systems are often responsible for their own backups. However, the reality is they do not always perform backups regularly or thoroughly. In some organizations, support personnel are charged with making backups periodically for smaller systems, either automatically (through server software) or manually (by visiting each machine).

Media Controls

Media controls include a variety of measures to provide physical and environmental protection and accountability for tapes, diskettes, CDs, Zip Disks, USB (Flash) drives, printouts, and other media. From a security perspective, media controls should be designed to prevent the loss of confidentiality, integrity, or availability of information, including data or software, when stored outside the system. This can include storage of information before it is input into the system and after it is output.

The extent of media control depends on many factors, including the type of data, the quantity of media, and the nature of the user environment. Physical and environmental protection is used to prevent unauthorized individuals from accessing media. It also protects against such factors as heat, cold, or harmful magnetic fields. When necessary, logging the use of individual media (e.g., a CD) provides detailed accountability—to hold authorized people responsible for their actions. Some of the common media controls are described in the sections below.

Marking Controlling media may require some form of marking or physical labeling. The labels can be used to identify media with special handling instructions, locate needed information, or to log media (e.g., with serial/control numbers or bar codes) to support accountability. Colored labels are often used to identify diskettes or tapes, and banner pages are used on printouts.

If labeling is used for special handling instructions, it is critical that people dealing with the labeled material are appropriately trained. The marking of PC input and output is generally the responsibility of the user, not the system support staff. Marking backup diskettes can help prevent them from being accidentally overwritten.

Logging Logging media supports accountability. Logs can include control numbers (or other tracking data), the times and dates of transfers, names and signatures of individuals involved, and other relevant information. Periodic spot checks or audits may be conducted to determine that no controlled items have been lost and that all are in the custody of individuals named in control logs. Automated media tracking systems may be helpful for maintaining inventories of tape and disk libraries.

Integrity Verification When electronically stored information is read into a computer system, it may be necessary to determine whether it has been read correctly or subjected to any modification. The integrity of electronic information can be verified using error detection and correction or, if intentional modifications are a threat, cryptographic-based technologies. In addition, the integrity of backup tapes or other media should be tested periodically so there are no surprises when it's time to rely on them to restore normal operations.

Physical Access Protection Media can be stolen, destroyed, replaced with a look-alike copy, or lost. Physical access controls that limit these problems include locked doors, desks, file cabinets, or safes. If the media requires protection at all times, it may be necessary to actually output data to the media in a secure location (e.g., printing to a printer in a locked room instead of to a general-purpose printer in a common area).

Physical protection of media should be extended to backup copies stored offsite. These offsite backup copies should generally be accorded an equivalent level of protection as media containing the same information stored onsite. Equivalent protection does not mean that the security measures need to be exactly the same. The controls at the off-site location are quite likely to be different from the controls at the regular site, but adequate controls must be present to preserve the integrity of media or systems used at off-site facilities.

Environmental Protection Magnetic media, such as diskettes or magnetic tape, require environmental protection, because they are sensitive to temperature, liquids, magnetism, smoke, and dust. Other media, such as paper and optical storage, may have different sensitivities to environmental factors.

Transmittal Media control may be transferred both within the organization and to outside elements. Possibilities for securing such transmittal include sealed and marked envelopes, authorized messenger or courier, or U.S. certified or registered mail.

Disposition When media is disposed of, it may be important to ensure that information is not improperly disclosed. This applies both to media that is external to a computer system (such as Zip Disks or diskettes) and to media inside a computer system, such as a hard disk. People often throw away old media, believing that erasing the files has made the data unretrievable. In reality, however, erasing a file simply removes the pointer to that file. The pointer tells the computer where the file is physically stored. Without this pointer, the files will not appear on a directory listing. This does not mean that the file was removed. Commonly available utility programs can easily retrieve information that is presumed deleted.

To prevent the threats from recovering information from disposed media, we turn to the technique of permanently removing information from media, called *sanitization*. Three techniques are commonly used for media sanitization:

- overwriting
- degaussing
- destruction

Overwriting is an effective method for clearing data from magnetic media. As the name implies, overwriting uses a program to write data (1s, 0s, or a combination) onto the media. Common practice is to overwrite the media three times. Overwriting should not be confused with merely deleting the pointer to a file, which typically happens when a delete command is used (see above).

Degaussing is a method to magnetically erase data from magnetic media. Two types of degausser exist: strong permanent magnets and electric degaussers.

The final, and the only sure method of sanitization, is destruction of the media by shredding or burning.

Documentation

Although it's the bane of most developers and IT professionals due to extra work involved, documentation of all aspects of computer support and operations is important to ensure continuity and consistency. Formalizing operational practices and procedures with sufficient detail helps to eliminate security lapses and oversights. It also gives new personnel sufficiently detailed instructions and provides a quality assurance function to help ensure that operations will be performed correctly and efficiently.

The security of a system also needs to be documented. This includes many types of documentation, such as security plans, contingency plans, risk analyses, and security policies and procedures. Much of this information, particularly risk and threat analyses, has to be protected against unauthorized disclosure. Security documentation also needs to be both current and accessible. Accessibility should take special factors into account (such as the need to find the contingency plan during a disaster).

Security documentation should be designed to fulfill the needs of the different types of people who use it. For this reason, many organizations separate documentation into policy and procedures. A security procedures manual should be written to inform various system users how to do their jobs securely. A security procedures manual for systems operations and support staff may address a wide variety of technical and operational concerns in considerable detail.

Maintenance

System maintenance requires either physical or logical access to the system. Support and operations staff, hardware or software vendors, or third-party service providers may maintain a system. Maintenance may be performed on site or it may be necessary to move equipment to a repair site. Maintenance may also be performed remotely via communications connections. If someone who does not normally have access to the system performs maintenance, security vulnerability is introduced.

In some circumstances, it may be necessary to take additional precautions, such as conducting background investigations of service personnel. Supervision of maintenance personnel may prevent some problems, such as "snooping around" the physical area. However, once someone has access to the system, the potential damage done through the maintenance process is very difficult to prevent.

Many computer systems provide default maintenance accounts. These special log-in accounts are normally preconfigured at the factory with preset, widely known passwords. One of the most common methods hackers use to break into systems is through maintenance accounts that still have factory-set or easily guessed passwords. It is critical to change these passwords or otherwise disable the accounts until they are needed. Procedures should be developed to ensure that only authorized maintenance personnel can use these accounts. If the account is to be used remotely, authentication of the maintenance provider can be performed using call-back confirmation. This helps ensure that remote diagnostic activities actually originate from an established telephone number at the vendor's site.

Other techniques can also help, including encryption and decryption of diagnostic communications, and strong identification and authentication techniques (such as tokens; see Chapter 10). Larger systems may have diagnostic ports. In addition, manufacturers of larger systems and third-party providers may offer more diagnostic and support services. It is critical to ensure that these ports are used only by authorized personnel and cannot be accessed by hackers.

Interdependencies

Support and operations components coexist in most computer security controls. These components are

- **Personnel:** Most support and operations staff have special access to the system. Some organizations conduct background checks on individuals filling these positions to screen out possibly untrustworthy individuals (see Chapter 4).

- **Incident handling:** Support and operations may include an organization's incident-handling staff. Even if they are separate organizations, they need to work together to recognize and respond to incidents (see Chapter 6).

- **Contingency planning:** Support and operations normally provides technical input to contingency planning and carries out the activities of making backups, updating documentation, and practicing responses to contingencies (see Chapter 6).

- **Security awareness, training, and education:** Support and operations staff should be trained in security procedures and be aware of the importance of security. In addition, they provide technical expertise needed to teach users how to secure their systems (see Chapter 4).

- **Physical and environmental:** Support and operations staff often control the immediate physical area around the computer system (see Chapter 8).

- **Technical controls:** The technical controls are installed, maintained, and used by support and operations staff. They create the user accounts, add users to access control lists, review audit logs for unusual activity, control bulk encryption over telecommunications links, and perform the countless operational tasks needed to use technical controls effectively. In addition, support and operations staff provide needed input to the selection of controls based on their knowledge of system capabilities and operational constraints.

- **Assurance:** Support and operations staff ensure that changes to a system do not introduce security vulnerabilities by using assurance methods to evaluate or test the changes and their effect on the system. Operational assurance is normally performed by support and operations staff (see Chapter 5).

Paying close attention to these operations controls helps in assuring overall secure operations and keeping auditors at bay as they review the data center's operation—which they often do in large organizations.

Summary

Operations security clarifies the controls needed to assure secure data center operations. It covers processes concerning hardware, media, software, and the operations staff who typically possess elevated privileges to maintain data center and computer program operations. The principle of least privilege, which limits operators' access rights or privileges, is essential to prevent abuses. A clear separation of duties is necessary to prevent abuses at a transaction or business process level. Even if process and human controls in data center operations are firmly in place and operating as intended, controls ensuring the maintenance of the operation must also be present and operating successfully.

Test Your Skills

MULTIPLE CHOICE QUESTIONS

1. Operations security seeks to primarily protect against which of the following?

    A. object reuse

    B. facility disaster

    C. compromising emanations

    D. asset threats

2. Which operations security control prevents unauthorized intruders from internally or externally accessing the system and lowers the amount and impact of unintentional errors that are entering the system?

    A. detective controls

    B. preventative controls

    C. corrective controls

    D. directive controls

3. What is the main objective of separation of duties?

    A. to prevent employees from disclosing sensitive information

    B. to ensure access controls are in place

    C. to ensure that no single individual can compromise a system

    D. to ensure that audit trails are not tampered with

4. It is a violation of the "separation of duties" principle when the security systems software is accessed by which individual?

    A. security administrator

    B. security analyst

    C. systems auditor

    D. systems programmer

5. What security procedure forces collusion between two operators of different categories to have access to unauthorized data?

    A. enforcing regular password changes

    B. management monitoring of audit logs

    C. limiting the specific accesses of operations personnel

    D. job rotation of people through different assignments

9

6. Intrusion response is a:

A. preventive control.

B. detective control.

C. monitoring control.

D. reactive control.

7. Which of the following are functions that are compatible in a properly separated environment?

A. security administration and software security testing activity

B. security administration and data entry

C. security administration and application programming

D. application programming and data entry

8. If a programmer is restricted from updating and modifying production software, what is this an example of?

A. rotation of duties

B. least privilege

C. separation of duties

D. personnel security

9. What is the most effective means of determining how controls are functioning within an operating system?

A. interview with computer operator

B. review of software control features and/or parameters

C. review of operating system manual

D. interview with product vendor

10. Which of the following is not concerned with configuration management?

A. hardware

B. software

C. documentation

D. They all are concerned with configuration management.

11. When backing up an application system's data, which of the following is a key question to be answered first?

A. when to make backups

B. where to keep backups

C. what records to backup

D. how to store backups

12. Operations security requires the implementation of physical security to control which of the following?

    A. unauthorized personnel access

    B. incoming hardware

    C. contingency conditions

    D. evacuation procedures

13. Which of the following is the *best* way to handle obsolete magnetic tapes before disposing of them?

    A. overwriting the tapes

    B. initializing the tape labels

    C. erasing the tapes

    D. degaussing the tapes

14. Which of the following is *not* a media viability control used to protect the feasibility of data storage media?

    A. clearing

    B. marking

    C. handling

    D. storage

15. What is the most secure way to dispose of information on a CD-ROM?

    A. sanitizing

    B. physical damage

    C. degaussing

    D. physical destruction

9

EXERCISES

Exercise 9.1: Separation of Duties

1. Construct a list of benefits for proper separation of duties in data center operations.

2. What threats are eliminated with a proper separation of duties?

3. What does separating duties force people who wish to abuse their privilege to do?

Exercise 9.2: Touring a Data Center

1. Arrange for a tour of your school's or employer's data center.

2. What controls over data center personnel can you identify?

3. Are there controls that you would expect to be there but are not?

Exercise 9.3: The Need for Current Backups

1. Why are current backups important?

2. Outline a recommendation for work-at-home users with respect to their backup habits and practices.

Exercise 9.4: Configuration and Change Control

1. Why is configuration and change management important?

2. What threats are mitigated through effective change management?

3. What are some of the activities you would expect to see in the process?

PROJECTS

Project 9.1: Designing Data Center Personnel Controls

1. Create a fictitious company or organization that requires a robust data center and operations.

2. Describe the data center and its operations schedule and personnel.

3. What roles are present?

4. What operations controls would you ensure are operating correctly?

Project 9.2: Sanitizing Media

Suggest some ways to erase the contents of these types of media so that no data can be recovered.

1. CD-ROMs

2. Zip Disks

3. Flash (USB) or thumb drives

4. Floppy diskettes

5. Magnetic tape cartridges

6. PC hard drives

You may find the article "Reminiscing about Remanence: Electronic Media Clearing and Transfer" **(https://infosec.navy.mil/ps/?t=main/main.tag&bc= main/tip21.html)** useful.

Project 9.3: Examples of Controls

1. List some preventative controls that you might expect to see in a data center.

2. List some detective controls that you might expect to see in a data center.

3. List some corrective or recovery controls that you might expect to see in a data center.

4. List some deterrent controls that you might expect to see in a data center.

5. List some application-level controls that you might expect to see in a data center.

6. List some transaction-level controls that you might expect to see in a data center.

Case Study

Section 404 of the Sarbanes-Oxley Act is an emphasis in most public corporations and is causing lots of confusion and wasted efforts as corporate personnel try to interpret the requirements and define controls to meet them. Your CIO has asked you to prepare a presentation to the IT executive team on what specific controls should be implemented in your organization.

Using an Internet search, what recommendations would you list? How would you prioritize these recommendations? How would you secure the funding within your organization that's necessary to implement the recommendations?

Chapter | 10

Access Control Systems and Methodology

Chapter Objectives

After reading this chapter and completing the exercises, you will be able to do the following:

- Apply access control techniques to meet confidentiality and integrity goals.
- Implement the major terms and concepts related to access control and relate them to system security.
- Apply discretionary access controls (DAC) and mandatory access controls (MAC) techniques as appropriate.
- Choose effective passwords and avoid password limitations.
- Implement password alternatives including smart cards, password tokens, and other multifactor techniques.
- Apply the goals of single sign-on concepts to business and common users.
- Use the techniques described to control remote user access.

Introduction

Access controls are a collection of mechanisms that work together to create security architecture to protect the assets of an information system. One of the goals of access control is personal accountability, which is the mechanism that proves someone performed a computer activity at a specific point in time.

This chapter will cover terminology and principles of *authentication* that are used in the Access Control Systems and Methodology domain, along with some of the more popular techniques and protocols used in commercial software to control access.

It will also cover single sign-on techniques and the methods commonly used to permit remote access to corporate and back-office systems (office networks and servers that front-office personnel access to do their jobs).

Terms and Concepts

Access control is the heart of an information technology (IT) security system and is needed to meet the major objectives of InfoSec: confidentiality and integrity.

There are a number of concepts and terms you need to be familiar with to gain an appreciation for access control needs and the techniques for meeting these needs. These terms are discussed in the following sections.

Identification

Identification credentials uniquely identify the users of an information system. Typically, identification equates to a user's offline identity through his or her name, initials, e-mail address, or a meaningless string of characters. Think of identification credentials in terms of how you identify yourself in the offline world: name, social security number, student ID number.

Authentication

Authentication credentials permit the system to verify one's identification credential. Authenticating yourself to a system tells it the information you have established to prove that you are who you say you are. Most often, this is a simple password that you set up when you receive the privilege to access a system. You may receive an assigned password initially with the requirement that you must reset it to something more personal—something that only you can remember. Offline, your picture on your credential (license, credit card, and so forth) allows the world to check the legitimacy of your identification claim. Your photo authenticates your identity. Another common authentication of your identity is your signature. If your signature matches the signature on your credential, the recipient can be reasonably assured that you are who your ID claims you are.

Least Privilege (Need-to-Know)

The principle of *least privilege* is the predominant strategy to assure confidentiality. The objective is to give people the least amount of access to a system that is needed to perform the job they're doing. The need-to-know dictates the privilege (authority) to perform a transaction or access a resource (system, data, and so forth). The military has a strict methodology to implement the concepts of need-to-know through assigning sensitivity labels (see Chapter 5) to stored information and clearance levels to personnel, but access is granted only when the subject also has the "need-to-know"—not all users (subjects) with Top Secret clearances can gain access to all Top Secret information.

Information Owner

An information owner is one who maintains overall responsibility for the information within an information system. In the corporate world, it may be a department head or a division executive. In the academic world, it might be a dean of records or it may be a university president. Information owners can delegate the day-to-day work to a subordinate or to an information technology department, but they cannot delegate the overall responsibility for the information and the system that maintains it. The information owner must be the one to make the decisions about who uses the system and how to recover the system in the event of a disaster (see Chapter 6).

Discretionary Access Control

The principle of discretionary access control (DAC) dictates that the information owner is the one who decides who gets to access the system(s). This is how most corporate systems operate. DAC authority may be delegated to others who then are responsible for user setup, revocation, and changes (department moves, promotions, and so forth). Most of the common operating systems on the market today (Windows, Macintosh, Unix, Novell's Netware, and so forth) rely on DAC principles for access and operation.

Access Control Lists

10

An access control list (ACL) is simply a list or a file of users who are given the privilege of access to a system or a resource (database, and so forth). Within the file is a user ID and an associated privilege or set of privileges for that user and that resource. The privileges are typically Read, Write, Update, Execute, Delete, or Rename. A system using ACLs to protect data files might encode the permissions as shown in Table 10.1.

TABLE 10.1 Example users and permissions.

Filename	User ID	Permissions
ABC.dat	User01	RW
ABC.dat	User02	R
ABC.dat	Admin1	RWD

Mandatory Access Control

In a system that uses mandatory access control (MAC; also called nondiscretionary access control), the system decides who gains access to information based on the concepts of *subjects*, *objects*, and *labels*, as defined below. MAC is most often seen in military and governmental systems and is rarely seen in the commercial world. In a MAC environment, objects (including data) are labeled with a classification (e.g. Secret, Top Secret, and so forth), and subjects, or users, are cleared to that class of access.

- **Subjects:** The people or other systems that are granted a clearance to access an object within the information system.

- **Objects:** The elements within the information system that are being protected from use or access.

- **Labels:** The mechanism that binds objects to subjects. A subject's clearance permits access to an object based on the labeled security protection assigned to that object. For example, only those who are cleared to access Secret objects may access those objects labeled Secret or less than Secret, provided that they also possess the need-to-know. Those who are cleared for Top Secret may access objects labeled Top Secret and objects with a lower classification label.

Role-Based Access Control

Role-based access control (RBAC) groups users with a common access need. You can assign a role for a group of users who perform the same job functions and require similar access to resources. Role-based controls simplify the job of granting and revoking access by simply assigning users to a group, and then assigning rights to the group for access control purposes. This is especially helpful where there is a high rate of employee turnover or frequent changes in employee roles.

Organizations using RBAC report significant reductions in time over conventional user-based access control systems for assigning privileges to new users and improved abilities to change, modify, and terminate user privileges (see **http://infosecuritymag.techtarget.com/articles/april01/cover.shtml**). "On average, when calculating the number of times these tasks are performed on a daily basis times the number of employees in an organization, a RBAC system could save an organization 7.01 minutes per employee, per year in administration functions. Annual cost savings range from $6,924 a year for organizations with 1,000 employees to $692,471 for organizations with 100,000 employees." RBAC methods are most appropriate where there is high turnover of employees and/or frequent movements between job roles. RBAC is also useful for rapid setup (provisioning of access rights) and can improve productivity and efficiencies.

Cost savings are extended when considering reductions in employee downtime because of waiting for access controls credentials in non-RBAC based systems. When new and transitioning employees can receive their system privileges faster through a RBAC system, their productivity is increased. Annual productivity cost savings yielded by a RBAC system ranges from $75,000 for organizations of 1,000 employees to $7.4 million for organizations of 100,000 employees.

IN PRACTICE: Classification and Clearances in Military Security

A security clearance investigation is an inquiry into an individual's loyalty, character, trustworthiness, and reliability to ensure eligibility for access to national security secrets. All investigations consist of a national records and credit check; some investigations also include interviews with individuals who know the candidate as well as the candidate herself.

In a military security model, information is ranked in a hierarchy from Unclassified to Confidential to Secret and finally to Top Secret. The principle of least privilege also applies; a subject has access to the fewest objects needed to perform her job duties successfully. The government compartmentalizes information to enforce the need-to-know principle and may spread it over several compartments. An indication of a certain level of trust is established by a security clearance classification. A subject can access an object only if she holds a clearance level that is at least as high as that of the information.

Following is a definition of the U.S. government classification labels (see **www.navysecurity.navy.mil/ocadecis.htm**):

- **Confidential:** Unauthorized disclosure of information may damage national security.
- **Secret:** Unauthorized disclosure of information may seriously damage national security.
- **Top Secret:** Unauthorized disclosure of information may cause *exceptionally* grave damage to national security.

Some classified information is so sensitive that even the extra protection measures applied to Top Secret information are not sufficient. This information is known as sensitive compartmented information (SCI) or special access programs (SAP). You need special SCI access, or SAP approval, to be given access to this information.

"For Official Use Only" is not a security classification. It is used to protect information covered under the Privacy Act and other sensitive data.

10

Principles of Authentication

The idea of authentication is that only the legitimate user possesses the secret information needed to prove to a system that she has the right to use a specific user ID. These secrets are commonly passwords, but history has shown that passwords are problematic.

The Problems with Passwords

Sometimes, passwords cause more problems than they solve. It is often said in the security field that people are the weakest link in the security chain. Because people are responsible for managing their passwords, there are inherent problems.

- **Passwords can be insecure:** Given the choice, people will choose easily remembered and easily guessed passwords such as names of relatives, pets, phone numbers, birthdays, hobbies, and other similar items.

- **Passwords are easily broken:** Free and widely available programs are available on the Internet to break the security afforded by passwords on most of the commonly used systems. The programs use dictionary attacks. A dictionary attack involves rapidly cycling through words, phrases, and common permutations of words and phrases to match a password and record it for someone to exploit at some future point.

- **Passwords are inconvenient:** In an attempt to improve security, organizations often issue users computer-generated passwords that are difficult if not impossible to remember. Rather than try to remember them, users will often write them down and put them where they can see them, like on a Post-it Note attached to a monitor, or on an index

---

IN PRACTICE: Password Cracking Tools

Password attack programs, such as crack, PWDUMP, John the Ripper, and NTCrack, are used to break the marginal protection afforded by weak UNIX, NetWare, and Microsoft Windows passwords. Dictionary and "brute-force attacks" (trying all possibilities) are possible because users tend to choose easily guessed passwords!

You can find more information about password attacks and links to tools and more in the Security Focus article "Password Crackers—Ensuring the Security of Your Password" (see **www.securityfocus.com/infocus/1192**).

card taped to the bottom of a keyboard. Clearly, this compromises the security of the system.

■ **Passwords are repudiable:** Unlike a written signature, when a transaction involves only a password, there is no real proof as to the identity of the individual that made the transaction. Repudiation is the act of denying participation in a transaction or system access. There's no way to prove that the user did not share his or her ID and password with someone else or that someone other than the user stumbled upon or cracked the user's password and logged on pretending to be the authorized user. Later in the chapter, you'll see a few alternatives to passwords alone that help information owners gain confidence that users are legitimate.

FYI: Creating Better Passwords

Good passwords are easy to remember and hard to crack using computerized password-cracking tools. The best way to create passwords that fulfill both criteria is to use two or more small and unrelated words or phonemes, ideally with a special character or number. Good examples might include *pa55w0rd* or *!l0g*me*1n*.

Don't use:

■ Common names, date of birth, spouse name, phone number, pet name, and so forth.

■ Words found in dictionaries.

■ "Password" as a password.

■ System default passwords (administrator, field-support, and so forth).

10

Passwords are an example of single-factor authentication, which is simply something that someone knows that is used to gain access to a system with no further requirements for proving identity.

Multifactor Authentication

It's possible to add more sophistication to authenticating users than passwords alone. With two or three factors (*multifactor authentication*) to authenticate, an information owner can gain confidence that users who access their systems are indeed authorized to access their systems. This is accomplished by adding more controls and/or devices to the password authentication process.

Two-Factor Authentication With a two-factor authentication system, a user has a physical device (a card, a token, a smart card, and so forth) that contains his or her credentials, protected by a personal identification number (PIN) or a password that the user keeps secret. This condition is described as *something you have + something you know* (SYH/SYK). An example of this is your debit card and PIN used to access an automated teller machine (ATM) at your bank. The card identifies you as the account holder and the PIN authenticates you to the device. Because these PINs are usually only 4 characters long and usually only numbers, the number of possibilities (entropy) of the system is 10,000 (0000 to 9999). Because a brute-force attack will eventually hit the right PIN, the ATM permits only three tries before it retains the card and notes the attempted breach of your account, forcing the user to contact the bank before the ATM privilege is restored.

FYI: What's a Password Token?

An example of two-factor authentication is a password token. A password **token** is a mechanism that generates passwords that change every minute or so. These devices are protected by a password so that when they're in use, a user is challenged to provide the one-time-password (OTP) displayed on the device at that moment in time as the *"dynamic"* password + *the password only the user knows* (*static password* to prove the device holder is the authorized user of the device). The mechanism behind these devices employs secret-key cryptography (discussed in Chapter 11) that encrypts and decrypts a time stamp that is unique each time the device is used. You'll learn more about these devices in the section *Remote User Access and Authentication* on page 219.

Three-Factor Authentication In a three-factor system, unique information related to the user is added to the two-factor authentication process. This unique information may be a biometric (fingerprint, retinal scan, and so forth) needed for authentication. These systems are common for physical access to secured areas and can be replicated for computer or logical access. The three-factor mechanism is described as *something you have + something you know + something you are* (SYH/SYK/SYA). An example of how this might be used is a person trying to access a data center door where she would be required to swipe a card (e.g., a badge), enter a PIN on a keypad to prove that she's the owner of the badge, and offer a fingerprint that proves that she is the person assigned the badge and PIN.

Biometrics

Biometric methods of identification work by measuring unique human characteristics as a way to confirm identity, for example, fingerprint recognition, iris or retinal scanning, dynamic signature verification, and face recognition. Some common biometric techniques in use today include

- Fingerprint recognition
- Signature dynamics
- Iris scanning
- Retina scanning
- Voice prints
- Face recognition

The most common biometric in use is fingerprint recognition. Some of the advantages of fingerprints include

- Fingerprints can't be lent out like a physical key or token and can't be forgotten like a password.
- Fingerprints are a good compromise between ease of use, cost, and accuracy.
- Fingerprints contain enough inherent variability to enable unique identification even in very large (millions of records) databases.
- Fingerprints last virtually forever or at least until some extraordinary circumstance prevents their use (amputation, dismemberment, and so forth).
- Fingerprints make network login and authentication effortless.

Some of the practical applications for biometric identification/authentication include

- Network access control

10

- Tracking staff time and attendance
- Authorizing financial transactions
- Distributing government benefits (Social Security, public assistance, and so forth)
- Verifying identities at point of sale
- Using in conjunction with ATM, credit or smart cards
- Controlling physical access to office buildings or homes
- Protecting personal property
- Preventing kidnapping in schools, play areas, and other locations
- Protecting children from fatal gun accidents
- Voting, passports, visas, and immigration

FYI: Fingerprint Readers

As of mid-2005, fingerprint readers are showing up as standard equipment on laptop computers and some corporate desktop computers.

You can view an online presentation of how IBM incorporates a fingerprint reader into ThinkPad laptops at **www.ibm .com/pc/us/thinkpad/3dtours/fingerprint/56/index. html**.

Single Sign-On

All the methods to authenticate described in this chapter assume that every system a user needs access to requires a unique ID and password, thus requiring the user to maintain a number of ID/password pairs. Internet sites exacerbate this problem by requiring users to register and create a user ID and password. To simplify this, a single sign-on (SSO) system could be implemented. In an SSO system, users have one password for all corporate and back-office systems and applications that they need in order to perform their jobs. That way, one consistent password can be remembered and used, thus increasing the security of the overall system of access controls. Although this goal sounds reasonable, in practice it's quite difficult to implement.

One common approach to managing IDs and passwords is to create a password or *PIN vault*. These programs use secure methods to locally store IDs and passwords that are protected by a master password that unlocks the vault when it's needed. A free, open-source version of this concept, developed by Bruce Schneier, principal of Counterpane Inc., is available from Source-forge.com and is called Password Safe. You can download a copy of it from **http://sourceforge.net/projects/passwordsafe/**.

Some of the mechanisms used to implement single sign-on include Kerberos (developed at MIT and described below), proprietary mechanisms that mimic Kerberos, and custom-developed solutions that actually maintain the discrete IDs and passwords. These types of programs make it transparent to users that different IDs and passwords are being used for access to different systems.

It's also possible using technologies like those from the Liberty Alliance (discussed later in this chapter) and Microsoft's Passport technology to authenticate users across security domains, like those between two or more companies or organizations. To permit such capability, the companies may establish a federated service or set of services that permit specific people the right to perform specific activities in a pre-established context. Under such a system, it is possible to log in to one Web site and jump to another site within the federation.

Kerberos

Kerberos is a network authentication protocol named from the three-headed dog that guarded the entrance to Hades according to Greek mythology.

Kerberos is designed to provide authentication for client/server applications by using symmetric-key cryptography (described in Chapter 11). A free implementation of Kerberos is available from the Massachusetts Institute of Technology (MIT). Kerberos is available in many commercial products as well. The Kerberos protocol uses robust cryptography so that a client can prove his or her identity to a server (and vice versa) across an insecure network connection, such as the Internet. After a client and server have used Kerberos to prove their identities, they can also encrypt all of their communications to assure privacy and data integrity as they go about their business. Kerberos works by assigning a unique key, called a ticket, to each user who logs on to the network. The ticket is then embedded in messages that permit the receiver of the message (programs or other users) to positively identify the sender of the message.

When using Kerberos, the user only needs to log in once and each resource they wish to access will check their tickets for currency and validity when a request for access is made.

For a view of the Kerberos Ticket Exchange Process, see Figure 10.1.

Federated Identities

So far, you have learned about mechanisms to implement single sign-on to manage the multiple corporate IDs and passwords needed to perform a job. But what about users who require multiple identities and passwords to access e-commerce and Web sites for conducting personal business?

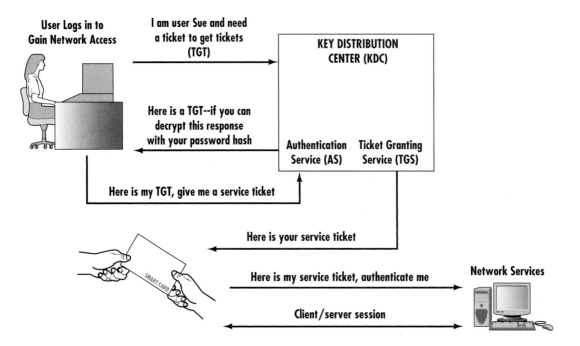

User Logs in to Gain Network Access

I am user Sue and need a ticket to get tickets (TGT)

KEY DISTRIBUTION CENTER (KDC)

Here is a TGT--if you can decrypt this response with your password hash

Authentication Service (AS) **Ticket Granting Service (TGS)**

Here is my TGT, give me a service ticket

Here is your service ticket

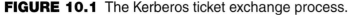

Here is my service ticket, authenticate me

Network Services

Client/server session

FIGURE 10.1 The Kerberos ticket exchange process.

Today's common user likely maintains a slew of IDs/passwords to access travel sites, online banking sites, credit card management sites, online brokerage sites, and so forth. All too often, users tire of trying to remember all these IDs and passwords and use the same IDs and passwords on each site, increasing their risk should a theft or compromise of their credentials occur. With modern problems like identity theft, e-scams, phishing, and offline social engineering attacks on consumers, users need to take extra precautions with their credentials to limit their risks.

An industry initiative that began at the end of 2001, called the Liberty Alliance, aims to increase the security of user credentials and simplify how businesses and individuals interact with one another.

The Liberty Alliance was developed to address the inefficiencies and complications of network identity management for businesses and consumers in today's world. There is a strong need for a federated network identity infrastructure that allows users to "link" elements of their identity between accounts without centrally storing all of their personal information. With a centralized store for all identities (e.g., using the MS Passport model), people are concerned about the potential for privacy breaches and are concerned about too much power being centralized into one specific company or organization. Federated identity reduces these concerns.

The benefits of a federated network identity infrastructure are many:

- Provides the end-user a far more satisfactory online experience, as well as new levels of personalization, security, and control over identity information.

- Enables the IT manager to more easily and securely provision accounts and provide access to the right resources.

- Enables businesses to create new relationships with each other and to realize business objectives faster, more securely, and at a lower cost.

Liberty Alliance operates through what it refers to as Expert Groups who are focused on one or more areas of identity management and authentication. These Expert Groups work together to collect business-related requirements and define them as protocol specifications to implement the required services and features. The structure of the Liberty Alliance Expert Groups can be found in Figure 10.3.

The Liberty Alliance's vision is one of a networked world in which individuals and businesses can more easily interact with one another while respecting the privacy and security of shared identity information. The Liberty Alliance serves as the premier open, nonproprietary industry-wide standards organization for federated network identity management and identity-based services. Its goals are to ensure operations across different computing platforms and operating systems, to support privacy, and to promote adoption of its specifications, guidelines, and best practices. The alliance began with 20 companies in 2001 and had grown to more than 200 companies by 2004. These companies represent a worldwide cross section of organizations, ranging from educational institutions and government organizations, to service providers and financial institutions, to technology firms and wireless providers. Some of the companies that participate in the Liberty Alliance include

- Computer Associates
- Verisign
- RSA Security
- Bank of America
- American Express Co.
- Fidelity Investments
- IBM Corporation
- Nokia
- NTT DoCoMo

10

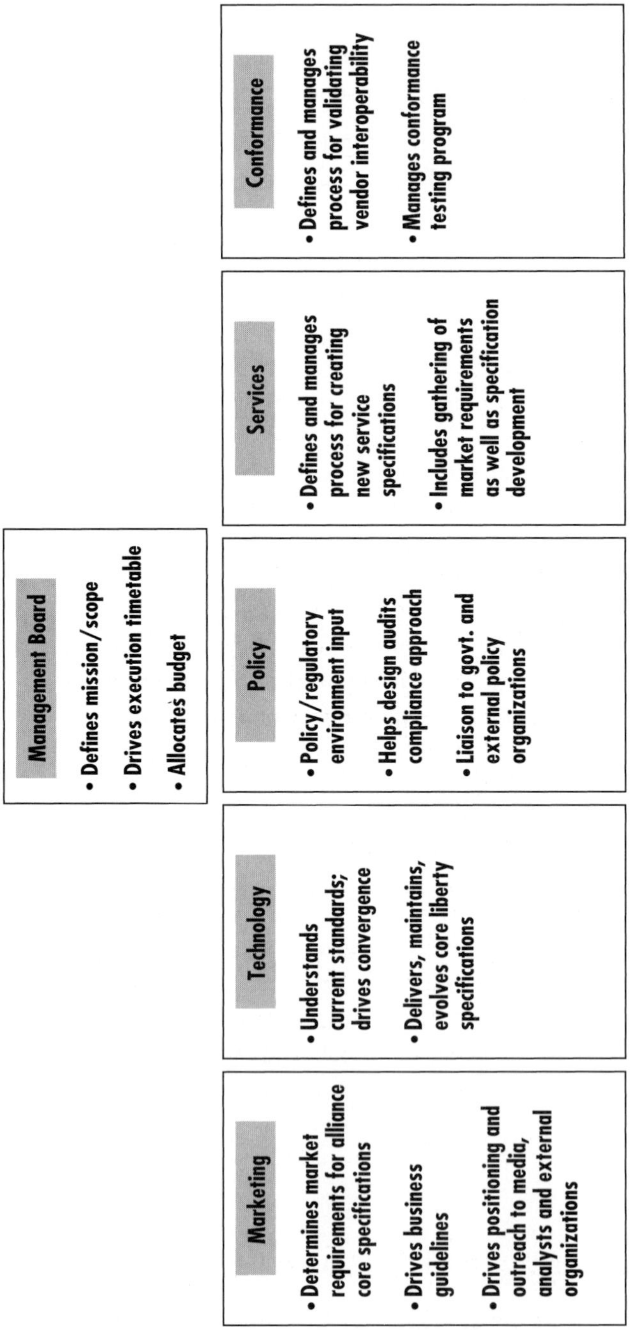

Management Board
- Defines mission/scope
- Drives execution timetable
- Allocates budget

Marketing
- Determines market requirements for alliance core specifications
- Drives business guidelines
- Drives positioning and outreach to media, analysts and external organizations

Technology
- Understands current standards; drives convergence
- Delivers, maintains, evolves core liberty specifications

Policy
- Policy/regulatory environment input
- Helps design audits compliance approach
- Liaison to govt. and external policy organizations

Services
- Defines and manages process for creating new service specifications
- Includes gathering of market requirements as well as specification development

Conformance
- Defines and manages process for validating vendor interoperability
- Manages conformance testing program

FIGURE 10.2 The Liberty Alliance Project Expert Groups structure.

- General Motors

- Gemplus

- Novell

- Hewlett-Packard

Memberships are categorized as:

- Mobile/Telephony

- Access Controls and Software

- Financial Services

- Government and Consumer

For more information about the Liberty Alliance, visit **www. projectliberty.org**.

FYI: What Is Phishing?

Internet scammers casting about for people's financial information have a new way to lure unsuspecting victims: They go "phishing."

Phishing is a high-tech scam that uses spam or pop-up messages to deceive you into disclosing your credit card numbers, bank account information, debit card PINs, Social Security number, passwords, or other sensitive information.

According to the Federal Trade Commission (FTC), phishers send an e-mail or pop-up message that claims to be from a business or organization that you deal with; for example, your Internet service provider (ISP), bank, online payment service, or even a government agency. The message usually says that you need to "update" or "validate" your account information. It might threaten some dire consequence if you don't respond. The message directs you to a Web site that looks just like a legitimate organization's site, but it isn't. The purpose of the bogus site is to trick you into divulging your personal information so the operators can steal your identity and run up bills or commit crimes in your name.

10

Remote User Access and Authentication

When working at remote locations or telecommuting from home, additional security problems are brought to bear because of the use of insecure networks (like the Internet) to create a connection to the corporate local area network (LAN). Addressing these problems requires additional access control mechanisms to protect both the LAN and user.

Remote Access Dial-In User Service

Remote Access Dial-In User Service (RADIUS) is a client/server protocol and software that enables remote access users to communicate with a central server to authenticate dial-in users and authorize their access to the requested system or service. For example, you may need to dial-up an external network to gain access for performing work, depositing a file, or picking up a file. The earliest versions of America Online (AOL) used RADIUS, or RADIUS-like technology, to authenticate legitimate AOL users.

RADIUS allows a company to maintain user profiles in a central database that all remote servers can share. RADIUS allows a company to set up a policy that can be applied at a single administered network point. Having a central service also means that it's easier to track usage for billing and for keeping network statistics. RADIUS is the *de facto* industry standard used by a number of network product companies and is in wide use throughout corporate networks.

Authenticating to a RADIUS server may require using an ID/password combination or, more often, a token or smart card for multifactor authentication.

Virtual Private Networks

A virtual private network (VPN) is another common means for remote users to access corporate networks. With a VPN, a user connects to the Internet via his or her ISP and initiates a connection to the protected network (often using a RADIUS server), creating a private tunnel between the end points that prevents eavesdropping or data modification. VPNs use strong cryptography to both authenticate senders and receivers of messages and to encrypt traffic so it's not vulnerable to a man-in-the-middle attack.

You'll find more details about VPNs in Chapter 12.

Summary

Access control is a central theme of information security. It is needed to meet the goals of confidentiality, integrity, and user accountability—essential for trust in an information system.

Access controls differentiate between identifying users of a system and authenticating them. This is done using discretionary means where an information owner decides who obtains access rights, mandatory means where the system decides access rights based on classifications and clearance, and role-based means that group people with a similar need for access together and tie access rights to the role people are assigned.

Passwords are the most common method that people use to authenticate their identities, but problems with passwords have led to the development of alternatives, such as tokens using one-time passwords and smart cards that use cryptography to prove a person's identity. Identification and authentication techniques sometimes use biometric information to add further confidence that users are legitimate when attempting physical or logical access to system resources.

Single sign-on and associated technologies and protocols aim to reduce the proliferation of IDs and passwords to better control the security of access control mechanisms both within and outside the organization. Industry alliances, such as the Liberty Alliance, are moving toward federated identities that permit single sign-on or reduced sign-on for e-commerce users.

Finally, remote access control technology, such as RADIUS and virtual private networks, permit travelers and work-at-home employees to access corporate networks without the need for expensive dial-up connections or additional hardware costs.

Test Your Skills

MULTIPLE CHOICE QUESTIONS

1. What is the term for the verification that the user's claimed identity is valid?

   A. authentication

   B. identification

   C. integrity

   D. confidentiality

2. Which access model is most appropriate for companies with a high employee turnover?

   A. role-based access control

   B. mandatory access control

   C. lattice-based access control

   D. discretionary access control

3. Identification and authentication are the keystones of most access control systems. Identification establishes:

   A. user accountability for the actions on the system.

   B. top management accountability for the actions on the system.

   C. IT department accountability for the actions of users on the system.

   D. authentication for actions on the system.

10

4. Controlling access to information systems and associated networks is necessary for the preservation of their

   A. authenticity confidentiality, and availability.

   B. confidentiality, integrity, and availability.

   C. integrity and availability.

   D. authenticity, confidentiality, integrity, and availability.

5. Which access control model is also called nondiscretionary access control?

   A. rule-based access control

   B. mandatory access control

   C. role-based access control

   D. label-based access control

6. An access control policy for a bank teller is an example of the implementation of which of the following?

   A. rule-based policy

   B. identity-based policy

   C. user-based policy

   D. role-based policy

7. What security model is dependent on security labels?

   A. discretionary access control

   B. label-based access control

   C. mandatory access control

   D. role-based access control

8. What can be defined as a table of subjects and objects indicating what actions individual subjects can take upon individual objects?

   A. a capacity table

   B. an access control list

   C. an access control matrix

   D. a capability table

9. Which of the following is the weakest authentication mechanism?

   A. pass-phrases

   B. passwords

   C. one-time passwords

   D. token devices

10. Which type of password provides maximum security because a new password is required for each new logon?

    A. one-time or dynamic password

    B. cognitive password

    C. static password

    D. pass-phrase

11. Which of the following would be the best password?

    A. golf001

    B. Elizabeth

    C. t1me4g0lf

    D. password

12. Tokens, smart cards, and biometric devices used for identification and authentication provide robust authentication of the individual by practicing which of the following principles?

    A. multiparty authentication

    B. two-factor authentication

    C. mandatory authentication

    D. discretionary authentication

13. Access control is the collection of mechanisms that permits managers of a system to exercise a directing or restraining influence over the behavior, use, and content of a system. It does not permit management to

    A. specify what users can do.

    B. specify which resources users can access.

    C. specify how to restrain hackers.

    D. specify what operations users can perform on a system.

14. The three classic ways of authenticating yourself to the computer security software are something you know, something you have, and something

    A. you need.

    B. you read.

    C. you are.

    D. you do.

10

15. The use of technologies such as fingerprint, retina, and iris scans to authenticate the individuals requesting access to resources is called

    A. micrometrics.

    B. macrometrics.

    C. biometrics.

    D. microbiometrics.

16. Which of the following addresses cumbersome situations where users need to log on multiple times to access different resources?

    A. single sign-on (SSO) systems

    B. dual sign-on (DSO) systems

    C. double sign-on (DSO) systems

    D. triple sign-on (TSO) systems

EXERCISES

Exercise 10.1: Access Controls and Confidentiality

1. How are access controls used to implement the security objective of confidentiality?

2. Determine what the features of a good access control system should include.

3. Can you determine the access control model that's found in Microsoft's Active Directory? (See **www.microsoft.com/windowsserver2003/ technologies/directory/activedirectory/default.mspx.**)

Exercise 10.2: Attacks on Passwords

1. Visit the Security Focus Web site to read the article "Password Crackers—Ensuring the Security of Your Password," found at **www.securityfocus.com/infocus/1192**.

2. Pay special attention to the section of the article with the heading, "Improving password quality."

3. Will reading this article change the way you establish and maintain passwords? What will you do differently?

Exercise 10.3: Biometrics and Privacy

People tend to resist biometrics as a method of identification because of their concerns that their privacy will be invaded or belief that the technology is too intrusive on their personal lives.

1. Research the Internet to determine some of the privacy problems related to biometrics.

2 Consider some of the mechanisms that could mitigate these problems and concerns.

3. Which method(s) of biometrics that would not meet with undue resistance from potential users would you recommend to a manager to replace password-based access controls?

Exercise 10.4: Single Sign-On Technologies in the Market

1. Visit one or more of the following single-sign-on product Web pages:

   - Single Sign-On in Windows 2000 Networks (**www.microsoft. com/technet/prodtechnol/windows2000serv/evaluate/feat func/nt2ksso.mspx**)

   - BMC Software Control SA (**www.bmc.com/products/products_ services_detail/0,,0_0_0_26,00.html**)

   - Netegrity SiteMinder (**www.netegrity.com/products/products_ SM_overview.cfm**)

2. Compare the differences between these single sign-on mechanisms.

3. Which product is most appealing to manage internal users throughout an enterprise? Which one would be most beneficial for Internet users?

Exercise 10.5: Phishing

1. Search the Internet for recent reported incidents on phishing.

2. Which organizations are the most frequent target of phishers?

3. What measures has this organization taken to protect their customers from phishing attacks?

10

PROJECTS

Project 10.1: Password Safe

1. On your home PC, download and install a copy of Password Safe from **http://sourceforge.net/projects/passwordsafe/.**

2. Load up your personal information for one or two of the sites you regularly visit while surfing the Internet.

3. Visit those sites and use Password Safe to supply your credentials to log in and fill out some of the information on forms.

4. What do you think of the experience in using this software? Is it easy to install and use? Is it easy to configure with your own IDs and passwords?

5. Would you consider using Password Safe for all your personal information management and security? Why or why not?

Project 10.2: Microsoft Passport

1. Visit the Microsoft Passport site at: **www.passport.net/ Consumer/default.asp?rollrs=11&lc=1033**.

2. Determine three advantages to Internet users from MS Passport.

3. Name some disadvantages of Passport.

4. Locate some sites that have signed on to use Passport for access control by their customers or users.

5. Compare the advantages and disadvantages of Passport with the Federated Identity Model from the Liberty Alliance Project (**www. projectliberty.org**).

Project 10.3: Smart Card Access Controls

1. Research the Internet for information about using smart cards for access controls.

2. Where are they being used most often?

3. What are some of the complications in implementing smart cards for network access?

4. Which access control model seems most appropriate for smart cards?

5. What changes to infrastructure would be necessary for an enterprise implementation of smart cards for PC access control?

▶▶ Case Study

The Mount Royal College in Calgary, Alberta, Canada, issues smart cards to students for identification, library access, food services, and laser printing. They have also established a complete support site for their program at: **www.mtroyal.ab.ca/ smartcard/**.

Visit their Web site and explore how they're using the card; then, using the information from this chapter on two-factor authentication, design a possible method whereby a university with a smart card infrastructure in place can add logical access to lab PCs and other equipment intended for student use.

10

Chapter  11

Cryptography

Chapter Objectives

After reading this chapter and completing the exercises, you will be able to do the following:

- Explain common terms used in the field of cryptography.
- Outline what mechanisms constitute a strong cryptosystem.
- Demonstrate how to encrypt and decrypt messages using the transposition method.
- Demonstrate how to encrypt messages using the substitution method.
- Support the role of cryptography in e-commerce systems.
- Explain the differences between symmetric and asymmetric cryptography.
- Outline the mechanisms used for digital signatures.
- Explain the purpose and uses of digital certificates.
- Evaluate commercial implementations of Public Private Key (PPK) cryptography.

Introduction

In the offline world, it's easy to ask someone for an ID to prove that they are who they claim to be. As a society, we've generally grown to trust photo IDs and written signatures as a way of verifying the legitimacy of certain rights, such as the right to use a credit card or drive a car.

In the online world, checking the same claims to access rights can only be performed through technology, primarily cryptography. Generally, this is accomplished by binding a person to a pair of cryptographic keys using tightly controlled and secure conditions. Once a trusted key issuance process is complete, these keys are used to keep messages private, authenticate the sender, and test the integrity of messages, achieving two of the objectives of security: confidentiality and integrity. Because most computer application-level security relies on cryptography, it's essential to have a strong foundational understanding of it.

Applying Cryptography to Information Systems

Applied cryptography—the science of secret writing—enables the storage and transfer of information in forms that reveal it only to those permitted to see it while hiding it from everyone else.

In the 20th century, international governments began to adopt the use of cryptography to protect their private and sensitive information and for communications purposes. Up until the past 25 years or so, governments and military organizations were the exclusive users of cryptography: securing private data and trying to crack everyone else's. The United States National Security Agency (NSA) is a large government agency devoted to developing and protecting robust cryptography to protect secrets. They also use their specialized skills in breaking cryptosystems to eavesdrop into foreign communications that are sent encrypted. Today, certain elements of cryptography are treated as munitions, and, as such, its uses and export are tightly controlled by various U.S. government agencies, including the NSA. United States encryption export policy rests on three principles: review of encryption products prior to sale, streamlined postexport reporting, and license review of certain exports and re-exports of strong encryption to foreign governments. As of December 2004, some controls have been relaxed and others clarified in a "Commercial Encryption Export Controls" fact sheet available at the U.S. Department of Commerce Web site (**www.bxa. doc.gov/Encryption/EncFactSheet12_02_04.htm**).

Since the 1970s, academic interest in cryptography has grown at a tremendous rate, and with the proliferation of research, private citizens have increasingly gained access to various cryptography techniques, permitting personal information protection and enabling the conduct of secure electronic transactions.

Although the U.S. government is not keen on carte blanche permission to permit the export or commercial accessibility to strong cryptography for nongovernment domestic and international uses, advancements in the field continue, primarily within academia. If the government continued to have its way, the National Security Agency would be the only user of strong cryptography, but in the Clinton administration, all that changed.

With the aid of supercomputers (i.e., massively parallel processors), communities of hackers who work together to try and crack the strongest cryptosystems, and the increasing sophistication of modern computer

> ## FYI: Encryption Controls Revised in 2000
>
> As of early 2000, any encryption devices (hardware) or software of any key length can now be exported under a license exception that may be granted after a technical review to any nongovernment end-user in any country *except for the seven state supporters of terrorism* (Cuba, Iran, Iraq, Libya, North Korea, Sudan, and Syria). Exports previously allowed only for a company's internal use can now be used for any activity, including communication with other firms, supply chains, and customers.
>
> A category of products called "Retail encryption commodities and software," defined in 2000, can be exported to any end user (except to those in the seven state supporters of terrorism). Retail encryption devices and software are those that are widely available and can be exported and re-exported to anyone (including any Internet and telecommunications service provider), and can be used to provide any product or service (e.g., e-commerce, client-server applications, or software subscriptions). The U.S. Department of Commerce Bureau of Export Administration (BXA) will determine which products qualify as retail through a review of their functionality, sales volume, and distribution methods. Products that are functionally equivalent to products classified as retail will also be considered retail.

technology, cryptography is becoming more tried and true, evolving into highly reliable and well-established practices.

Basic Terms and Concepts

Cryptography is a domain loaded with new terms and concepts. Following are some of the more common terms you're likely to encounter when studying the field of cryptology.

- A *cryptosystem* disguises messages, allowing only selected people to see through the disguise.

- *Cryptography* is the science (or art) of designing, building, and using cryptosystems.

- *Cryptanalysis* is the science (or art) of breaking a cryptosystem.

- *Cryptology* is the umbrella study of cryptography and cryptanalysis.

Cryptographers rely on two basic methods of disguising messages—*transposition*, where letters are rearranged into a different order, and *substitution*, where letters are replaced by other letters and/or symbols.

FYI: Codebooks

Cryptography, the art and science of secret codes, has evolved dramatically over the centuries, especially since World War II. For most of their history, codes have relied on sharing secrets between small groups of people who needed to communicate safely and privately. The shared secret might be a codebook that translated important words and phrases into short, nonsense words. This not only concealed a message's meaning but also made it shorter. Codebooks were popular among wealthy individuals and large companies during the days of the telegraph. Because one had to pay for each word in a telegram, a well-designed code could reduce telegraph costs. Private companies produced codebooks that they sold to anyone who asked for them. The most effective codebooks were custom-made to be shared among a restricted group of business associates, who maintained their privacy by keeping their codes secret.

In the days of the telegraph, business executives often had real worries about the secrecy of their telegrams. Unlike a telephone call, which travels automatically without human intervention, each telegram had to be keyed in by a telegraph operator at the sending office, transcribed by an operator at the receiving office, and occasionally transcribed by other operators along its route. Telegraph operators were not always paid well enough to resist bribery, so sensitive business information could occasionally find its way into competitors' hands. Secret telegraph codes gave businessmen confidence that their private traffic remained private.

Secrecy doesn't always guarantee safety, however. Mary, Queen of Scots, learned this lesson more than 400 years ago, when agents of Queen Elizabeth I unmasked a plot against her by Mary's supporters. Mary used a codebook to communicate with her associates, but Elizabeth's spies succeeded in deducing the codebook's contents by reading numerous coded messages, guessing their contents, and systematically testing the guesses by trying to decode other messages. Although Elizabeth's agents didn't break Mary's entire code, they figured out enough of it to identify and arrest the plotters. While in prison, the plotters revealed the rest of the code, and Mary's decoded letters helped convict her of high treason.

Mary's code was not sophisticated enough to resist a systematic attack, but its present-day analogues generally are. Modern codes, particularly those used in computers, generally consist of two separate parts: the coding procedure, called the algorithm, and the key, which tells the algorithm how to scramble a message. The algorithm might be public knowledge, but the key is always kept secret. In essence, the secrecy of encrypted data relies entirely on the secrecy of the key. Instead of worrying about how to keep the data confidential, you need only concern yourself with keeping the key itself secret.

Plaintext is the message that is passed through an encryption algorithm, or cipher, and becomes ***ciphertext***. When ciphertext is passed through a decryption algorithm, it becomes plaintext again.

An understanding of these basic terms will help you as you move forward in this chapter.

Strength of Cryptosystems

A strong cryptosystem is considered strong only until it's been cracked. Although that may sound like common sense, one can never *prove* that a cryptosystem is strong—all that can be done is to assure that certain properties are present within it. Each defeat of an attempt to crack a cryptosystem serves to strengthen the belief in its ability to secure. Similar to monetary currency, a cryptosystem has value because its users believe in its worth. Once that worth is proven to be unfounded, the cryptosystem collapses and no one relies on it anymore.

The most popular commercial cryptosystems found in software products have similar characteristics. Their algorithms are made readily available to the public (through published standards and public posting), and the strength of the algorithm rests in the keys used to encrypt and decrypt (in general, the longer the key, the better). The basic idea is to keep the keys a secret rather than keep the algorithm a secret. Many government cryptosystems are kept secret and are not intended for public or commercial use.

FYI: Random Number Requirements

Perfectly random numbers, thought to exist in nature, are impossible to achieve using deterministic devices such as computers. The best a computer can do is to generate pseudorandom numbers. Cryptography demands far more pseudorandomness than most other applications, such as computer games, for example. For a string of bits to be considered cryptographically random, it must be computationally infeasible to predict what the *n*th random bit will be when given full knowledge of the algorithm and the values of the bits already generated. Because computers are deterministic, at some point a random number generator becomes periodic (i.e., it begins to repeat). The challenge then is to build random number generators that won't predictably repeat values generated. Some of the pseudorandom number generators available today show randomness through 2 raised to the 256 power (2^{256}, a very large number), making them more suitable for use in cryptography than the kinds of random number generators built into programming languages, such as the random number generation function in C or C++ rnd().

11

Strong cryptosystems produce ciphertext that always appears random to standard statistical tests. They also resist all known attacks on cryptosystems and have been brutally tested to ensure their integrity. Those cryptosystems that have not been subjected to brutal testing are considered suspect.

IN PRACTICE: A Simple Transposition Encryption Example

Although a firm grasp of the actual mechanics of cryptosystems is not directly required to understand how they are used in securing systems, some understanding of the complexities involved helps one appreciate what is going on behind the curtain.

Using the transposition technique with a symmetric key (shared secret), we can take a look at how encryption and decryption might operate manually.

Assume the plaintext message you want to encrypt is

```
SECURITY BEGINS WITH YOU
```

You choose the word TEACUPS as your keyword and send it to your intended recipient using a secure channel other than the one you will use to send the message. This is for added security and to assure our recipient has the key when the ciphertext arrives.

Encrypt the message through the following steps:

1. Write the key horizontally as the heading for columns:

```
T   E   A   C   U   P   S
```

2. Assign numerical values to each letter based on the letter's order of appearance in the alphabet.

```
T   E   A   C   U   P   S
6   3   1   2   7   4   5
```

3. Align the plaintext message across each key/value column heading, skipping to the next line when the last column of the matrix is reached.

```
T   E   A   C   U   P   S
6   3   1   2   7   4   5
S   E   C   U   R   I   T
Y   B   E   G   I   N   S
W   I   T   H   Y   O   U
```

4. Read down along each column according to the ordinal value of the column to produce the ciphertext (A-1 is the first column, C-2 the second and so forth):

```
CET   UGH   EBI   INO   TSU   SYW   RIY
```

5. Send the ciphertext to the recipient using any channel desired. Because they already possess the shared secret, you don't need to worry about it getting into the wrong hands.

Upon receipt of the ciphertext, the recipient will decrypt it through the following steps:

1. Write the key horizontally as the heading for columns:

```
T   E   A   C   U   P   S
```

2. Assign numerical values to each letter based on the letter's order of appearance in the alphabet.

```
T   E   A   C   U   P   S
6   3   1   2   7   4   5
```

3. Transpose the ciphertext, three letters at a time, using the ordinal value of each column to determine its placement. Because A is column value 1, the first group of letters, CET, is written vertically under A-1. Group two belongs under C-2, and so forth:

```
T   E   A   C   U   P   S
6   3   1   2   7   4   5
S   E   C   U   R   I   T
Y   B   E   G   I   N   S
W   I   T   H   Y   O   U
```

4. Read the message horizontally to reveal the plaintext message:

```
SECURITY BEGINS WITH YOU
```

If the message had been longer, for example,

```
SECURITY BEGINS WITH EVERYONE AT HOME
```

the ciphertext groups would have consisted of four letters instead of three, growing with the length of the message. If this example had included the use of numbers or special characters, they would have to be treated separately and agree with their positional values in the alphabet; otherwise your algorithm would not work.

Even with a simple example like this, you can begin to see the protocol developed to make it work. Steps must be performed:

- in order
- cannot be skipped
- cannot be altered in any way

Cryptosystems Answer the Needs of Today's E-Commerce

Before you move on to specific implementations of data encryption and secure networks, it's important to understand that different situations call for different levels of security.

A college student sending an e-mail home to his parents for money is mainly concerned that the note reaches its intended destination and that no one tampers with the contents of the note. An internal corporate memo to all employees, on the other hand, might contain sensitive information that should not go beyond the company's intranet. The CEO assumes that when he sends the note, only the intended audience will read the note. Likewise, the employees assume that the note did indeed come from the president and no one else. No real authentication is performed because the company's e-mail system relies on the notion of trust. Each employee must have an ID and password to access the e-mail system, but beyond that, any guarantees of authenticity require implicit trust in the users of the system.

To ensure that electronic commerce is secure, however, requires an *implicit distrust* in users of the Internet and public networks. Most users are law-abiding citizens who use the network for legitimate purchases. They are who they say they are, and they enjoy the convenience that Internet shopping affords. However, the decentralized design of the Internet enhances the potential for an unscrupulous few to wreak havoc on the many. Electronic commerce can never be made too secure. And the bad press resulting from a security failure could destroy a business.

The Role of Keys in Cryptosystems

Keys (secrets) used for encryption and decryption come in two basic forms—symmetric and asymmetric—simply meaning either the same key is used to both encrypt and decrypt or a pair of keys is needed.

When the same key is used to both encrypt and decrypt messages, it's called **symmetric key** or **shared secret cryptography**. When different keys are used, it's called **asymmetric key cryptography**. The Data Encryption Standard (DES) uses the former technique, while RSA, named after its inventors—Rivest, Shamir, and Adelman—uses the latter technique. Pretty Good Privacy (PGP), which is discussed later in this chapter, is a public-domain cryptosystem that also uses asymmetric key cryptography.

Symmetric Keys When you use the same key to both encrypt and decrypt a message, it's called symmetric key cryptography and is the method used in the previous example. The most common form of symmetric key cryptography is the Data Encryption Standard. It was developed by IBM at the request of the U.S. government. DES was adopted as a Federal Information Processing Standard (FIPS) in 1976 for use with unclassified government communications between agencies. It uses 64 bits of data (8 bytes)

IN PRACTICE: A Simple Substitution Example

An even easier method of cryptography is the substitution cipher. The Caesar cipher uses simple letter substitution. It originated with the Greeks long before Caesar's time and first appeared in one of the earliest works on military science, *On the Defense of Fortified Places*, by Aeneas the Tactician, and, as Julius Caesar claimed in his *Gallic Wars*, was only subsequently applied to Roman military strategy.

According to history, Caesar wrote to Cicero and others in a cipher in which the plaintext letters were replaced by letters standing three places or rotated three places further down the alphabet.

On the Internet, the most popular example of a Caesar cipher is called ROT13 from "rotate alphabet 13 places" and can be found in most Internet Network News or Usenet (NNTP) groups. It is used to enclose the text in a wrapper that the reader must choose to open; for instance, to post things that might offend some readers.

This simple Caesar-cipher encryption replaces each English letter with the one 13 places forward or back along the alphabet, so that "The butler did it!" becomes "Gur ohgyre qvq vg!"

The following is an example of how to convert plaintext to ciphertext using ROT13.

1. Write down the alphabet, splitting it across two rows in the middle:

A	B	C	D	E	F	G	H	I	J	K	L	M
N	O	P	Q	R	S	T	U	V	W	X	Y	Z

2. With the plaintext message "THE BUTLER DID IT," substitute the letter above or below each letter in the sentence to come up with the ciphertext, so T becomes G, U becomes H, and so forth.

One major advantage of ROT13 over other Caesar rotation values is that it is self-inverse, so the table shown above can be used for encoding and decoding.

Computer-based cryptography, though far more robust than anything that could be accomplished by hand, uses the same approaches, if not the same algorithms as those illustrated here but with far more complexity and processing requirements.

11

with a 56-bit (7 byte) key within it. Triple DES (3DES) is identical but uses a double-length key (128 bits) that encrypts, then encrypts, then encrypts again (called "folding" in crypto-speak). Triple DES is commonly used by banks to protect your PIN number when you enter it on an ATM or Point Of Sale keypad (where you swipe your credit or debit card at the cash register). Your PIN is never stored by the bank as you know it: it's always stored in encrypted forms to prevent its use in the event of theft. If the ATM enciphers your PIN exactly as your bank stores it, then access is granted.

One of the most significant challenges of symmetric key cryptography lies in sharing keys prior to needing them. Asymmetric key cryptography helps out with this task.

Asymmetric Keys With asymmetric key cryptography, two keys are needed. A message encrypted using one key can only be decrypted using the other and vice versa. One of the keys is called a public key and the other is called a private key. Fundamental to operating properly, it must be assured that the private key *always* remains private and is never shared or copied from where it was generated.

Using asymmetric key cryptography, you share your public key with everyone you want to communicate with privately, but keep your private key a secret. Your private key essentially is your identity so that when someone can successfully decrypt a message you sent encrypted with your private key, they know that it could only have come from you if the decryption using the public key succeeds. That's the basis of asymmetric key or Public-Private Key (PPK) cryptography.

The two keys that compose a key pair are mathematically related, but neither can be derived from the other. Typically, the key lengths that are used with strong asymmetric key cryptography are 1024 bits long (128 bytes) and are meant to foil a brute-force attack on messages that are signed and encrypted using standard PPK applications.

PPK cryptography enables you to communicate over any open channel with high degrees of confidence and permits you to trust in these ways:

- **Authentication:** Messages you receive are from their advertised source.

- **Privacy:** Messages you send can be read only by their intended receiver(s).

- **Message integrity:** All messages sent and received arrive intact.

Putting the Pieces to Work

Now that you've begun to understand the principles of public and private key pairs, it's time to examine how PPK systems are used for authentication, privacy, and message integrity. To start, you need to be familiar with a computer programming technique called ***hashing***. A hash is a transformation of data into distilled forms that are unique to the data and is a one-way function. A one-way function is easy to do and next to impossible to undo. Think of how hamburger is made—whole chunks of meat are run through a grinder (easy to do), but once ground up, can never be reassembled into chunks of meat (hard to undo). With a computer program, a document is run through a one-way hashing formula to produce a small numeric value that's unique but easily repeatable for that exact stream of data. This process is also called digesting data or creating a message digest. The UNIX operating system employs this principle for storing passwords in the */etc/passwd* file.

Digesting Data

Several well-known digest-creation techniques, including the Secure Hashing Algorithm (SHA-1) and the Message Digest 5 (MD5) algorithm, are common. Using SHA-1, unique message digests (fingerprints) are computed such that the chances of two different messages computing to the same digest values are 1 in 10^{48}. After computing the message digest for your message, you'll encrypt it using your private key and append (attach) the encrypted message digest to your original message. This process is called *creating a digital signature* or *digitally signing* a message.

At this point, if you send your message to your recipient (who already holds a copy of your public key), he can "test" your signature to see if the message really came from you and arrived unaltered.

Here is how digital signing works: Because the digital signature can only be decrypted using your public key, your recipient knows that you created the digest because you never shared your private key with anyone else. Your recipient's software also uses the same hashing algorithm that you used to compute message digests, so he runs the message he received through it. His software then compares the newly calculated message digest to the one that he successfully decrypted from you. If they match, he's now also assured that the message he received is the same message that you sent without any alteration.

Think of digital signatures in a similar vein as notary public services. If you receive a notarized document, you have a high degree of assurance that the person who signed it is the person he or she claims to be—because we, as a society, trust notaries. Digital signatures actually enhance the process and security of communications. If I were to send you a nine-page document bearing a notary seal, you'd know it came from me, but you wouldn't know if the document was altered after the notary attested to my signature. With a digital signature, if even a single byte of data were changed, the message digest computes to a completely different value. If your recipient's comparison of the two digests doesn't match, the software will indicate that the message should not be trusted and recommend that it be discarded.

11

FYI: What Is SHA-1?

Described in Federal Information Processing Standards (FIPS) Standard 180-1, the Secure Hash Algorithm, SHA-1, is specified for computing a condensed representation of a message or a data file. SHA-1 is considered secure because it is computationally infeasible (hard to undo) to find a message that corresponds to a specific message digest or to find two different messages that produce the identical message digest. Any change to a message in transit will, with very high probability, result in a different message digest, and the signature will fail to verify. SHA-1 is based on principles similar to those used by Professor Ronald L. Rivest of MIT when designing the MD4 message digest algorithm (predecessor to the MD5 algorithm).

For example, when the message "This is a unique message" is run through a SHA-1 calculator, the output is "fcc6a03cb4 dbb02fcdaf842d1084a0e6dd1ea1de." When the message "This is a unique message too" is run through the calculator, the result is "f687b5becf5e48d739ea62a2c3f9c1815be2044a," which is nothing like the first value calculated. You can play with a SHA-1 calculator yourself at **www.cs.eku.edu/faculty/styer/ 460/Encrypt/JS-SHA1.html**.

With a single process, sender authentication and message integrity can be added to the otherwise untrusted communication channel called the Internet. But, privacy still needs to be addressed.

In practice, you would never send a digitally signed message out without further encryption. Because the digest is appended to the plaintext message, the message itself could still be read by anyone who intercepted it en route. Instead, you'll need to put the message and its digest into a safe and secure envelope before you send it on its way. To accomplish this, you'll use your recipient's public key (of which you already have a copy or know where to find it) to encrypt both the message and digest, creating what's called a *digital envelope*. Because no one else has the private key from your recipient's key pair, you're assured that no one else can "open" the envelope. Now you have all the elements you want: sender authentication, privacy, and message integrity. A graphical look at the digital signing process is found in Figure 11.1. A look at the process to create digital envelopes is found in Figure 11.2.

In summary, Table 11.1 shows the purposes and uses of public and private keys to secure electronic communications.

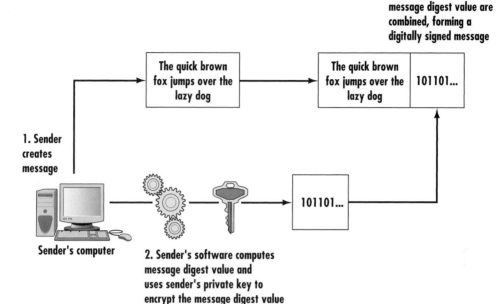

3. Message and encrypted message digest value are combined, forming a digitally signed message

1. Sender creates message

Sender's computer

2. Sender's software computes message digest value and uses sender's private key to encrypt the message digest value

FIGURE 11.1 Using public-private key pairs to create a digital signature.

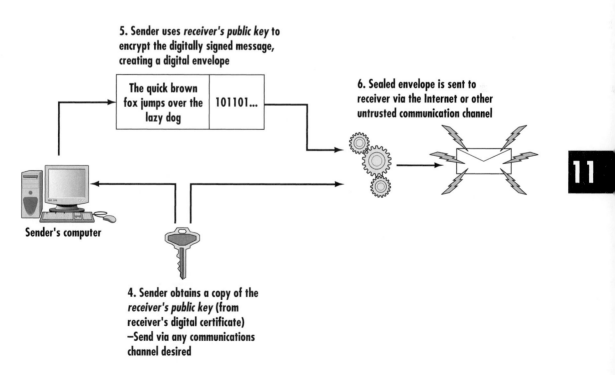

5. Sender uses *receiver's public key* to encrypt the digitally signed message, creating a digital envelope

6. Sealed envelope is sent to receiver via the Internet or other untrusted communication channel

Sender's computer

4. Sender obtains a copy of the *receiver's public key* (from receiver's digital certificate) –Send via any communications channel desired

FIGURE 11.2 Using public-private key pairs to create a digital envelope.

TABLE 11.1 Public/Private Key Uses

	Create Digital Signature	Verify Digital Signature	Create Digital Envelope	Open Digital Envelope
Sender's private key	X			
Sender's public key		X		
Receiver's public key			X	
Receiver's private key				X

So, with all the keys needed for security, where do they come from and how are they managed?

You cannot rely on the users of a computer system to manage their own cryptographic keys and provide the amount of trust that's needed for secure implementation. Because of the need for high levels of trust, businesses require a predictable infrastructure under which key management is the only theme. Because e-commerce is an environment of trusted relationships, it requires a *Public Key Infrastructure (PKI)* for establishing and maintaining trusted digital certificates.

Digital Certificates

Digital certificates behave in the online world the same way driver's licenses, passports, and other trusted documents behave outside the online world. Digital certificates use the basic PPK cryptography principles discussed above to offer the security that people demand for private communications and electronic commerce. The digital certificate standard, X.509, governs how certificates are constructed and used between communicating parties.

When used for signing electronic messages (creating digital signatures), the private key associated with the public key that's contained in the digital certificate creates the unforgeable fingerprint (digest) for the message.

In order for PPKs to operate successfully, the principles dictate that public-private key pairs are obtained in a manner that's impervious to attack. The primary assumption is that a person's private key will always remain private. Digital certificates help to implement this principle.

In 1988, X.509 became an International Telecommunications Union (ITU) recommended standard and has since become a de facto industry standard for user authentication on open systems, such as the Internet. X.509 certificates are similar to notary seals in that they bind a person's identity to a pair (or pairs) of cryptographic keys.

Digital certificates are issued by a trusted party, called a certificate authority, or CA. These CAs operate on behalf of those who wish to operate a Public Key Infrastructure (PKI) using X.509 recommended standards.

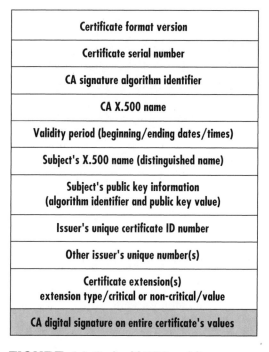

Certificate format version
Certificate serial number
CA signature algorithm identifier
CA X.500 name
Validity period (beginning/ending dates/times)
Subject's X.500 name (distinguished name)
Subject's public key information (algorithm identifier and public key value)
Issuer's unique certificate ID number
Other issuer's unique number(s)
Certificate extension(s) extension type/critical or non-critical/value
CA digital signature on entire certificate's values

FIGURE 11.3 An X.509 public key certificate's structure.

Figure 11.3 illustrates the structure and contents of a typical X.509 public key certificate.

Certificates often contain extensions (shown near the bottom of Figure 11.3) that describe how the certificate may be used and under which conditions. For example, a certificate that's used to access network resources cannot be used to access bank accounts. Each certificate is issued for specific uses and with guidelines described within the certificate's extensions. Extensions can be labeled "critical," "mandatory," or "optional" depending on the issuer's requirements.

CAs maintain a "tree of trust" that's checked each time a certificate is presented as proof of one's identity. Once the tree of trust is successfully traversed, proof of identity and proof of a person's right to use the key can be ascertained by the recipient.

Many of the higher order e-commerce protocols, such as Secure Sockets Layer (SSL), use a robust set of digital certificates to authenticate people and resources for assurance that all parties possess the rights needed to transact. A corporation may issue digital certificates to its employees as an alternative to IDs and passwords for access to network services, mainframe applications, and other locations of secure data. These certificates will normally be stored in software that resides on the user's PC within a Web browser. Certificates may also be stored on smart cards (see Chapter 10) to permit access.

Using digital certificates, system users are offered high degrees of security along several dimensions of communications. Because of the cryptography used to process messages, anyone receiving a signed message, along with the public key in the sender's digital certificate, can be confident that the message came from the specific person (user authentication) and that the message itself arrived intact (integrity).

PKIs are often rather challenging to develop. Not only do they require extremely tight security measures to protect CA private keys, they're also difficult to transition from electronic forms to the real world.

Now that you are armed with a basic understanding of the principles of modern cryptography, in the next sections we will examine some common implementations that are mixed and matched to produce useful work in effectively securing digital resources and data.

Examining Digital Cryptography

Several types of cryptosystems have come into the mainstream over the years. The most significant categories are

- hashing functions (SHA-1 and MD5)

- block ciphers (DES, 3DES, and AES)

- implementations of RSA Public-Private Key (PPK)

Each of these categories is discussed in greater detail in the following sections.

Hashing Functions

Thus far, you've seen some of the most common hashing functions to create the message digest for digitally signed messages. Hashing-type functions can also be used with symmetric key cryptography, and the result of the operation is called a *message authentication code*, or *MAC*. When you hear the term hash, think of digital signatures, and when you hear the term MAC, think of shared secret cryptography operations.

Hashing is a powerful mechanism to protect user passwords. Should a system require IDs and passwords for any reason, it is best to store the passwords that people create in the form of a hash value. That way, even if hackers steal the security database records, they won't be able to use the data to impersonate customers directly. Instead, they'll need to use additional resources and time to attempt to find out what passwords are associated with which user IDs. UNIX operating systems implemented this technique right from the start. Microsoft Windows NT implementations are similar but are considered weaker because of backward-compatibility issues to older versions of Microsoft operating systems.

The Secure Hashing Algorithm 1 (SHA-1) and Message Digest 5 (MD5) are the two most common variants of hashing functions that you'll encounter with most commercial software.

Block Ciphers

Earlier you read about DES and Triple-DES as the most common forms of symmetric key block cipher cryptosystems. DES uses a 56-bit (7 bytes + checksum byte) key, which is considered weak today. Triple DES uses a 112-bit (14 bytes + 2 checksum bytes) key, which is adequate by today's standards.

Block ciphers are important for encrypting/decrypting data in bulk, such as files or batches of data. They're also useful for encrypting data in storage systems to prevent unauthorized access. Block ciphers may be used to encrypt data fields (attributes) in records and tables, entire records of data, or entire files or database tables.

Besides DES and 3DES, there are plenty of other block cipher algorithms out there, and many of them have already been subjected to brutal cryptanalysis attacks. In early October 2000, the National Institute of Standards and Technology (NIST) announced the end of a 4-year search for a successor to the aging DES, used to protect nonclassified government information and systems. The Advanced Encryption Standard (AES) is based on the Rijndael algorithm, which takes its name from its Belgium co-creators, Vincent Rijmen and Joan Daemon. AES was adopted by the U.S. Department of Commerce as the Federal Information Processing Standard (FIPS) in 2001. AES will likely also be adopted by the private sector (just as DES was) and will find its way into encrypting sensitive corporate, e-commerce, and banking data.

FYI: The Great Cryptography Bake-Off

In early October 2000, NIST announced the end of 4-year search for a successor to the aging Data Encryption Standard, used to protect nonclassified government information and systems. On January 2, 1997, NIST announced the initiation of the Advanced Encryption System development effort and made a formal call for algorithms on September 12, 1997. The call required that the AES would specify an unclassified, publicly disclosed encryption algorithm(s), available royalty-free, worldwide. In addition, the algorithm(s) must implement symmetric key cryptography as a block cipher and (at a minimum) support block sizes of 128 bits and key sizes of 128, 192, and 256 bits.

In 1999, the AES finalist candidate algorithms were MARS, RC6, Rijndael, Serpent, and Twofish, and NIST developed a report describing the selection of the finalists. On October 2, 2000, NIST announced that it had selected Rijndael to replace DES.

11

Implementations of PPK Cryptography

Public-Private Key cryptography has found its way into numerous implementations intended to better secure Internet communications and prove identities. These systems include:

- Secure Sockets Layer (SSL)

- Transport Layer Security (TLS)

- Pretty Good Privacy (PGP)

- Secure Multipurpose Internet Mail Extensions (S/MIME)

- Secure Electronic Transactions (SET)

- XML Digital Signatures

Each of these is explained in greater detail in the following sections.

The SSL Protocol Secure Sockets Layer (SSL) is the most popular form of PPK and has become the *de facto* standard for transporting private information across the Internet. People have not only grown more comfortable with entering their payment card information into SSL-protected sessions, but they demand it and have grown to expect it.

SSL addresses some of the concerns of transporting confidential data via the Internet. The goals of SSL are to ensure the privacy of the connection, to authenticate a peer's identity, and to establish a reliable transport mechanism for the message using integrity checks and hashing functions.

SSL was designed for client/server applications, to prevent the unwanted tampering of data transmission, whether eavesdropping, data alteration, or message forgery. It's intended to ensure the privacy and reliability of communications between two applications. When you shop online, you're already very likely using SSL, whether you know it or not. Two signs that SSL is active during an Internet session:

- The URL begins with "https//. . ." rather than "http://. . ."

- A little padlock appears on the status bar of the browser

Transport Layer Security The Transport Layer Security (TLS) protocol is designed to provide communications privacy over the Internet. The protocol allows client/server applications to communicate in ways that are designed to prevent eavesdropping, tampering, or message forgery. The goals of TLS protocols are to provide:

- **Cryptographic security:** TLS should be used to establish a secure connection between two parties.

- **Interoperability:** Independent programmers should be able to develop applications using TLS that will then be able to successfully exchange cryptographic parameters without knowledge of one another's code.

- **Extensibility:** TLS seeks to provide a framework into which new public key and bulk encryption methods can be incorporated as necessary. This will also accomplish two subgoals: prevent the need to create a new protocol, which would risk the introduction of possible new weaknesses, and avoid the need to implement an entire new security library.

- **Relative efficiency:** Cryptographic operations tend to be highly CPU intensive, particularly public key operations. For this reason, the TLS protocol has incorporated an optional session caching scheme to reduce the number of connections that need to be established from scratch. Additionally, care has been taken to reduce network activity.

Pretty Good Privacy Pretty Good Privacy (PGP) is a distributed key management approach that does not rely on certificate authorities. Users can sign one another's public keys, adding some degree of confidence to a key's validity. Someone who signs someone else's public key acts as an introducer for that person to someone else, with the idea that if they trust the introducer, they should also trust the person who's being introduced.

PGP was written by Phil Zimmerman in the mid-1980s and remains popular because of its ability primarily to encrypt electronic mail. Zimmerman distributed his first version of PGP over the Internet as freeware and then ran into legal problems because he didn't realize he had given away the rights to public key cryptography patents (most notably the patent that was issued to protect the RSA Cryptosystem). Legal matters were eventually straightened out in 1993 when ViaCrypt, a company with a valid license for the RSA patent, worked out a deal with Zimmerman to distribute a commercial version of PGP.

PGP is often used to encrypt documents that can be shared via e-mail over the open Internet. Users of PGP will password-protect the file, and the password is used in the process of encryption, and upon arrival, the password is requested. Only at the point the exact password is entered can the file be decrypted. Users will share the password "out of band" by sending it in a separate message or leaving the recipient a voice message with the password to use.

Secure/Multipurpose Internet Mail Extensions Based on technology from RSA Data Security, the Secure/Multipurpose Internet Mail Extensions (S/MIME) offers another standard for electronic-mail encryption and digital signatures. S/MIME, along with a version of PGP called Open PGP, are implemented in Netscape Communications Corporation Web browsers.

11

Unfortunately, the dual electronic-mail encryption standards are creating problems for users while vendors continue to clash over whose standard should dominate.

S/MIME and Open PGP use proprietary encryption techniques and handle digital signatures differently. Simply put, if Person "A" uses a Web browser that supports S/MIME and tries to communicate with Person "B" who uses a different browser supported by PGP, the two individuals most likely will not be able to communicate successfully.

Secure Electronic Transactions Secure Electronic Transactions (SET) addresses most of the consumer demands for privacy when using a credit card to shop online. SET uses are specific to the payment acceptance phases of the shopping experience. It covers the steps from the point a particular payment card is selected for use through the point the merchant completes the transaction and settles the batch with their acquirer bank or processor.

On May 31, 1997, SET Version 1.0 was released to the public. SET addresses seven major business requirements:

- Provides confidentiality of payment information and enables confidentiality of order information that is transmitted along with the payment information.

- Ensures the integrity of all transmitted data.

- Provides authentication that a cardholder is a legitimate user of a branded payment card account.

- Provides authentication that a merchant can accept payment card transactions through its relationship with an acquiring financial institution.

- Ensures the use of the best security practices and system design techniques to protect all legitimate parties in an electronic commerce transaction.

- Creates a protocol that neither depends on transport security mechanisms nor prevents their use.

- Facilitates and encourages interoperability among software and network providers.

SET uses a robust set of strictly controlled digital certificates to identify cardholders, merchants, and acquiring payment gateways to assure the security of messages passing through open channels like the Internet. It also uses multiple forms of symmetric key cryptography (such as DES) to provide confidentiality of payment card and transaction data.

SET never really caught on in the commercial world due to a number of factors, including costs beyond what an immature sales channel would bear to implement the system within banks, merchants, and credit processors, a lack of any mandate from the banks to implement the protocol, and incompatibilities in software implementations of SET that sometimes prevented end-to-end communications. Lessons learned from SET have influenced other activities in the financial services industry to protect online credit card payments (e.g., Verified by Visa.)

XML Digital Signatures Extensible Markup Language (XML) has exploded as an effective solution to many of the stickiest Internet communications problems but suffers from a lack of security mechanisms to protect XML documents and messages.

As of this writing, digital signature discussions and standard setting are occurring throughout the industry and are at the heart of the Web services formulation strategies. Web services and XML digital signatures are becoming prevalent in business-to-business e-commerce and are easing the communication incompatibilities between organizations conducting secure business via the Internet.

Summary

Cryptography is needed by computer applications to implement the privacy and security that users demand.

Cryptography is commonly found in security systems and security mechanisms. It's useful as a tool to protect confidential information and to assure the identity of people who send electronic messages and conduct electronic transactions.

The strength of a cryptosystem rests in the size and means used to protect cryptographic keys; in general, the longer the key, the harder it is to break the encryption. The same key can be used to both encrypt and decrypt information and is called a symmetric key, or different keys can be used for encryption and decryption and are called asymmetric keys.

Cryptography relies on two basic methods: transposition and substitution. With transposition, ciphertext is created by scrambling a message based on a shared secret key. In substitution, letters are exchanged with other letters based on a substitution pattern known by both the sender and receiver.

Digital signatures are used in asymmetric key cryptography to protect a message's content from disclosure, prove the integrity of a message upon receipt, and verify that the sender of the message is indeed who he or she claims to be. Digital signature technology relies on a Public Key Infrastructure for implementation and is at the heart of many commercial products that are used in modern electronic commerce.

11

Test Your Skills

MULTIPLE CHOICE QUESTIONS

1. What are two types of ciphers?

   A. transposition and permutation

   B. transposition and shift

   C. transposition and substitution

   D. substitution and replacement

2. What is called the substitution cipher that shifts the alphabet by 13 places?

   A. Caesar cipher

   B. polyalphabetic cipher

   C. ROT13 cipher

   D. transposition cipher

3. The DES algorithm is an example of what type of cryptography?

   A. symmetric key

   B. two-key

   C. asymmetric key

   D. public key

4. Which of the following statements is most accurate of digital signature?

   A. It is a method used to encrypt confidential data.

   B. It is the art of transferring handwritten signatures to electronic media.

   C. It allows the recipient of data to prove the source and integrity of data.

   D. It can be used as a signature system and a cryptosystem.

5. A message is said to be digitally signed if sent with which of the following?

   A. message digest

   B. message digest encrypted with sender's public key

   C. message digest encrypted with sender's private key

   D. message and sender's digital certificate

6. Why does a digital signature contain a message digest?

    A. to detect any alteration of the message

    B. to indicate the encryption algorithm

    C. to confirm the identity of the sender

    D. to enable transmission in a digital format

7. What is called a mathematical encryption operation that cannot be reversed?

    A. one-way hash

    B. DES

    C. transposition

    D. substitution

8. Which of the following statements related to a private key cryptosystem is *false*?

    A. The encryption key should be secure.

    B. Data Encryption Standard (DES) is a typical private key cryptosystem.

    C. The key used for decryption is known to the sender.

    D. Two different keys are used for the encryption and decryption.

9. Which of the following standards concerns digital certificates?

    A. X.400

    B. X.25

    C. X.509

    D. X.75

10. Which of the following offers confidentiality to an e-mail message?

    A. the sender encrypting it with its private key

    B. the sender encrypting it with its public key

    C. the sender encrypting it with the receiver's public key

    D. the sender encrypting it with the receiver's private key

11. What attribute is included in an X.509 (digital) certificate?

    A. secret key of the issuing CA

    B. distinguished name of the subject

    C. the key pair of the certificate holder

    D. telephone number of the department

12. The Secure Hash Algorithm (SHA-1) creates:

   A. a fixed-length message digest from a fixed-length input message.

   B. a variable-length message digest from a variable-length input message.

   C. a fixed-length message digest from a variable-length input message.

   D. a variable-length message digest from a fixed-length input message.

13. The primary purpose for using one-way encryption of user passwords within a system is which of the following?

   A. It prevents an unauthorized person from trying multiple passwords in one log-on attempt.

   B. It prevents an unauthorized person from reading or modifying the password list.

   C. It minimizes the amount of storage required for user passwords.

   D. It minimizes the amount of processing time used for encrypting passwords.

14. Which of the following best provides e-mail message authenticity and confidentiality?

   A. signing the message using the sender's public key and encrypting the message using the receiver's private key

   B. signing the message using the sender's private key and encrypting the message using the receiver's public key

   C. signing the message using the receiver's private key and encrypting the message using the sender's public key

   D. signing the message using the receiver's public key and encrypting the message using the sender's private key

15. Which of the following identifies the encryption algorithm selected by NIST for the new Advanced Encryption Standard?

   A. Twofish

   B. Serpent

   C. RC6

   D. Rijndael

16. Which of the following algorithms is used today for encryption in PGP?

   A. RSA

   B. IDEA

   C. Blowfish

   D. RC5

17. Which of the following mail standards relies on a "Web of Trust"?

    A. Secure Multipurpose Internet Mail Extensions (S/MIME)

    B. Pretty Good Privacy (PGP)

    C. MIME Object Security Services (MOSS)

    D. Privacy Enhanced Mail (PEM)

18. Which of the following was developed in 1997 as a means of preventing fraud from occurring during electronic payments?

    A. Secure Electronic Transaction (SET)

    B. MONDEX

    C. Secure Shell (SSH-2)

    D. Secure Hypertext Transfer Protocol (S-HTTP)

EXERCISES

Exercise 11.1: Practicing Encryption Using Transposition

1. Encrypt the following message using the keyword CAUTION and the transposition method:

   MARCH FORWARD INTO THE NIGHT TUESDAY NEXT

2. What result did you get?

Exercise 11.2: More Practice of Encryption Using Transposition

1. Using the shared secret PRIVACY, encrypt the following message with the transposition method:

   ANYONE CAN HIDE MESSAGES

2. What result did you get?

Exercise 11.3: Practicing Decryption Using Transposition

1. Decrypt the following message using the keyword CAUTION and the transposition method:

   RAU CRM TYF GSN OIU PHH YPC

2. What result did you get?

11

Exercise 11.4: More Practice of Decryption Using Transposition

1. Decrypt the following message using the keyword CAUTION and the transposition method:

   OYES NTRE ECMG UNMS BAYE NUDA OOAS

2. What result did you get?

Exercise 11.5: Practicing Encryption Using Substitution

1. Encrypt the following using the substitution method with a rotate value of 13:

   ALL GOOD MEN SHOULD COME TO THE AID OF THEIR COUNTRY

2. What result did you get?

Exercise 11.6: More Practice of Decryption Using Substitution

1. Decrypt the following using the substitution method with a rotate value of 13:

   PELCGBTENCUL VF SHA

2. What result did you get?

PROJECTS

Project 11.1: Researching the RSA Cryptosystem

1. Visit the RSA Security Web site (**www.rsa.com**) to begin your research.

2. Using your favorite search engine, search for commercial products that implement the RSA Cryptosystem to protect electronic commerce transactions and communications.

3. Up to this point, how aware were you of when you were using the RSA system?

4. As you continue using the Internet, what signs would you look for to verify that the RSA system is active?

Project 11.2: Desktop Encryption Products

Laptop theft has become rampant, and companies are becoming very concerned about the loss or theft of business confidential data and are adopting desktop encryption products at a rapid pace.

1. Use the Internet to research products that perform PC desktop encryption to protect locally stored files.

2. What differences in how they implement and manage the cryptography do you find?

3. How do these different approaches offer different types of protection (file encryption, disk encryption, and so forth)?

4. Which product would you recommend to management for use throughout the organization?

5. Which product would you consider adopting for yourself?

Project 11.3: Issues with MD5 and SHA-1

MD5 and SHA-1 have come under fire since 2004 because of research findings that demonstrate that these algorithms may not be as secure as previously thought.

1. Find out what problems researchers cite with MD5.

2. Find out what problems researchers cite with SHA-1.

3. Determine if the problems cited are a vulnerability that should be addressed immediately or if they are theoretical issues that would only cause problems in extremely rare circumstances.

4. What are researchers and experts recommending to commercial users about these findings?

5. What would you recommend to your managers when you're asked what your organization should do?

11

Case Study

XML digital signatures and Web services are taking the e-commerce world by storm. In a rush to accelerate business-to-business e-commerce, companies and organizations are offering more and more Web services to share information. XML digital signatures are needed to assure the receivers of Web services communications that they are *bona fide* and not altered. One of the drawbacks to adoption of secure Web services is the number of competing and emerging industry standards that will specify how to construct and use XML digital signatures. Your CIO has asked you to develop a position paper for your company to help decide a direction for your software developers.

Research some of these competing standards to determine which one(s) may become prevalent in future software systems. You may find the following sites useful in your research:

- Liberty Alliance Project: **www.projectliberty.org**

- OASIS: **www.oasis-open.org/committees/tc_home.php ?wg_abbrev=security**

- WS-Security: **http://webservices.xml.com/pub/a/ws/ 2003/06/24/ws-trust.html**

Chapter 12

Telecommunications, Network, and Internet Security

Chapter Objectives

After reading this chapter and completing the exercises, you will be able to do the following:

- Classify the International Standards Organization/Open Systems Interconnection (ISO/OSI) layers and characteristics.

- Summarize the fundamentals of communications and network security and their vulnerabilities.

- Analyze the Transmission Control Protocol/Internet Protocol (TCP/IP) protocol.

- Distinguish between wide area networks (WANs), local area networks (LANs), and the Internet, intranets, and extranets.

- Outline the roles of packet-filtering routers, firewalls, and intrusion detection technology in network perimeter security.

- Classify the various configurations and architectures for firewalls.

- Illustrate the elements of IP security (IPSec) and how virtual private networks implement IPSec.

Introduction

The Internet is growing faster than any telecommunications system in history, including the telephone system. Often, however, users of the Internet fail to realize that Internet-attached corporate and internal networks are attractive targets for intruders who use the Internet to attack systems and create computer security incidents. New Internet sites in particular are often prime targets for malicious activity, including break-ins, file tampering, vandalism, and service disruptions. Not only is this activity difficult to discover and correct, it is highly embarrassing to the organization and costly in terms of lost productivity and damage to data, company reputation, and customer goodwill.

Information security practitioners must be aware of the risk of computer security incidents from the Internet and the steps they can take to secure public and private sites. This chapter discusses management and technical concerns related to telecommunications and network security.

The chapter contains some of the more technical and challenging information that the security professionals must understand in detail. Designing a secure network is rigorous but interesting and fulfilling work. Many people depend on the network engineers and security specialists to design, implement, and maintain the networks that keep businesses humming while simultaneously protecting them from ever-present threats to corporate computing resources.

Network and Telecommunications Security from 20,000 Feet Up

Telecommunications, Network, and Internet Security is one of the largest of the domains in the Common Body of Knowledge (in terms of content) and one of the most essential areas of focus.

Topics in this domain include:

- Open Systems Interconnection (OSI) Reference Model to promote interoperability for disparate network communications.

- TCP/IP, the Transmission Control Protocol/Internet Protocol, developed by the U.S. Department of Defense in the 1970s and widely used on the Internet.

- Security services to protect networks from attack: authentication, access control, data confidentiality, data integrity, nonrepudiation, and logging.

- Data network types that include local area networks (LAN), wide area networks (WAN), and the Internet, intranets, and extranets.

- Devices for network security: routers, firewalls, and intrusion detection systems (IDSs).

- Virtual private networks, or VPNs, a kind of private "tunnel" through the Internet that use IP security (IPSec) to perform encryption and authentication to address the lack of security on IP-based networks.

Using the building blocks of network security (the bricks) along with the objectives and principles (the mortar) for protecting networks from unauthorized access and unauthorized changes, you can mix and match technologies, architectures, and processes to meet any security requirements you'll encounter in the real world.

Network Security in Context

Information security (IS) practitioners must never lose sight of the security mantra—confidentiality, integrity, and availability (CIA)—explained in Chapter 2.

We refer to this again to remind you that to an IS specialist, a discussion about network architecture is not done in and for itself, but in the context of CIA. Will the network architecture guarantee the confidentiality, reliability, integrity, and accessibility of the data?

Confidentiality touches upon the topics of network authentication and data encryption. Integrity protects the data from unauthorized or accidental modification through the use of firewalls, cryptography, and intrusion detection tools. Availability—as you have seen in Chapter 6—involves sound disaster recovery planning procedures based on an accepted business continuity plan. Without these guarantees, the phrase "information security" is like a toothless lion—all roar and no bite.

The Open Systems Interconnection (OSI) Reference Model

Any discussion of network and Internet security necessarily begins with an overview of the Open Systems Interconnection (OSI) Reference Model; the model for network communications. The International Standards Organization (ISO) developed OSI in the early 1980s to promote interoperability of network devices. Think of OSI as the translation services at the United Nations that allows speakers from different nations to communicate with each other, and imagine what the Internet would be like today had ISO not promoted such a standard.

The remainder of this section will look at the seven layers of the data flow "stack," as it is called, and follow up with a discussion of the OSI security services.

The Protocol Stack

When ISO sat down to develop the Open Systems Interconnection Reference Model, they realized that they had to define a standard set of communication protocols. These protocols would allow dissimilar networks and equipment from different manufacturers to communicate with each other.

The OSI Reference Model is exactly what it says: a reference to help people to understand highly complex activities by using an abstract description. As an organizing framework for humans, it does not exist exactly as specified in the computing and networking industry. Its usefulness is in the "seams" between the layers that describe the specifications on how one layer interacts or interfaces with another layer. This means that an implementation of a layer written by one manufacturer that follows the specifications can operate with an implementation of another layer (above or below) written by another manufacturer.

The seven layers create a top-down hierarchy of ***protocol services*** on the client side of the model, protocols being the rules and standards that enable communication between computers over the Internet. This hierarchy works in reverse order on the server side of the model. The hierarchy in no way represents levels of importance. It simply represents a series of different protocols with different tasks to perform.

Figure 12.1 shows the seven layers of the OSI protocol stack.

This model defines the standard by which two computers share data over the network. A quick look at this illustration shows how data moves from the Application Layer on the client or "application" side of the model down through several other layers until it reaches the bottom of the stack, the Physical Layer. The data then crosses the network to the server or "application services" side of the model and climbs back up the ladder of the protocol stack. Each layer in the stack performs a specific set of tasks and is able to communicate with adjacent layers. For example, the Network Layer is able to communicate with the level above it (the Transport Layer) and the layer beneath (the Data Link Layer). Another reason ISO developed the standard was to help computer scientists break the protocols into a structured representation and facilitate a discussion of how the model works.

Layer No.	Layer Name	Description
7	Application	Consists of standard communication services and applications that everyone can use.
6	Presentation	Ensures that information is delivered to the receiving machine in a form that it can understand.
5	Session	Manages the connections and terminations between cooperating computers.
4	Transport	Manages the transfer of data and assures that received and transmitted data are identical.
3	Network	Manages data addressing and delivery between networks.
2	Data Link	Handles the transfer of data across the network media.
1	Physical	Defines the characteristics of the network hardware.

FIGURE 12.1 The OSI Data Flow Reference Model.

Following is a discussion of the layers on a superficial level. You need not understand the mechanics of how the protocols work. What you do need to understand is the general purpose of each layer. A discussion of the OSI Security Services will then follow.

Application Layer (Layer 7) The Application Layer, the highest layer in the stack, is the one most directly related to the computer user. It provides several application services such as file transfer, resource allocation, and the identification and verification of computer availability. For example, your program may be trying to obtain resources on a network server that currently are unavailable for whatever reason. Programs no doubt familiar to you at this level include:

- e-mail
- discussion groups
- WWW (the World Wide Web)

Each time you send an e-mail, you are invoking protocols at the Application Layer level.

Presentation Layer (Layer 6) As its name indicates, this layer translates or "presents" data to the Application Layer. Data encryption and decryption may occur in this layer along with data translation. Whenever you view a photograph in the JPEG (a compressed photo storage standard) format on the Internet, or watch the family reunion video a relative has sent you in MPEG format (a compressed movie storage format), or listen to an MP3 (a compressed audio storage format), you are interacting with OSI Presentation Layer protocol services.

Session Layer (Layer 5) Now the water begins to get a little deeper, and murkier. The protocols at this level establish, maintain, and manage sessions between computers. When you request information about your checking account balance from your bank's Web application, the Session Layer makes the initial contact with the host computer, formats the data you are sending for transmission, establishes the necessary communication links, and handles recovery and restart functions. If you have selected various options from drop-down lists to obtain information from a Web site on the network (for example, looking for a home with certain characteristics in a specific price range and location or entering an artist name for a song search), you used data formatting routines at the OSI Session Layer level.

Transport Layer (Layer 4) Protocols at this level provide the point-to-point integrity of data transmissions. They determine how to address the other computer, establish communication links, handle the networking of messages, and generally control the session. The *Transmission Control*

12

Protocol (TCP) operates at this level. TCP allows two computers to connect with each other and exchange streams of data while guaranteeing delivery of the data and maintaining it in the same order. Although the context of communications works at the higher layers of the protocol stack, the transport of this context over the network occurs at Layer 4.

Network Layer (Layer 3) The Network Layer decides how small bundles, or "packets," of data route between destination systems on the same network or interconnected networks. A packet (sometime called a *protocol data unit*, or PDU) is a bundle of data organized for transmission, containing control information (destination, length, origin, and so forth), the data itself (payload), and error detection and correction bits. Packets traverse *packet switching* networks that divide messages into standard-sized packets for greater efficiency of routing and transport.

Unlike the Transport Layer, the Network Layer doesn't know where the destination to deliver your data is found—it only knows how to address the data and drop the packet onto the network for the Transport Layer to route.

Data Link Layer (Layer 2) Now the water is extremely deep and dark. The Data Link Layer transfers units of information to the other end of the physical link. Protocols at this level establish communication links between devices over a physical link or channel, converting data into bit streams for delivery to the lowest layer, the Physical Layer. Token Ring and Ethernet LAN topologies operate at this level.

Physical Layer (Layer 1) Finally, protocols at the Physical Layer transmit bit streams on a physical medium. They manage the interfaces of physical devices with physical transmission mediums—coax cable, for example. This layer has the fewest tasks to perform. It sends bit streams across the network to another device and receives a bit stream response in return. The High Speed Serial Interface (HSSI) is one example of a standard interface working at the Physical Layer level.

Assuming everyone does their jobs correctly, when you send a request from an application down through the layers of the protocol stack, your data traverses the network to the Physical Layer of the receiving device and winds its way back up the stack to the receiving application on the other side. Data—e-mail, financial transactions, MP3 downloads—streams back and forth in this way at millions of bits per second from a myriad of users, all because the ISO and other dedicated computer scientists established common routines for the transmission and receipt of data.

The OSI Reference Model and TCP/IP

As mentioned earlier, the OSI seven-layer model is commonly used as a reference model to help people organize their thinking about abstract layers

OSI Ref. Layer No.	OSI Layer Equivalent	TCP/IP Layer	TCP/IP Protocol Examples
5, 6, 7	Application, Session, Presentation	Application	NFS, NIS +, DNS, telnet, ftp, "r" commands ("r" commands include rlogin, rsh, annd rcp), RIP, RDISC, SNMP, others
4	Transport	Transport	TCP, UDP
3	Network	Network	IP, ARP, ICMP
2	Data Link	Data Link	PPP, IEEE 802.2
1	Physical	Physical Network	Ethernet (IEEE 802.3) Token Ring, RS-232, others

FIGURE 12.2 TCP/IP mapped to the OSI Model.

of networking. A real-world implementation, the Transmission Control Protocol/Internet Protocol (TCP/IP), described below, is an implementation of a more compact network protocol that roughly maps onto the seven layers of the OSI Model as shown in Figure 12.2.

It's useful to refer to activities of the seven-layer model even though they don't actually exist as distinct clear-cut layers in the TCP/IP world. By using the principle of defense in depth (see Chapter 2), the principle whereby each system on the network is protected to the greatest degree possible, you can gain clarity of thought when deciding how to secure communications at all levels of the protocol.

TCP/IP is the collection of protocols used by the U.S. Department of Defense in the 1970s to build the predecessor of the Internet, called ARPANET, or the Advanced Research Projects Network. Among other things, TCP/IP provides universal connectivity across the Internet using a reliable delivery mechanism. It handles data in bundles called "packets," keeping them from getting lost, damaged, or disordered.

The primary protocols in TCP/IP are bundled in each layer and are briefly described below.

Transport Layer (Host-to-Host) Protocols The Transport Layer consists of two elements:

- **Transmission Control Protocol:** TCP is a reliable service that maintains the proper sequence of incoming packets and acknowledges receipt to the user.

- **User Datagram Protocol (UDP):** UDP is a less robust version of TCP. It does not acknowledge receipt of packets and is a connectionless and less reliable service. Its advantage over TCP is its faster speed and lower overhead.

12

Network (Internet) Layer Protocols The Network Layer is responsible for these services and protocols:

- **Internet Protocol:** The protocol of protocols, IP addresses are assigned by the Internet Assigned Numbers Authority (**www.iana.org/**) to each host computer on the network. This serves as a logical ID. The IP address assists with the routing of information across the Internet. Outgoing data packets have the originator's IP address and the IP address of the recipient.

- **Address Resolution Protocol (ARP):** Matches an IP address to an Ethernet address, which is a physical device (network adapter) that has a unique media access control (MAC) address assigned by the manufacturer of the device. MAC addresses are much longer numbers than are IP addresses and humans tend to work better with IP addresses than with MAC addresses, thus ARP and RARP (below) exist to help with network addressing tasks.

- **Reverse Address Resolution Protocol (RARP):** If ARP translates an IP address to a MAC address, then RARP translates hardware interface (MAC) addresses to IP protocol addresses.

- **Internet Control Message Protocol (ICMP):** The ICMP is tightly integrated with the IP protocol. Some of its functions include announcing network errors and congestion, troubleshooting, and reporting timeouts. ICMP is the management protocol for TCP/IP and is often found as the source of security issues or is found useful by network hackers to select targets and determine network level information about these targets. For example, the common PING Command, used to determine if an IP or host name is online, is an ICMP command.

The primary applications using TCP/IP include

- **File Transfer Protocol (FTP):** FTP is one of the oldest Internet protocols. It facilitates the transfer of data files (e.g., customer purchase information from a mainframe to a data warehouse) between two similar or dissimilar FTP devices. The FTP can also perform certain directory functions.

- **Remote Login (Telnet):** First published in 1983, Telnet was originally designed to facilitate remote logins to a computer via the Internet for terminal (interactive) sessions. A user running a local Telnet program (client) can execute a login session on a remote computer, for example to access a university library catalog, using a Telnet server program for communication.

- **Electronic Mail or Simple Mail Transfer Protocol (SMTP):** This is the protocol used to send e-mail via the Internet in a host-to-host configuration that will relay messages from source to destination through as many intermediate relay systems along the route.

You can think of these application programs running at the Application Layer of the OSI Model, along with all other network-based services that require external connectivity. Because TCP/IP was built for resilience in the face of nuclear war, the designers did not consider security of the network an issue to consider at the time.

The OSI Model and Security

Now that you have seen the complexity of the OSI protocol stack and its relationship to the real-world TCP/IP, you can begin to think of the layers as interdependent links in a chain. Each link is subject to security attacks and, in keeping with the old saying about the chain and its weakest link, the OSI had to address security services and the mechanisms needed to keep the chain strong.

ISO Security Services ISO has in fact identified six security services to protect networks from attack. They are

- **Authentication:** Access to documents can be restricted in one of two ways: by asking for a username and password or by the hostname of the browser being used. The former, referred to as "user authentication," requires creating a file of user IDs and passwords (an access control list; see Chapter 5), and defining critical resources (e.g., files/documents) to the server.

- **Access control:** Unlike authentication, which is security-based on the user's identity, restricting access based on something other than identity is called "access control." "Allow and deny" directives allow or deny access to network services based on host name or address (see Chapter 5).

- **Data confidentiality:** This service protects data against unauthorized disclosure and has two components: content confidentiality and message flow confidentiality. The former protects the plaintext message from unauthorized disclosure; the latter allows the originating network to conceal the path or route that the message followed on its way to the recipient. *Message flow confidentiality* is useful in preventing an attacker from obtaining information from the observation of the message.

- **Data integrity:** The goal is to protect data from accidental or malicious modification whether during data transfer, data storage, or from an operation performed on it, and to preserve it for its intended use.

- **Nonrepudiation:** A service guaranteeing that the sender of a message cannot deny having sent the message and the receiver cannot deny having received the message.

12

- **Logging and monitoring:** These services allow IS specialists to observe system activity during and after the fact by using monitoring and logging tools. These include operating system logs, server records, application log errors, warnings, and observation of network switch and router traffic between network segments.

The OSI model additionally identifies eight security mechanisms that implement the aforementioned security services. They are

- **Encipherment:** The conversion of plaintext messages into ciphers or encoded messages that only the person with the cipher key can unlock.

- **Digital signature:** In general, the use of public and private key encryption that allows the sender to encrypt his message and the intended recipient to decrypt the message.

- **Access control:** See description above.

- **Data integrity:** See description above.

- **Authentication:** See description above.

- **Traffic padding:** The technique by which spurious data is generated in order to disguise the amount of real data being sent, thus making data analysis or decryption more difficult for the attacker.

- **Routing control:** The Internet has routes between networks. When a network drops, the routing control processor determines in real-time the optimal path in order to reduce downtime to a minimum.

- **Notarization:** Digital notarizations, the counterpart to the paper notary with which you are probably familiar, prove that electronic files have not been altered after they were digitally notarized. (See Chapter 11 for more information on digital signatures.)

FYI: Wireless LANs (WLANs)

Wireless (802.11) networks have taken the home and corporate networking world by storm. The convenience, freedom, and low cost of wireless access points and network adapters is too irresistible to pass up by many regular users of the Internet. Despite their attractiveness and compelling business case, the security of WLANs continues to be a problem well into 2005. Appendix C includes a wireless LAN security standard to help in configuring an access point for an acceptable level of security for most purposes.

Data Network Types

Now that you have an understanding of the OSI protocol stack and some of the services and mechanisms used to protect it, this section will step back to look at basic network configurations. The three types of data networks are:

- local area networks
- wide area networks
- Internet, intranet, and extranet

Local Area Network

A local area network, or LAN, is a network configuration designed for a limited space or geographic area such as a series of offices in the same building (e.g., a university administration building). LANs share network services such as databases, e-mail, and application services by connecting workstations and servers through a set of LAN protocols and access methods. Two common types of LANs are the campus area network (CAN) used to connect buildings through a network "backbone" and the metropolitan area network (MAN) that is used to connect branches of an organization using wireless (satellite or cellular) devices over a long distance between branches. A MAN can cover an area between 5 to 50 kilometers, roughly the size of a city.

Wide Area Network

A group of smaller LANs connected logically or physically is referred to as a Wide Area Network, or WAN. As you might suspect, the WAN covers a larger geographic area than a LAN (technically, a network that covers an area larger than a single building). A WAN can span the entire nation or even the globe using satellites. The WAN is inherently more complex than a LAN because of its size and use of multiple network protocols and configuration. WANs can combine other subnetworks such as intranets, extranets, and virtual private networks (VPNs) to provide enhanced network capabilities.

12

Internet

Sometimes referred to as a "network of networks," the Internet is an interconnection of different-sized networks (LANs) around the world. Evolving from the U.S. military's ARPANET in the late 1960s and early 1970s, the Internet uses the TCP/IP protocols (see below) in a scheme decentralized by design. Each host computer on the Internet is independent. Its operators can choose the Internet services and local services they wish to offer.

FYI: What Makes the Internet Tick?

The Internet is a store and forward network, meaning that TCP/IP packets can be sent to (and stored on) any number of computers along the way to their destination. If there is a direct network link between two host computers—that is, a physical cable linking them—the packets can fly right through. Most of the time, however, there is no direct link. In this case, the sending computer (host) sends the packets to one that's a little closer to the destination. That machine moves the packets further down the line, and so on, until the packets reach their destination. It's not uncommon for a cross-country trip to make 20 or 30 hops on different routers along the way. Most of the time, this happens very, very quickly (at the speed of electricity, roughly the speed of light).

Intranet

An intranet is a local or wide area network, based on TCP/IP, but with fences (firewalls) that limit the network's access to the Internet. Intranets use the standard software and protocols you find on the Internet with the difference that they are for private use and are not accessible to the public via the Internet. Companies can use low-cost Internet software such as browsers to build internal sites, such as human resources and internal job postings. An intranet is more secure than the Internet because it has a restricted user community and local control.

Extranet

An extranet is an intranet that allows select users on the outside of the firewalls to access the site. For example, a company may choose to allow vendors and suppliers to have limited access to the intranet while excluding the general public.

Protecting TCP/IP Networks

Protecting computer networks is a challenging job and is best approached by applying the principle of defense in depth. The following sections will begin to examine the pieces of the security puzzle to see how to best fit them together for effective defenses and coverage. We will explore several types of security approaches that are usually present wherever the Internet and corporate networks intersect. These include the uses of:

- routers
- firewalls
- intrusion detection systems (IDSs)

Basic Security Infrastructures

Figure 12.3 illustrates the basic design for network security. As you see, the infrastructure relies on layers of devices that serve specific purposes and provide multiple barriers of security that protect, detect, and respond to network attacks, often in real-time.

The following sections focus on the individual building blocks that are needed to complete the network security picture.

Routers

A router is a network traffic management device that, unbeknownst to the user, sits in between subnetworks (LANs) and routes traffic intended for or leaving the network segments to which it's attached. Because of their special role in network management, routers are sensible places to implement packet-filtering rules, based on the security policies already developed for the routing of network traffic

Packet Filtering

A packet filter is a simple and effective form of protection. It matches all packets against a series of rules. If the packet matches a rule, then an action is performed; the packet is accepted, rejected, logged, and so forth. Because malicious network activity can harm network users and because all network communications are packet-based, packets can be inspected as they traverse the network, and those that contain commands that are disallowed can be filtered out of the network and discarded before they cause harm or unauthorized activity.

Basic Packet Filtering Basic or straight packet-filtering mechanisms allow communication originating from one side of the communication path or the other. To enable two-way traffic, you must specify a rule for each direction. Packet-filtering firewalls identify and control traffic by examining the source, destination, port number, and protocol types (for example, UDP or TCP).

Stateful Inspection Packet Filtering Stateful inspection filtering is a more complex packet-filtering technology that filters traffic based on more than just source, destination, port number, and protocol type. Stateful inspection keeps track of the state of the current connection to help assure that only desired traffic passes through. This allows the creation of one-way rules, for example, inside to outside.

A packet-filtering router yields a permit or deny decision for each packet that it receives. The router examines each IP datagram to determine whether it matches one of its packet-filtering rules.

12

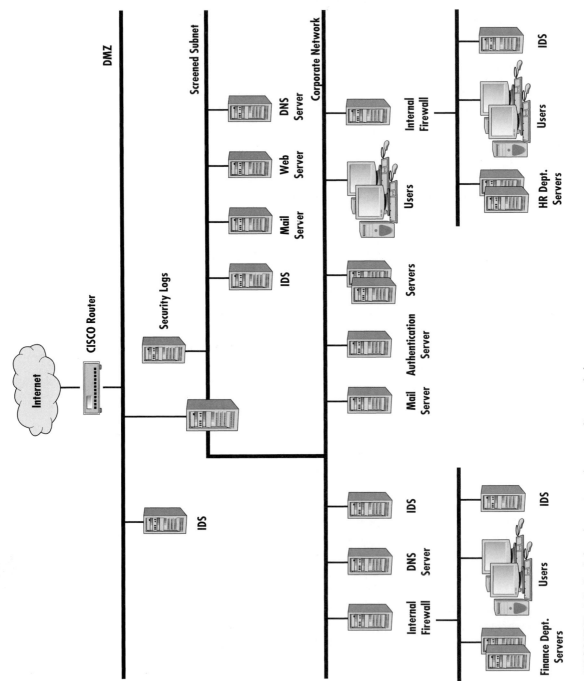

FIGURE 12.3 A basic network security model.

Benefits of Packet-Filtering Routers

A number of Internet firewall systems are deployed using only a packet-filtering router. Other than the time spent planning the filters and configuring the router, there is little or no cost to implement packet filtering because the feature is included as part of standard router software releases. Because a WAN interface usually provides Internet access, there is little impact on router performance if traffic loads are moderate and few filters defined. Packet-filtering routers are generally transparent to users and applications, eliminating the need for specialized user training or specific software on each connected host system.

Limitations of Packet-Filtering Routers

Defining packet filters can be a complex task because network administrators need to have a detailed understanding of the various Internet services, packet header formats (packets typically have "header" and "trailer" records marking the beginning and end of the data packet), and the specific values they expect to find in each field. If complex filtering requirements must be supported, the filtering rule set can become robust and complicated, increasing in difficulty to manage and comprehend. Finally, there are few testing facilities to verify the correctness of the filtering rules after they are configured on the router. This can potentially leave a site open to untested vulnerabilities.

Any packet that passes directly through a router could potentially be used to launch a data-driven attack. Data-driven attacks occur when seemingly harmless data is forwarded by the router to an internal host. The data may contain hidden instructions that cause the host to modify access control and security-related files, making it easier for the intruder to gain access to the system.

Generally, the packet throughput of a router decreases as the number of filters increase. Routers are optimized to extract the destination IP address from each packet, make a relatively simple routing table lookup, and then forward the packet to the proper interface for transmission. If filtering is enabled, the router must not only make a forwarding decision for each packet but also apply all of the filter rules to each packet. This can consume CPU cycles and impact the performance of a system.

IP packet filters may not be able to provide enough control over traffic. A packet-filtering router can permit or deny a particular service, but it is not capable of understanding the context/data of a particular service. For example, a network administrator may need to filter traffic at the Application Layer in order to limit access to a subset of the available FTP or Telnet commands or to block the import of mail or newsgroups concerning specific topics. This type of control is best performed at a higher layer by application-level gateways often called *firewalls*.

Firewalls

Firewalls insulate a private network from a public network using carefully established controls on the type of requests they'll route through to the private network for processing and fulfillment. For example, an HTTP request for a public Web page will be honored whereas an FTP request to a host behind the firewall may be dishonored.

Firewalls typically run monitoring software to detect and thwart external attacks on the site and protect the internal corporate network. When you install a firewall, you essentially *break* the network so that no communications can occur until the rules for permissible communications are established and implemented. Firewalls are an essential device for network security, and many of the architectures needed for security rely on one or more firewalls within an intelligent design.

Several firewall architecture models are used to protect the perimeter of a network and control the flow of permitted communications. Nonpermitted traffic (requests for services that are not authorized) is discarded by the firewall prior to entering the protected network or network segment. Two of the most common firewall building block architectures—application-level gateways and bastion hosts—are described in the following sections.

Application-Level Gateway Firewall

An application-level gateway allows the network administrator to implement stricter security policies than packet-filtering routers can manage. Rather than relying on a generic packet-filtering tool to manage the flow of Internet services through the firewall, special-purpose code (a proxy service) is installed on the gateway for each desired application. If the network administrator does not install the proxy code for a particular application, the service is not supported and cannot be forwarded across the firewall. Also, the proxy code can be configured to support only those specific features of an application that the network administrator considers acceptable while denying all other features.

This enhanced security comes with increased costs in terms of:

- purchasing the dedicated gateway hardware

- configuring the proxy service applications

- time, knowledge, and skills required to configure the gateway system

- degradation in the level of service that may be provided to users due to the overhead of firewall operation

- lack of transparency for remote users, resulting in a less user-friendly system

Note that users are permitted access to the proxy services, but they are never permitted to log in to the application-level gateway itself. If users are permitted to log in to the firewall system, the security of the firewall is threatened, as an intruder could potentially perform some activity that compromises the effectiveness of the firewall. To that end, it is crucial that the firewall software you purchase is operated exclusively on a ***hardened server*** (a server whose software has been modified to make it more difficult to attack), with all unnecessary services eliminated from the host.

FYI: Proxy Server

A proxy server sits between the user's application such as a Web browser and the server providing the application services and resources. Proxy servers are designed to filter Web sites and improve performance. For example, the bastion host is the ideal location for installing strong authentication using a one-time password technology like a smart card or token that generates a unique access code (see Chapter 11). Additionally, each proxy service may require its own authentication before granting user access. Characteristics of the proxy server include

- Each proxy is configured to support only a subset of the standard application's command set. If a standard command is not supported by the proxy application, it is simply not available to the authenticated user.

- Each proxy is configured to allow access only to specific host systems. This means that the limited command/feature set may be applied only to a subset of systems on the protected network.

- Each proxy maintains detailed audit information by logging all traffic, each connection, and the duration of each connection. Audit logs are essential tools for discovering and terminating intruder attacks. Each proxy is a small and uncomplicated program specifically designed for network security.

- Each proxy is independent of all other proxies on the bastion host. If there is a problem with the operation of any proxy or if a future vulnerability is discovered, it can be uninstalled without affecting the operation of the other proxy applications.

- Each proxy runs as a nonprivileged user in a private and secured directory on the bastion host. If users require support for new services, the network administrator can easily install the required proxies on the bastion host. A proxy generally performs no disk access other than to read its initial configuration file. This makes it difficult for an intruder to install Trojan horse sniffers or other dangerous files on the bastion host.

12

Bastion Hosts

An application-level gateway is often referred to as a bastion host because it is a designated system that is specifically armored and protected against attacks. Unlike packet-filtering routers, which allow the direct flow of packets between inside systems and outside systems, application-level gateways allow information to flow between systems but do not allow the direct exchange of data. The primary risk of allowing packet exchange between inside systems and outside systems is that the host applications residing on the protected network's systems must be secured against any threat posed by the allowed services. The application-level gateway firewall configuration is illustrated in Figure 12.4.

Several design features are used to provide security for a bastion host. The bastion host hardware platform operates a secure (hardened) version of its operating system. For example, if the bastion host is a UNIX platform, it executes a secure version of the UNIX operating system that is specifically designed to protect against operating system vulnerabilities and ensure firewall integrity.

Network administrators only install services they consider essential on the bastion host. An uninstalled service is not vulnerable to attack. Generally, a limited set of proxy applications such as Telnet, DNS, FTP, SMTP, and user authentication are installed on a bastion host. The bastion host may be configured to require additional authentication before a user is allowed access to the proxy services.

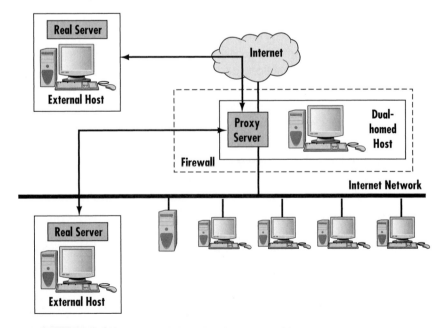

FIGURE 12.4 Application-level gateway firewall configuration.

Benefits of Application-Level Gateways

There are many benefits to the deployment of application-level gateways. They give the network manager complete control over each service, as the proxy application limits the command set and determines which internal hosts may be accessed by the service. In addition, the network manager has complete control over permitted services, as the absence of a proxy for a particular service means that the service is completely blocked. Application-level gateways also have the ability to support strong user authentication and provide detailed logging information. Finally, the filtering rules for an application-level gateway are much easier to configure and test than for a packet-filtering router.

Limitations of Application-Level Gateways

The greatest limitation of an application-level gateway is that it requires either that users modify their behavior or that specialized software be installed on each system that accesses proxy services. For example, Telnet access via an application-level gateway requires two user steps to make the connection rather than a single step.

Firewall Implementation Examples

The following are a few examples of common implementations using firewall technologies.

Packet-Filtering Router The most common Internet firewall system consists of nothing more than a packet-filtering router deployed between the private network and the Internet. This configuration is shown in Figure 12.5.

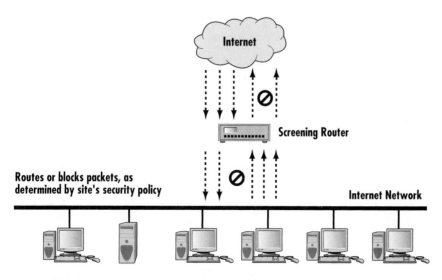

FIGURE 12.5 Packet-filtering router firewall.

A packet-filtering router performs the typical routing functions of forwarding traffic between networks as well as using packet-filtering rules to permit or deny traffic. Typically, the filter rules are defined so that hosts on the private network have direct access to the Internet, while hosts on the Internet have limited access to systems on the private network. The external posture of this type of firewall system dictates that all traffic that is not specifically permitted be denied.

Although this firewall system has the benefit of being inexpensive and transparent to users, it possesses all of the limitations of a packet-filtering router such as exposure to attacks from improperly configured filters and attacks that are tunneled over permitted services. Because the direct exchange of packets is permitted between outside systems and inside systems, the potential extent of an attack is determined by the total number of hosts and services to which the packet-filtering router permits traffic. This means that each host directly accessible from the Internet needs to support sophisticated user authentication and needs to be regularly examined by the network administrator for signs of an attack. Also, if the single packet-filtering router is penetrated, every system on the private network may be compromised.

Screened Host Firewalls The second firewall example employs both a packet-filtering router and a bastion host as illustrated in Figure 12.6. This firewall system provides higher levels of security than the previous example because it implements both Network-Layer security (packet-filtering) and

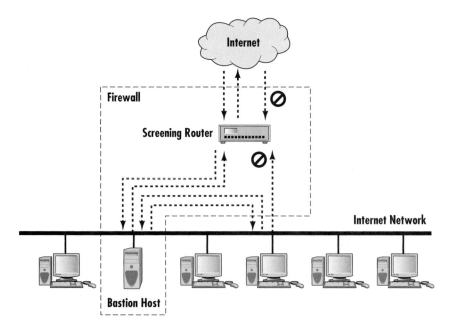

FIGURE 12.6 Screened host firewall system (single-homed bastion host).

Application-Layer security (proxy services). Also, an intruder has to penetrate two separate systems before the security of the private network can be compromised.

For this firewall system, the bastion host is configured on the private network with a packet-filtering router between the Internet and the bastion host. The filtering rules on the exposed router are configured so that outside systems can access only the bastion host; traffic addressed to all other internal systems is blocked. Because the inside hosts reside on the same network as the bastion host, the security policy of the organization determines whether inside systems are permitted direct access to the Internet or whether they are required to use the proxy services on the bastion host. Inside users can be forced to use the proxy services by configuring the router's filter rules to accept only internal traffic originating from the bastion host.

One of the benefits of this firewall system is that a public information server providing Web and FTP services can be placed on the segment shared by the packet-filtering router and the bastion host. If the strongest security is required, the bastion host can run proxy services that require both internal and external users to access the bastion host before communicating with the information server. If a lower level of security is adequate, the router may be configured to allow outside users direct access to the public information server.

An even more secure firewall system can be constructed using a dual-homed bastion host system, like the one illustrated in Figure 12.7. A dual-homed bastion host has two network interfaces, but the host's ability to directly forward traffic between the two interfaces bypassing the proxy

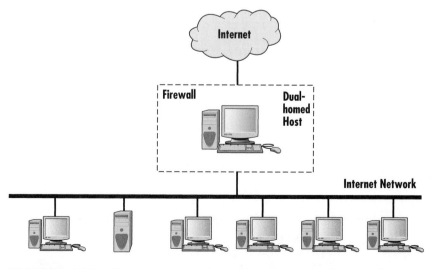

FIGURE 12.7 Screened host firewall system (dual-homed bastion host).

services is disabled. The physical topology forces all traffic destined for the private network through the bastion host and provides additional security if outside users are granted direct access to the information server.

Demilitarized Zone or Screened-Subnet Firewall The final firewall example employs two packet-filtering routers and a bastion host, as shown in Figure 12.8. This firewall system creates the most secure firewall system, as it supports both Network-Layer and Application-Layer security while defining a "demilitarized zone" (DMZ) network. The network administrator places the bastion host, information servers, modem pools, and other public servers on the DMZ network. The DMZ network functions as a small, isolated network positioned between the Internet and the private network. Typically, the DMZ is configured so that systems on the Internet and systems on the private network can access only a limited number of systems on the DMZ network, but the direct transmission of traffic across the DMZ network is prohibited.

For incoming traffic, the outside router protects against the standard external attacks (source IP address spoofing, source routing attacks, and so forth) and manages Internet access to the DMZ network. It permits external systems to access only the bastion host (and possibly the information server). The inside router provides a second line of defense, managing DMZ access to the private network by accepting only traffic originating from the bastion host.

For Internet-bound traffic, the inside router manages private network access to the DMZ network. It permits internal systems to access only the

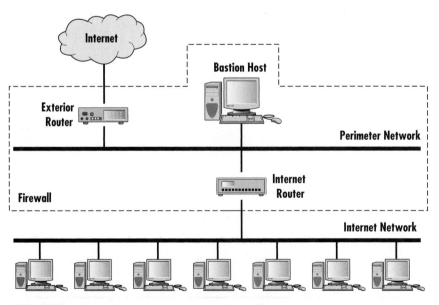

FIGURE 12.8 Screened-subnet firewall system.

bastion host (and possibly the information server). The filtering rules on the outside router require use of the proxy services by accepting only Internet-bound traffic from the bastion host.

There are several key benefits to the deployment of a screened-subnet firewall system:

- An intruder must crack three separate devices without detection (see next section of this chapter) to infiltrate the private network: the outside router, the bastion host, and the inside router.

- Because the outside router advertises the DMZ network only to the Internet, systems on the Internet do not have routes to the protected private network. This allows the network manager to ensure that the private network is "invisible" and that only selected systems on the DMZ are known to the Internet via routing table and DNS information exchanges.

- Because the inside router advertises the DMZ network only to the private network, systems on the private network do not have direct routes to the Internet. This guarantees that inside users must access the Internet via the proxy services residing on the bastion host. Packet-filtering routers direct traffic to specific systems on the DMZ network, eliminating the need for the bastion host to be dual-homed. The inside router supports greater packet throughput than a dual-homed bastion host when it functions as the final firewall system between the private network and the Internet. Because the DMZ network is a different network than the private network, a network address translator (NAT) can be installed on the bastion host to eliminate the need to renumber or re-subnet the private network.

Choose Wisely!

In considering the deployment of an Internet firewall, there is no single answer or any one correct design. Decisions on how to build firewall architecture are influenced by many different factors related to corporate security policies, technical background of the staff, costs, and the perceived threat level. However, because the benefits of connecting to the Internet are certain to exceed the related costs to implement and maintain a secure connection, network managers can design a level of safety commensurate with the needs, resources, and risk tolerance of a client. A network can be made as safe as need be if the proper precautions are taken.

By adding one more element to the building blocks for secure networks—intrusion detection systems—you can keep an eye out for problems before they get out of hand. IDSs work in conjunction with routers and firewalls by monitoring and standing as a sentry on guard to protect your networks against attacks.

12

Intrusion Detection Systems

An intrusion detection system attempts to detect an intruder breaking into your system or an authorized user misusing system resources. The IDS operates constantly on your system, working in the background, and only notifies you when it detects something it considers suspicious or illegal.

There are two major classifications of potential intruders:

- outside intruders
- inside intruders

IDSs are needed to detect both types of intrusions: break-in attempts from the outside and knowledgeable insider attacks. Effective intrusion detection systems detect both.

As you have seen all along, security policies define what's permitted and what's denied on your computer systems. The two basic philosophical options in designing policy are

- Prohibit everything that is not expressly permitted.
- Permit everything that is not expressly denied.

Generally, people more concerned about security will exercise the first option. Policies are put in place to describe exactly what operations are allowed on a system. Any operation that is not detailed in the policy will be considered banned on the system.

Others who operate their systems under the spirit of cooperative computing will likely adopt the second philosophy. Unfortunately, this philosophy does not work well in today's hostile computing environments.

What Kind of Intrusions?

Before discussing the detection of intrusions, it is important to understand what is meant by an intrusion. Intrusions are defined relative to a security policy. Unless you decide what is and what is not allowed on your system, it is pointless to try and detect intrusions.

An intrusion is defined as any set of actions that attempt to compromise the integrity, confidentiality, or availability of a resource. Intrusions can be categorized into two main classes:

- Misuse intrusions are well-defined attacks on known weak points within a system. They can be detected by watching for certain actions being performed on certain objects.

- Anomaly intrusions are based on observations of deviations from normal system usage patterns. They are detected by building up a profile of the system in question and detecting significant deviations from this profile.

As misuse intrusions follow well-defined patterns, they can be detected by doing pattern matching on audit-trail information. Anomalous intrusions are detected by observing significant deviations from normal behavior. An anomaly may be a symptom of a possible intrusion. Given a set of metrics that can define normal system usage, security violations may be detectable from abnormal patterns of system usage.

Anomaly detection can also use other mechanisms, such as neural networks (networks that learn with experience and can remember patterns of behavior that it witnesses), machine learning classification techniques (pattern matching), and even trying to mimic biological immune systems (such as antivirus and cell repair).

Anomalous intrusions are harder to detect. There are no fixed patterns that can be monitored and so a more complex approach is needed. Ideally, a system that combines human-like pattern matching capabilities with the vigilance of a computer program could eliminate most problems.

Many intrusion detection systems base their operations on analysis of operating system audit trail data. This data forms a footprint of system usage over time. Audit trails are convenient sources of data and are readily available on most systems. Using audit trail observations, the IDS can compute metrics about a computer network's overall state and decide whether an intrusion is occurring.

Characteristics of Good Intrusion Detection Systems

An intrusion detection system should address the following issues, regardless of what mechanism it uses:

- It must run continually without human supervision. The system should be reliable enough to run autonomously in the background of the system being observed.

- It must be fault tolerant. It must survive a system crash without requiring the rebuilding of the IDS's knowledge base each time the system is restarted.

- It must resist subversion. The system should monitor itself to assure that it has not been subverted.

- It must impose minimal overhead on the attached network.

- It must observe deviations from normal behavior.

- It must be easily tailored to the network in question. Every system has different usage patterns, and the defense mechanisms should adapt easily to these patterns.

- It must cope with changing system behavior over time as new applications are being added. The system profile will change over time, and the IDS must be able to adapt.

12

False Positives, False Negatives, and Subversion Attacks

IDS processing errors are categorized as false positives, false negatives, or subversion errors. A false positive occurs when the system classifies an action as anomalous (a possible intrusion) when it is a legitimate action. A false negative occurs when an actual intrusive action has occurred but the system allows it to pass as nonintrusive behavior. A subversion error occurs when an intruder modifies the operation of the intrusion detector to force false negatives to occur.

False positive errors will lead users of the intrusion detection system to ignore its output, as it will classify legitimate actions as intrusions. The occurrences of this type of error should be minimized (it may not be possible to completely eliminate them) so as to provide useful information to the operators. If too many false positives are generated, the operators will come to ignore the output of the system over time, which may lead to an actual intrusion being detected but ignored.

A false negative error occurs when an action proceeds even though it is an intrusion. False negative errors are more serious than false positive errors because they give a misleading sense of security. By allowing these actions to proceed, a suspicious action will not be brought to the attention of the operator. The intrusion detection system is now a liability as the security of the system is less than it was before the intrusion detector was installed.

Subversion errors are more complex and tie in with false negative errors. An intruder could use knowledge about the internals of an intrusion detection system to alter its operation, possibly allowing anomalous behavior to proceed. The intruder could then violate the system's operational security constraints. This may be discovered by a human operator examining the logs from the intrusion detector, but it would appear that the intrusion detection system still seems to be working correctly.

Another form of subversion error is fooling the system over time. As the detection system is observing behavior on the system over time, it may be possible to carry out operations that when taken individually pose no threat but when taken as an aggregate form a threat to system integrity. How would this happen? As mentioned previously, the detection system is continually updating its notion of normal system usage. As time goes by, a change in system usage patterns is expected and the detection system must cope with this. But if an intruder could perform actions over time that are just slightly outside of normal system usage patterns, then it is possible that the actions could be accepted as legitimate even though they form part of an intrusion attempt. The detection system would come to accept each of the individual actions as slightly suspicious but not a threat to the system. It would not recognize that the combination of these actions is a serious threat to the system.

With packet-filtering routers, firewalls, proxies, and intrusion detection systems in place, network managers can protect their networks from both internal and external threats while still keeping the channels of communications open for customers and employees on the outside.

Virtual Private Networks

A virtual private network, or VPN, is a network technology that makes it possible to establish private "tunnels" over the public Internet, which reduces the cost of dedicated private network connections, like leased lines and dial-up networks. The three primary uses for VPNs are for employee remote access to corporate networks, extranet connections with business partners and suppliers, and branch office networks. All that is needed for a VPN is a specialized firewall, client, or server software (to initiate and maintain a connection), and an Internet service provider (ISP) connection for Internet connectivity.

The current version and the one in widest use today on the Internet is IP Version 4, or IPv4. The next generation of IP, called IP Version 6, or IPv6, mandates the use of a new set of security features that are optionally available for IPv4. These features, called IP security, or IPSec, operate at both the Network Layer and Session Layer of the TCP/IP protocol stack. IPSec VPNs are the most common form in use today and are widely available from network and firewall providers.

To answer some of the enhanced security requirements that are mandatory as Internet demand increases, certain vendors of networking systems are responding with both proprietary (customized specific to a manufacturer and not based on industry standards) and nonproprietary (standardized) solutions that tunnel private traffic over public networks such as the Internet.

IPSec

IPSec was developed by the Internet Engineering Task Force (IETF) as RFC1825-9, based on the work conducted in the Automotive Network exchange (ANX) project (now run by Covisint) by the Big 3 automakers. IPSec performs both encryption and authentication to address the inherent lack of security on IP-based networks. Its design supports most of the security goals—sender authentication, message integrity, and data confidentiality. IPSec operates by encapsulating an IP packet with another packet that surrounds it and then encrypts the result. IPSec provides security without requiring organizations to modify user applications.

Just as TCP/IP networks operate using a series of layers, security processing can also occur at one or more layers of the protocol stack. IPSec is designed to operate at the Network Layer of TCP/IP, enabling those applications operating at higher layers (e.g., public key cryptography) to enhance the security that an IPSec-compliant network already provides.

12

Communications using computer networks can only be deemed secure when it meets three characteristics:

- sender authentication to prove that messages originate from their advertised source

- message integrity to assure that messages arrive intact and unaltered

- confidentiality to assure that only the intended receiver can successfully read private messages that are sent

IPSec meets these requirements using two security mechanisms: authentication header (AH) and Encapsulating Security Protocol (ESP).

Authentication header modifies IP datagrams by adding an additional field (attribute) that enables receivers to check the authenticity of the data within the datagram.

AH provides connectionless data integrity, data authentication, and protection against replay attacks.

FYI: Replay Attack

A "replay attack" is a repeat transmission of a valid data transmission that was already conducted, typically a malicious action meant to masquerade the perpetrator's fraudulent intent—like replaying a log-in activity that was recorded when the legitimate user first logged in. These attacks can occur when a **man-in-the-middle** of a conversation stream collects and stores the communication, and then goes back through the stream looking for authentication credentials or session initiation messages.

The added block of data on IPSec packets is called an integrity value check (IVC), which is generally used to carry a message authentication code (MAC) or a digital signature (a message digest signed using sender's private key; see Chapter 11). Protection against replay attacks is provided by adding a sequence number to the packet to prevent reprocessing if it's received multiple times. IPSec may be operated in one of two basic modes:

- Transport mode, where protection is applied to upper layer protocols (TCP or UDP).

- Tunnel mode, where an entire IP packet is wrapped inside a new IP packet and attached with a new IP header before it's transmitted through the public network.

The destination address contained in the new header is an IPSec-capable host that will unwrap the packet and send it to its ultimate destination. A benefit of tunneling is the ability to hide source and destination addresses before data is sent, thus increasing communications security.

Because IPSec defines the framework for using IP securely, it does not mandate specific cryptographic algorithms. Rather, it's written to permit the uses of a variety of cryptosystems for MAC and/or digital signatures.

Encapsulating Security Protocol The Encapsulating Security Protocol (ESP) is used to assure one or more of these security services:

- confidentiality (in IPSec tunnel mode)

- connectionless data integrity

- data origin authentication

- protection against replay attacks

Unlike AH, ESP operates under the principle of encapsulation; encrypted data is sandwiched between an ESP header and ESP trailer.

Again, IPSec does not mandate the use of any specific cryptosystem for confidentiality or sender authentication but supports the use of a number of cryptographic algorithms.

Security Associations AH and ESP require a number of parameters that both senders and receivers must agree on before communications can take place. To manage these parameters, IPSec uses the concept of a security association (SA).

A security association is a secure "connection" between two endpoints that applies a security policy and keys to protect information. You can think of an SA as the set of data that describes how a given communication will be secured. An SA is uniquely identified by the combination of these three fields:

- IP destination address

- security protocol identifier (AH or ESP)

- security parameter index (SPI)

IPSec stores these security associations in a database called the security association database (SAD). The database stores all the parameters used for a specific SA and is consulted each time a packet is sent or received.

SAs contain the actual keys used for encrypting data or signing message authentication codes or message digests. Because key exchange is normally performed out-of-band to the communication that will use these keys to communicate, IPSec provides a separate protocol for exchanging security associations. Using this approach, IPSec separates its key management mechanisms from other security mechanisms, enabling the substitution of

12

key management protocols without affecting the implementation of the security mechanism (see Chapter 11).

The protocol to negotiate security associations under IPSec is called Internet Security Association and Key Management Protocol (ISAKMP).

FYI: Out-of-Band Communications

Out-of-band communications occur when a secondary mode of communications is established to share information needed to communicate successfully in the primary channel. An example is sharing a secret key to encode or decode messages using postal mail and then applying the secret key to Internet-based communications.

Say you and your friend want to encrypt your e-mail to one another but you don't want to share the key that you use for encryption and decryption using e-mail. You can send your friend the key using FedEx and she can load it into her e-mail program so she can encrypt messages she sends you and can decrypt the messages that you send to her.

Internet Security Association and Key Management Protocol Internet Security Association and Key Management Protocol (ISAKMP) is not usable on its own, as it defines a general framework or structure to use one of any number of possible key exchange protocols. To make ISAKMP useful, IPSec associates it with other session-key exchange and establishment mechanisms. The Oakley Key Determination Protocol is one such mechanism. Together, ISAKMP and Oakley result in a new protocol called Internet Key Exchange (IKE).

Oakley Key Determination Protocol Oakley uses a hybrid Diffie-Hellman key exchange protocol to exchange session keys on Internet hosts and routers. (Diffie-Hellman protocol enables two users to exchange a key over an insecure medium without any prior association or set of steps.) Oakley optionally provides the security property called perfect forward secrecy (PFS). In addition to providing traditional key exchange under Diffie-Hellman, Oakley may be used to derive new keys from old keys or distribute keys by encrypting them with a different shared secret key. Oakley consists of three components:

- cookies exchange for stateless connections (such as the Internet)
- Diffie-Hellman public key values exchange mechanism
- authentication mechanism with the options of anonymity, perfect forward secrecy on the identities, and/or nonrepudiation

Security Policies

IPSec protects traffic based on the policy choices defined in the security policy database (SPD). The SPD is used for decision making on each packet of traffic. Information in the SPD is consulted to determine whether or not a packet will undergo IPSec transformation, be discarded, or be allowed to bypass IPSec. The database contains an ordered list of rules that define which IP packets within the network will be affected by the rule and enforces the scrutiny or transformation by the IPSec gateway server(s). SPD rules correspond to SAs in the SA database. The SPD, which is configured by the network administrator, is consulted with each receipt or transmission of IPSec (AH or ESP) packets and refers to entries within the SAD.

IPSec Key Management

As you've seen, IPSec requires the generation and sharing of multiple keys to carry out its security features. Following are three of the most common methods used for key exchanges:

- manual key exchange
- Simple Key Interchange Protocol (SKIP)
- ISAKMP/Oakley

The simplest and most widely used method for key exchange is the manual key exchange as defined in Internet Engineering Task Force RFC 1825. Using the manual exchange, a person manually configures each system with its own keys and those needed to communicate with other VPNs. Keys generated and managed under this approach are manually entered in the security association database.

Simple Key Exchange Protocol is a key management standard proposed by Sun Microsystems. SKIP is based on the generation of a shared secret using Diffie-Hellman with already authenticated public key values.

ISAKMP was selected as the key management protocol for IPSec by the IETF in September 1996. ISAKMP is used to negotiate security associations using the parameters (keys, protocols, and so forth) related to any security mechanism. ISAKMP is needed to negotiate, establish, modify, and delete security associations and their corresponding data.

12

Summary

The content of the Telecommunications, Network, and Internet Security domain is broad, deep, and complex and forms one of the most important areas that security practitioners must understand well, as modern computing is highly reliant on communications for success.

Once you have gained a level of comfort in how network communications operate through the aid of the OSI Model, you can begin to determine where the network is threatened by malicious activity, then you can begin to mix and match the building blocks of network security tools and techniques to implement defense in depth in preserving confidentiality, integrity, and availability.

It's not essential to memorize all the various firewall architectures or how VPNs operate under the covers, but it is important to know how to find this information and how to decide which architecture is most appropriate for a given situation. Because there are no cookbooks or recipes that work for all conditions, you'll find that the principles of network security will guide you to the right solutions at the right time.

Test Your Skills

MULTIPLE CHOICE QUESTIONS

1. Which OSI/ISO layer defines how to address the physical devices on the network?

    A. Session Layer

    B. Data Link Layer

    C. Application Layer

    D. Transport Layer

2. The ISO/OSI Layer 6 is which of the following?

    A. Application Layer

    B. Presentation Layer

    C. Data Link Layer

    D. Network Layer

3. What is an extranet?

    A. an intranet on steroids

    B. an intranet providing extra services

    C. an intranet that allows specific users outside the network to access its services

    D. None of the above.

4. Intrusion detection has which of the following sets of characteristics?

    A. It is adaptive rather than preventative.

    B. It is administrative rather than preventative.

    C. It is disruptive rather than preventative.

    D. It is detective rather than preventative.

5. A firewall is

    A. a pass-through device that allows only certain traffic in and out.

    B. a network segment off the firewall in which you would put systems that require different levels of access than other network components.

    C. an external DNS server.

    D. a mail relay.

6. Application-level firewalls operate at the

    A. OSI protocol Layer 7, the Application Layer.

    B. OSI protocol Layer 6, the Presentation Layer.

    C. OSI protocol Layer 5, the Session Layer.

    D. OSI protocol Layer 4, the Transport Layer.

7. Which of the following is the simplest type of firewall to implement?

    A. stateful packet-filtering firewall

    B. packet-filtering firewall

    C. dual-homed host firewall

    D. application gateway

8. The Telecommunications, Network, and Internet Security domain of information security is also concerned with the prevention and detection of the misuse or abuse of systems, which poses a threat to the tenets of

    A. confidentiality, integrity, and entity (CIE).

    B. confidentiality, integrity, and authenticity (CIA).

    C. confidentiality, integrity, and availability (CIA).

    D. confidentiality, integrity, and liability (CIL).

9. Which of the following is most affected by Denial-of-Service (DoS) attacks?

    A. confidentiality

    B. integrity

    C. accountability

    D. availability

12

10. Which of the following protocols is used by the Internet?

    A. SNA

    B. DECnet

    C. TCP/IP

    D. MAP

11. A DMZ is located

    A. right behind your first Internet firewall.

    B. right in front of your first Internet firewall.

    C. right behind your first network active firewall.

    D. right behind your first network passive Internet HTTP firewall.

12. Which protocol of the TCP/IP suite addresses reliable data transport?

    A. Transmission Control Protocol (TCP)

    B. User Datagram Protocol (UDP)

    C. Internet Protocol (IP)

    D. Internet Control Message Protocol (ICMP)

13. Another name for a VPN is a

    A. tunnel.

    B. one-time password.

    C. pipeline.

    D. bypass.

14. What advantages does a VPN offer?

    A. reduced cost of dedicated network services

    B. generally more secure than shared network services

    C. allows employees and business partners access to the organization's network in a secure fashion

    D. All of the above.

15. IPSec

    A. performs encryption and authentication.

    B. provides redundant security for IP-based networks.

    C. is an acronym for International Policy on Security Enforcement Committee.

    D. existed prior to the birth of the Internet.

EXERCISES

Exercise 12.1: Research the
International Standards Organization

1. Visit the ISO Web site at **www.iso.org**.

2. How is ISO organized?

3 How does ISO function?

4 What services does ISO provide in addition to the standardization of computer networks?

Exercise 12.2: Investigate In-Depth
One Layer of the OSI

1. Review the OSI Seven-Layer Model.

2. Choose one of the several layers of the OSI protocol stack to research in detail.

Exercise 12.3: Focus on a Security Mechanism

1. Investigate in greater detail one of the eight security mechanisms defined by ISO for network security (digital signatures, traffic padding, access control, or others).

2. Be prepared to discuss where and how the mechanism is implemented in some computer networks.

Exercise 12.4: Compare the
Three Major Data Network Types

1. Describe the form and function of a LAN.

2. Describe the form and function of a WAN.

3. Describe the form and function of an intranet.

12

PROJECTS

Project 12.1: Research Building a Home Computer Network

Home computer systems are becoming increasingly sophisticated as the availability of tools at a reasonable price improves.

1. Research articles on the Internet about building a home computer network complete with firewalls.

2. What would the basic configuration look like?

3. How would you decide how to configure the firewall? What document would you need to prepare? (*Hint*: See Chapter 4.)

4. What commercial tools are available to secure your home network? (*Hint*: Go to the following site to begin your research: **http://compnetworking.about.com/cs/homenetworking/a/homenet guide.htm**.)

5. How would you go about making sure the security of your network is working as intended?

Project 12.2: Interview a Network Administrator

1. Interview a network administrator at your company or school to learn about the type of security controls in place on your network.

2. What types of firewalls are used? For what purposes?

3. Are intrusion detection systems present? Who monitors them?

4. Ask the network manager what different methods are used to protect the networks that operate the school's record-keeping systems versus the network that's open for student educational uses.

5. Which security posture is adopted on which network segments?

Project 12.3: Research In-depth
Intrusion Detection Systems

Intrusion detection systems look for attacks originating from outside and inside the network.

1. Visit the distributed intrusion detection system called DShield at **www.dshield.org/**.

2. Which types of attacks are more prevalent at the time of your visit to the site?

3. Where is the origin of most of the attacks?

4. What is the status of the Internet Storm Center at the time of your visit?

5. What is the FightBack program all about?

▶▶ **Case Study**

Your public library system must protect the computer resources in its local area network (LAN) at each location from the rising number of malicious attacks that originate from the Internet, including Denial of Service (DoS) attacks. As the network administrator, you must protect the assets of the primary network, such as application servers at the main branch, without compromising service to the branch libraries that are connected to the network at the central library. You have also been instructed to keep your eye on the security budget as funding for the public library was recently cut back.

As the network security administrator, how would you approach this problem of securing a central computer network that is accessed by other branches and staff, sometimes in remote physical locations?

12

Chapter | 13

Application Development Security

Chapter Objectives

After reading this chapter and completing the exercises, you will be able to do the following:

- Determine the importance of security considerations as a part of the system development life cycle (SDLC).
- Outline an accelerated history of the SDLC and its purpose.
- Analyze the structure and roles of the SDLC Task Force committee subgroups.
- Categorize application development issues related to InfoSec.
- Apply your understanding of these issues to the distributed software environment (i.e., the client/server implementation).
- Distinguish among several major types of malicious software (malware).
- Outline the types and uses of antivirus software.

Introduction

You have probably heard the football cliché "the best offense is a good defense" more than once in your lifetime, as well as the old adage "an ounce of prevention is worth a pound of cure." The lesson behind these truisms is to be prepared for whatever comes at you—a 280-pound offense lineman or the flu bug. What does football or influenza have to do with information security?

More than you might think.

As the software development process continues to mature, software designers build more safeguards into their applications that prevent intrusion attacks instead of relying on security administrators to react to attacks after they occur. Just as the American Medical Association recommends annual health checkups to detect diseases and prevent them from undermining a patient's health, software designers now increasingly anticipate attacks based on the best practices developed by the software industry as a result of painful and, unfortunately, costly experiences reacting to software attacks.

This chapter introduces you to the concepts of the software development life cycle (SDLC). The SDLC has had to change over the past two decades to accommodate the increased rigor and exposure of network architectures compatible with hardware and software from different vendors (referred to as *open architecture systems* that rely on industry standards, thus permitting different manufacturers to produce systems that can operate with systems from competing manufacturers; e.g., IBM servers and Sun servers). In the early days of computing using mainframe computers and dumb terminals that could only communicate with the mainframe, application developers had little concern for the security of their programs as they were running in the "Glass House," which is what mainframe data centers were called. As computer systems became increasingly available and as computing power moved out of the Glass House into server rooms and user desktops, the concomitant risk of malicious computer use rose. As you shall see, threats to computer systems have forced the software industry to anticipate and defend against malicious users rather than reacting after an attack.

The Practice of Software Engineering

The art of software development evolved from its infancy decades ago to the more structured and "scientific" approach of today. In the early days of software development, programmers mainly had to worry about making programs as efficient as possible so as not to waste highly precious but limited computer memory. Their concern was not so much the vulnerability of their code to attacks from unauthorized individuals as making the code perform as efficiently and accurately as possible. These software developers worked in a more isolated environment at a time when large mainframe computers did not communicate with the outside world on today's complex networks. They were stand-alone computers, and only those who worked on the internal operating system could access the systems running on them. Software security was little more than a system ID, a password, and a set of rules determining the data access rights of users on the machine.

The evolution of open systems architecture made it possible for software engineers (as they prefer to be called today) to accomplish tasks thought inconceivable just a few decades ago. Users can now share resources on networked computers on the other side of the globe, sending e-mails with video and audio attachments to friends and relatives across the country and around the planet. There is no need to discuss the Internet boom here. In fact, we may have already become a little too complacent about the revolution it has spawned.

However, there is a need to discuss the risks inherent in making software systems available to a theoretically unlimited and largely anonymous audience. With the power and advantages of the Internet comes the responsibility to protect the individuals who use it from computer criminals.

Once upon a time, building security into software components was a luxury—a "nice-to-have" that outside of the U.S. Department of Defense was perhaps a novel leg-up over competitors. Those days have long since gone. Today, security in software is no longer an "add-on" but a requirement that software engineers must address during each phase of the SDLC. The "methodology," as software engineers call it, can no longer afford to ignore the principles of security procedures when designing and building systems. Instead, they must anticipate attacks to their systems and rethink the old ways of securing them. They must build defensive mechanisms into their computer systems to anticipate, monitor, and prevent attacks on their software systems. Simply waiting for and recovering from a hacker attack is no longer viable in an interconnected world where billions of dollars and personal identities are at stake.

Software Development Life Cycles

What is an SDLC? Some call it a methodology, others a religion, still others a set of handcuffs that restricts their creative energies. To some degree, everyone who has an opinion on the subject is right. Software engineers have followed a number of different software engineering processes over the years, beginning with no process at all (a.k.a., "spaghetti code" for its resemblance to a disorganized mess and using what was called "code and fix" methodology without any ability to repeat successes from one project to the next), moving on to higher levels of maturity and structure, and finally, to the more recent object-oriented techniques and languages. Regardless of the process, the software engineer will undoubtedly perform the same fundamental tasks to build information technology systems, namely:

- Understand the requirements of the system.

- Analyze the requirements in detail until the detailed business model is complete.

- Determine the appropriate technology for the system based on its purpose and use.

- Identify and design program functions.

- Code the programs.

- Test the programs, individually and collectively.

- Install the system into a secure "production" environment.

13

FYI: Developing Systems Using Object Orientation

Object orientation (OO) describes a view of solving a software development problem by modeling the problem space with components or objects that are

- modular (self-contained)
- reusable
- abstract (adequately represent the physical world context)
- easy to locate using technology (searchable over a network)
- easy to use (deploy)

This is in contrast to procedural orientation, where programs are written as a collection of functions or procedures that perform useful work.

An object is best described through an example of a physical world situation. In a university setting, objects are found wherever you look and become interesting to software developers when placed within a context that requires the building of a virtual model for what occurs in the real world. For a class-scheduling subsystem, some potentially interesting objects are identified by looking for people, places, artifacts, and events.

A CLASS object requires modeling information: name, line number, location, days, times, maximum number of students permitted, and so forth. This information is sometimes referred to as object attributes and is contained within an object definition (template). Each instance of a real class leads to the capture and management of actual data that's assigned to the selected attributes. Methods, or things that the object needs to do, are also modeled for the object and implemented via the object definition. Some methods in a CLASS object may include, among others:

- supply class name
- supply class location
- add a student to the class
- drop a student from the class
- supply class enrollment
- assign teacher to class

Objects within the subsystem communicate with other objects by sending a message indicating the service required, along with parameter values for the attributes within the object in question.

CONTINUED

As a simple example, a message sent to the CLASS object in the form of: CLASS.ShowLocation("classABC") would return the value of the location in which ClassABC is being held.

The method that the CLASS object implements to determine the location of where the class is held is of no consequence to the requesting object—the requester simply needs to know that the service is available and how to properly format a request to obtain the information. This principle of OO is called information hiding and eliminates many of the problems found in procedural approaches to software development. If an object's method requires changes, no other objects within the subsystem are affected, as only the CLASS object needs to implement the ShowLocation service. Because of this, changes that might otherwise affect many parts of a procedurally developed system are localized into a single point of maintenance when OO techniques are used.

If you are an aspiring or practicing software engineer, you are most likely familiar with several of these methodologies: the simple SDLC, the "Waterfall" model, and the Spiral model. Where these approaches differ is not so much in their content as in the weighting and ordering of specific tasks within the SDLC. One approach may be more data driven; for example, the data model takes precedence over all else (e.g., data flow diagramming). Another will focus more on the user and his interaction with the system (rational unified process/use cases). Regardless, one area where all methodologies fall short is on security in their systems. Security risks must be considered and mitigated in all phases of the SDLC.

Table 13.1 shows the security components related to the stages of the SDLC. Consider these a roadmap of security concerns as you traverse the system life cycle process.

Distributed Systems

This section will turn from the discussion of the SDLC to the real-world implementation of systems in a distributed environment, known more commonly as a client/server implementation. Prior to the advent of client/server systems, the user requested services from a local, centralized system, typically a large mainframe computer where resources were restricted to a finite set of users. In a distributed system such as a client/server system, resources are shared in a decentralized fashion. Whereas the user of a distributed system may think that his application is running locally, in fact he calls resources from a number of distributed systems across an array of networks.

13

TABLE 13.1 SDLC phases and associated security activities.

SDLC Phase	Security Component
Project inception (initiation)	Business stakeholders and project team members should refer to company information security policies and review any overarching legal or regulatory issues that might become risks to the project. The Health Insurance Portability and Accountability Act of 1996, or HIPAA, for example, would be a concern for a system that will process confidential medical information. This phase is required to identify which security policies are applicable for the software under development.
System requirements	Project team members should consider threats to the application and potential vulnerabilities as part of the system design. What level of protection is needed for the system data? Who should have access to the data? At what level? Will the data be available for external users? If so, how broad will the user community be? What kind of testing will be required to test system security? Security personnel should be included as part of the requirements gathering activity to assure that corporate security requirements are included.
System design	Security specifications created in the previous step should be incorporated into the system design. What access controls are needed, for example?
Detailed design	At the program level, identify security measures/controls needed to meet system security requirements including all legal and regulatory requirements and audit trails to assure user accountability and responsibility. Is data encryption required? If so, how robust must the encryption be? What kind of security testing will be needed at the module (program) level? At the subsystem (collection of programs) level or at the operating system level?
Coding	Ensure that individual modules adhere to the security specification requirements. Perform code walkthroughs to validate security features. Adjust test plans as needed.
System testing	Perform subsystem, string, and full system testing to eliminate coding errors, bugs, undesirable behavior, and measuring results against test plans.

Distributed systems are no longer the exception but the rule. Whether you are downloading music from the Internet, paying bills, looking up stock quotes, checking the weather, or e-mailing a friend or relative, you are executing a client that requests services that are processed by a server. The client software is your interface to a large distributed network that retrieves and presents the information that you requested (such as checking a bank account balance or paying your bills online). For example, you request financial information and find the Dow was down today and the NASDAQ was up. What you may not realize is the information you requested comes from a remote server that performs a number of different services to protect the confidentiality, integrity, and the availability of the information that you need.

Distributed systems come in several forms. Decentralized distributed systems may be connected or unconnected systems running independent copies of software using independent copies of data (e.g., accounting functions at different subsidiary companies of a large corporation). Dispersed distributed systems are interconnected, meaning that they run the same software and share the same data (like multiple branches of the same company). Cooperative distributed systems share interconnected platforms that use independent copies of software but use shared data (like retailers who can check on the inventories of other stores within the same sales districts). Distributed systems have come into being for some obvious and not-so-obvious reasons. Some of the not-so-obvious reasons are

- Improved performance because of reduced contention for centralized resources. The work is "spread out" across multiple networks.

- Increased availability, as the risk of system failure is lower. If a particular server crashes, traffic is rerouted to the next available server, for example.

- Greater versatility through the combined processing of disparate platforms.

You probably have realized the benefits of such interconnectedness and interoperability, but you have also undoubtedly experienced the downside of such technological expansiveness, the weakening of security, and the increasing risk of security attacks.

The distributed software environment introduces a number of risks foreign to a centralized computing system. They include the following features.

Software Agents

Think of the agent as a delegate or proxy program or service running in one operating environment at the behest of a calling program in another environment. An example of an agent is the Windows Updater function built into Microsoft Windows XP. The agent is a piece of software that "calls home" periodically looking for new updates to Windows that are not already installed on a local machine. The agent has no other purpose but to notify a user that a new update to Windows is ready and requests the user's permission to install it. Software agents are attractive targets for intruders because they tend to operate with operating system levels of authority, and their compromise or misuse are more difficult to detect. Think for a moment of the damage that can be caused if an intruder placed an agent on your PC that promised to perform essential operating system maintenance but in fact sent your personal information to a remote system for nefarious uses, such as ID theft or credit card fraud.

Java

Java is an object-oriented programming language used to create applets, servlets (small server-based programs), and JavaBeans. Java has become the mother language of many programs you use on the World Wide Web. One of the benefits of Java—its ability to download other Java programs to your machine—is also a security risk, especially when dealing with an unknown source on an insecure network. Although security experts generally feel the security architecture of Java is robust, its implementation is less so and has been plagued with a number of security flaws since its inception.

Java Applets

A Java applet is a dynamic program module written in the Java programming language, in a sense a miniature Java application embedded in a Web page and downloaded to the user's machine for execution. Although applets have made the World Wide Web more than a place to view static pages, they have also introduced security risks to your computer. Hostile applets, for example, can take control of your computer's operating system, corrupt or compromise data on your hard drive, fake e-mail, and bypass firewalls, particularly firewalls permitting unlimited outbound connections.

ActiveX Controls

If you see an authenticity certificate pop up while accessing a Web site in a browser such as Internet Explorer, you are most likely being asked if you want to install an ActiveX control. This security mechanism, known as Authenticode, recommends that commercial content and software providers digitally sign their ActiveX controls (see Chapter 11). Some experts compare ActiveX controls to Java applets, but usually not in a favorable way. Java applets theoretically are safer than ActiveX controls because they cannot access your machine's operating system and have a more limited range of functionality and versatility (called "operating in a sandbox").

Java applets, however, do not use the MS Authenticode feature and for that reason are considered by ActiveX proponents to be a bigger security risk. However, Java has its own security mechanism called Signed Objects. Object signing allows you to obtain reliable information about software code you download in much the same way you get reliable information about shrink-wrapped, off-the-shelf software. You can then make informed decisions about the software you download and make choices about whether to allow a signed Java applet to access specific resources or not.

FYI: What Is Authenticode?

Authenticode is Microsoft's security system for ActiveX controls to help people who download active content from Web sites to determine its authenticity and, by extension, its safety for use. Authenticode is based on a digital signature system to help users to verify that the software has not changed since it was signed and that the private key used to sign the code is tied to the digital certificate originally issued by the Authenticode certificate authority (CA). For more information, visit: **http://msdn.microsoft.com/ library/default.asp?url=/library/en-us/dnauth/ html/msdn_codewp.asp**.

Distributed Objects

Distributed object model, or DOM, allows "objects" to interact across different operating platforms in a distributed processing environment. It is also an attempt to define standards for open object interfaces. The Common Object Request Broker Architecture, or CORBA, defines an architecture that allows client software (such as a Java applet) to request a server process or object without the client software having to know the precise location of the server object. Think of an application where a client program needs information such as the shipping rates from all potential shippers but does not know where this information is available. Using distributed objects, the client simply invokes a request for such information—in a specified format—and the network determines the location, invokes the service, and returns the results. The object request broker (ORB) controls the messaging between objects residing on different platforms (see Figure 13.1).

The most attractive features of distributed object computing such as transparent and open access to objects on other systems also pose certain security risks as you have probably already guessed. Specific areas requiring greater security include the ability to restrict access to Web pages, to secure distributed objects such as CORBA communications, and to coordinate disparate security systems such as Web security with database security systems.

13

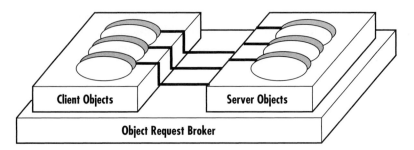

FIGURE 13.1 The object request broker.

Malware

What are some of the potential vulnerabilities of a distributed system? If a user accesses a Web site on an insecure network, he may risk downloading malicious code sometimes referred to as malware. Malware is malicious in that the code's intention is to wreak havoc on the host computer, as opposed to inept or poorly written code that opens itself up to exploitation. You have undoubtedly received e-mails warning you about the latest malware exploits. A few of the more recognizable types of malicious code are

- **Trojan horse:** A program containing hidden and malicious functions that's disguised as a utility program that performs useful work.

- **Virus:** Malicious code that propagates itself by infecting other programs, including operating systems. Viruses often use a local copy of a user's address book to obtain new recipients to target and may use the infected system's user identity to create an e-mail message that appears to originate from a trusted user but in fact has malicious directives.

- **Logic bomb:** Hidden code that is triggered by meeting or reaching a specific condition (date, time, event), much like a time bomb. Omega Engineering, a company that manufactures measuring devices for agencies such as NASA and the U.S. Navy, learned first-hand the dangers of the disgruntled employee after a logic bomb wiped out all of its research, development, and production programs all at once and wiped out the back-up tapes as well. Timothy Lloyd, a programmer at Omega, was charged with coding and releasing the logic bomb that detonated 10 days after he was terminated. Estimates of losses at Omega went as high as $10 million to rewrite their systems from scratch.

- **Worm:** A program that propagates itself by "worming" its way through communication protocols with no assistance or intervention from a user. The MS Blast worm attack in 2003 is an example.

- **Applet:** The aforementioned Java object that once downloaded can cause undue harm on the host computer. Because of vulnerabilities found in the Java programming implementations on some browsers, it's possible for an applet to gain elevated privileges and then access local machine information or cause the browser to crash.

Information security specialists must be well versed in the various types of malware exploits in order to include security concerns as important components of system design. Just as technology has become increasingly sophisticated over the relatively short life span of distributed systems, so too has the inventiveness of those who attack the systems.

Antivirus Software

Finally, what would a discussion of malware be without a brief look at several of the more popular antivirus software systems on the marketplace? Antivirus systems serve different purposes. Some attempt to prevent infection in the first place by blocking the downloading of malicious code on the host computer. Others attempt to repair the damage once it is done. Many vendors tout their software as the best antivirus tool on the market, and there are plenty to choose from.

Users should look for the following functionality and features when selecting antivirus software:

- Software updates are automatically downloaded when the consumer is online.

- Updated virus definitions are provided by the vendor, preferably downloadable from the Internet.

- The software protects, but does not inhibit, other software (such as e-mail).

- An experienced and respected vendor; some of the better known tools include Network Associates McAfee VirusScan, F-Secure AntiVirus, and Symantec Norton AntiVirus.

- A vendor that provides timely information about new viruses.

Any reputable software provider will admit that despite his or her best intentions, no software system is completely impervious to intrusion. Only through running software based on sound system design including the latest security features and the best antivirus tools can a user hope for a reasonable level of system security.

Improving Security Across the SDLC

The Security Across the Software Development Lifecycle Task Force published the report *Improving Security Across the Software Development Lifecycle* in early April 2004. The SDLC Task Force, a group composed of

13

software experts from both the public and private sectors, intended to increase software security throughout the SDLC. The task force includes representatives from universities, charitable organizations, and publicly traded and privately held companies. Although the task force also includes federal government employees, it is not an advisory group to any governmental department. Rather, the task force receives guidance from the National Cyber Security Partnership, itself a coalition of organizations including the U.S. Chamber of Commerce, TechNet, the Business Software Alliance, and the Information Technology Association of America.

Their 150-page report resulted from the work of four subgroups working under the guidance of co-chairs Ron Moritz, of Computer Associates, and Scott Charney, of Microsoft. These subgroups recommended the following guiding principles to increase software security throughout the SDLC:

- The Education Subgroup called for the increased training and educating of software engineers, present and future, to make software security an integral part of software design, not an afterthought.

- The Software Process Subgroup called for the development and sharing of enhanced software security processes and practices to make software systems safe from attack.

- The Incentives Subgroup recommended that software engineers be given incentive to develop an awareness of software security and to translate that understanding into practical techniques while punishing those individuals who behave maliciously (e.g., hackers).

- Finally, the Patching Subgroup wanted to make the process of applying software security patches "simple, easy, and reliable."

Given the timeliness of the task force's report and its sense of urgency, a closer look at the individual subgroup findings will set up the rest of this chapter for a discussion of some of the processes and procedures needed to implement their recommendations.

Education Subgroup

According to the Education Subgroup, the lack of adequate education in software security for software developers has cost the United States dearly. The industry sustains tens of billions of dollars per year in losses from software security flaws patch-management costs for critical security-related patches. The economy has also been harmed by the offshoring of software industry jobs to well educated and less expensive programmers from across the world. All these costs will only continue to rise until this educational need is addressed at a national level.

At the heart of the Education Subgroup's recommendation is a call for a change in the fundamental way people think about software, from the development of the simplest programs to the complex interdependencies of global systems. Their concern is not just about the present moment but also about the United States falling behind other nations that are already teaching security practices and procedures as part of their SDLC. For that reason, the Education Subgroup insists that universities, their faculty, and students must receive the funding and training necessary to revamp outdated information security curricula. They specifically recommend the following:

- Begin a new public-private effort to modernize educational and research programs to promote secure software development.

- Create a software security certification/accreditation program to promote increased security requirements in software design and development.

- Request that IT centers and software assurance groups outside mainstream academia also include security components as part of their SDLC.

Software Process Subgroup

The primary finding of this subgroup (and it is cause for alarm) is the gaping vulnerability of much of the U.S. "cyber infrastructure" to attack and the fact that the problem is getting worse. The Software Process Subgroup wants software engineers to follow standard processes and procedures to produce secure software. The Software Process Subgroup's recommendations include a number of short-, medium-, and long-range steps to build more secure software systems:

Short-term recommendations include

- Following software development processes that reduce defects in all phases of the SDLC (called "zero defects" in the quality assurance world).

- Following best practices for building secure software systems.

- When relevant, software developers should measure the results of their efforts and publish them to promote common practices across the industry.

Mid-term recommendations include

- Creating a security verification/validation program to review existing software development processes.

- Establishing measurable annual security goals for the U.S. cyber infrastructure through the joint efforts of private industry and the U.S. Department of Homeland Security.

13

Long-term recommendations include

- Certifying processes with demonstrated results in producing secure software.

- Continuing to research and teach new techniques while broadening the scope and depth of this research.

Software assurance testing and secure coding practices are discussed at length in Chapter 5. Even with secure software in the marketplace, new vulnerabilities and bugs continue to be revealed, and patch management is needed to close these holes and fix flaws in operations.

Patch Management Subgroup

Unlike a flat bicycle tire that won't ride without a patch, software usually can still operate with "holes" in it, frequently to the detriment of its users. A complex computer system contains thousands of instructions, many of which an experienced attacker can exploit. Inevitably, software engineers must apply fixes or "patches" to the software to prevent the code from breaking or, worse yet, opening the door to would-be attackers. A software patch can be much more difficult to install than a bicycle tire patch and can expose organizations to greater risk if not installed carefully. The Patch Management Subgroup states that the process is complex and should include impact and risk evaluation, rigorous testing, and controlled installation into production.

This subgroup has a number of recommendations for different audiences, including technology providers, critical infrastructure providers, and independent software vendors, mainly because the installation of software patches can be a collaborative effort among these three groups. A few of the many recommendations of the Patch Management Subgroup include

- Technology providers should include backup and risk mitigation plans for each patch including alternative actions technology consumers might use in place of installing the patch. The providers should give the technology consumer sufficient and relevant information about the nature of the patch and the risks of installing it in order to make an informed decision.

- For critical infrastructure companies, the Department of Homeland Security (DHS) should set up guidelines and procedures for critical infrastructure companies responsible for patch management, much like the Federal Deposit Insurance Corporation (FDIC) guidelines for financial institutions.

- Furthermore, the DHS should encourage independent software vendors to stay current with the most advanced secure software techniques and products.

Incentives Subgroup

The Incentives Subgroup may have the toughest job of all the task force groups as they are chartered with encouraging or "incenting" technology providers to take software security seriously. In the task force report, this subgroup says, "To be successful in our efforts to improve the security of cyber space, we must educate each person in the software industry about the direct impact they have on our collective security. Proper incentives can help to develop ownership of the problem at both a personal and corporate level" (*Improving Security Across the Software Development Lifecycle*, **www.cyberpartnership.org/SDLCFULL.pdf**).

But what exactly are the incentives needed to get the attention of the industry? Some of the Incentives Subgroup recommendations include

- basing job performance criteria on the quality and security of the software.

- creating industry awards for companies and individuals who promote software security practices.

- creating and distributing sample performance metrics for IT departments as a call to arms.

- setting up a National IT Security Certification Accreditation Program.

- banding together to catch cyber criminals.

Summary

In spite of all the network controls that security and network engineers deploy, without also considering the threats to confidentiality, integrity, and availability at the Application Layer, those controls could only provide marginal protection.

It's essential that security professionals are fully involved throughout the SDLC to help assure high-quality systems. As the rigor of software design has increased with technological advances, so has the need for enhanced security procedures built into the software. The far reach of the Internet and client/server applications increases the risk of malicious attacks against widely distributed software.

The SDLC Task Force, a group comprising software experts from both the public and private sectors, issued an April 2004 report aimed at increasing software security throughout the SDLC. The task force is composed of four subgroups including the Education, Software Process, Patch Management, and Incentives Subgroups.

The SDLC is not a newly minted approach to software delivery. The basic "phases" of the methodology include requirements gathering, analysis,

13

technical design, program design, coding, testing, and implementation. These phases have remained essentially the same over the past several decades. What has changed is the increasing emphasis on security in systems design and the need to anticipate the attacks of malicious users. Distributed applications have increased the reach and flexibility of software systems, but they have also increased the risk of attacks against weaknesses in software design.

Malware is an example of malicious attacks against computer systems that exploit vulnerabilities in software design. Code such as Trojan horses or viruses once introduced into a computer system can undermine the confidentiality, integrity, and availability of system services and data.

Test Your Skills

MULTIPLE CHOICE QUESTIONS

1. The process of software development
   A. has remained fundamentally the same over the past several decades.
   B. has changed from a passive to an active acceptance of security needs.
   C. has outgrown the need for methodology because of increased maturity of development models.
   D. has had a diminishing importance since the threat of terrorism has increased.

2. The SDLC is
   A. a task force committed to promoting consistent software development methodologies across operating platforms.
   B. a branch of the Department of Homeland Security.
   C. a learning center for software design.
   D. a series of activities describing the process of building computer systems.

3. Most computer industry experts view security in software as a (n):
   A. requirement.
   B. nice-to-have feature.
   C. elective.
   D. foolproof mechanism to thwart computer attacks.

4. The primary reason for enabling software audit trails is which of the following?

   A. improve system efficiency

   B. improve response time for users

   C. establish responsibility and accountability

   D. provide useful information to track down processing errors

5. What was the impetus behind the SDLC Task Force's report of April 2004?

   A. to improve security across the SDLC

   B. to raise awareness of the importance of system security

   C. to coordinate security efforts across the private and public sectors

   D. all of the above

6. What was one of the recommendations of the SDLC Task Force's Patch Management Subgroup?

   A. improving the reliability of applying software security updates

   B. developing new software traps such as "honey pots" to attract and catch would-be attackers

   C. combining "best practices" from international security groups to build quilted approaches or "patches" to software security

   D. identifying attacks from computer hackers known as "pirates" or "patches"

7. Which of the following phases of a system development life cycle is most concerned with establishing a sound policy as the foundation for design?

   A. development/acquisition

   B. implementation

   C. initiation

   D. maintenance

8. Which of the following best describes the purpose of debugging programs?

   A. to generate random data that can be used to test programs before implementing them

   B. to ensure that program coding flaws are detected and corrected

   C. to protect, during the programming phase, valid changes from being overwritten by other changes

   D. to compare source code versions before transferring to the test environment

13

9. Which of the following tests make sure the modified or new system includes appropriate access controls and does not introduce any security holes that might compromise other systems?

   A. recovery testing

   B. security testing

   C. stress/volume testing

   D. interface testing

10. Risk reduction in a system development life cycle should be applied:

    A. mostly to the initiation phase.

    B. mostly to the development phase.

    C. mostly to the disposal phase.

    D. equally to all phases.

11. At what stage of the applications development process should the security department become involved?

    A. prior to the implementation

    B. prior to systems testing

    C. during unit testing

    D. during requirements development

12. When considering an IT system development life cycle, security should be

    A. mostly considered during the initiation phase.

    B. mostly considered during the development phase.

    C. treated as an integral part of the overall system design.

    D. added once the design is completed.

13. What is a distributed system?

    A. an implementation of a client/server application

    B. a system using networked services and resources

    C. system resources located on disparate servers

    D. all of the above

14. Which of the following is not a risk with distributed systems?

    A. Java applets

    B. a firewall

    C. CORBA interfaces

    D. ActiveX controls

15. Antivirus software should

    A. have a track record of successful implementations.

    B. be self-updating.

    C. protect a computer system without inhibiting normal processing.

    D. All of the above.

EXERCISES

Exercise 13.1: Reasons for Security in Application Development

1. Why is application development security important?

2. What elements of application development should security professionals be most concerned with?

3. How can application developers stay current on threats to application software?

Exercise 13.2: What Is a "Buffer Overflow" Condition?

1. Conduct an Internet search for "buffer overflow."

2. Read through a number of the sites that appear and try to find what causes this condition in software.

3. What can developers do to discover buffer overflow problems in their own software and eliminate them before releasing the program to users?

Exercise 13.3: Investigate the Importance of the "Sandbox"

1. Conduct an Internet search of "Java sandbox."

2. Why are Java applications less susceptible to buffer overflow problems?

3. What are the security benefits of the sandbox?

13

Exercise 13.4: Logic Bombs

1. Examine one of the different kinds of malware mentioned in this chapter such as the "logic bomb."

2. Describe in greater detail how the attack works, and cite specific cases when the attack was launched.

3. What was the extent of the damage caused? Was the perpetrator caught? What punishment if any did he or she receive?

PROJECTS

Project 13.1: Research Efforts to Address Software Security

1. Find some of the industry and public efforts in the marketplace to address software security.

2. Address each issue below separately:

   ■ Patch management

   ■ Security testing for commercial software

   ■ Software liability issues

   ■ Developer education and awareness

Project 13.2: Offshore Software Development Security

Increasingly, U.S. organizations are outsourcing software development activities to countries like India, Pakistan, China, and other emerging economies to gain the benefits of reduced costs and faster turnaround times. But these efforts come at a price.

1. What security issues does overseas development of software raise in commercial and custom systems intended for use in the United States?

2. What privacy issues are raised?

3. How are these issues being addressed?

4. What trends can you determine on the future of offshore development?

5. What is the IT security industry doing to counter the threats from offshore development? (*Hint*: Visit **www.fdic.gov/regulations/examinations/offshore/ for more information.**)

Project 13.3: SDLC and Government Regulations

1. Review the provisions of the Security Rule for the Health Insurance Privacy and Accountability Act (HIPAA) as it relates to software development activities (see **www.securityfocus.com/infocus/1764**).

2. Review the provisions of Section 404 of the Sarbanes-Oxley Act as it relates to software development activities (see **www.cfodirect.com/ cfopublic.nsf?opendatabase&content=http://www.cfodirect.com/ cfopublic.nsf/vContent/THUG-66JS3C?open**).

3. What role does the SDLC play in compliance with these regulations?

4. What should software security specialists do to help their organizations comply?

5. How can software security specialists help IT auditors to best understand what controls are necessary and operating as intended?

13

Case Study

The U.S. Department of Justice (DOJ) recently adopted a 10-phase SDLC "to ensure privacy and security when developing information systems, to establish uniform privacy and protection practices, and to develop acceptable implementation strategies for these practices."

The DOJ needs a systematic and uniform methodology for information systems development. Using this SDLC will ensure that systems developed by the department meet IT mission objectives, are compliant with the current and planned information technology architecture (ITA), and are easy to maintain and cost-effective to enhance. Sound life-cycle management practices include planning and evaluation in each phase of the information system life cycle. The appropriate level of planning and evaluation is commensurate with the cost of the system, the stability and maturity of the technology under consideration, how well defined the user requirements are, the level of stability of the program, and user requirements and security considerations (cited from **www.usdoj.gov/jmd/irm/lifecycle/ch1.htm#para1**).

You are the chief information officer (CIO) of a major U.S. intelligence department tasked to review the DOJ methodology for completeness and consistency with industry standards. Using the above URL as a guideline, make a case for adopting, modifying, or wholesale rejecting of the DOJ's recommendation.

Chapter | 14

Securing the Future

Chapter Objectives

After reading this chapter and completing the exercises, you will be able to do the following:

- Establish plans for continuous monitoring and compliance enforcement.
- Discuss the future of information technology (IT) software security developments and the outlook for InfoSec professionals.
- Discuss the issues that drive the growth of the industry, technology, and regulations.

Introduction

Each chapter from Chapter 4 through Chapter 13 of this text discussed key concepts within the 10 domains of the Common Body of Knowledge, or CBK. Students with a solid grounding in these subject areas will be well on the way to earning the professional certification of their choosing. If this is not your intent and you simply want to understand the importance of information security as part of a larger computer science curriculum, you now have a good grasp of the basic principles of this discipline. If you are an information technology (IT) business manager or even a consumer worried about the computer attacks and threats you read about in the news—and perhaps more importantly threats you do not hear about—you have become more mindful of the importance of the subject. Regardless of your goal, this text has aimed at giving you additional guidance in case you want to investigate a specific topic in greater depth.

With this understanding of IT security in the context of modern business, you can begin to map solutions to problems that you'll encounter in both personal and organizational security issues. In this chapter, we wrap up with a view into securing the future and protecting the networks that modern-day lives depend on.

Continuous Monitoring and Constant Vigilance

The U.S. Department of Energy's Sandia National Laboratories use science-based technologies to support the U.S. national security program. This includes ensuring the safety, security, and reliability of the nuclear stockpile, reducing the proliferation of weapons of mass destruction (WMDs), monitoring and assessing new threats to national security, protecting energy sources and other critical infrastructures, and, more recently, helping the U.S. Department of Homeland Security protect the United States against terrorist attacks.

Information security is not an elective at Sandia. Information systems programs critical to national security and the infrastructure of the United States simply cannot be compromised by intruders from within or without. In order to test the security of their systems, Sandia created a group of self-described "bad guys" whose purpose was to break into Sandia's computer systems. Informally dubbed the "Red Team," this group set out to prove that competent outsiders can break into practically any networked computer no matter how well it is guarded. The Red Team performed so well that over the past two years, outside organizations including several key U.S. agencies invited the Red Team to break into their systems. In every instance, at 35 different sites, the Red Team was able to invade or create a mock attack on the information systems by adopting the mindset of outlaws. Through these staged attacks, the Red Team has helped develop and test concepts in information security, some of which are not declassified or publicly available.

Ruth Duggan, team leader of the Red Team, said after staging these attacks, "Right now, information system defenders have a very difficult job. Our goal is to improve the security of information systems to make the attacker's job difficult instead." Duggan added, "Fortified positions do take us longer to break in, but on the order of minutes, not hours."

The activity Sandia's Red Team engages in is a form of "ethical hacking" sometimes referred to as "white-hat" hacking. Ethical hackers use the same tactics as malicious hackers to perform penetration and intrusion testing; however, their goal is to uncover and not exploit holes in security systems. The U.S. government first used ethical hackers in the 1970s, and the practice has spread ever since. Governments and big businesses, like IBM, keep teams of ethical hackers to test their systems.

Ethical hackers typically follow scripts describing specific types of hackers, such as the cyber terrorist—people who attack weak points in information systems such as undefended modems instead of attacking robust defenses such as firewalls. Their goal is to show their client the weaknesses of their security systems and help them adopt better security measures in their systems architecture.

As new technologies continue to evolve, so do the threats to those technologies. As an organization counters each new security breach, a new threat appears, thus continuing the cycle. The problem with this approach is that technology companies are usually playing catch-up, reacting to the latest attack rather than anticipating it. Often, if academic and professional researchers do manage to anticipate attacks, the market is too slow to react and procure and implement the necessary protective measures.

Several measures can be taken to put a halt to this cycle of "hack-and react":

- Security needs to predict, not react to, attacks on information systems. By promoting information security in college curriculums, universities will begin to produce a new generation of highly trained InfoSec specialists with the skills and creativity to anticipate attacks.

- Educate the public. Consumers are becoming increasingly aware of attacks involving identity theft, credit card fraud, and social engineering. As consumer demand for safe systems increases, organizations will have to reassure the public with more robust security.

- Red Teams and ongoing frequent penetration testing are essential to vigilant intelligence gathering and uncovering problems early enough to prevent intrusions from nefarious sources.

- Build intelligence in systems. The capabilities of traditional network-layer firewalls can no longer keep up with worms, viruses, and the sophistication of malicious hackers. Countermeasures for preventing intrusions using technology that can recognize potential security compromises are being developed that thwart attempted attacks before damage can be done.

- Creating a national "security culture" whereby information security is a key component of every system designed and developed, both in public and commercial systems.

Operation Eligible Receiver

In 1997, Operation Eligible Receiver demonstrated the potential vulnerability of the U.S. government's information systems. The National Security Agency hired 35 hackers to launch simulated attacks on the national

14

information structure. The hackers obtained "root access"—the highest level of control—in 36 of the government's 40,000 networks. If the exercise had been real, the attackers would have been able to create power outages across Los Angeles, Chicago, Washington, and New York. They could have disrupted the U.S. Department of Defense's communication systems (taking out most of the Pacific Command) and gained access to computer systems aboard U.S. Navy vessels.

It was a disturbing exercise. So much so that several top White House officials at the time spoke of the possibility of an "electronic Pearl Harbor" attack on the U.S. mainland. Added to these vulnerabilities is the fact that most Americans have no sense of how information warfare would affect them.

The exercise also set the stage for a widespread national initiative called Critical Infrastructure Protection, or CIP. In 1998, President Clinton signed Presidential Decision Directive (PDD) Number 63 to establish the program.

From the White House Fact Sheet dated May 22, 1998:

> This Presidential Directive builds on the recommendations of the President's Commission on Critical Infrastructure Protection. In October 1997, the Commission issued its report calling for a national effort to assure the security of the United States' increasingly vulnerable and interconnected infrastructures, such as telecommunications, banking and finance, energy, transportation, and essential government services.

Today, most of the government activity that began from PDD63 has continued and matured into the Information Analysis and Infrastructure Protection (IAIP) Directorate, found in the U.S. Department of Homeland Security. The IAIP helps deter, prevent, and mitigate acts of terrorism by assessing vulnerabilities in the context of continuously changing threats. IAIP strengthens the nation's protective posture and disseminates timely and accurate information to our federal, state, local, private, and international partners and includes these subareas:

- Homeland Security Operations Center (HSOC)

- Information analysis (IA)

- Infrastructure protection

Information Sharing and Analysis Centers (ISACs) have been expanded from the original 8 sectors to 12 sectors, with varying degrees of participation and maturity. Many of these follow the model established for the banking and finance sector, called the Financial Services ISAC, or the

FS/ISAC (**www.fsisac.com**). Annually, an ISAC Congress meets to coordinate the activities across all sectors and to develop strategies for the following year. The ISAC Coordinating Council meets monthly to discuss issues from each sector and ways the government can help in assuring CIP.

Identity Theft and the U.S. Regulatory Environment

By the end of the first quarter of 2005, there were more than 25 bills working their way though state governments and the U.S. Congress and Senate in response to the ever-growing scourge of theft from information brokers such as Choicepoint (a credit reporting firm) and Lexis-Nexis (an information aggregator), and banking data theft, such as the loss of computer tapes containing account information on 1.2 million government expense management account users, including data from 47 U.S. Senators who use the service. Phishing attacks are also on the rise, and constituents are pressuring lawmakers to propose regulations for disclosing information breaches and implementing stronger controls to secure information. California's Senate Bill 1386 (SB1386) to mandate U.S. businesses to disclose to California citizens any suspected compromise of their personal or financial data led several other states to propose regulations.

Growing Threats

One of the more pressing threats today is the "knowledgeable insider"—employees, contractors, vendors, or strategic partners who access a network or computer environment for nonbusiness purposes. The annual security study from the Computer Security Institute (CSI) and the FBI (**http:// i.cmpnet.com/gocsi/db_area/pdfs/fbi/FBI2004.pdf**) has long indicated that one of the greatest threats to an enterprise is the insider.

The CSI/FBI report estimated that insiders waste up to three hours each day on the Internet engaged in activities that deplete resources and business productivity. Although most companies allow some personal use of the Internet, through the monitoring of Internet usage by their employees and partners, companies are discovering shocking information, such as regular access to pornographic sites or abuse of external instant messaging (IM) systems such as AIM, Yahoo!, and Instant Messenger.

Intellectual property is threatened by the ease with which individuals can walk into an environment with a thumb drive and copy large quantities of data practically undetected. Instant messaging (IM) is another problem. In the past, information security professionals have placed so much emphasis on protecting and regulating corporate e-mail structures that few organizations have looked at IM as a security issue and don't recognize the need to control it as they do e-mail.

14

As you read earlier in this chapter, companies are also experiencing pressure from external regulators and new corporate governance rules such as Sarbanes-Oxley to require publicly traded companies to adequately protect their systems and information assets that impact their financial position.

Vendors Try to Silence Security Researchers

Chapter 2 explained why security through obscurity is a bad idea and that Disclosure of Vulnerabilities Is a Good Thing for users of IT products. It seems Sybase (a database company) does not agree. In March 2005, Next Generation Security Software Ltd. (NGS), a security research company in England, was threatened by Sybase with a lawsuit if it published the details of a batch of vulnerabilities in Sybase Adaptive Server that it discovered in 2004. NGS initially notified Sybase of the problems, and Sybase issued patches for the holes and distributed them to customers. When NGS decided to publish the details of the vulnerabilities after waiting a period of time to allow Sybase to develop and issue patches, Sybase sent NGS a letter communicating their intent to sue if NGS released the details. NGS co-founder David Litchfield stated in *Computerworld* (March 28, 2005), "They claim that looking for security bugs comes under the banner of database performance testing and benchmarking." According to Sybase, the license agreement for the Development Edition of Sybase ASE prohibits the publication of performance testing and benchmarking results without their permission.

As of this writing, the case remains pending (see **www.computerworld.com/securitytopics/security/story/0,10801,100667,00.html**).

Pharming Supplements Phishing Attacks

A new class of network attacks that redirects consumers to potentially malicious Web servers—*pharming*—is sweeping the Internet. This type of attack redirects a victim attempting to visit a legitimate site (e.g., her online bank) to a malicious Web site that harvests user IDs and passwords. Criminals change the records used to convert domain names to numerical addresses (called domain-name system, or DNS), hijacking traffic intended for one site to pay-per-click Web sites that install aggressive advertising software (adware) on victims' computers.

The Internet Storm Center (**http://isc.sans.org/**), which collects and analyzes firewall log data to detect Internet threats, found that at least three attacks have used DNS cache poisoning since early March 2005. Two of the attacks aimed to drive victims to adware installation sites, while the other appeared only to redirect browsers to a Web site advertising herbal supplements.

Trends in Security Threats

In March 2005, a press release from Symantec Corporation entitled "Symantec Internet Security Threat Report" highlighted increases in attacks against Web applications, newfound threats to MS Windows, severe and easy-to-exploit vulnerabilities in popular software and systems, and an increase in phishing scams (see **www.symantec.com/press/2005/ n050321.html**). Symantec sees an increase in the use of "bots" (software robots for short) that are widely distributed to vulnerable PCs, laptops, and servers and are centrally controlled to activate on demand as a distributed Denial of Service (see Chapter 13), primarily against financial institutions. They report that mobile devices (PDAs, MP3 players, mobile phones) are becoming more vulnerable to malicious code attacks, and those attacks are on the rise. Spyware and adware attacks will increase or at least remain at the current level of threat, despite increased legislation that attempts to further criminalize the activities. Finally, hidden malicious code in otherwise trusted image files and music files raises the stakes for downloading content over the Internet.

Clearly, security specialists have their work cut out for them.

The Rosy Future for InfoSec Specialists

To neutralize the threats and comply with new regulations, organizations are increasingly looking to highly trained information security professionals for answers. Companies understand that they need to hire the right professionals with the right expertise. Otherwise, the potential negative impact on their business could be enormous.

Unlike other areas of the once-flourishing IT industry, InfoSec specialists should see an expansion of the security workforce through 2008, thanks to an estimated 13.7 percent annual increase in worker numbers to 2.1 million. This optimistic estimate is based on a survey that the International Data Corporation (IDC) conducted on behalf of the Information Systems Security Certifications Consortium (ISC^2).

IDC based its projections on several factors affecting the IT industry:

- A wider use of Internet technologies, creating even more challenges for security experts.

- An increasingly divergent set of technologies including wireless technologies that potentially introduce more and greater risks.

- Increased government regulation including laws protecting personally identifying information and national security.

In a November 2004 *Computerworld* article, more than 90 percent of the hiring managers stated that professional certification was important

14

when recruiting new information security professionals, and that a good understanding of business practices was becoming equally important. According to Allan Carey, the IDC analyst who conducted the study, "The study shows a shift in the information security profession, indicating that business acumen is now often required along with technology proficiency. This widening responsibility means information security professionals not only have to receive a constant refresh of the best security knowledge but also must acquire a solid understanding of business processes and risk management to be successful in their roles."

The goal of the IDC study was to provide comprehensive, meaningful research data about the information security profession to professionals, corporations, government agencies, academia, and others. More than 5000 information security professionals were interviewed for the study. They had an average 13 years experience in IT, 7 years of which were specifically in information security. To give you some idea of the kind of earning power these professionals have, 22 percent of residents of the United States who participated in the survey earned $100,000 to $120,000 a year ("Hackers force creation of more IT security jobs," **www.computerworld.com/print this/2004/0,4814,97912,00.html**).

Demand Outpaces Security Skills

Demand for specific security skill sets and capabilities has outpaced the demand for more generalized IT knowledge, and the population of IT security professionals has grown quickly. Career opportunities are abundant in the field today. People can make security their career choice but develop a concentration in other areas such as voice, data, or video. Other career paths may lead to a management position, ranging from privacy officer to chief information security officer (CISO).

More than 97 percent of the survey's respondents had moderate to very high expectations for career growth. The study stated that security professionals have experienced growth in job prospects, career advancement, higher base income, and salary premiums for certification at faster rates than other areas of information technology. All this for a profession that barely existed 10 years ago.

In addition to a highly positive outlook for career opportunities, information security professionals may find themselves in positions of higher responsibility in coming years.

Although these numbers bode well for those considering a career in InfoSec, what do they mean for the industry in general? Does an increase in the numbers of the local police force mean that that the town is getting serious about fighting crime or that the crime rate is out of control? Should we take an increase in the number of InfoSec professionals as a preventative measure on the part of organizations or a type of damage control? No one knows for sure, partly because organizations that have been hacked are reluctant to make this generally known. However, with heightened interest in Internet security from the consumer, and increased pressure from governments to make systems safer, we can safely surmise that those who specialize in this field will be highly sought-after individuals in IT in the years to come.

Summary

The Common Body of Knowledge (CBK) comprises 10 areas of study and discipline ranging from Security Management Practices to Laws, Investigations, and Ethics. Although the future direction of information security is as uncertain as the technology it protects, experts indicate that constant vigilance and monitoring are critical to keeping systems safe and secure.

Security experts must improve their ability to predict and not just react to the future. Colleges need to improve their curriculums in information security, and the industry as a whole must do a better job of educating the public about the importance of information security.

Improved technologies such as intelligent agents and more "proactive" diagnoses such as "Red Team" attacks should improve the security design of new applications. Creating a culture of information security specialists is critical to advances in information security.

Finally, according to a recent International Data Corporation survey, the job prospects for information specialists through 2008 look bright with a projected annual increase of 13.7 percent. Reasons cited are a wider use of Internet technologies, a more divergent technology including wireless, and increased government regulation.

Test Your Skills

MULTIPLE CHOICE QUESTIONS

For each of the following topics, identify the domain of the CBK to which it belongs.

1. Encryption/decryption:
    A. Security Architecture and Models
    B. Cryptography
    C. Business Continuity Planning
    D. Operations Security

14

2. Risk assessment:

   A. Physical Security

   B. Law, Investigations, and Ethics

   C. Telecommunications, Network, and Internet Security

   D. Security Management Practices

3. Virtual private networks (VPNs):

   A. Telecommunications, Network, and Internet Security

   B. Physical Security

   C. Security Management Practices

   D. Access Control Systems and Methodology

4. Perimeter alarm systems:

   A. Access Control Systems and Methodology

   B. Operations Security

   C. Security Management Practices

   D. Physical Security

5. Software copyrighting:

   A. Cryptography

   B. Telecommunications, Network, and Internet Security

   C. Law, Investigations, and Ethics

   D. Business Continuity Planning

6. OSI Model:

   A. Security Architecture and Models

   B. Application Development Security

   C. Access Control Systems and Methodology

   D. Operations Security

7. Retina scanning:

   A. Physical security

   B. Access Control Systems and Methodology

   C. Operations Security

   D. Law, Investigations, and Ethics

8. Intrusion-detection:
    A. Physical security
    B. Cryptography
    C. Operations Security
    D. Access Control Systems and Methodology

9. Cold-site facility:
    A. Business Continuity Planning
    B. Security Architecture and Models
    C. Security Management Practices
    D. Physical Security

10. CGI scripting:
    A. Application Development Security
    B. Telecommunications, Network, and Internet Security
    C. Operations Security
    D. Access Control Systems and Methodology

Select the most appropriate answer for the following questions.

11. What is a Red Team?
    A. hackers operating within the Soviet Union
    B. "white-hat" hackers
    C. republican congressmen promoting increased government regulation of information security
    D. germ-warfare agents

12. Which of the following factors may account for an increasing need for information security specialists?
    A. increased government regulation
    B. heightened public awareness
    C. growth of Internet technologies
    D. All of the above

13. What was the purpose of "Operation Eligible Receiver"?
    A. test the readiness of the NFL's computer systems
    B. detect the robustness of Iraqi computer systems
    C. test the strength of our national computer systems
    D. determine if hackers were compromising the National Security Agency's e-mail system

14

14. The President's 1998 Commission on Critical Infrastructure Protection:

    A. was the result of the Presidential Decision Directive 63 signed by President Clinton in 1998.

    B. was a national effort to secure critical U.S. infrastructures.

    C. was an interagency effort to recommend a holistic framework for solving problems with critical systems such as finance, energy, and communications.

    D. All of the above.

15. Which of the following is *not true* of the Information Analysis and Infrastructure Protection (IAIP) Directorate?

    A. helps deter acts of terrorism

    B. disseminates timely information about security threats to federal, state, and local agencies

    C. was modeled after the OSI Security Model

    D. cooperates with agencies such as the Department of Homeland Security

EXERCISES

Exercise 14.1: A Hacker by Any Other Name

1. Using your favorite Internet search engine, find some stories about "white-hat" hackers (like NGS in the Sybase story above).

2. How do white-hat hackers differ from the "gray-hat" hackers?

3. How do white-hat hackers differ from the "black-hat" hackers?

Exercise 14.2: Presidential Decision Directive 63

1. Download and read the Fact Sheet for the Presidential Decision Directive 63 (**www.fas.org/irp/offdocs/pdd-63.htm**).

2. What are the main points of the directive?

3. Why do you think President Clinton felt a Presidential Decision Directive was needed at that time?

Exercise 14.3: Private Sector versus Public Sector Careers in IT Security

1. Investigate the pros and cons of pursuing a career in information security in the private and public sectors.

2. What are some of the advantages and disadvantages in working for industry versus working for the government?

Exercise 14.4: Attitudes in Security

1. Describe some of the ways your personal attitude toward information security has changed as a result of this course.

2. Can you imagine that your behavior when using computers will change as a result of this course? What will you do differently?

PROJECTS

Project 14.1: Staying Current in the Field

1. From the ISC^2 Web site, download a copy of the *2005 Resource Guide for Today's Information Security Professional - Americas Edition* (**www.isc2.org/download/2005ISC2RGEDUandEvents.pdf**). (*Note:* Adobe Acrobat Reader is required.)

2 Scroll through the guide looking for resources and publications to help practitioners remain current in the field.

3. Why do you think that there are dozens of security conferences and events held throughout the year and throughout the world?

4. What value can security professionals gain from attending and participating in these conferences and seminars?

14

Project 14.2: U.S. Government Roles in National Security

1. Visit the Web site of the National Security Agency (NSA; **www.nsa.gov**) to determine their mission in protecting the national interest in computer use.

2. Visit the Web site of the U.S. Department of Homeland Security (DHS; **www.dhs.gov**) to determine their mission in protecting the national interest in cybersecurity.

3. Visit the Web site of the U.S. Department of Commerce NIST Computer Security Resource Center (**http://csrc.nist.gov**) to determine their mission in protecting the national interest in cybersecurity.

4. How are these agencies alike, and what are some of the overlapping elements of their mission statements?

5. How are these agencies different, and how is their work compatible or complementary?

Project 14.3: The Price of Spam

A notorious spammer in Raleigh, North Carolina, was able to generate 10 million e-mails a day using 16 high-speed lines, the equivalent capacity to support a company with more than 1000 employees. The spammer's business grossed more than $750,000 per month, pitching everything from work-at-home businesses to pornography. His weeklong trial ended with a 9-year sentence for the former distributor of physical junk mail (e.g., the unsolicited circulars you receive in your U.S. Postal Service mail box) (**http://securityfocus.com/news/10852**).

1. Investigate the current laws regarding the dissemination of spam on the Internet.

2. Does sending spam on the Internet deserve a 9-year sentence?

3. Do you believe the sentence for the first spam purveyor to be found guilty of a felony was too severe or too lenient?

4. How do the actions of the spam purveyor on the Internet differ (if at all) from "junk mail" distributors?

Project 14.4: Career Outlook

1. Visit the U.S. Department of Labor's Outlook for Computer Support Specialists (**www.bls.gov/oco/ocos268.htm**).

2. Prepare a want ad for an information security specialist. Include in your position announcement the nature of the work, working conditions, qualifications, work environment, salary information, and so forth.

3. Prepare a list of criteria and questions you would ask a prospective employee for the position.

4. What (if any) certifications would you seek in a candidate?

5. Would a certified prospective employee have an advantage over an equally skilled but not-certified candidate? Why or why not?

▶▶ Case Study

You have just accepted the position as the chief security officer (CSO) for a software development company selling human resources and payroll systems that until now has only done business within the United States. You accepted the position knowing that the organization's immediate goal is to expand overseas and address the needs of global businesses.

Prepare a brief executive presentation (e.g., PowerPoint) for the company's board of directors that explains the importance of information security to a purveyor of HR and payroll systems and makes a case for a twofold increase in the organization's security budget. Include international regulatory and privacy issues.

14

Appendix A

Common Body of Knowledge

The ISC^2 Common Body of Knowledge (CBK) is an organization and collection of topics that are relevant to information security professionals. The CBK establishes a common framework of information security terms and principles collected to assist worldwide information security professionals with discussions, debates, and to resolve matters within a common understanding. The 10 Domains of the CBK, along with the major topics and major subject areas follows.

Security Management Practices

Key Areas of Knowledge

Security Management Concepts and Principles

- Privacy
- Confidentiality
- Integrity
- Availability
- Authorization
- Identification and Authentication
- Accountability
- Non-Repudiation
- Documentation
- Audit
- CIA Triad

Protection Mechanisms

- Layering
- Abstraction
- Data Hiding
- Encryption
- Change Control/Management
- Hardware Configuration
- System and Application Software
- Change Control Process

Data Classification

- Objectives of a Classification Scheme
- Criteria by Which Data Is Classified
- Commercial Data Classification
- Government Data Classification
- Information/Data
- Worth/Valuation
- Collection and Analysis Techniques

Employment Policies and Practices

- Background Checks/Security Clearances
- Employment Agreements
- Hiring and Termination Practices
- Job Descriptions
- Roles and Responsibilities
- Separation of Duties and Responsibilities
- Job Rotations
- Policies, Standards, Guidelines, and Procedures

Risk Management

- Principles of Risk Management
- Threats and Vulnerabilities

- Probability Determination
- Asset Valuation
- Risk Assessment Tools and Techniques
- Qualitative vs. Quantitative Risk Assessment Methodologies
- Single Occurrence Loss
- Annual Loss Expectancy (ALE) Calculations
- Countermeasure Selection
- Countermeasure Evaluation
- Risk Reduction/Assignment/Acceptance

Roles and Responsibilities
- Management
- Owner
- Custodian
- Users
- IS/IT Function
- Other Individuals
- Security Awareness Training
- Security Management Planning

Security Architecture and Models

Key Areas of Knowledge

Principles of Common Computer and Network Organizations, Architectures, and Designs
- Addressing (Physical and Symbolic)
- Address Space versus Memory Space
- Hardware, Firmware, and Software
- Machine Types (Real, Virtual, Multi-State, Multi-Tasking, Multi-Programming, Multi-Processing, Multi-Processor, Multi-User)
- Network Protocol Functions (OSI 7 Layer Model)
- Operating States (Single State, Multi-State)

- Operating Modes (User, Supervisor, or Privileged)

- Resource Manager Functions

- Storage Types (Primary, Secondary, Real, Virtual, Volatile, Non-Volatile, Random, Sequential)

- Protection Mechanisms (Layering, Abstraction, Data Hiding, Process Isolation, Hardware Segmentation, Principle of Least Privilege, Separation of Privilege, Accountability)

- System Security Techniques (Preventive, Detective, and Corrective Controls)

Principles of Common Security Models, Architectures, and Evaluation Criteria

- Certification and Accreditation

- Closed and Open Systems

- Confinement, Bounds, and Isolation

- Controls (Mandatory and Discretionary)

- IETF Security Architecture (IPSEC)

- ITSEC Classes and Required Assurance and Functionality

- Objects and Subjects (Purpose and Relationship)

- Security Perimeter and DMZ

- Reference Monitors and Kernels (Purpose and Function)

- Trusted Computing Base (TCB)

- Security Models (Bell-LaPadula, Clark-Wilson, Biba) (Confidentiality, Integrity, and Information Flow; Commercial versus Government Requirements)

- TCSEC Classes and Required Functionality

- Tokens, Capabilities, and Labels (Purpose and Functions)

Common Flaws and Security Issues Associated with System Architectures and Designs

- Covert Channels (Memory, Storage, and Communications)

- Initialization and Failure States

- Input and Parameter Checking

- Maintenance Hooks and Privileged Programs (Superzap/Su)

- Programming (Techniques, Compilers, APIs, and Library Issues)
- Timing (TOC/TOU), State Changes, and Communication Disconnects
- Electro-Magnetic Radiation

Business Continuity Planning (BCP) and Disaster Recovery Planning (DRP)

Key Areas of Knowledge

Business Continuity Planning

- Project Scope and Planning
- Business Organization Analysis
- Resource Requirements
- Legal and Regulatory Requirements
- Business Impact Assessment
- Emergency Assessment
- Business Success Factors
- Critical Business Functions
- Establishment of Priorities
- Development of Alternative Means of Accomplishing Objectives

Containment Strategy

- Developing a Strategy, Provisions, and Processes

Recovery Strategy

- Business Unit Priorities
- Crisis Management
- Work Group Recovery
- Alternatives
- Cold/Warm/Hot/Mobile Sites
- Electronic Vaulting
- Selection Criteria
- Processing Agreements

- Reciprocal/Mutual

Recovery Plan Development

- Emergency Response
- Developing Emergency Response Teams and Procedures

Personnel Notification

- Handling Personnel Notification and Communications to Management

Backups and Off-Site Storage

- Determining What to Back Up (Data, Software, Parameters, Tables, Formulas, Documentation) and How Often (Backup Cost versus Cost to Recreate or Update)
- Selecting a Proper Storage Facility for Backups

Software Escrow Arrangements

External Communications

Utilities

- Determining Proper Applications of UPSs
- Logistics and Supplies
- Fire and Water Protection
- Documentation
- Implementation
- Work Group Recovery

Recovery Techniques

- Developing a Containment Strategy
- Determining Provisions to Stock and Where to Store Them
- Developing Recovery Processes (Facilities, Telecommunications, Software, Data)
- Developing a Recovery Strategy (Networks, Systems, Applications, Training/Testing/Maintenance)
- Developing a Training Strategy
- Testing the Plans and Frequency

- Keeping the Plans Up to Date

Disaster Recovery Planning

- Recovery Plan Development
- Emergency Response
- Developing Emergency Response Teams and Procedures
- Personnel Notification
- Handling Personnel Notifications and Communications to Management
- System Software, Application Software, and Data
- Reconstruction from Backups
- Movement of Files from Off-Site Storage
- Loading All Software and Installation of Applicable Updates
- Loading of Data, Parameter, and Supporting Files
- External Communications
- Crisis Management
- Utilities
- Logistics and Supplies
- Documentation
- Implementation
- Work Group Formation
- Recovery Techniques
- How to Develop Recovery Processes
- Facilities
- Telecommunications
- Software
- Data
- How to Develop a Recovery Strategy
- Networks
- Systems
- Applications

- Restoration
- Cleaning
- Procurement
- Data Recovery
- Software Recovery
- Training/Testing/Maintenance
- How to Develop a Training Strategy
- How to Test the Plans and How Often
- How to Keep the Plans Up to Date
- Relocation to Primary Site
- Elements of Business Continuity Planning
- Awareness and Discovery
- Contingency Planning Goals
- Statement of Importance
- Statement of Priorities
- Statement of Organizational Responsibility
- Statement of Urgency and Timing
- Risk Assessment
- Vital Records Program
- Emergency Response Guidelines
- Emergency Response Procedures
- Mitigation
- Preparation
- Testing

BCP/DRP Events

- Bombings
- Explosions
- Earthquakes
- Fires
- Floods

- Power Outages
- Other Utility Failures
- Storms
- Hardware/Software Failures
- Strikes
- Testing Outages
- Hazardous Material Spills
- Employee Evacuation/Unavailability

Law, Investigations, and Ethics

Key Areas of Knowledge

Laws

- Licensing
- Intellectual Properties
- Import/Export
- Liability
- Transborder Data Flow

Major Categories and Types of Laws

- Criminal Law
- Civil Law
- Administrative Law

Investigations
Evidence

- Types of Admissible Evidence
- Collection and Preservation of Evidence
- Chain of Evidence

Investigation Processes and Techniques

- Target

- Object/Subject
- Team Composition
- Forensics
- Privacy
- Interrogation
- Internal/External Confidentiality

Major Categories of Computer Crime

- Military and Intelligence Attacks
- Business Attacks
- Financial Attacks
- Terrorist Attacks
- Grudge Attacks
- "Fun" Attacks

Incident Handling

- Common Types of Incidents
- Abnormal and Suspicious Activity
- Generally Accepted Guidelines for Confiscating Equipment, Software, and Data
- Generally Accepted Guidelines for Incident Data Integrity and Retention
- Generally Accepted Guidelines for Reporting Incidents

Ethics

- (ISC^2) Code of Ethics
- Request for Comment 1087 — Internet Activity Board "Ethics and the Internet"

Physical Security

Key Areas of Knowledge

Facility Requirements

- Restricted Areas/Work Areas

- Escort Requirements/Visitor Control
- Fences, Gates, Turnstiles, Mantraps
- Security Guards/Dogs
- Badging
- Keys and Combination Locks
- Lighting

Site Selection, Facility Design, and Configuration

- Motion Detectors, Sensors, and Alarms
- CCTV
- Technical Controls
- Smart/Dumb Cards
- Audit Trails/Access Logs
- Intrusion Detection
- Biometric Access Controls
- Environment/Life Safety
- Power and HVAC Considerations
- Water Leakage and Flooding
- Fire Detection and Suppression
- Natural Disasters
- Physical Security Threats
- Fire and Smoke
- Water (Rising/Falling)
- Earth Movement (Earthquakes, Slides, Volcanoes)
- Storms (Wind, Lightning, Rain, Snow, Sleet, Ice)
- Sabotage/Vandalism
- Explosion
- Building Collapse
- Toxic Materials
- Utility Loss (Power, Heating, Cooling, Air, Water)
- Communications Loss (Voice, Data)

- Equipment Failure
- Personnel Loss (Strikes, Illness, Access, Transport)
- Elements of Physical Security

Threat Prevention, Detection, and Suppression

- Fire (Sensors, Sprinklers, Flooding Systems, Extinguishers)
- Water (Leakage and Flooding)
- Toxic Materials (Detection and Control)
- Electrical (UPS and Generators)
- Environmental (Location, Air Temperature, Humidity, Contamination, HVAC, Water)
- Public, Private and Restricted Areas (Perimeter Security, Prevention, Detection)
- Guns, Guards, Fences and Gates
- Swat Teams, Armored Personnel Carriers
- Guard Towers, PIDAS Fences
- Man Traps and Turnstiles
- Locks
- Enclosures, Safes, Cabling Systems
- Dogs and X-Ray Equipment
- CCTV
- Detectors (Motion, Heat, Laser Beam, Glass-Breakage)
- Alarms (Silent and Audio)

Operations Security

Key Areas of Knowledge

Administrative Management

- Job Requirements/Specifications
- Background Checking
- Separation of Duties and Responsibilities
- Least Privilege

- Job Rotation
- Mandatory Vacation in One-Week Increments
- Terminations

Concepts

- Antivirus Management
- Backup of Critical Information
- Changes in Workstation/Location
- Need-to-Know/Least Privilege
- Privileged Operations Functions
- Standards of Due Care/Due Diligence
- Privacy and Protection
- Legal Requirements
- Illegal Activities (Fraud Detection, Collusion)
- Record Retention

Sensitive Information and Media

- Marking
- Handling
- Storage
- Destruction

Control Types

- Directive Controls
- Preventive Controls
- Detective Controls
- Corrective Controls
- Recovery Controls
- Operations Controls
- Resource Protection

- Privileged Entity Controls
- Change Control Management
- Hardware Controls
- Input/Output Controls
- Media Controls
- Administrative Controls (Separation of Duties and Responsibilities, Rotation of Duties, Least Privilege)

Trusted Recovery Process

- Communications Hardware/Software
- Processing Equipment
- Password Files
- Application Program Libraries
- Application Source Code
- Vendor Software
- Operating System
- System Utilities
- Directories and Address Tables
- Proprietary Packages
- Main Storage
- Sensitive/Critical Data
- System Logs/Audit Trails
- Violation Report
- Backup Files
- Sensitive Forms and Printouts

Auditing

- Compliance Checks
- Internal and External
- Frequency of Review
- Standard of Due Care
- Audit Trails

- Individual Accountability
- Reconstruction of Events
- Problem Identification (Intrusion Detection)
- Problem Resolution
- Reporting Concepts (Content, Format, Structure, Hierarchy, Escalation, Frequency)
- Reporting Mechanisms
- Audit Logging
- Security Events
- System Audit Trails
- Sampling and Data Extraction
- Retention Periods
- Media
- Protection Against Alteration
- Protection Against Unavailability
- Audit Log Backup (Importance of System Backups, Frequency, Availability, Media, Off-Site Storage Location and Protection Mechanisms, Quality, Readability)

Monitoring

- Event Monitoring
- Hardware Monitoring (Fault Detection, Port)
- Illegal Software Monitoring

Monitoring Tools and Techniques

- Warning Banners
- Keystroke Monitoring
- Traffic Analysis
- Trend Analysis
- Available Tools
- Real Time
- Ad Hoc

- Passive
- Closed Circuit Television (CCTV)

Failure Recognition, Response, and Alternatives

- Problem Identification
- Problem Resolution
- Reporting Concepts (Content, Format, Structure, Hierarchy, Escalation, Frequency)
- Reporting Mechanisms

Intrusion Detection

- Intrusion Prevention (Identification, Authentication)
- Intrusion Detection (Data Extraction, Sampling, Recognition, Traffic)
- Intrusion Response

Types of Intrusion Detection

- Pattern Recognition and Baselines
- Anomaly Identification
- Attack Signature Identification
- Penetration Testing Techniques
- War Dialing
- Sniffing
- Eavesdropping
- Radiation Monitoring
- Dumpster Diving
- Social Engineering

Inappropriate Activities

- Fraud
- Collusion
- Sexual Harassment
- Pornography
- Waste

- Abuse
- Theft

Threats and Countermeasures

- Errors and Omissions
- Fraud and Theft (Internal or External)
- Employee Sabotage
- Loss of Physical and Infrastructure Support
- Malicious Hackers/Crackers
- Espionage
- Malicious Code
- Violations, Breaches, and Reporting

Access Control Systems and Methodology

Key Areas of Knowledge

Accountability

- Access Control Techniques
- Discretionary Access Control
- Mandatory Access Control
- Lattice-Based Access Control
- Rule-Based Access Control
- Role-Based Access Control

Access Control Lists

- Access Control Administration
- Account Administration
- Account, Log, and Journal Monitoring
- Access Rights and Permissions
- Establishment (Authorization)
- File and Data Owners, Custodians, and Users
- Principle of Least Privilege

Segregation of Duties and Responsibilities

- Maintenance
- Revocation

Access Control Models

- Bell-LaPadula
- Biba
- Clark and Wilson
- Non-Interference Model
- State Machine Model
- Access Matrix Model
- Information Flow Model

Identification and Authentication Techniques

- Knowledge-Based Passwords, Personal Identification Numbers (PINs), Phrases
- Passwords
- Selection
- Management
- Control
- Characteristic-Based (Biometrics, Behavior)
- Tokens
- Tickets
- One-Time Passwords
- Token-Based (Smart Card, Key Card)
- Administrative
- Single Sign-On (SSO)

Access Control Methodologies and Implementation

Centralized/Remote Authentication Access Controls

- RADIUS
- TACACS

Decentralized Access Control

- Domains

- Trust

- File and Data Ownership and Custodianship

Methods of Attack

- Brute Force

- Denial of Service

- Dictionary

- Spoofing

- Man-in-the-Middle Attacks

- Spamming

- Sniffers

- Crackers

- Monitoring

Intrusion Detection

- Types of Intrusions

- Intrusion Prevention (Identification, Authentication)

- Intrusion Detection (Data Extraction, Sampling, Recognition, Traffic)

- Attack Signature Identification

- Intrusion Reactive Response

- Anomaly Identification

Intrusion Response

- Alarms

- Signals

- Audit Trails

- Violation Reports

- Corrections

- Penetration Testing

Cryptography

Key Areas of Knowledge

Use of Cryptography

- Confidentiality
- Integrity
- Authentication
- Non-Repudiation

Cryptographic Concepts, Methodologies, and Practices

- Symmetric Algorithms
- Asymmetric Algorithms

Message Authentication

- Digital Signatures
- Non-Repudiation

Encryption/Decryption

- Basic Functionality of Cryptographic Algorithms (DES, RSA, SHA, MD5, HMAC, and DSA)
- Strengths and Weaknesses of Cryptographic Algorithms and Effects of Key Length

Basic Functions Involved in Key Management

- Key Distribution Methods and Algorithms (Manual, Kerberos, and ISAKMP)
- Error Detecting/Correcting Features
- Hash Functions
- Message Digests (MD5, SHA, and HMAC)
- One-Time Cipher Keys (Pads)
- Stream Ciphers and Block Ciphers
- Key Escrow and Key Recovery

Private Key Algorithms

- Applications and Uses
- Algorithm Methodology
- Key Distribution and Management
- Key Generation/Distribution
- Key Recovery
- Key Storage and Destruction
- Key Strength
- Complexity
- Secrecy
- Weak Keys

Public Key Algorithms

- Applications and Uses
- Algorithm Methodology
- Key Distribution and Management
- Key Generation
- Key Recovery
- Key Storage and Destruction
- Key Strength
- Complexity
- Secrecy
- Weak Keys
- Public Key Infrastructure (PKI)
- Certificate Authorities
- Components
- Hierarchical Structure

Certificates

- Types and Classes
- How Certificates Are Issued, Verified, Distributed, and Revoked
- Hierarchy Chain

System Architecture for Implementing Cryptographic Functions

- Use of Application and Network-Based Protocols (PEM, S/MIME, SSL, HTTPS or SHTTP, SET, IPSEC)

- Application of Hardware Components (Smart Cards and Tokens)

- Application of Cryptographic Components (IPSEC)

- Nodes/ISAKMP

Methods of Attack

- COA

- KPA

- CTA (CPA, ACPA, and CCA)

- Brute Force

- CRACK

- Replay

- MIM

- Birthday

Telecommunications and Network Security

Key Areas of Knowledge

International Standards Organization/Open Systems Interconnection (ISO/OSI) Layers and Characteristics

- Physical Layer

- Data Link Layer

- Network Layer

- Transport Layer

- Session Layer

- Presentation Layer

- Application Layer

Communications and Network Security

- Physical Media Characteristics (Fiber Optics/Coaxial/Twisted Pair)

- Network Topologies (Star/Bus/Ring)

- IPSEC Authentication and Confidentiality

- TCP/IP Characteristics and Vulnerabilities
- Local Area Networks (LANs)
- Wide Area Networks (WANs)
- Remote Access/Telecommuting Techniques
- Secure Remote Procedure Call (S-RPC)
- Remote Access Dial-In User System/Terminal Access Control
- Access System (RADIUS/TACACS)
- Network Monitors and Packet Sniffers
- Internet/Intranet/Extranet
- Firewalls
- Routers
- Switches
- Gateways
- Proxies

Protocols

- Transmission Control Protocol/Internet Protocol (TCP/IP)
- Network Layer Security Protocols (IPSEC, SKIP, SWIPE)
- Transport Layer Security Protocols (SSL)
- Application Layer Security Protocols (S/MIME, SSL, SET, PEM)
- Challenge Handshake Authentication Protocol (CHAP) and Password Authentication Protocol (PAP)
- Point-to-Point Protocol (PPP)/Serial Line Internet Protocol (SLIP) Services
- HDLC
- Frame Relay
- SDLC
- ISDN
- X.25

Communications Security Techniques

- Tunneling
- Virtual Private Network (VPN)

- Network Monitors and Packet Sniffers
- Network Address Translation
- Transparency
- Hash Totals
- Record Sequence Checking
- Transmission Logging
- Transmission Error Correction
- Retransmission Controls
- E-mail Security
- Facsimile Security
- Secure Voice Communications
- Security Boundaries and How to Translate Security Policy to Controls

Network Attacks and Countermeasures

- ARP
- Brute Force
- Worms
- Flooding
- Eavesdropping
- Sniffers
- Spamming
- PBX Fraud and Abuse

Applications and Systems Development Security

Key Areas of Knowledge

Application Issues

- Distributed Environment
- Agents
- Applets

- ActiveX
- Java
- Objects
- Local/Non-Distributed Environment
- Viruses
- Trojan Horses
- Logic Bombs
- Worms

Databases and Data Warehousing

- Aggregation
- Data Mining
- Inference
- Polyinstantiation
- Multi-Level Security
- Database Management System (DBMS) Architecture

Data/Information Storage

- Primary
- Secondary
- Real
- Virtual
- Random
- Volatile
- Sequential
- Knowledge-Based Systems
- Expert Systems
- Neural Networks
- Systems Development Controls
- System Development Life Cycle

- Conceptual Definition
- Functional Requirements Determination
- Protection Specifications Development
- Design Review
- Code Review or Walk-Through
- System Test Review
- Certification
- Accreditation
- Maintenance

Security Control Architecture

- Process Isolation
- Hardware Segmentation
- Separation of Privilege
- Accountability
- Layering
- Abstraction
- Data Hiding
- System High
- Security Kernel
- Reference Monitor
- Modes of Operation
- Supervisor
- User
- Integrity Levels
- Network/System
- Operating System
- Database
- File
- Service Level Agreement

Malicious Code

- Definitions
- Jargon
- Myths/Hoaxes

Hackers, Crackers, Phreaks, and Virus Writers

- Antivirus Protection
- Antivirus Software

Computer Viruses

- Multi-Partite
- Macro
- Boot Sector Infectors
- Macintosh
- File Infectors
- Logic Bombs
- Trojan Horses
- ActiveX
- Java
- Trap Doors

Methods of Attack

- Brute Force or Exhaustive Attack
- Denial of Service
- Dictionary Attacks
- Spoofing
- Pseudo Flaw
- Alteration of Authorized Code
- Hidden Code
- Logic Bomb
- Trap Door
- Interrupts

Remote Maintenance

- Browsing
- Inference
- Traffic Analysis
- Flooding
- Cramming
- Time of Check/Time of Use (TOC/TOU)

Appendix | B

Security Policy and Standards Taxonomy

As described in Chapter 4 (Security Management Domain), a complete Policy and Standards Library is essential to a comprehensive security programme. An outline of the policies and standards that one would expect to see, derived from ISO/IEC 17799–Code of Practice for Information Security Management, follows. The first level indicates where a policy would be expected, the second level where a standard would be expected, and the third level indicates which topics within the standard should be covered.

Security Management Policy

Information Security Organization

- Mission, Purpose, and Charter
- Authority and Responsibility
- Information Security Oversight
- Information Security Council
- Security-Related Organizational Responsibilities
- Cooperation Between Organizations
- Policy Framework
- Information Security Strategy

Training and Awareness

- Information Security Training and Awareness
- Communication of Policies

Risk Management Policy

Information Ownership

- Information Owners
- Resource Administrators
- Information Users

Information Classification

- Classification Levels
- Data Classification Prefixes
- Classification Reviews

Risk Assessments

- Risk Assessment Process
- Inventory of Information Resources
- Initial Risk Assessment
- Re-evaluation Process
- Risk Classification Process

Security Baselines

Security of Hard Copy Media

- Handling and Labeling
- Copying
- Distribution
- Storage
- Transport
- Disposal
- Printing

Security of Electronic Media

- Handling and Labeling
- Duplication
- Distribution
- Storage
- Transport
- Disposal

Personnel Security Policy

Pre-Employment Controls

- Personnel Screening
- User Acknowledgement of Security Awareness

Separation of Duties

- Separation of Duties Requirements
- Critical Functions to be Separated

During Employment Controls

- Security in Job Definitions
- Confidentiality Agreements
- Information Security Training
- Periodic Re-Screening
- Acknowledgement of Information Security Responsibilities

Personnel Administration

- Performance Monitoring
- Disciplinary Actions
- Third Party Compliance with Security Policies
- Depth of Expertise
- Mandatory Vacation Time
- Rotation of Critical Personnel

Transfer/Resignation/Termination Controls

- Transfers
- Terminations
- Resignations

Physical Security Policy

Security of Facility

- Securing Computing Facilities
- Construction and Design
- Physical Entry Controls
- Securing Offices, Rooms and Facilities
- Working in Secure Areas
- Isolated Delivery and Loading Areas

Security of Information Systems

- Workplace Protection
- Power/Telecommunications Cabling
- Power Supplies
- Network/Server Equipment
- Equipment Maintenance
- Security of Equipment Off-Premises
- Secure Disposal or Re-Use of Equipment
- Removal of Equipment
- Unused Ports and Cables

Fire Protection

- Non-Smoking Restriction
- Fire Detection
- Fire Suppression
- Monitoring Systems

- Systems Testing
- Fire Prevention Training
- Storage of Flammables
- Computing Facility Separation Requirements

Water Protection

- Water Detection
- Waterproof Covering
- Equipment Location
- Water Monitoring Systems
- Systems Testing
- Water Protection Training
- Computing Facility Water Protection

Environmental Controls

- Electrical Protection
- Emergency Lighting
- Climate Controls
- Backup Ventilation
- Monitoring Environmental Controls
- Environmental Controls Training
- Emergency Shutdown Controls

Operations Management Policy

Operational Management and Controls

- Organization and Management
- Operations Manual
- Information Resource Configuration
- Network Documentation
- Emergency Access

- Patches, Fixes and Updates
- Vendor Supplied Operational Software
- Operational Change Control
- System Logs
- System Documentation
- System Acceptance
- Capacity Planning
- Single Points of Failure
- Separation of Development, Test and Protection Environments
- Segregation of Duties
- Never Alone Principle
- Security Diagnostic Tools
- Developer Access to Production Systems

Malicious Code and Viruses

- Responsibilities, Training and Actions
- Antivirus Software

Backup and Recovery

- Periodic Backup
- Off-site Storage
- Record Retention Schedules
- Destruction of Records
- Annual Review/Testing

Software Support

- Use of Approved Software products
- Control of Proprietary Software
- Use of Public Domain Software
- Software Escrow
- Ownership of Software

Security Monitoring and Response Policy

Monitoring Activities

- Network/System Monitoring
- Access Monitoring
- Intrusion Detection Systems (IDSs)
- Internal Communications Monitoring
- Control of Monitoring Devices
- Review of Monitoring Activities

Incident Response

- Reporting Security Incidents/Violations
- Documenting Security Incidents
- Investigation of Incidents/Violations
- Learning from Incidents
- Public Relations

Communications Management Policy

Encryption

- Use of Encryption
- Digital Signatures
- Key Management

Exchange of Information

- Information Exchange Agreements
- Electronic Data Interchange (EDI
- Publically Available Information

E-mail, Internet and Other Electronic Communications

- Business Use
- Use of Encryption

- Acceptable Use
- Retention/Deletion of Electronic Mail
- Personal Web Sites

Voice/Fax/Video Communications

- Business Use
- Acceptable Use
- Phone Calls
- Voice Mail
- Facsimile
- Conference Calls/Video Teleconferences
- Limitations on Confidential and Restricted Information

Meetings and Conversations

- Meetings and Conferences
- Public Conversations

Access Control Policy

User Enrollment and Authorization

- User Enrollment Process
- User Registration
- Review of User Access Privileges
- Password Management Systems

Identification

- User IDs
- Shared/Group IDs
- Default User IDs
- Temporary User IDs
- Group Membership

Authentication

- Access Control Features
- Password Length/Composition
- Password Expiration
- User Password Change
- Password Storage
- One-Time Use of Initial Passwords
- Password Resets
- Default Passwords
- Inactive Accounts
- Failed Login Attempts
- Password History
- Display and Printing of Passwords and User IDs
- Simultaneous Logins
- Automatic Logoff/Timeout
- Duress Alarms

Privileged and Special Account Access

- Special Privileges
- Need to Know
- Least Privilege
- Identification of Privileges
- Use of System Routines
- Logging Privileged Account Activity
- System Utilities/Commands
- Third Party Access

Remote Access

- Requesting/Granting Access
- Remote Computing Devices

- Remote Control Software
- Modem Connections

Network Security Policy

Network Access

- Use of Network Services
- Enforced Path
- Inventory of Network Access Points
- Authentication
- Remote Diagnostic Ports
- Network Segregation
- Network Connections
- Network Routing
- Limitation of Connection Time
- System Login Banner
- Avoidance of Trust Relationships

Network Security Control Devices

- Use of Firewalls
- Use of Demilitarized Zones (DMZs)
- Packet Filter Configuration
- Router Configuration
- Host Configuration
- E-mail
- Remote login
- File Transfer Protocol (FTP)
- Hyper Text Transfer Protocol (HTTP)
- Network News Transfer Protocol (NNTP)
- Trivial File Transfer Protocol (TFTP)
- Non-Essential Services
- UNIX-to-UNIX Copy Protocol (UUCP) Restrictions

- Domain Name Server (DNS)
- Logging and Auditing
- Automatic Terminal Identification
- Requirements for Network Traffic Filtering
- Honey Pots
- Network Address Translation

Third Party Services Policy

Third Party Services

- Selection Process
- Third Party Service Agreements
- Outsourcing Contract Requirements
- Monitoring Outsourcing Contracts

Application Development Policy

Application Development Process

- Methodology
- Development Environment
- Access to Program Source Library
- Business Requirements
- Risk Assessment
- Installation Process
- Electronic Commerce Development
- Software Acquisition
- Restrictions on Changes to Software Packages
- User Procedures and Training

System Business Requirements

- Design
- Design Exceptions

- Input Data Validation
- Control of Internal Processing
- Message Authentication
- Output Data Validation
- Application Auditing/Logging

Application Testing

- Application Review
- Acceptance Testing Criteria
- User Acceptance Testing
- Post Implementation Review
- Protection of System Test Data

Recovery and Business Continuity Area

Business Continuity Management Process

- Roles and Responsibilities
- Business Continuity Planning Framework
- Business Continuity Impact Analysis
- Business Continuity Plan Development
- Annual Inventory

Recovery/Business Continuity Plan Testing Requirements

- Recovery/Business Continuity Plan Testing
- Documentation of Plan Testing
- Testing Requirements for Highly Critical Systems
- Testing Requirements for Moderately Critical Systems
- Third Party Testing

Recovery Sites

- Hot Recovery Sites
- Cold Recovery Sites

Legal, Compliance, and Regulatory Requirements

- Intellectual Property Rights
- Safeguarding of Organizational Records
- Privacy of Personal Information
- Customer Privacy

Security Compliance Testing

- Testing Concepts and Processes
- Testing Results
- Compliance Tools

Appendix C

Sample Policies

Appendix C provides real-world examples of security policies you're likely to find in use in a typical security program as described in Chapter 4. These standards are illustrative of the types of security documentation that you can find at the SANS Security Policy Project, where boiler-plate documentation is available for the taking to reduce the need to reinvent the wheel each time a new policy is required. You can find the Security Policy Project at: **www.sans.org/resources/policies/**

Sample Computer Acceptable Use Policy

1.0.0 Acceptable Use Policy

1.1.0 Overview

<Company Name Here> intentions for publishing an Acceptable Use Policy are not to impose restrictions that are contrary to <Company Name Here> established culture of openness, trust and integrity. <Company Name Here> is committed to protecting <Company Name Here> employees, partners and the company from illegal or damaging actions by individuals, either knowingly or unknowingly. Internet/Intranet/Extranet-related systems, including but not limited to computer equipment, software, operating systems, storage media, network accounts providing electronic mail, WWW browsing, and FTP, are the property of <Company Name Here>. These systems are to be used for business purposes in serving the interests of the company, and of our clients and customers in the course of normal operations. Please review Human Resources policies for further details. Effective security is a team effort involving the participation and support of every <Company Name Here> employee and affiliate who deals with information and/or information systems. It is the responsibility of every computer user to know these guidelines, and to conduct their activities accordingly.

1.2.0 Purpose

The purpose of this policy is to outline the acceptable use of computer equipment at <Company Name Here>. These rules are in place to protect the employee and <Company Name Here>. Inappropriate use exposes <Company Name Here> to risks including virus attacks, compromise of network systems and services, and legal issues.

1.3.0 Scope

This policy applies to employees, contractors, consultants, temporaries, and other workers at <Company Name Here>, including all personnel affiliated with third parties. This policy applies to all equipment that is owned or leased by <Company Name Here>.

1.4.0 Policy

1.4.1 General Use and Ownership

- While <Company Name Here> network administration desires to provide a reasonable level of privacy, users should be aware that the data they create on the corporate systems remains the property of <Company Name Here>. Because of the need to protect <Company Name Here> network, management cannot guarantee the confidentiality of information stored on any network device belonging to <Company Name Here>.

- Employees are responsible for exercising good judgment regarding the reasonableness of personal use. Individual departments are responsible for creating guidelines concerning personal use of Internet/Intranet/Extranet systems. In the absence of such policies, employees should be guided by departmental policies on personal use, and if there is any uncertainty, employees should consult their supervisor or manager.

- <Company Name Here> recommends that any information that users consider sensitive or vulnerable be encrypted.

- For security and network maintenance purposes, authorized individuals within <Company Name Here> may monitor equipment, systems and network traffic at any time, per <Company Name Here> Audit Policy.

- <Company Name Here> reserves the right to audit networks and systems on a periodic basis to ensure compliance with this policy.

1.4.2 Security and Proprietary Information

- The user interface for information contained on Internet/Intranet/Extranet-related systems should be classified as either confidential or not confidential, as defined by corporate confidentiality guidelines, details of which can be found in Human Resources policies. Examples of confidential information include but are not limited to: company private, corporate strategies, competitor sensitive, trade secrets, specifications, customer lists, and research data. Employees should take all necessary steps to prevent unauthorized access to this information.

- Keep passwords secure and do not share accounts. Authorized users are responsible for the security of their passwords and accounts. System level passwords should be changed quarterly; user level passwords should also be changed quarterly.

- All PCs, laptops and workstations should be secured with a password-protected screensaver with the automatic activation feature set at 10 minutes or less, or by logging-off (*control+ alt + delete* for Win2K users) when the host will be unattended.

- Use encryption of information in compliance with <Company Name Here> Acceptable Encryption Use policy.

- Because information contained on portable computers is especially vulnerable, special care should be exercised.

- Postings by employees from a <Company Name Here> e-mail address to newsgroups should contain a disclaimer stating that the opinions expressed are strictly their own and not necessarily those of <Company Name Here>, unless posting is in the course of business duties.

- All hosts used by the employee that are connected to the <Company Name Here> Internet/Intranet/Extranet, whether owned by the employee or <Company Name Here>, shall be continually executing approved virus-scanning software with a current virus database. Unless overridden by departmental or group policy.

- Employees must use extreme caution when opening e-mail attachments received from unknown senders, which may contain viruses, e-mail bombs, or Trojan horse code.

1.4.3 Unacceptable Use

The following activities are, in general, prohibited. Employees may be exempted from these restrictions during the course of their legitimate job responsibilities (e.g., systems administration staff may have a need to disable the network access of a host if that host is disrupting production services). Under no circumstances is an employee of <Company Name Here> authorized to engage in any activity that is illegal under local, state, federal or international law while utilizing <Company Name Here> -owned resources.

The lists below are by no means exhaustive, but attempt to provide a framework for activities, which fall into the category of unacceptable use.

1.4.3.1 System and Network Activities The following activities are strictly prohibited, with no exceptions:

- Violations of the rights of any person or company protected by copyright, trade secret, patent or other intellectual property, or similar laws or regulations, including, but not limited to, the installation or distribution of "pirated" or other software products that are not appropriately licensed for use by <Company Name Here>.

- Unauthorized copying of copyrighted material including, but not limited to, digitization and distribution of photographs from magazines, books or other copyrighted sources, copyrighted music, and the installation of any copyrighted software for which <Company Name Here> or the end user does not have an active license is strictly prohibited.

- Exporting software, technical information, encryption software or technology, in violation of international or regional export control laws, is illegal. The appropriate management should be consulted prior to export of any material that is in question.

- Introduction of malicious programs into the network or server (e.g., viruses, worms, Trojan horses, e-mail bombs, etc.).

- Revealing your account password to others or allowing use of your account by others. This includes family and other household members when work is being done at home.

- Using a <Company Name Here> computing asset to actively engage in procuring or transmitting material that is in violation of sexual harassment or hostile workplace laws in the user's local jurisdiction.

- Making fraudulent offers of products, items, or services originating from any <Company Name Here> account.

- Making statements about warranty, expressly or implied, unless it is a part of normal job duties.

- Effecting security breaches or disruptions of network communication. Security breaches include, but are not limited to, accessing data of which the employee is not an intended recipient or logging into a server or account that the employee is not expressly authorized to access, unless these activities are within the scope of regular duties. For purposes of this section, "disruption" includes, but is not limited to, network sniffing, pinged floods, packet spoofing, Denial of Service, and forged routing information for malicious purposes.

- Port scanning or security scanning is expressly prohibited unless prior notification to <Company Name Here> is made.

- Executing any form of network monitoring which will intercept data not intended for the employee's host, unless this activity is a part of the employee's normal job/duty.

- Circumventing user authentication or security of any host, network or account.

- Interfering with or denying service to any user other than the employee's host (for example, Denial of Service attack).

- Using any program/script/command, or sending messages of any kind, with the intent to interfere with, or disable, a user's terminal session, via any means, locally or via the Internet/Intranet/Extranet.

- Providing information about, or lists of, <Company Name Here> employees to parties outside <Company Name Here>.

1.4.3.2 E-mail and Communications Activities The following activities are strictly prohibited, with no exceptions:

- Sending unsolicited e-mail messages, including the sending of "junk mail" or other advertising material to individuals who did not specifically request such material (e-mail spam).

- Any form of harassment via e-mail, telephone or paging, whether through language, frequency, or size of messages.

- Unauthorized use, or forging, of e-mail header information.
- Solicitation of e-mail for any other e-mail address, other than that of the poster's account, with the intent to harass or to collect replies.
- Creating or forwarding "chain letters," "Ponzi" or other "pyramid" schemes of any type.
- Use of unsolicited e-mail originating from within <Company Name Here> networks of other Internet/Intranet/Extranet service providers on behalf of, or to advertise, any service hosted by <Company Name Here> or connected via <Company Name Here> network.
- Posting the same or similar non-business-related messages to large numbers of Usenet newsgroups (newsgroup spam).

1.5.0 Enforcement

Any employee found to have violated this policy may be subject to disciplinary action, up to and including termination of employment.

1.6.0 Definitions

Term   Definition

Spam Unauthorized and/or unsolicited electronic mass mailings.

1.7.0 Revision History

7/24/2004: Initial Section Creation.

Sample E-mail Use Policy

1.0.0 E-mail Use Policy

1.1.0 Purpose
The purpose of this policy is to prevent tarnishing the public image of <Company Name Here>. When e-mail goes out from <Company Name Here> the general public will tend to view that message as an official policy statement from <Company Name Here>.

1.2.0 Scope
This policy covers appropriate use of any e-mail sent from a <Company Name Here> e-mail address and applies to all employees, vendors, and agents operating on behalf of <Company Name Here>

1.3.0 Policy

1.3.1 Prohibited Use
The <Company Name Here> e-mail system shall not to be used for the creation or distribution of any disruptive or offensive messages, including offensive comments or attachments about race, gender, hair color, disabilities, age, sexual orientation, pornography, religious beliefs and practice, political beliefs, or national origin. Employees who receive any e-mails with this content from any <Company Name Here> employee should report the matter to their supervisor immediately.

1.3.2 Personal Use
Using a reasonable amount of <Company Name Here> resources for personal e-mails is acceptable, but non-work related e-mail should be saved in a separate folder from work related e-mail. Sending chain letters or joke e-mails from a <Company Name Here> e-mail account is prohibited. Virus or other malware warnings and mass mailings from <Company Name Here> shall be approved by <Company Name Here> VP Operations before sending. These restrictions also apply to the forwarding of mail received by a <Company Name Here> employee.

1.3.3 Monitoring
<Company Name Here> employees shall have no expectation of privacy in anything they store, send or receive on the company's e-mail system. <Company Name Here> may monitor messages without prior notice. <Company Name Here> is not obliged to monitor e-mail messages.

1.4.0 Enforcement
Any employee found to have violated this policy might be subject to disciplinary action, up to and including termination of employment.

1.5.0 Definitions

E-mail The electronic transmission of information through a mail protocol such as SMTP or IMAP. Typical e-mail clients include Eudora and Microsoft Outlook.

Forwarded e-mail E-mail resent from an internal network to an outside point.

Chain e-mail or letter E-mail sent to successive people. Typically the body of the note has direction to send out multiple copies of the note and promises good luck or money if the direction is followed.

Sensitive information Information is considered sensitive if it can be damaging to <Company Name Here> or its customers' reputation or market standing.

Virus warning A warning consists of an e-mail containing warnings about virus or malware. The overwhelming majority of these e-mails turn out to be a hoax and contain bogus information usually intent only on frightening or misleading users.

Unauthorized disclosure The intentional or unintentional revealing of restricted information to people, both inside and outside <Company Name Here>, who do not have a need to know that information.

1.6.0 Revision History

Sample Password Policy

1.0.0 Password Policy

1.1.0 Overview

Passwords are an important aspect of computer security. They are the front line of protection for user accounts. A poorly chosen password may result in the compromise of <Company Name Here>'s entire corporate network. As such, all <Company Name Here> employees (including contractors and vendors with access to <Company Name Here> systems) are responsible for taking the appropriate steps, as outlined below, to select and secure their passwords.

1.2.0 Purpose

The purpose of this policy is to establish a standard for creation of strong passwords, the protection of those passwords, and the frequency of change.

1.3.0 Scope

The scope of this policy includes all personnel who have or are responsible for an account (or any form of access that supports or requires a password) on any system that resides at any <Company Name Here> facility, has access to the <Company Name Here> network, or stores any non-public <Company Name Here> information.

1.4.0 Policy

1.4.1 General

- All system-level passwords (e.g., root, enable, NT admin, application administration accounts, etc.) must be changed on at least a quarterly basis.
- All production system-level passwords must be part of the VSI administered global password management database.
- All user-level passwords (e.g., e-mail, Web, desktop computer, etc.) must be changed at least every three months. The recommended change interval is every month.
- User accounts that have system-level privileges granted through group memberships must have a unique password from all other accounts held by that user.
- Passwords must not be inserted into e-mail messages or other forms of electronic communication.
- Where SNMP is used, the community strings must be defined as something other than the standard defaults of "public," "private" and "system" and must be different from the passwords used to log in interactively. A keyed hash must be used where available (e.g., SNMPv2).

- All user-level and system-level passwords must conform to the guidelines described below.

1.4.2 Guidelines

A. General Password Construction Guidelines

Passwords are used for various purposes at <Company Name Here>. Some of the more common uses include: user level accounts, Web accounts, e-mail accounts, screen saver protection, voicemail password, and local router logins. Since very few systems have support for one-time tokens (i.e., dynamic passwords which are only used once), everyone should be aware of how to select strong passwords.

Poor, weak passwords have the following characteristics:

- The password contains less than eight characters.
- The password is a word found in a dictionary (English or foreign).
- The password is a common usage word such as:
  - Names of family, pets, friends, co-workers, fantasy characters, etc.
  - Computer terms and names, commands, sites, companies, hardware, software.
  - The words "<Company Name Here>" or any derivation.
  - Birthdays and other personal information such as addresses and phone numbers.
  - Word or number patterns like aaabbb, qwerty, zyxwvuts, 123321, etc.
  - Any of the above spelled backwards.
  - Any of the above preceded or followed by a digit (e.g., secret1, 1secret)

Strong passwords have the following characteristics:

- Contain both upper- and lowercase characters (e.g., a-z, A-Z).
- Have digits and punctuation characters as well as letters (e.g., 0-9, !@#$%^&*()_+|~-=\`{}[]:";'<>?,./)
- Are at least eight alphanumeric characters in length.
- Are not comprised of any words in any language, slang, dialect, jargon, etc.
- Are not based on personal information, names of family, etc.
- Passwords should never be written down or stored online. Try to create passwords that can be easily remembered. One way to do this is create a password based on a song title, affirmation, or other phrase. For example, the phrase might be: "This May Be One Way To Remember" and the password could be: "TmB1w2R!" or "Tmb1W>r~" or some other variation.

NOTE: Do not use either of these examples as passwords!

B. Password Protection Standards

Do not use the same password for <Company Name Here> accounts as for other non-<Company Name Here> access (e.g., personal ISP account, option trading, benefits, etc.). Where possible, don't use the same password for various <Company Name Here> access needs. For example, select one password for the Engineering systems and a separate password for IT systems. Also, select a separate password to be used for an NT account and a UNIX account.

Do not share <Company Name Here> passwords with anyone, including administrative assistants or secretaries. All passwords are to be treated as sensitive, confidential <Company Name Here> information.

Here is a list of "don'ts":

- Don't reveal a password over the phone to ANYONE.
- Don't reveal a password in an e-mail message.
- Don't reveal a password to the boss.
- Don't talk about a password in front of others.
- Don't hint at the format of a password (e.g., "my family name").
- Don't reveal a password on questionnaires or security forms.
- Don't share a password with family members.
- Don't reveal a password to co-workers while on vacation.
- If someone demands a password, refer them to this document or have them call someone in the Information Security Department.
- Do not use the "Remember Password" feature of applications (e.g., Eudora, Outlook, Netscape Messenger).
- Again, do not write passwords down and store them anywhere in your office. Do not store passwords in a file on ANY computer system (including Palm Pilots or similar devices) without encryption.
- Change passwords at least once every three months (just as system-level passwords which must be changed quarterly). The recommended change interval is every month.
- If you suspect that an account or password has been compromised, report the incident to someone in the Information Security Department immediately and change all the passwords.
- Password cracking or guessing may be performed on a periodic or random basis. If a password is guessed or cracked during one of these scans, the user will be required to change it.

C. Application Development Standards

Application developers must ensure their programs contain the following security precautions. Applications:

- Support authentication of individual users, not groups.

- Do not store passwords in clear text or in any easily reversible form.

- Provide for some sort of role management, such that one user can take over the functions of another without having to know the other's password.

- Support TACACS+ , RADIUS and/or X.509 with LDAP security retrieval, wherever possible.

D. Use of Passwords and Pass Phrases for Remote Access Users

Access to the <Company Name Here> networks via remote access is to be controlled using either a one-time password authentication or a public/private key system with a strong pass phrase.

E. Pass phrases

Pass phrases are generally used for public/private key authentication. A public/private key system defines a mathematical relationship between the public key that is known by all, and the private key, that is known only to the user. Without the pass phrase to "unlock" the private key, the user cannot gain access.

Pass phrases are not the same as passwords. A pass phrase is a longer version of a password and is, therefore, more secure. A pass phrase is typically composed of multiple words. Because of this, a pass phrase is more secure against "dictionary attacks."

A good pass phrase is relatively long and contains a combination of upper- and lowercase letters and numeric and punctuation characters. An example of a good pass phrase:

"The*?#>*@TrafficOnThe101Was*&#!#ThisMorning"

All of the rules above that apply to passwords apply to pass phrases.

1.5.0 Enforcement

Any employee found to have violated this policy might be subject to disciplinary action, up to and including termination of employment.

1.6.0 Definitions

Application Administration Account Any account that is for the administration of an application (e.g., Oracle database administrator, NT administrator, etc.).

1.7.0 Revision History

Sample Wireless (Wi-Fi) Use Policy

1.0.0 Wireless Communication Policy

1.1.0 Purpose
This policy prohibits access to <Company Name Here> networks via unsecured wireless communication mechanisms. Only wireless systems that meet the criteria of this policy or have been granted an exclusive waiver are approved for connectivity to <Company Name Here> networks.

1.2.0 Scope
This policy covers all wireless data communication devices (e.g., personal computers, cellular phones, PDAs, etc.) connected to any of <Company Name Here> internal networks. This includes any form of wireless communication device capable of transmitting packet data. Wireless devices and/or networks without any connectivity to <Company Name Here> networks do not fall under the purview of this policy.

1.3.0 Policy

1.3.1 Register Access Points and Cards
All wireless Access Points / Base Stations connected to the corporate network must be registered and approved. These Access Points / Base Stations are subject to periodic penetration tests and audits. All wireless Network Interface Cards (i.e., PC cards) used in corporate laptop or desktop computers must be registered.

1.3.2 Approved Technology
All wireless LAN access must use corporate-approved vendor products and security configurations.

1.3.3 VPN Encryption and Authentication
All computers with wireless LAN devices must utilize a corporate-approved Virtual Private Network (VPN) configured to drop all unauthenticated and unencrypted traffic. To comply with this policy, wireless implementations must maintain point-to-point hardware encryption of at least 56 bits. All implementations must support a hardware address that can be registered and tracked, i.e., a MAC address. All implementations must support and employ strong user authentication which checks against an external database such as TACACS+, RADIUS or something similar.

1.3.4 Setting the SSID

The SSID shall be configured so that it does not contain any identifying information about the organization, such as the company name, division title, employee name, or product identifier.

1.4.0 Enforcement

Any employee found to have violated this policy might be subject to disciplinary action, up to and including termination of employment.

1.5.0 Definitions

User Authentication A method by which the user of a wireless system can be verified as a legitimate user independent of the computer or operating system being used.

1.6.0 Revision History

Appendix  D

An Insider's Look at a Security Policy and Standards Management System

In Chapter 4 you saw the structure and requirements for a policy manual that's accessible to employees, to help them quickly locate security requirements and determine how to comply with them. There are several commercial products on the market that automate the tasks of policy management to help both executives and those who must live up to these requirements. Notable products in this market space are the Vigilent Policy Center (VPC) from NetIQ (**www.netiq.com**), Polivec (**www.polivec.com**), and the Archer Technologies Management System (**www.archer-tech.com**). We chose to use the Archer Tecnologies system here as an example of automated policy and standards management because of it robustness, ease of use, and comprehensive content library that's linked from regulatory guidance documents all the way through to the procedures that implement the required controls.

This Appendix demonstrates how Archer can be useful to application software developers by quickly extracting system security requirements prior to design and development activities. To do this, we've created the following scenario:

A programmer is charged with the development of an accounting system for a new medium-sized manufacturing firm. The target development and operating environment is a MS Windows 2003 Server internally called the Corporate Exchange Server. The firm must also meet the compliance requirements of the Sarbanes-Oxley (SOX) Act for corporate accountability.

To begin, it's useful to understand how the Archer Technologies Security Management System organizes policies, standards, and documentation that deal with requirements of compliance. Figure D.1 shows how a policy is used to define a control standard that is tied to one or more industry references. The policy statement, related to Password Expiration, is further refined in the Standard on password expiration that places system requirements on password expiration processes. The Policy and Standard appear in the company library because the management of the firm mandates that IT systems comply with ISO17799 (described in Chapter 4). ISO17799 is the firm's choice for comprehensive controls to comply with the Sarbanes-Oxley Act (SOX) for internal control processes.

Figure D.2 expands upon Figure D.1, showing the internal structure of a Control Standard and its relationship to policies, industry references, and Baseline Standards—which are specific to operating platforms, such as Windows 2003 Server. Baselines include guidance information and procedural instructions on how to implement the control on the target system (in this case how to make sure that passwords expire as prescribed by the standard.)

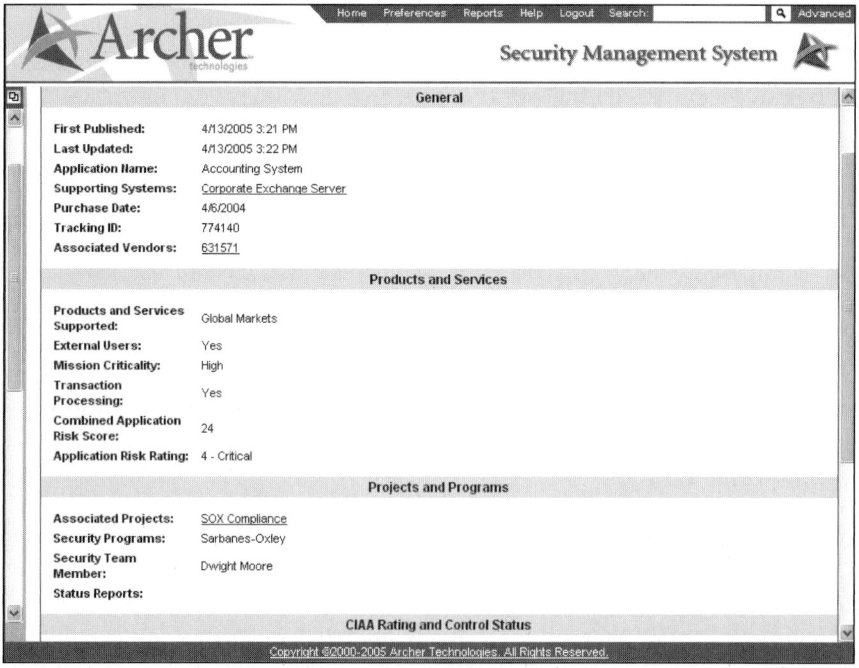

Credit: Archer Technologies

FIGURE D.1 Archer Security Management System control standards data structure.

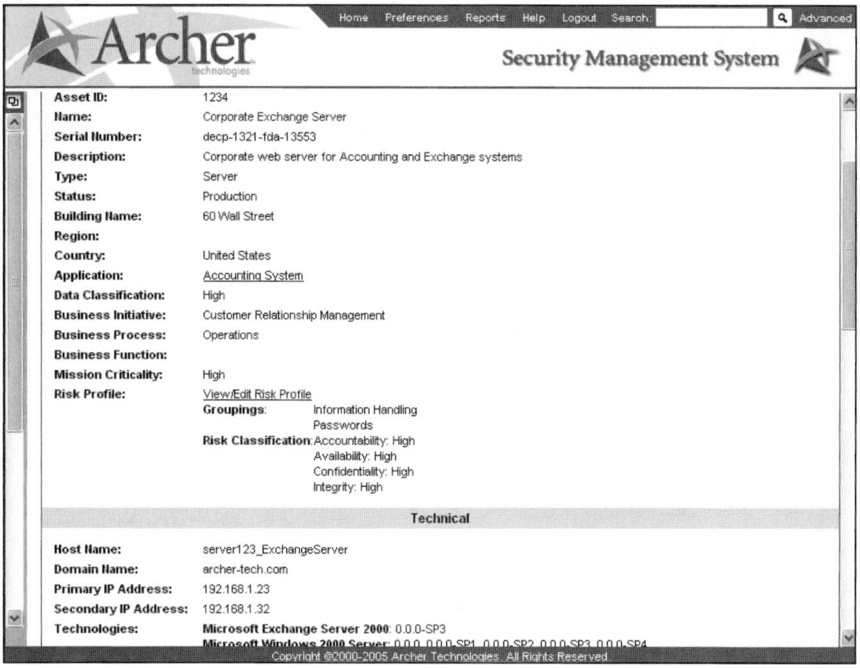

Credit: Archer Technologies

FIGURE D.2 Archer Security Management System policy relationships.

Figure D.3 begins the process that a programmer would see when using the system to set up the project and determine the design, development, and implementation requirements are for the new system. The first step is an "Application Profile" where information about the project is collected to determine the scope of the system (where it will be used, who will use it, and how critical it is to the firm's mission). Following the scope section, any associated projects and programs are indicated. In this scenario, the SOX Compliance program is selected.

Once the Application Profile is completed, information about the target platform is collected, as shown in Figure D.4. Because the Archer system is also an Asset Manager for IT systems, the specific production asset is selected and a risk profile is determined based on the needs for confidentiality, integrity, availability, and accountability of the users. These risk classifications are used to begin determining which Control Standards and Baseline Standards are in effect.

With the basic Risk Profile completed in the Asset Profile, an application-specific risk assessment is performed to determine if financial transactions will be processed and characteristics of the user population (Figure D.5). Since financial transactions are present, the SOX requirements for verification of internal controls are present.

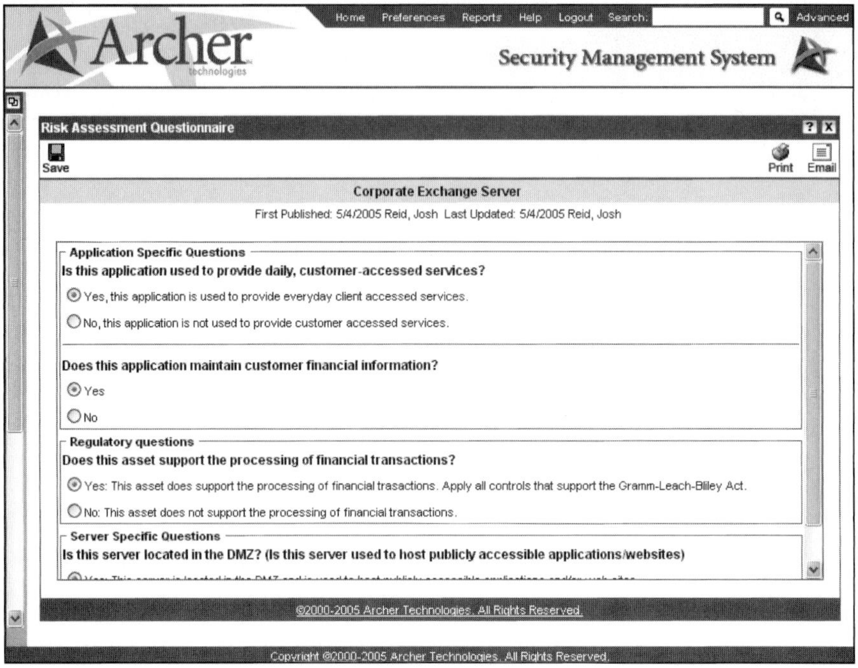

Credit: Archer Technologies

FIGURE D.3 Application profile interface.

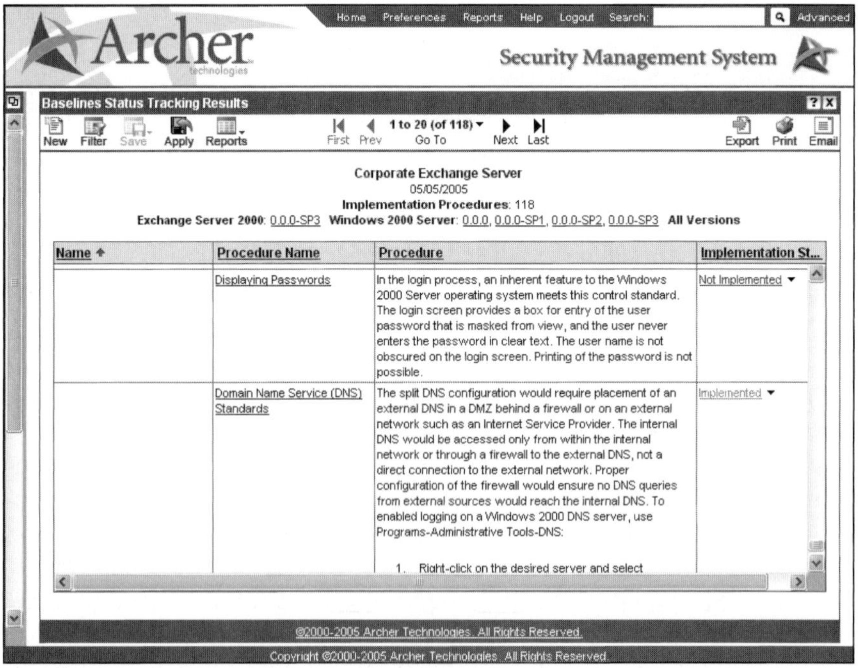

Credit: Archer Technologies

FIGURE D.4 Asset and risk profile interface.

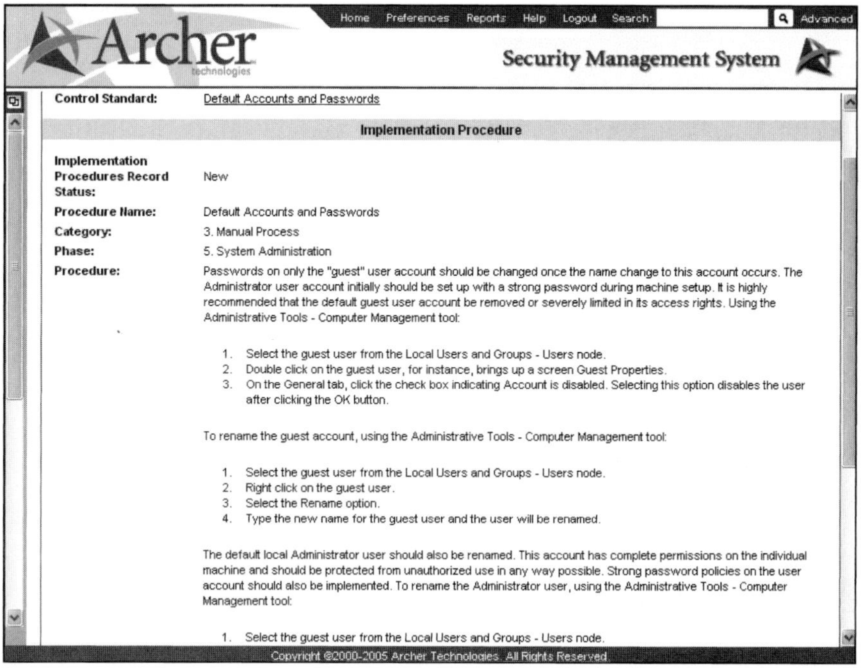

FIGURE D.5 Risk assessment interface.

Upon completion of the Asset and Risk Profiles, the Archer system uses its Policy database to extract the procedures that the system and development must follow in order to be compliant, and permits the operator to indicate if the control has already been implemented or is pending, as shown in Figure D.6.

When the programmer selects the "Default Accounts and Passwords" procedure, a detail screen (Figure D.7) appears. The procedure describes the requirements (as dictated by the standard(s)), and lists the steps the administrator should perform to implement the control using the Administrative Tools console on Windows Server 2003.

Figure D.8 illustrates how the Control Standard (Default Accounts and Passwords) is related internally to one or more policies, sections of other standards, and industry references. A user can click on a hypertext link for additional details.

Now that system development and operational standards are known, it's time to address the Baseline Standards related to the development and operating environment (Windows 2003 Server). Figure D.9 shows the Baseline Standards that are required for a given operating requirement, along with information on whether they are manually implemented, required, or inherent in the system. It also indicates the average time it would take a user to implement the Baseline control.

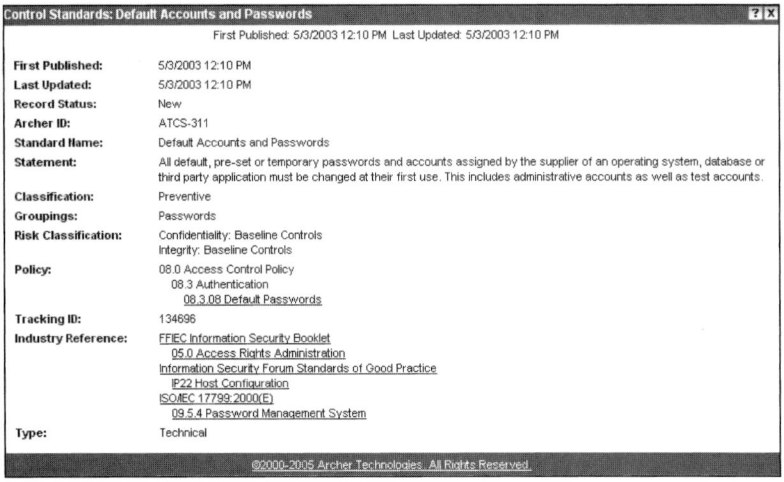
Control Standards: Default Accounts and Passwords

First Published: 5/3/2003 12:10 PM Last Updated: 5/3/2003 12:10 PM

First Published:	5/3/2003 12:10 PM
Last Updated:	5/3/2003 12:10 PM
Record Status:	New
Archer ID:	ATCS-311
Standard Name:	Default Accounts and Passwords
Statement:	All default, pre-set or temporary passwords and accounts assigned by the supplier of an operating system, database or third party application must be changed at their first use. This includes administrative accounts as well as test accounts.
Classification:	Preventive
Groupings:	Passwords
Risk Classification:	Confidentiality: Baseline Controls Integrity: Baseline Controls
Policy:	08.0 Access Control Policy 08.3 Authentication 08.3.08 Default Passwords
Tracking ID:	134696
Industry Reference:	FFIEC Information Security Booklet 05.0 Access Rights Administration Information Security Forum Standards of Good Practice IP22 Host Configuration ISO/IEC 17799:2000(E) 09.5.4 Password Management System
Type:	Technical

©2000-2005 Archer Technologies. All Rights Reserved.

Credit: Archer Technologies

FIGURE D.6 Development and operating requirements based on risk profile.

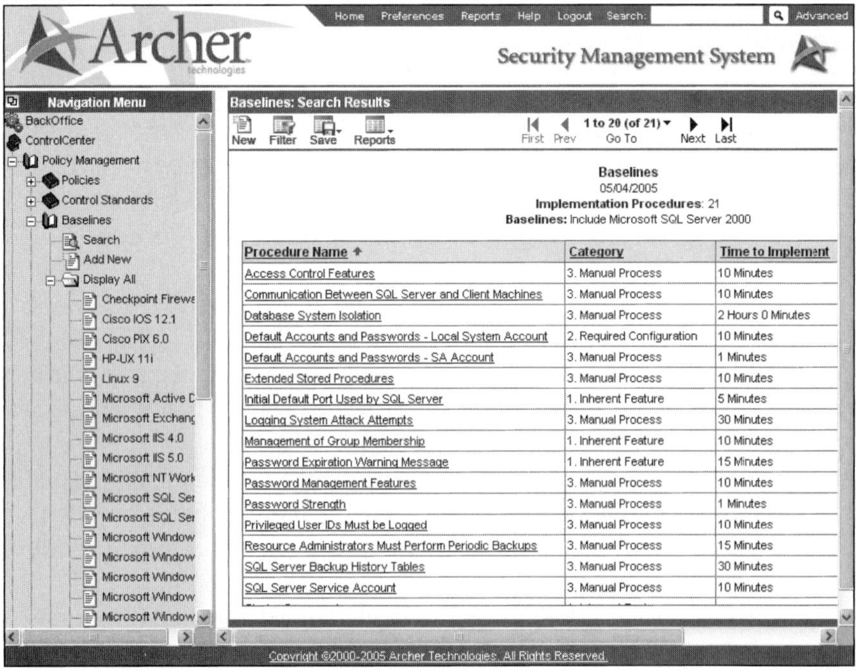

Procedure Name	Category	Time to Implement
Access Control Features	3. Manual Process	10 Minutes
Communication Between SQL Server and Client Machines	3. Manual Process	10 Minutes
Database System Isolation	3. Manual Process	2 Hours 0 Minutes
Default Accounts and Passwords - Local System Account	2. Required Configuration	10 Minutes
Default Accounts and Passwords - SA Account	3. Manual Process	1 Minutes
Extended Stored Procedures	3. Manual Process	10 Minutes
Initial Default Port Used by SQL Server	1. Inherent Feature	5 Minutes
Logging System Attack Attempts	3. Manual Process	30 Minutes
Management of Group Membership	1. Inherent Feature	10 Minutes
Password Expiration Warning Message	1. Inherent Feature	15 Minutes
Password Management Features	3. Manual Process	10 Minutes
Password Strength	3. Manual Process	1 Minutes
Privileged User IDs Must be Logged	3. Manual Process	10 Minutes
Resource Administrators Must Perform Periodic Backups	3. Manual Process	15 Minutes
SQL Server Backup History Tables	3. Manual Process	30 Minutes
SQL Server Service Account	3. Manual Process	10 Minutes

Credit: Archer Technologies

FIGURE D.7 Procedure detail interface.

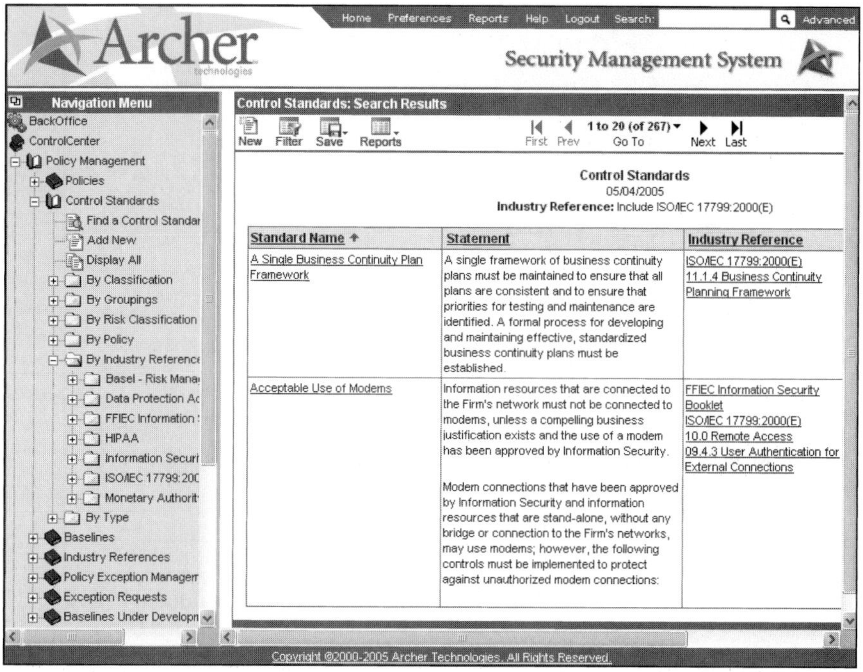

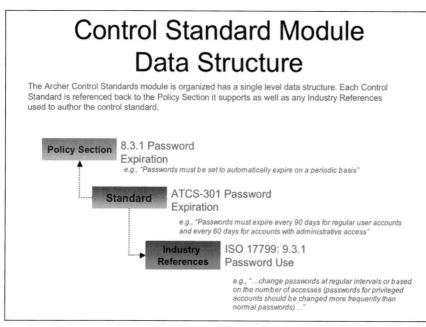

Credit: Archer Technologies

FIGURE D.8 Control standard details.

Control Standard Module Data Structure

The Archer Control Standards module is organized has a single level data structure. Each Control Standard is referenced back to the Policy Section it supports as well as any Industry References used to author the control standard.

Policy Section — 8.3.1 Password Expiration
e.g., "Passwords must be set to automatically expire on a periodic basis"

Standard — ATCS-301 Password Expiration
e.g., "Passwords must expire every 90 days for regular user accounts and every 60 days for accounts with administrative access"

Industry References — ISO 17799: 9.3.1 Password Use
e.g., "...change passwords at regular intervals or based on the number of accesses (passwords for privileged accounts should be changed more frequently than normal passwords)..."

Credit: Archer Technologies

FIGURE D.9 Baseline standards by target platform interface.

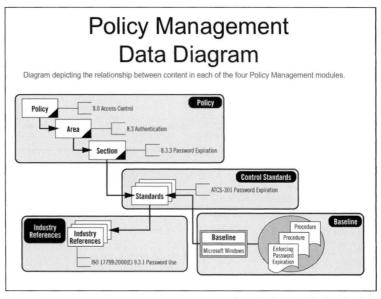

Credit: Archer Technologies

FIGURE D.10 Archer Security Management System Control Standards by industry reference.

Finally, the Archer Security Management System permits the user to determine what Control Standards are required by industry references. Figure D.10 shows an excerpt of the control standards required by ISO/IEC 17799, along with the standard statement and links to additional details (Figure D.8).

With a policy and standards management system like this one, users, developers, managers, associated third parties who perform services for the firm, and auditors can rapidly locate and understand what is expected of them for security compliance and what the current state of security compliance is. It offers greater accuracy and efficiency over paper-based policy manuals.

Appendix  E

HIPAA Security Rule Standards

As mentioned in Chapter 4, HIPAA is the Health Insurance Portability and Accountability Act. Passed in 1996, HIPAA is designed to protect confidential healthcare information through improved security standards and federal privacy legislation. It defines requirements for storing patient information before, during and after electronic transmission. It also identifies compliance guidelines for critical business tasks such as risk analysis, awareness training, audit trail, disaster recovery plans and information access control and encryption.

HIPAA Security Standards

The proposed HIPAA security regulations establish a minimum framework of standard procedures for ensuring the protection of all individually identifiable health information that is maintained, transmitted or received in electronic form. These standards guard the integrity, confidentiality, and availability of electronic data. The safeguards are intended to protect data from accidental or intentional release to unauthorized persons, and from alteration, destruction or loss. For more information on the proposed HIPAA security standards, visit the US Government Department of Health and Human Services Web site at: **www.dhhs.gov**.

There are 18 information security standards in four areas that must be met to ensure compliance with the *HIPAA Security Rule*. The three areas are:

- Administrative Safeguards: documented policies and procedures for day-to-day operations; managing the conduct of employees with electronic protected health information (EPHI); and managing the selection, development, and use of security controls.

- Physical Safeguards: security measures meant to protect an organization's electronic information systems, as well as related buildings and equipment, from natural hazards, environmental hazards, and unauthorized intrusion.

- Technical Security Services for stored data: security measures that specify how to use technology to protect EPHI while stored.

- Technical Security Mechanisms (particularly controlling access to data and data transmissions).

The Final Rule adopting HIPAA standards for the security of electronic health information was published in the Federal Register on February 20, 2003. This final rule specifies a series of administrative, technical, and physical security procedures for covered entities to use to assure the confidentiality of electronic protected health information. The standards are delineated into either required or addressable implementation specifications.

Administrative Procedures

Policies and procedures must be implemented and documented in each of these twelve areas:

- Training programs in security management and process issues

- Formal data processing protocols

- Formal protocols for controlling access to data

- Internal audit procedures

- Certification of data systems for compliance with DHHS security standards

- Chain of Trust agreements with covered entities with whom we exchange electronic information

- Contingency plan to ensure continuity and preservation of data in the event of an emergency

- Security features for initial clearance of all personnel who have access to health information along with ongoing supervision, training and monitoring of this personnel

- Security configuration management procedures such as virus checking, hardware and software systems review, and documentation

- Specific procedures when personnel terminate employment

- Security management structure that maintains continual risk assessment and sanction policies and procedures

Physical Safeguards

Data and data systems must be physically protected from intrusion and environmental hazards via seven basic elements:

- Designation of a specific person for responsibility of security
- Controlling access to and altering of computer hardware
- Enforcement of "need to know" clearances
- Implementation of work station security activities
- Development of disaster/intrusion response and recovery plans
- Maintenance of security records
- Implementation of identity verification procedures for personnel in order to physically access sites

Technical Security Services

Software control and procedures regarding stored data include these requirements:

- Providing for internal audits and controls within data systems
- Controlling access by users through authentication
- Ensuring that stored data is neither altered nor inappropriately accessed/processed
- Allowing data access to particular privileged classes of personnel, including during crises

Technical Security Mechanisms

These requirements relate to accessed data and the transmission of stored data, to ensure that data cannot easily be accessed, intercepted or interpreted by unauthorized third parties. These proposed procedures include:

- Validation that stored data being transmitted is accurate
- Validation that received data is identical to sent data
- Data transmissions either encrypted or controlled by a dedicated, secure line. If transmissions are not encrypted, DHHS would also require three elements:
- Alarms to signal abnormal communication conditions
- Automatic recording of audit trail information
- A method for authentication of the entity receiving the data

Glossary

A

abstract machine   Software model that mediates access from any subject to any object.

abstraction   Process that defines a specific set of permissible values for an object and the operations that are permissible on that object.

administrative law   Legal system in which disputes are resolved before an administrative tribunal and not in a court. Also referred to as natural law, this concept stemmed from the belief that certain legal principles were "natural" or self-evident and did not need to be codified by statute.

assurance requirements   Describe how functional requirements should be implemented and tested.

asymmetric key cryptography   When different keys are used to encrypt and decrypt messages.

authentication   Process of verifying the identity of a person or an application.

B

baseline   Specific set of requirements for a technology implementation.

biometrics   Methods of identification that work by measuring unique human characteristics as a way to confirm identity.

buffer overflow   Intentional overloading of an input area that crashes or disables a program.

business impact analysis   Process of assessing risks to a business if critical services are discontinued.

C

Canadian Trusted Computer Product Evaluation Criteria (CTCPEC)   Formal computer security testing model published in 1993 as a combination of the ITSEC and TCSEC approaches.

ciphertext   Text that results when a message is passed through an encryption algorithm, or cipher.

closed systems   Use specific operating systems and hardware to perform tasks and generally lack standard interfaces to allow connection to other systems.

Common Body of Knowledge (CBK)   Compilation and distillation of all international security information relevant to security professionals.

Common Criteria   Standardization efforts of formal computer security testing models established in the early 1990s in the United States that supplanted the FC criteria.

common law   Legal system that developed from judicial cases based on precedent and custom. Common law is either unwritten or written as statutes or codes and contains the three primary categories of civil law, criminal law, and regulatory law.

computer forensics   Investigating crimes committed with computers.

confidentiality model   Model intended to preserve the principle of least privilege.

configuration and change management controls   Used for tracking and approving changes to a system by identifying, controlling, and auditing any changes by administrative personnel.

copyright infringement   When a law protecting intellectual property has been broken, such as downloading music from a Web site without paying for it.

cryptanalysis   Science (or art) of breaking a cryptosystem.

cryptography   Science (or art) of designing, building, and using cryptosystems.

cryptology   Study of cryptography and cryptanalysis.

cryptosystem   Disguises messages, allowing only selected people to see through the disguise.

D

data hiding   Mechanism to assure that information available at one processing level is not available in another, regardless of whether it is higher or lower; also called information hiding.

de facto   Accepted practices in the industry.

degaussing   Method to magnetically erase data from magnetic media.

dejure   Official standards passed by international and industry standards committees.

digital envelope   Envelope created when you use a recipient's public key to encrypt both the message and digest, therefore ensuring that no one else can open the envelope.

dual control   Computer security practice borrowed from the military in which two people are required to initiate an action; one person acts as a countermeasure to another.

E

exploit Program that describes how to take advantage of a specific vulnerability.

F

Federal Criteria for Information Technology Security (FC) Formal computer security testing model published in early 1993 as an attempt to develop criteria to replace the TCSEC and harmonize North American and European concepts for security evaluation criteria.

finite-state machine Any device that stores the status or state of something at a given time that can operate based on inputs to change the stored status and/or cause an action or output to take place.

firewall Insulates a private network from a public network by using carefully established controls on the type of requests that they will route through to the private network for processing and fulfillment.

functional requirements Describe what a system should do.

H

hardened server Server whose software has been modified to make it more difficult to attack.

hardware segmentation Specifically relates to the segmentation of memory into protected segments.

hashing One-way function that transforms data into distilled forms that are unique to the data.

information storage Refers to the parts of a computer system that retain a physical state (information) for some interval of time, possibly even after electrical power to the computer is removed.

I

Information Technology Security Evaluation Criteria (ITSEC) A formal computer security testing model published in 1991 by the European Commission after joint development by France, Germany, the Netherlands, and the United Kingdom.

International Information Systems Security Certifications Consortium (IISSCC or ISC^2) Organization that administers the most prominent and most demanded information security certifications.

intrusion detection Detectors and alarms that alert security personnel when an unauthorized person attempts to access a system or building.

K

Kerberos Network authentication protocol designed to provide authentication for client/server applications by using symmetric-key cryptography.

L

labels   Mechanisms that bind objects to subjects.

layering   Process operation that is divided into layers by function, with each layer dealing with a specific activity.

logical systems   Software that runs on computer hardware.

M

mandatory access control (MAC)   In deciding who may gain access to what information, MAC requires that access control policy decisions are beyond the control of the individual owner of an object, thus requiring the system to make the decisions.

media viability controls   Needed for the proper marking and handling of assets.

Message Authentication Code (MAC) key   Key that is used to generate a keyed hash.

message flow confidentiality   Allows the originating network to conceal the path or route that the message followed on its way to the recipient.

multifactor authentication   Adding more controls and/or devices to the password authentication process.

multiprocessing   Provides for simultaneous execution of two or more programs by a processor (CPU).

multiprogramming system   Allows for the interleaved execution of two or more programs on a processor.

multitasking   Technique used by a system that is capable of running two or more tasks in a concurrent performance or interleaved execution.

N

need-to-know   Defines a minimum set of access rights or privileges needed to perform a specific job description.

O

object   Something within a trusted system that people wish to access or use, such as a program.

open architecture system   Permits different manufacturers to produce systems that can operate with systems from competing manufacturers.

open system   Based on accepted standards and promotes interoperability by employing standard interfaces to allow connections between different systems.

P

packages   Permit the expression of requirements that meet an identifiable subset of security objectives.

packet switching   Division of messages into standard-sized packets for greater efficiency of routing and transport.

patent   Grants an inventor the right to exclude others from producing or using the inventor's discovery or invention for a limited period of time.

personnel security investigation   Meticulous background check for security clearance.

pharming   Network attack that redirects consumers to potentially malicious Web servers.

physical security plan   Developed by executive management, department managers, and physical security site personnel as one of the many policy and standards documents that all effective security programmes require.

physical systems   Computer hardware.

PIN vault   Approach to managing IDs and passwords by using secure methods to locally store IDs and passwords that are protected by a master password that unlocks the vault when it is needed.

plaintext   Message that is passed through an encryption algorithm.

policies   Statements of management intent.

primary storage   Computer's main memory that is directly addressable by the central processing unit. It is a volatile storage medium.

principle of least privilege   Dictates that a process (program) has no more privilege than what it really needs in order to perform its functions.

privileged entity controls   Given to operators and system administrators as special access to computing resources.

process isolation   Design objective in which each process has its own distinct address space for its application code and data.

programme   Ongoing management activity intended to preserve and advance an organization.

protection profiles   Implementation-independent collection of objectives and requirements for any given category of products or systems that must meet similar needs.

protocol data unit   Bundle of data organized for transmission containing control information, the data itself, and error detection and correction bits.

protocol services   Services that define the rules and standards that enable communication between computers over the Internet.

Public Key Infrastructure (PKI)   Public key, known to anyone, and a private key held in secret by a single individual.

R

random memory   Computer's primary working and storage area.

read up, write down   Computer security model in which subjects cannot read objects of lesser integrity and subjects cannot write to objects of higher integrity.

real memory Refers to when a program has been given a definite storage location in memory and direct access to a peripheral device.

record retention process Refers to how long transactions and other types of computerized or process records should be retained.

reference monitor Software model or abstract machine that mediates all access from any subject to any object and cannot be bypassed.

resource protection Needed to protect company resources and assets such as modem pools, network routers, storage media, and documentation.

ring of trust Trust in a system moves from the outside to the inside in a unidirectional mode.

role-based access control (RBAC) Groups users with a common access need.

S

sanitization Technique of permanently removing information from media.

secondary storage Nonvolatile storage format in which application and system code plus data can be stored when the system is not in use.

separation of duties Security practice in which no one person in an organization has the ability to control or close down a security activity.

sequential storage Computer memory that is accessed sequentially (magnetic tape).

session laws Laws arranged by subject matter in the order, or session, in which they are enacted.

shared secret cryptography When the same key is used to both encrypt and decrypt messages; also called symmetric key cryptography.

smart card Resembles a regular payment (credit) card with the major difference being that it carries a semiconductor chip with logic and nonvolatile memory.

standard What is needed for a system or process to be considered secure.

subjects People or other systems that are granted a clearance to access an object within the information system.

substitution Basic method of disguising messages whereby letters are replaced by other letters and/or symbols.

symmetric key cryptography When the same key is used to both encrypt and decrypt messages; also called shared secret cryptography.

T

target of evaluation (TOE) Refers to the product or system under evaluation.

token Mechanism that generates passwords that change every minute or so.

trade secret Usually denotes a patent in process or an unofficial and legally unprotected idea.

trademark   Any word, name, symbol, or device or any combination thereof that an individual intends to use commercially and wants to distinguish as coming from a unique source.

Transmission Control Protocol (TCP)   Connection-oriented protocol utilizing the TCP/IP stack to provide reliable, full duplex communication between hosts.

transposition   Basic method of disguising messages whereby letters are rearranged into a different order.

Trusted Computer System Evaluation Criteria (TCSEC)   Formal computer security testing model originated in the United States in the early 1980s.

trusted computing base (TCB)   The totality of protection mechanisms within a computer system including hardware, firmware, and software.

trusted recovery controls   Ensure that security is not breached when a computer system crashes.

V

volatile memory   Complete loss of any stored information when the power is removed.

References

Amoroso, Edward. 1994. *Fundamentals of Computer Security Technology.* Upper Saddle River, NJ: Prentice Hall

Anderson, Ross. 2001. *Security Engineering: A Comprehensive Guide to Building Dependable Distributed Systems.* New York: John Wiley & Sons

Anonymous. 1998. *Maximum Security, A Hacker's Guide to Protecting Your Internet Site and Network,* 2nd Edition. Upper Saddle River, NJ: Sams Publishing

Atkins, Derek, Buis, Paul, Hare, Chris, Kelley, Robert, Nachenberg, Carey, Nelson, Anthony B., Phillips, Paul, Ritchey, Tim, and Steen, William. 1996. *Internet Security Professional Reference.* Upper Saddle River, NJ: New Riders Publishing

Bates, Regis J., Gregory, Donald W., and Ranade, J. 1998. *Voice and Data Communications Handbook.* New York: McGraw-Hill

Brenton, Chris. 1999. *Mastering Network Security.* Alameda, CA: Sybex

Cobb, Stephen. 1996. *The NCSA Guide to PC and LAN Security.* New York: McGraw-Hill

Cooper, James Arlin. 1989. *Computer and Communications Security: Strategies for the 1990's.* New York: McGraw-Hill

Daley, Bill. 2005. *Computers Are Your Future.* Upper Saddle River, NJ: Prentice Hall

Dam, Kenneth W., Lin, Herbert S. 1996. *Cryptography's Role in Securing the Information Society.* Washington, DC: National Academy Press

Deborah, Russell, and Gangemi, G. T. 1991. *Computer Security.* Sebastopol, CA: O'Reilly & Associates

Denning, Dorothy. 1998. *Information Warfare and Security.* Boston: Addison-Wesley

Denning, Dorothy, 1997. *Internet Besieged.* Boston: Addison-Wesley

Ermann, M. David, Williams, Mary B., and Shauf, Michele S. 1997. *Computers, Ethics, and Society,* 2nd Edition. Oxford: Oxford University Press

Escamilla, Terry. 1998. *Intrusion Detection, Network Security Beyond the Firewall.* New York: John Wiley & Sons

Fites, Phillip E., and Kratz, Martin P. J. 1996. *Information Systems Security: A Practitioner's Reference.* London: International Thomson Computer Press

Ford, Warwick. 1994. *Computer Communications Security: Principles, Standard Protocols and Techniques.* Upper Saddle River, NJ: Prentice Hall

Garfinkel, Simson, and Spafford, Gene. 1996. *Practical Unix & Internet Security.* Sebastopol, CA: O'Reilly & Associates

Garfinkel, Simson, and Spafford, Gene 1997. *Web Security and Commerce.* Sebastopol, CA: O'Reilly & Associates

Ghosh, Anup. 1998. *E-Commerce Security: Weak Links, Best Defenses.* New York: John Wiley & Sons

Gollmann, Dieter. 1999. *Computer Security.* New York: John Wiley & Sons

Harley, David, Slade, Robert, and Gattiker, Urs. 2001. *Viruses Revealed.* New York: McGraw-Hill

Held, Gilbert. 1994. *Understanding Data Communications,* 4th Edition. Upper Saddle River, NJ: Sams Publishing

Hutt, Arthur E., Bosworth, Seymour, and Hoyt, Douglas B. 1995. *Computer Security Handbook,* Third Edition. New York: John Wiley & Sons

Icove, David, Seger, Karl, and VonStorch, William. 1995. *Computer Crime: A Crime Fighter's Handbook.* Sebastopol, CA: O'Reilly & Associates

Kabay, Michel E. 1996. *The NCSA Guide to Enterprise Security: Protecting Information Assets.* New York: McGraw-Hill

Klarder, Lars. 1997. *Hacker Proof: The Ultimate Guide to Network Security*. Ashburton, Devon, UK: Jamsa Press

Konicek, Joel, and Little, Karen. 1997. *Security, ID Systems and Locks, The Book on Electronic Access Control.* Burlington, MA: Elsevier Butterworth-Heinemann

Kovacich, Gerald L. 1998. *Information Systems Security Officer's Guide, Establishing and Managing an Information Protection Program.* Burlington, MA: Elsevier Butterworth-Heinemann

Krause, Micki, and Tipton, Harold F. 1999. *Information Security Management Handbook, Fifth Edition.* Boca Raton, FL: Auerbach Publications

Krist, Martin A. 1999. *Standard for Auditing Computer Applications.* Boca Raton, FL: Auerbach Publications

Kruegle, Herman. 1995. *CCTV Surveillance, Video Practices and Technology.* Burlington, MA: Elsevier Butterworth-Heinemann

McClure, Stuart, Scambray, Joel, and Kurtz, George. 1999. *Hacking Exposed: Network Security Secrets and Solutions.* New York: Osborne/McGraw-Hill

Merkow, Mark, and Breithaupt, James. 2001. *Complete Guide to Internet Security.* New York: AMACOM Books

Merkow, Mark, and Breithaupt, James. 2004. *Computer Security Assurance Using the Common Criteria.* Clifton Park, NY: Thomson Delmar Learning

Morrison, Perry, and Forester, Tom. 1995. *Computer Ethics,* 2nd Edition. Cambridge, MA: MIT Press

Nichols, Randall K., Ryan, Daniel J., and Ryan, Julie. 2000. *Defending Your Digital Assets Against Hackers, Crackers, Spies, and Thieves.* New York: McGraw-Hill

Nichols, Randall K. 1998. *ICSA Guide to Cryptography.* New York: McGraw-Hill

Northcutt, Stephen. 1999. *Network Intrusion Detection: An Analysis Handbook.* Old Tappan, NJ: New Riders Publishing

Oaks, Scott. 1998. *Java Security.* Sebastopol, CA: O'Reilly & Associates

Parker, Donn B. 1998. *Fighting Computer Crime: A New Framework for Protecting Information.* New York: John Wiley & Sons

Ranum, Marcus. 2003. *The Myth of Homeland Security.* New York: John Wiley & Sons

Rubin, Aviel D., Geer, Daniel, and Ranum, Marcus J. 1997. *Web Security Sourcebook, A Complete Guide to Web Security Threats and Solutions.* New York: John Wiley & Sons

Russell, Deborah, and Gangemi, G. T. 1991. *Computer Security Basics.* Sebastopol, CA: O'Reilly & Associates

Schneier, Bruce. 1995. *Applied Cryptography: Protocols, Algorithms, and Source Code in C, Second Edition.* New York: John Wiley & Sons

Schneier, Bruce. 1995. *E-Mail Security: How to Keep Your Electronic Messages Private.* New York: John Wiley & Sons

Schwartau, Winn. 1999. *Time Based Security.* Seminole, FL: Interpact Press

Scott, Charlie, Wolfe, Paul, and Erwin, Mike. 1999. *Virtual Private Networks, 2nd Edition.* Sebastopol, CA: O'Reilly & Associates

Simonds, Fred. 1996. *Network Security, Data and Voice Communications.* New York: McGraw-Hill.

Singh, Simon. 1999. *The Code Book: The Secret History of Codes & Code-breaking.* London: Fourth Estate Limited

Slade, Robert. 1996. *Computer Viruses: How to Avoid Them, How to Get Rid of Them, and How to Get Help, 2nd Edition.* New York: Springer

Smith, Martin. 1993. *Commonsense Computer Security, Your Practical Guide to Information Protection, 2nd Edition.* New York: McGraw-Hill

Summers, Rita C. 1997. *Secure Computing: Threats and Safeguards.* New York: McGraw-Hill

Tiwana, Amrit. 1999. *Web Security.* Burlington, MA: Elsevier Butterworth-Heinemann

Umbaugh, Robert E. 1997. *Handbook of IS Management, 5th Edition.* Boca Raton, FL: Auerbach Publications

U.S. Department. of Health, Education and Welfare. 1973. Records, Computers, and the Rights of Citizens, Report of the Secretary's Advisory Committee on Automated Personal Data Systems, p. viii

Walrand, Jean. 1998. *Communications Networks, A First Course, 2nd Edition.* New York: McGraw-Hill

Winkler, Ira. 1999. *Corporate Espionage: What It Is, Why It Is Happening in Your Company, What You Must Do About It.* New York: Prima Publishing

Wood, Charles C. 1999. *Information Security Policies Made Easy.* Houston: Information Shield

Index